"OK, I'm Karl's wife, so judge for yourself the value of my testimony—but I can tell you that Karl is a happier, easier to live with, more fun, more loving, more outgoing, and more relational person since he has been testing and proving the principles in *Outsmarting Yourself* in his own life—and that's evidence from the twenty-three years of our marriage. He effectively teaches this material because it has changed his own life, and mine too. Furthermore, I use these principles in my job as a pastor every day, since dealing with people is foundational to the work of the Kingdom of God."

Charlotte Lehman, M.Div.
Pastor, pastoral counselor, Dr. Lehman's wife

"People have an almost universal desire to be in strong, healthy, nurturing relationships where they are loved, known, and understood. However, finding and developing these types of relationships is often easier said than done. Dr. Karl Lehman gives the reader profound insights into why our relationships with ourselves, others, and God are not as life-giving and satisfying as we would like them to be. But don't despair. He also gives clear solutions and guidelines that will radically transform your life and your relationships. I have personally used the information in this book to address and resolve my own relational difficulties, with life-changing results. Dr. Lehman's writing style is engaging and often humorous. He is able to explain complex ideas in a simple, understandable manner, often using his own life experiences as an example. I highly recommend this book for those who want to maximize the quality and depth of their relationships."

Andrea Bacon, M.D.
Board-certified in both child and adult psychiatry

"We have all had the experience of having emotional content from our past flood into a present moment, supercharging our reaction to the situation in front of us, and impacting not only our feelings and thoughts, but unfortunately our actions as well. Often we have done or said things we later regret. Dr. Lehman explains, with eloquence and wit, the answer to our question, "What just hit me?"

In order to demonstrate the principles that cause these emotional reactions, as well as the effective interventions he has developed, Dr. Lehman humbly shares examples from his own healing journey. I think Dr. Lehman's openness and sense of humor about his own experiences are two of the most important strengths of this book. He not only provides vivid and concrete examples, but also gives permission for each of us to be just where we are in our own process of healing. Dr. Lehman then outlines a path to freedom from the painful and destructive influences of these emotional intrusions by combining the latest in brain science and a dynamic connection with Jesus, our Immanuel.

Dr. Lehman goes to great lengths to present this material in a way that is understandable to a lay person who is just being introduced to emotional healing, and at the same time is informative and exciting to a professional with years of experience. The insights Dr. Lehman presents have been very beneficial to me both as a psychologist in private practive as well as in my own marriage and other relationships. I have been tremendously blessed to have Dr. Lehman as a friend and a colleague. I was an original member of his first mentoring group and have had the privilege to learn from him for the last ten years. Thank you, Karl, for all you have given me."

Wanda K. Morgan, Ph.D.
Psychologist and psychotherapist with thirty years of clinical experience

Outsmarting Yourself

Catching Your Past Invading the Present and What to Do about It

Second Edition

Karl Lehman, M.D

This JOY! Books

Libertyville, Illinois

Outsmarting Yourself: Catching Your Past Invading the Present and What to Do about It, second edition
by Karl Lehman

Published by This JOY! Books—A Division of Three Cord Ministries, Inc.
1117 S. Milwaukee Ave., Suite A4, Libertyville, IL 60048
www.thisjoybooks.com

First edition published 2011. Second edition 2014.
Printed in the United States of America
22 21 20 19 18 17 16 15 14   2 3 4 5 6

ISBN: 978-0-9834546-9-4

Typesetting by Joanna Tsuyuki
Cover design by Laura Sebold
Figure illustrations by Charlotte Lehman

To Charlotte

My sister in Christ,

my professional colleague,

my partner in ministry,

my life-journey companion,

my soul mate,

my sweetheart, . . .

and my best friend.

Contents

*Note that a much more detailed outline is available at the Outsmarting
Yourself website (www.outsmartingyourself.com).*

Acknowledgments

First and foremost I want to thank Jesus, Immanuel, God with us: thank you, Lord, for guidance and grace in the process of developing this material; thank you for the privilege of watching your powerful, beautiful, elegant work in emotional healing sessions; and thank you for your patience and forgiveness regarding the many ways in which I have transferred the unresolved pain in my life onto you.

Thank you, Mom and Dad Lehman, for the strength, persistence, faithfulness, obedience, and radical discipleship that I learned from you and that have helped me to develop this material. And thank you for the integrity, humility, and grace that enables you to be two of my biggest fans, even though I share so openly about the ways in which our family was not perfect. Thank you to my patients, colleagues, friends, and family for being such good sports as I have developed and practiced these principles and tools in the context of our friendships. Thank you, Dr. E. James Wilder, for the many hours you have spent brainstorming with me regarding brain science, emotional healing, and spirituality. I would never have developed the material regarding the pain-processing pathway and relational circuits without your input, and it has been tremendously satisfying to work together in developing the group Immanuel exercises. Thank you, Mom Tsuyuki, for your faithful administrative support, and especially for preparing this material for print. Thank you to Pastor Velotta and Calvary Way International Fellowship, for the many ways you have supported and encouraged us. Thank you to our friend, Colleen Delaney, for your help with proof-reading. Thank you to Mary Anne Pfitzinger and her team at This Joy! Books—this book is greatly improved because of your expertise, patience, and care. And thank you to the reference librarians at the Evanston Public Library, for tracking down the *many* books and journal articles that have contributed to this project.

Last but not least, I want to thank my wife, Charlotte: thank you for your patience, especially during the years before I began to recognize and deal with my woundedness; thank you for your many valuable suggestions—this book (and practically everything else I have written) has been greatly improved by your editorial input; thank you for your support, care, and patience during the many times my relational circuits were off due to my being triggered by working on this project; and thank you for being my number one guinea pig. I love you and I couldn't have done this without you!

Introduction

Our hope is that the material presented in this book will be valuable for those who already have experience and training regarding psychological trauma, implicit memory, triggering, relational connection circuits, and emotional healing; and also that this material will be effective as the first exposure for people not yet familiar with these important concepts and phenomena. Since we are writing only one book, rather than providing separate "advanced" and "newcomers" versions, it's as if we are presenting a single mathematics curriculum to a large class, with some of the material geared toward students who are just learning algebra and other material geared toward students who have already mastered calculus. We thought it would be helpful to name this reality so that you recognize it as you encounter it, and that it would also be helpful to make some suggestions regarding how readers might best embrace this challenge.

For readers who have already been working with psychological trauma and emotional healing, especially the first half of the book will include a lot of material with which you are already familiar. As you review chapters 1 through 8, where the content will be more familiar, I invite you to start thinking like teachers. Hopefully the material in these chapters will give you language, examples, and research that you will find helpful in sharing these concepts with others.

For readers who have *not* already been working with psychological trauma and emotional healing, especially part 3 will be presenting answers to questions you are not yet asking. I want to explicitly name my goal for you with respect to the more advanced material: your goal is not to even *try* to remember or master the details, but rather to take in the big picture, so that as you begin applying the more basic tools and principles, as you begin to encounter the phenomena we discuss in chapters 9 through 13, and as the more advanced material starts to become relevant, you will remember that it's here and come back for it.

At this point I would also like to provide an overview with respect to content (like a satellite picture of a country you are visiting), so that you will have reference points that can help you stay oriented as you explore and learn through the next twenty-nine chapters.

- In part 1 (chapters 1 through 6), I present basic information about psychological trauma, and then also discuss *implicit memory, the Verbal Logical Explainer,* and *central nervous system extrapolation*—three related phenomena that will be especially important in helping us understand how psychological trauma affects us, how it behaves, and what to do about it.

- In part 2 (chapters 7 and 8), I present an initial discussion of how to neutralize the negative effects of psychological trauma: the first half of the basic plan is to engage in the ongoing process of permanently resolving traumatic memories; and the second half of the basic plan is to recognize when we are being affected by traumatic memories, and then make behavioral choices based on truth.

- In part 3 (chapters 9 through 13), I talk about exacerbating factors that can make it very difficult to implement this basic plan: maturity from the age of memory, memory-based negative reactions to the suggestion that old trauma might be contributing to our thoughts and emotions, and loss of access to the circuits in our brains responsible for handling relational connection.

- In part 4 (chapters 14 through 23), I describe additional resources and insights that are helpful for working with both straightforward and more difficult situations: additional insights regarding the importance of taking responsibility for *our own* stuff, additional resources for recognizing when our traumatic memories are getting stirred up, and tools for reestablishing access to the circuits in our brains responsible for handling relational connection.

- In part 5 (chapters 24 through 27), I describe specific interventions for helping *others* who are impaired by traumatic memories getting stirred up.

- And in part 6 (chapters 28 and 29), I provide summary points, synthesis conclusions, and answers to frequently asked questions.

I hope this book will help you to better understand yourself and others, that it will teach you to recognize when unresolved pain from the past is invading the present, and that it will give you practical tools for helping yourself and others to minimize (and even eliminate) the wide variety of problems caused when old pain comes into the present.

Part One

Psychological Trauma, Implicit Memory, and the Verbal Logical Explainer (VLE)

1

Psychological Trauma

When I present this material as a seminar, I start with the question: "How many of you have ever had a painful experience?" and people laugh. They laugh because we all have painful experiences, and this reality is so obvious that the question is absurd. The question should not be *whether* we encounter pain, but rather "What do we do *when* we encounter pain?" So, what *do* we *do* when we encounter pain?

The Pain-Processing Pathway

When we encounter pain, our brain-mind-spirit system always tries to process the painful experience. There is a very deliberate pathway that this pain-processing attempt will follow, and there are specific processing tasks that we must complete as we travel along this pathway, such as maintaining organized attachment, staying emotionally connected, staying relational, navigating the situation in a satisfying way, and correctly interpreting the meaning of the experience (figure 1.1).[1] When we are able to successfully

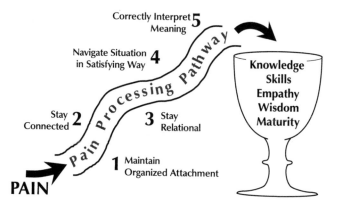

Figure 1.1   The pain-processing pathway, with a representative task from each of the five levels of processing

---

1.   Just in case you are concerned that you don't know what I mean by "maintaining organized attachment" or "staying relational," mostly all you need to know for the purposes of this book is that there is a pathway for processing painful experiences, and it includes a series of specific processing tasks. At the few points where you will need to know more, I will provide the additional information when we get there.

complete this processing journey, we get through the painful experience without being traumatized—we emotionally and cognitively "metabolize" the experience in a healthy way, and instead of having any toxic power in our lives, the adequately processed painful experience contributes to our knowledge, skills, empathy, wisdom, and maturity. That is, when we successfully process a painful experience we don't just stuff it down into our unconscious, or teach ourselves to think about other things. We actually get through it, stronger and wiser. There's an old saying, "Suffering will either make you bitter or better." Successfully completing the pain-processing pathway is what ensures that we get better rather than bitter.

Unfortunately, various problems and/or limitations can block successful processing; and when we are *not* able to complete the processing journey, then the painful experience becomes a traumatic experience and the memories for these traumatic experiences carry unresolved toxic content.[2] As described in much more detail below, this unresolved toxic content has lots of negative effects, and these negative effects often include the bitterness mentioned in the old saying.

Trauma Is More Easily Caused and More Common Than Most Realize

Recognizing that psychological trauma comes from failure to successfully complete the journey through the pain-processing pathway leads to a very important point regarding what kind of experiences can end up being traumatic. This point is discussed in much greater detail in the "Brain Science, Psychological Trauma, and the God Who Is with Us" essays, but the short summary is: *you don't need the overwhelming negative emotions and physical pain of military combat or tsunami disasters to create psychological trauma.* In fact, if you are a child without anyone in your community who can help make sure you get through the processing pathway successfully, and a painful experience presents a challenge where your personal processing skills are especially weak, *even a fairly minor painful experience can result in psychological trauma.*

For example, I grew up in the turbulent 1960s in a church with a heavy emphasis on social justice and radical discipleship. The zealous young

---

2. Note that this *very, very* brief summary of the pain-processing pathway and psychological trauma is specifically designed to provide context for the material presented in this book. Processing tasks at each of the five levels of the pain-processing pathway, psychological trauma, traumatic memories, and tools for resolving traumatic memories are all discussed in much greater detail in the "Brain Science, Psychological Trauma, and the God Who Is with Us" essay series (parts 1 through 6), all available as free downloads from www.kclehman.com.

leaders constantly challenged us to follow the Lord no matter what the cost, and repeatedly emphasized that there should be nothing in our lives that we weren't willing to sacrifice for Jesus. To my young mind it felt like every other sermon was on "Take up your cross and follow me," and that the ones in between were distributed equally between "If your eye causes you to sin, pluck it out," the story of Abraham being told to sacrifice his son, Isaac, and the story where Jesus tells the rich young ruler: "Sell all you have, give it to the poor, and then come and follow me."

These challenges and exhortations were appropriate for the grown-ups in the congregation—from the foundation of adult maturity, it was appropriate that they hear these invitations to *choose* sacrifice, and they also had the cognitive maturity to be able to correctly understand how Jesus intended these passages to be received. However, as a four-year-old still working on the child maturity task of learning how to take care of myself, I was frightened and overwhelmed by these teachings that I received with the very concrete, literal understanding of a small child. I remember thinking about what it would be like to pluck out one of my eyes—visualizing ramming my fingers into my eye socket as hard as I possibly could, and wondering if I would ever have the courage and strength to actually do it. And I remember thinking about the "Sell all you have, give it to the poor, and then come and follow me" passage. I had no idea where one went in response to the "and then come and follow me" part of the passage, but I was pretty sure it meant that I couldn't stay in my house. I remember imagining what it would be like to walk out into the alley naked (at four years old, "sell *all* you have" includes clothing), with no home to go back to and no parents to care for me. At first the whole scenario felt totally overwhelming—it seemed like the shame would be unbearable, and I was frightened by the prospect of slowly starving to death. Fortunately, I eventually figured out that I could hide under people's porches during the day, to escape the embarrassment of everybody seeing me running around the neighborhood naked, and then I could come out at night and get food out of people's trash cans.

During this same time in my life, small group fellowship meetings were often held in our living room, next to my bedroom. My bed was right by the door, and I often overheard what was being said as I lay in bed waiting to fall asleep. On a number of occasions, one person especially talked about how God had taken away her jobs, boyfriends, and other treasures so that she wouldn't have any idols—so that "nothing would be before God" in her life. When I think back on this, my perception is that she totally missed the dynamic of the request on God's part, she missed the appropriate place for free will in the equation, and she didn't talk as if she perceived God as her friend. That is, she did *not* seem to be saying, "I *want* to love God more than anything else, and I've been asking him to help me dismantle idolatry in my life. Even though it's been very painful, I'm *grateful* that he has removed the things I was wrongly worshiping." Instead, there was more of the sense that God was her adversary, and that he was taking and destroying the precious things in her life *without her permission or agreement*. The adults in the sharing group with her probably realized that her perception of God's heart was distorted, and they may even have discussed this at some point; but as a four-year-old in the next room, hearing only pieces of these conversations, I was frightened and confused by her comments.

As part of my unsuccessful attempts to process these experiences I came to distorted conclusions about God's character and heart. Instead of feeling safe in God's love for me, trusting that his plans were good, and being truly willing to lay down anything in my life if it were necessary, I felt that God was pathologically insecure and controlling—I felt that he spent a lot of his time prowling around snatching things away from his children, demanding that we give up anything that might be precious to us in order to prove our allegiance, submission, and obedience, and in order to "keep our priorities straight." For example, as I grew older I wanted very much to get married, so I feared that God would demand that I remain single in order to prevent me from loving some*one* more than him; I had been able to purchase a pair of binoculars and a ten-speed bicycle after years of saving my paper-route money, so I feared that God would take these treasured possessions to prevent me from loving some *thing* more than him; and doing well in school was very important to me, so I feared that God would intentionally mess up my studies and give me bad grades to prevent me from getting too attached to academic success. I can remember trying to "hide" my bicycle and binoculars by thinking about them as little as possible, while deliberately focusing more of my attention on less important possessions, like my pocketknife and my pet turtle. My hope was that God would follow the focus of my attention, erroneously conclude that the knife and the turtle were the idols that needed to be confiscated, but then miss the hidden treasures that were actually more precious. I can even remember bargaining with God: "You can have all my other stuff if I can keep my bicycle and binoculars," or even "I'll throw in the bicycle AND the binoculars if you just let me get married and don't mess up my grades."

I never *wanted* to believe these perceptions regarding the Lord's character and heart, and truth carried in my non-traumatic memories told me that this picture of a petty, insecure, and mean God was distorted. I fought these distorted perceptions whenever they came forward, and the struggle slowly improved through years of discipleship and personal spiritual growth, as I spent thousands of hours studying the Bible, studying a wide variety of books arguing for God's goodness, praying, receiving pastoral care, reading true stories that provided examples of the Lord's goodness, and reminding myself of the evidence for God's goodness in my own life. It took larger and larger triggers to bring them out, and I got better and better at stuffing them back in. But if it looked like I was about to lose something *really* important, I would rediscover these memory-anchored distorted beliefs about the Lord.

The good news is that Charlotte and I were able to pray through these experiences, and the Lord helped resolve the toxic content in these memories.[3] But before this happened, there were more than thirty years during which the unresolved traumatic content from these experiences powerfully affected what I believed about God's character and heart.

One of Charlotte's childhood experiences, described in the following first-person account, provides another example of the way in which minor painful events can result in trauma.

When I was in fifth grade, there was a boy in my class who dominated the social dynamics of the group. He wasn't really a bad kid, but he was a little too smart regarding how to manipulate others, and he didn't yet have the maturity to use his power for the good of the whole group versus his own ego. And he also was, in a basic fifth-grade sort of a way, quite misogynistic. That is, he was always saying that boys were better than girls, and he would often try to make any classroom election or competition to be about boys versus girls. For example, when we were voting for which one student would have the privilege of doing some coveted task (such as cleaning out the gerbil cage), he would coach all the boys in the classroom to only have one boy nominated—because he had observed that if the girls' votes were divided over more than one girl candidate, then the one boy on the slate usually won. And everything he succeeded in getting to happen *his* way seemed to prove his assertion that girls were inferior to boys.

One day at recess we were all playing boxball—called four square in some parts of the country—and I don't remember exactly how it happened, but this young man started giving orders to others. He'd tell one "You get yourself out" and another "Now you go over there"—and none of these "moves" were the usual competitive

---

3. Now I believe that I should love the Lord with all my heart and all my mind and all my strength, and that I should love and obey the Lord before all else; but now it also feels true that I *choose* this and that the Lord is trying to bring me to this place in the most gentle way possible, as a loving Father. I realize that he might allow pain in this process, but only if it's the only possible way to accomplish a greater good.

process of the game, but rather his capricious preferences, which for some reason on that day he decided to try to impose on the rest of us. He wasn't physically forcing or threatening anyone. He wasn't verbally threatening, using foul language, or even calling anyone names. He was just issuing commands in a forceful way.

I don't really remember what everyone else's reaction was to this ordering about, but I know that in me, something sort of snapped, or gave way. I just didn't have the strength or sense of self or whatever it was I needed to fight back. So when he told me to get myself out, I did. On the sidelines, my friend Anne, who was a healthier, stronger person than I, was appalled that I would cave in to this boy's orders. "Charlotte! Charlotte! What are you doing?! Don't listen to him!!" she was saying. But I just didn't have it in me to resist. At the time it occurred, I wasn't even aware of this event having any affect on me, but in retrospect I can see that in my unsuccessful attempt to process the experience I internalized the distorted belief: "I'm not as good as a boy/man."

This distorted belief and the shame it caused were actually so subtle that I was never even consciously aware of them until they came forward in an emotional healing session many years later. In this session one of my friends was praying for me, and this memory came to mind. I gave her a brief account of the scenario, just as I have described it here—very matter of fact, with no big swell of emotion—and I was thinking, "Well, this isn't anything traumatic." But then as I pressed in to describing how it felt, the words "He's better than me" popped out of my mouth. And as I said the words, a wave of shame passed over me, like a shudder. And then, as suddenly as it had appeared, the shame was gone and I realized that "He's better than me" no longer felt true.

This was all so low key that I might doubt the significance of both the original childhood experience and the prayer session, but for two things. The first was an incident that happened shortly after the prayer time. Sometime in the next day or so, I was sitting at my desk in my office, and Karl was at his desk across the hall. Out of nowhere, a thought came to me. So since there was no one else in the office, I called out to Karl across the hall, and said, "You know, Dallas Willard isn't better than me." Dallas Willard is an author whom I greatly admire. And Karl said, "Yes, honey." And maybe an hour or so later, another thought came to me, and I said, "You know, Virgil isn't better than me." Virgil was our pastor at the time—a wonderful, godly man. And Karl said, "Yes, honey." And a little while later, the thought came to me, "Even you—you aren't better than me." And Karl patiently said, "Yes, honey," one more time.

The second piece of evidence indicating the importance of the original experience and confirming God's healing work is that there have been changes inside of myself that have been both significant and lasting. Since this curious day in which the new truth seemed to be "sinking in," I have had more confidence, particularly when it comes to relating to men with authority of one kind or another. I can "look them in the eye," so to speak, in a way that I couldn't quite do so clearly before. In retrospect, I can also now see that this distorted "I'm not as good as a man" belief contributed to my lifelong lack of confidence and sense of insecurity.

This point about "small" painful experiences sometimes resulting in trauma is so important that I would like to provide another example from my childhood. On my grade-school playground there was a lot of cheating. The biggest, toughest kids were particularly prone to cheat, since no one could stop them, and they found ways to cheat in most of the games we played. They might add points to their scores if they were losing, they might make up new rules that gave them a needed advantage, or they might simply insist that they had made it safely to first base when we could all see that this was not the case. The scenario that bothered me the most was kids cutting in line during batting practice. Each time they finished their turn at the plate, the three or four toughest fifth graders would appear to go to the back of the line, but then every ten seconds or so they would cut forward by three or four kids. Day after day I would stand in line, watching these toughs cut in front of me, knowing that there was nothing I could do about it unless I wanted to get beaten up. And the gym teacher never seemed to notice that these guys got to bat four or five times as often as the rest of us. He was the person with the size and the designated authority to maintain appropriate order, but he did nothing to protect the smaller, more vulnerable kids (like me).

As a result of being unable to successfully process these experiences, bitterness, judgment, feelings of powerlessness, and feelings of helplessness remained in the memories of these events. Then, for many years (until this stuff got resolved), whenever I encountered situations in which others were cheating, and especially situations in which others were "cutting in line" in one way or another, the toxic content carried in these unresolved playground memories would come forward and I would become both very miserable and very unpleasant to be with. For example, when we would come to a construction zone where some drivers were using the "merge" lane as a personal bypass lane, and zipping to the front of the line where they were cutting in front of those of us who had been waiting in the good citizen lane for the last forty-five minutes, I would have a sense of being helpless and powerless, I would feel intense anger toward the cheaters, I would feel intense frustration toward "somebody" for not imposing order and fairness in the situation, and I would go back and forth between fuming (with lots of words I won't use here) and indulging in a macabre little daydream. My little fantasy was that the government would pass a law making it legal to blow these people up, and I would get one of those rocket launchers you can hold on your shoulder (you know—the ones you always see the special forces teams using in the action movies). Then, when one of these guys zips by in the cheater lane, I would lean out my window and send one of those little rockets right through his rear license plate and into his back seat. KABOOM! One less cheater! And then we would roll the burning wreckage to the side of the road and put a sign on it: "This is what happened to the last guy who used the merge lane for a cheater lane."

Charlotte, on the other hand, was an example of how a person might react in this situation if she were *not* being affected by old trauma. Charlotte could acknowledge that it was frustrating to see people whizzing by and then cutting in at the front of the line, and that these people were being inconsiderate, but she wasn't all bent out of shape. Her attitude was more along the lines of "We can't do anything about it, so we might as well make the best of it—let's just enjoy being together while we're waiting in line." Furthermore, she would even offer charitable thoughts regarding the cheaters, such as "They might not be *maliciously* inconsiderate—maybe they just haven't learned the maturity skill of being able to wait for their turn—maybe being able to go to the front of the line will prevent them from hitting their children when they get home," or "We don't know what's happening in their lives—maybe they're single parents who've had especially hard days, and just can't deal with waiting longer in the 'good citizen lane'." And then she would make additional gracious suggestions, such as: "Even if they do know what they're doing, we could be part of the solution by choosing to forgive them and pray for them."[4]

---

4. In the interest of truth, justice, and humility I will confess my own use of the "cheater lane": for years as a young driver I was oblivious to the complexity of construction zone traffic flow, and innocently zipped along in the merge lane without even realizing that I was cheating. Even more narcissistically mortifying is the humbling truth that for several years after coming to understand the whole cheater lane phenomena, I found it so unbearable to feel like a helpless victim waiting in the "good citizen lane" that I actually used the cheater lane *fully aware of the fact that I was cheating.*

So, when we came to a construction zone where people were using the merge lane as a cheater lane, the toxic content from my unresolved memories would make me miserable, as I felt powerless, helpless, and furious; Charlotte had to endure the unpleasant experience of being trapped in the car with a husband who was alternating between openly fuming and silently fantasizing about killing people; and instead of participating in the Lord's vision for redemption by forgiving these people and praying for them, I gave the enemy a foothold in my own life by indulging in bitterness, and I contributed to the enemy's schemes for destruction by spewing toxic waste into the spiritual environment.

As you may have noticed, two of these traumatic experiences were caused by kids playing games on grade-school playgrounds in the middle of the day with teachers present, and the third trauma was caused by comments made in the context of Sunday morning church services and small group fellowship meetings. There was no wreckage from a semi running into a passenger car at seventy miles per hour. There weren't any suicide bombers, crazed gunmen, or burning buildings. There weren't any tornadoes, earthquakes, or tidal waves. And there were no rescue squads, no ambulances, and no mangled bodies. In fact, there was no physical violence or physical danger of any kind. Nobody was being forced, violated, or touched inappropriately, and nobody was intoxicated or out of control. Nobody even raised their voices. However, there *were* children who were unable to successfully process painful experiences, and the resulting unresolved toxic content carried in the memories for these experiences caused trouble for many years.

The point here is that psychological trauma is *not* a rare phenomenon carried only by those who have survived overwhelmingly painful experiences, such as natural disasters, military combat, or child abuse. Our perception is that psychological trauma, especially from minor painful events, is much more common than most people realize, and that nobody is completely free of memories carrying unresolved traumatic content.

As you wrestle with whether or not to accept this very important point regarding the commonness of psychological trauma, make sure to note that our formulations of "trauma" and "traumatic" are fundamentally different from the ways most people use these terms. "Traumatic" is often used synonymously with "disastrous," "life threatening," "catastrophic," and other terms you expect to see on the front page of the newspaper; and most definitions of trauma focus on the magnitude/intensity of the painful event. However, our definitions are based *solely* on whether or not the person successfully processes the experience. A trauma is a painful experience that has not been successfully processed. That's it. This means that no matter how bad an experience is, if it successfully completes the journey through the pain processing pathway, then it will *not* be traumatic. And no matter how *small* a painful experience is, if it does *not* successfully complete the journey through the pain processing pathway, then it *will* be traumatic, and it will have negative, ongoing effects on the person (even though the effects may be small).[5]

The Effects of Trauma Can Be Found Everywhere, and Are Amazingly Variable in Presentation

When something in the present activates or "triggers" a traumatic memory, the unresolved toxic content comes out of where it's stored and becomes part of what a person thinks and feels in the present. This coming forward of incompletely processed memory content into the present causes a wide variety of problems, such as addictions, mysterious physical symptoms, post-traumatic stress disorder, anxiety disorders, depression, eating disorders, impaired parenting, difficulty receiving new truth, impaired discernment, and blocked peak performance.[6] As I will describe shortly, unresolved trauma coming forward and blending with our experience in the present especially causes and/or exacerbates relational conflict, and this applies to every kind of relational conflict you can imagine—marital discord, conflicts between family members, conflicts between friends, conflicts in church, conflicts on the mission field, conflicts between neighbors, conflicts between employers and employees, conflicts between professional colleagues, conflicts between students and teachers, conflicts between warring tribal groups in Africa, conflicts between Arabs and Israelis, and conflicts between drivers in the good citizen lane and drivers using the merge lane to cut in line.

The Effects of Trauma Can Be Subtle

As you struggle with whether or not to accept my assertions about the effects of trauma being so ubiquitous and diverse, it is important to note that these effects can sometimes be very subtle. For example, you may not have

---

5. For a much more detailed discussion regarding our formulation of trauma, including discussion of published case studies and clinical research that provide extensive supporting evidence, see section 7 ("Definition of Type B Psychological Trauma") in "Brain Science, Psychological Trauma, and the God Who Is with Us ~ Part II: The Processing Pathway for Painful Experiences and the Definition of Psychological Trauma."

6. See section 5 ("Implicit Memory vs Explicit Memory") in "Brain Science, Psychological Trauma, and the God Who Is with Us ~ Part III: Traumatic Memories vs Non-Traumatic Memories" for additional discussion of how unresolved trauma contributes to each of these issues.

a flaming addiction to cocaine that is destroying every aspect of your life, but subtle impaired maturity and restlessness caused by unresolved trauma contributes to your problem with spending too much time playing games on your computer when important tasks are waiting for your attention. You may not have clinical anorexia, bulimia, or binge eating disorder; but a vague sense of emptiness, loneliness, and lack of satisfaction contributes to your pattern of snacking even when you're not hungry, and this subtle form of using food to moderate emotional discomfort from underlying painful memories causes your weight to ride twenty pounds higher than the set point your body would otherwise maintain. You may not have full-blown panic attacks; but subtle, memory-anchored fears about not being able to meet other people's expectations contributes to chronic, background tension that increases your vulnerability to headaches and impairs the quality of your sleep.

You may not be physically or emotionally abusing your children, but frustration from unresolved painful experiences subtly contributes to unpleasant scenarios where you respond to your kids with irritated harshness instead of patient gentleness. You may not be demonstrating obvious poor judgment by making dramatic blunders; but content from traumatic memories may be subtly blunting the edge of your discernment, especially when you are facing intense, complex challenges. You may be doing a pretty good job of fulfilling your work responsibilities and caring for your family, but traumas getting stirred up subtly undermine peak performance that could be even better. And you may be far from thinking about divorce; but unresolved traumas coming forward and blending with your experience in the present cause subtle exacerbations of the conflicts in your marriage, and these exacerbations of conflict result in small but frequent losses of joy and intimacy.

Chapter 1 Summary

To summarize the most important points so far:

- Trauma occurs when we encounter a painful experience but are unable to successfully complete each of the tasks in the pain-processing pathway.

- Trauma can be caused by surprisingly small painful experiences.

- Trauma is much more common than most people realize.

- Unresolved trauma can manifest in many, many different ways, and these effects of trauma are everywhere.

- Unresolved trauma especially contributes to relational conflicts.

- The effects of unresolved trauma can be subtle.

2

Implicit Memory vs. Explicit Memory

An important aspect of the unresolved content carried in traumatic memories is that it comes forward as *implicit* memory. Allow me to clarify the difference between explicit memory and implicit memory, and to explain why it's so important that unresolved traumatic content comes forward as implicit memory.

Explicit Memory

Explicit memory recall is what we all think of as "remembering." Explicit memory *feels* like "normal" memory. When we recall events through the explicit memory system, it feels, subjectively, like "I'm remembering something from my personal past experience." For example, if I ask you, "What did you do this morning?" you might tell me about getting woken up by the paper boy throwing the newspaper through your living room window at 5:30 a.m., and how you spent the next hour picking up broken glass, and you will *feel* like you are remembering something from your personal past. This *conscious, autobiographical*[1] memory about your personal experiences is explicit memory.

Implicit Memory

Implicit memory is all memory phenomena that *does not* include the subjective experience of "I'm remembering something from my personal past experience." Implicit memory content *does not* feel like "normal" memory. When the implicit memory systems are activated, our minds and brains recall memory material, but it does not feel, subjectively like explicit autobiographical memory. Since implicit memory does not *feel* like what we think of as memory, we usually *do not* have any awareness that we are remembering or being affected by past experience when memory material comes

---

1. Autobiographical memory is memory for the *story of your life*. For example, your memory for the story of your morning adventures with the paper boy would be autobiographical memory. Remembering the meaning of the word "autobiography" helps me to remember the definition of autobiographical memory: If I wrote a *book* about the story of my life, it would be called an *autobiography*; similarly, *memory* for the story of my life is *autobiographical memory*.

forward through one of the implicit memory systems. In fact, we sometimes refer to implicit memory as "invisible" memory, since it usually affects us without being "seen" by our conscious minds.

If this is the first time the reader has ever heard of implicit memory these statements might sound strange and hard to believe: "What do you mean, 'We don't have any awareness that we're remembering'? I can always feel that I'm remembering when I think about past experiences!" It may therefore surprise you to discover that you have probably remembered and applied implicit memory within the last hour. What could I be referring to? Well, were you born with the ability to walk? Certainly not. You had to *learn* how to walk, and as you *learned* to walk your brain *remembered* the various motor skills involved. Every time you walk, your brain is *remembering* learned motor skills. Even though you have no conscious awareness of it, you are recalling and using implicit memory every time you walk, every time you ride a bike, every time you drive a car, and every time you type an e-mail. As you are probably realizing by now, one of the most important and most common kinds of implicit memory is motor-skill memory.

Actually, there is a LOT of rigorous medical, scientific evidence proving the existence of implicit memory as separate from explicit memory. Some of the most easily understood data demonstrating the reality of implicit memory are observations from medical situations in which a particular neurological injury totally knocks out explicit memory while leaving a variety of implicit memory systems intact. For example, Dr. Oliver Sacks describes a carefully documented case study of a young man with complete loss of ability to lay down new explicit autobiographical memory due to a brain tumor that destroyed a part of his brain called the hippocampus. Within minutes after the actual event, Greg would lose every trace of explicit autobiographical memory for any personal experience—if you spoke with him for an *hour*, and then left briefly to use the restroom, when you returned *five minutes* later, he would have no conscious memory of ever having met you before. However, his implicit memory systems were still intact.

For example, he could learn new pieces of factual information—even though he did *not* have any *explicit autobiographical* memories of his conversations with Dr. Sacks, *he could remember the facts of news trivia from these conversations.* If you asked him, "Greg, have you spoken with Dr. Sacks today?" He would respond with something along the lines of, "Who's Dr. Sacks? I've never met the man." But if you then asked him, "Who won the baseball game last night?" He could often respond with accurate sports trivia from his conversation with Dr. Sacks earlier that morning: "The Mets won, 7 to 5, with two runs in the ninth inning." And he could learn to find his way around the hospital—even though he did *not* have any *explicit auto-biographical* memories of his years of living at the hospital, *he could walk from his room to the cafeteria without getting lost.* If you asked him, "Greg, can you show me the way to the cafeteria?" He would respond with some-thing along the lines of "I've never seen this place before this morning! How could I know the way to the cafeteria?" But when it was time for lunch, he would get up and walk to the cafeteria.

He could learn new physical skills, such as typing or playing the guitar—even though he did *not* have any *explicit autobiographical* memories of his many practice sessions, *if you put him in front of a typewriter he could type, and if you gave him a guitar he could play.* He could learn new songs—even though he did *not* have any *explicit memories* of ever hearing the new songs before, if someone started humming the tune he could sing the rest of the song. And he could form new emotional associations—even though he did *not* have any *explicit autobiographical* memories of previous interactions with people on the staff, *his face would light up when he met those who had been especially kind to him.*

The most dramatic demonstration of the difference between his *severely damaged* explicit memory and his *perfectly intact* implicit memory was his experience with attending a rock concert. Dr. Sacks took him to a Grateful Dead concert—a band he loved, but that he had not heard for many years. Rock concerts are not particularly subtle—not something you would forget easily. This concert was an *all day* event, and Greg participated *enthusias-tically* and *passionately.* The next day, he had **no** explicit autobiographical memory of going to the concert—*the morning after the concert,* when Dr. Sacks asked him about the Grateful Dead, he reported that he really liked the group but that it had been many years since he had been to one of their concerts. But he *could* remember and sing the new songs from the concert, and he had new positive emotional associations. For example, if Dr. Sacks played one of the new songs from the concert, Greg would immediately begin to sing along—accurately remembering both the words and the melody; and after the concert, whenever Dr. Sacks came to visit, Greg's face would light up and he would greet Dr. Sacks as a fellow Grateful Dead fan.[2]

Another especially dramatic case study is presented by Dr. Claparede. Dr. Claparede describes a forty-seven-year-old woman who had neurologi-cal injury that, like Greg's brain tumor, destroyed her ability to form new explicit autobiographical memory. Like Greg, she would lose all conscious, explicit autobiographical memory of personal experiences in a matter of minutes. Her inability to record new explicit autobiographical memory was

2. Oliver Sacks, *An Anthropologist on Mars* (New York: Vintage Books, 1995), pages 42–76.

so severe that she still did not recognize her physical surroundings (even after living at the chronic care facility for *five years*), she did not recognize the doctors she saw every day, and she continued to greet her nurse as a complete stranger (even after this nurse had been with her for six months).

However, her implicit memory systems remained intact, as demonstrated by a famous experiment performed by Dr. Claparede. While shaking hands with the patient, Dr. Claparede stuck her with a pin hidden between his fingers. Several minutes later, when Dr. Claparede again reached out for her hand, she pulled it back and refused to shake his hand. When questioned about her behavior, she persisted in her refusal to shake his hand, but appeared to have no conscious memory or insight regarding the recent incident with the pin. Any normal person would have responded to his questions with something direct and obvious, such as "Why do you *think* I don't want to shake your hand? You just stuck me with a pin! (You Jerk!)" Instead, this patient seemed confused and had difficulty explaining her persistent refusal to shake his hand. Eventually she commented, "Is there perhaps a pin hidden in your hand?" When asked why she would have this fear she again had difficulty explaining herself, and eventually responded with comments such as "That was an idea that went through my mind," or "Sometimes pins are hidden in people's hands."

Even though she did not have any *explicit autobiographical memory* of getting stuck a few minutes earlier, some kind of *implicit memory* correctly warned her that Dr. Claparede might have a pin hidden in his hand—the thought came into her mind that she might get stuck by a pin if she shook his hand, and it *felt true*.[3]

Traumatic Memory Content Comes Forward as Implicit Memory, and Why This Is Important

For this discussion, the relevant point with respect to explicit memory vs implicit memory is that the toxic content from unresolved trauma also comes forward as various kinds of implicit memory. *When something in the present triggers a traumatic memory, the unresolved content from the trauma, such as the distorted beliefs and emotions associated with the original painful experience, will come forward as "invisible" implicit memory **that feels true and valid in the present**.* For example, if questions from a person's boss trigger unresolved trauma from grade school, instead of having the

3.   Edouard Claparede, "Recognition and 'me-ness'," in *Organization and Pathology of Thought*, ed. D. Rapaport (New York: Columbia University Press, 1951), pages 58–74, specific quotes pages 69–70 (translated from E. Claparede. "Recognition et moiite." *Archives de Psychologie*. Vol. 11 (1911): pages 79–90).

explicit memory subjective experience of "I'm remembering the time when the teacher hit me with a ruler because I couldn't answer his questions," the person will just have the thoughts "I don't know the answer, and now he's going to hurt me," he will feel intense anxiety, *and he will perceive that these thoughts and emotions are **true and valid in the present**.*

My experience with dyslexia provides another good example of unresolved traumatic content coming forward as unrecognized, "invisible" implicit memory. I have dyslexia, but this was not discovered until second grade. Unfortunately, this meant that my teachers did not understand the problem or know how to help me during kindergarten and first grade as I was having tremendous difficulty learning how to read. There were incidents of particular unpleasantness, like getting laughed at by the whole class while trying to do some kind of reading/writing exercise on the chalkboard, but the more significant part of the pain was the day-after-day-after-day experience of being unable to learn how to read. When I tried and tried, but could not do something all the other kids appeared to be handling easily, I felt hopeless, I felt inadequate, and I concluded that I was stupid. Then, for most of the rest of my life (until these traumatic experiences got healed), whenever I would encounter a problem where I could not make some kind of progress fairly quickly I would have the thought, "I'm just stupid," I would feel hopeless and inadequate, and I would expect to fail. *But I never realized that this was memory content.* When this content from my kindergarten and first-grade experiences would get activated as implicit memory, these thoughts and emotions would *feel true in the present*, and I would have *no awareness that these thoughts and emotions were actually coming from my childhood memories.*

Note: It's really, really important to understand the phenomena of implicit memory, and the way in which the toxic content in unresolved trauma comes forward *invisibly* by coming forward as implicit memory. Many readers will already be familiar with these phenomena, but if you are not already familiar with this material, and not fully convinced by this brief summary presentation, then please see "Basic Memory Phenomena, Explicit and Implicit Memory," and "Brain Science, Psychological Trauma, and the God Who Is with Us ~ Part III." (Both of these essays are available for free download from our website, www.kclehman.com.)

The Verbal Logical Explainer and Confabulation

When dealing with unresolved traumatic content coming forward as "invisible" implicit memory, there are two intriguing, subtle, and ubiquitous phenomena that make the situation even more difficult.

What are the Verbal Logical Explainer (VLE) and Confabulation?

THE VERBAL LOGICAL EXPLAINER (VLE)
The first of these "particular phenomena" is the part of our brain/mind/spirit that I call our Verbal Logical Explainer, or VLE. The VLE's job is to come up with *explanations* that help us organize and make sense out of our experiences and the world around us. Most of the time this is a good thing. Our VLEs are constantly coming up with explanations that help us make sense out of our lives, and they usually work so quickly and smoothly that we don't even notice them. In fact, *your* VLE is busily working at this very moment, making sense out of your experience as you read this book. For example, your VLE is explaining to you that you are reading a book about psychological trauma and the Verbal Logical Explainer (as opposed to other things you might be doing, such as watching a soap opera, hang gliding in Hawaii, or driving to work in rush hour traffic).

Our VLEs also usually start with basically adequate and accurate data, and come up with basically valid explanations. However, if our VLEs start with distorted and/or inadequate data, they can come up with profoundly flawed explanations. For example, if my VLE starts with thoughts and emotions that are actually from my playground cheating trauma, but these thoughts and emotions are coming forward as "invisible" implicit memory so that they *feel true in the present* and I have *no awareness of their real origin*, my VLE will make up explanations for how these thoughts and emotions are being caused by *circumstances in the present*, such as people using the merge lane to go to the front of the line in a construction zone.

CONFABULATION

The second of these "particular phenomena" is confabulation. Confabulation is a special kind of fabrication in which the person makes something up based on her best guess regarding what might be the answer, but with *no conscious awareness that she is just guessing* and with *no deliberate intent to deceive*. Confabulation is most dramatically seen in people who have severely damaged explicit memory combined with minimal conscious awareness of their explicit memory deficit, such as people with Korsakov's syndrome. However, we all engage in much more subtle forms of confabulation when our VLEs are unknowingly working with raw material that includes "invisible" implicit memory content.

Fascinating Examples from Research and Case Studies

There are fascinating research studies and clinical case studies that demonstrate the sobering ability of the VLE to come up with flawed, confabulated explanations when it starts with flawed and/or inadequate raw material. One of the most dramatic sources of information about the Verbal Logical Explainer comes from split-brain research. Most seizure disorders can be controlled with medication, but some people have extremely severe seizure disorders that do not respond adequately to medication. Even on several simultaneous medications, each at maximum dosage, these patients might still be having twenty, thirty, or even fifty seizures every day; and if this kind of seizure activity is allowed to continue, it will cause progressive brain damage that eventually ends in death. For these patients, one of the last-ditch treatment options is to cut the pathways that connect the right and left sides of the brain, so that seizures starting on one side will not spread to the whole brain. This is pretty drastic, but it's better than progressive brain damage and death.

When the two sides of the brain are separated in this way, the Verbal Logical Explainer on the left side no longer receives communication from the right side, and this leads to some very interesting results when the left-sided VLE tries to explain right-sided behavior. For example, in one study the patient was first shown a card with a single image, and then shown a card with a number of different images, from which he was asked to pick the item most related to the first picture (figure 3.1). Because of how the neurology of the visual system is designed, it is possible to simultaneously show one image to the right side of the brain and a different image to the left side of the brain, and the research team designed special equipment that could do this. The patient was then shown an initial image that presented a picture

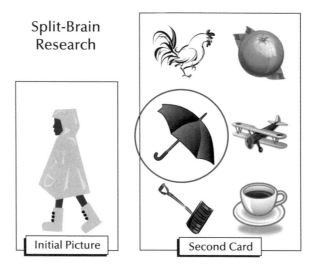

Figure 3.1   Split-brain research: The subject is instructed to pick the image from the second card that is most related to the initial picture.

of a chicken foot to the left side of his brain and a picture of a snowstorm to the right side of his brain. As indicated in figure 3.2, when he was shown the second set of pictures, his right hand (corresponding to the left side of his brain) immediately pointed to the picture of the chicken, while his left hand (corresponding to the right side of his brain) pointed to the picture of the snow shovel. The left side of his brain saw the chicken foot and then chose

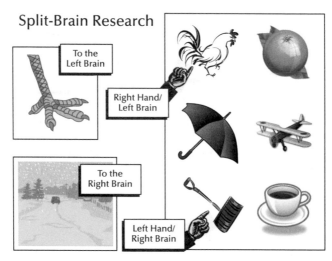

Figure 3.2   The left brain sees the chicken foot and points to the chicken, while the right brain sees the snowstorm and points to the snow shovel.

the chicken, while the right side of his brain saw the snowstorm and then chose the snow shovel.

This was not particularly surprising. But then the researchers thought to ask the patient to *explain* his choices. He first explained that he had chosen the chicken to go with the chicken foot, which again surprised no one. However, when they asked him to explain why he had also chosen the snow shovel, instead of acknowledging "I don't know," or even "I'm not sure," he promptly responded that if you had chickens, you would need something with which to clean out the chicken shed. Aware that he had chosen the snow shovel, *but completely unaware of the fact that this picture was chosen in response to the initial image of the snowstorm,* his left-sided Verbal Logical Explainer *just made something up* (figure 3.3). Furthermore, the patient appeared to have no awareness that his Verbal Logical Explainer had just made up an explanation that had *absolutely nothing to do with the real reason he had chosen the picture of the snow shovel.*[1]

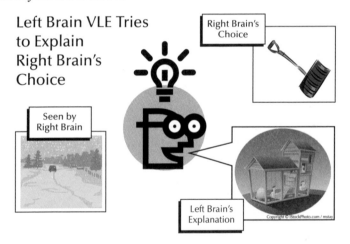

Figure 3.3   When the *left*-brain Verbal Logical Explainer is asked to explain the snow shovel chosen by the *right* brain: "If you had chickens, you would need something with which to clean out the chicken shed."

Research with hypnosis provides another source of dramatic information regarding the Verbal Logical Explainer. For example, a well-known and often-repeated demonstration, in which the person is not consciously aware of a post-hypnotic suggestion as the true cause of a particular action,

---

1.   For a thorough discussion of the original research, see Michael S. Gazzaniga and Joseph E. LeDoux, *The Integrated Mind* (New York: Plenum Press, 1978), pages 146–150; for Dr. Gazzaniga's account of his personal subjective experience and thoughts as he performed the experiment, see Carl Zimmer, "A Career Spent Learning How the Mind Emerges From the Brain," *New York Times*, May 10, 2005, page F3.

again exposes the VLE making something up when the person is asked to explain his behavior. While the demonstration subject is in hypnotic trance, the hypnotist makes the post hypnotic suggestion: "When I tap three times on the table with my pencil, you will get up and open the window, and you will not remember that I gave you these instructions until I give you permission to do so." The subject is brought out of hypnotic trance, the hypnotist pretends to end the demonstration, and then several minutes later the hypnotist "absent mindedly" taps his pencil on the table. The subject gets up and opens the window, and as he's returning to his seat the hypnotist asks "Why did you open the window?"

You might think the person would pause, look confused, anxious, and maybe also embarrassed, and then respond with something along the lines of: "Well, I—I don't really know. This is actually kind of weird. I was sitting there listening to your presentation, and then I suddenly had this irrational impulse to get up and open the window. I hope I'm not going crazy or something!" However, this is not what happens. The person might pause for the *briefest* moment, an expression of confusion might *flicker* across his face, and then he responds with something like: "It was getting stuffy in here, so I thought I'd open the window." With most subjects, the moment of hesitation is barely discernible, and the person appears to be *completely unaware* of the fact that his VLE has just given an explanation that is only a wild guess—a guess that actually has *nothing* to do with the real reason for his actions.[2]

Children have Verbal Logical Explainers that are still quite primitive, and therefore provide yet another place where it's easy to recognize that the VLE often makes things up. For example, a number of years ago Charlotte and I spent a week with my sister, Emily, and her family, and after we left, our four-year-old niece, Miranda, was having a terrible, horrible, no good, very bad day.[3] Throughout the day she became increasingly fussy, irritable,

---

2. Some people think hypnosis is just a joke, some believe it is a valuable tool that can be used safely in certain situations, and some believe that it is an occult practice in which Christians should never participate. I am convinced that hypnosis is a real phenomenon because colleagues in the medical center where I obtained my psychiatric training routinely used hypnosis as the only anesthetic for major oral surgery procedures (procedures that involved scalpels and stitches). However, I encourage people to be **very** cautious with respect to using it. At this point, my perception is that hypnosis *may* simply come out of science that is not yet understood, in which case it is not *inherently* non-Christian/occult, and it may be possible for careful, competent practitioners to use it safely. On the other hand, my perception is that hypnosis *may* include spiritual components that are inherently non-Christian/occult, and are therefore inherently unsafe. For additional thoughts regarding practices that may be non-Christian/occult, see "Non-Christian/Occult Spiritual Activities" (available as a free download from www.kclehman.com).

3. This description should have special meaning for those of you familiar with Judith Viorst's wonderful children's book, *Alexander and the Terrible, Horrible, No Good, Very Bad Day* (New York: Aladdin Paperbacks, 1972).

whiny, and frustrated with everything and everybody. Finally, as Miranda was brushing her teeth in preparation for going to bed, Emily asked her, "What's the matter, honey? Why are you so unhappy?" And Miranda, looking at the toothbrush she was holding in her hand at that moment, responded with, "BECAUSE THE TOOTHBRUSH IS *ORANGE*!!!"

When asked to come up with an explanation for why she was so unhappy, her four-year-old Verbal Logical Explainer, seeing the toothbrush in front of her face and having no insight regarding the attachment pain caused by Charlotte and me leaving, came up with an explanation that had *nothing* to do with the real reason for her emotional distress: "I'm upset because the toothbrush is orange!!" And we know the problem really was attachment pain because after Miranda's angry accusation blaming the terrible orange toothbrush, Emily gently suggested, "I wonder if you miss Aunt Charlotte and Uncle Karl?" There was a long pause as Miranda's face slowly crumpled, and then she burst into tears, "Yeee-ee-ee-ee-ss." Emily held her, comforted her, and talked with her about how much fun it had been to spend time with Charlotte and me, about how it was okay to be sad that we had left, and about how we would come back again next year. After having a good cry and receiving the comfort Emily was offering, Miranda's usual pleasant disposition promptly returned.[4]

Patients with Korsakov's syndrome provide some of the most dramatic opportunities to observe the Verbal Logical Explainer making things up. Korsakov's syndrome produces a very specific kind of brain damage that results in a form of memory impairment very similar to Greg's, in which the person retains memory for events prior to the illness but is totally unable to form any *new* autobiographical memories; and just as with Greg's injury, this amnesia for new autobiographical memory can be so severe that you can talk with one of these patients for an hour, leave the room to get a drink of water, and when you return forty-five seconds later the person is convinced that he has never met you before. Furthermore, in some cases of Korsakov's syndrome, the person's Verbal Logical Explainer also seems to be particularly unaware of the memory impairment. This results in a dramatic situation in which the person's Verbal Logical Explainer has *no* autobiographical information regarding the many months (and often many years) between

---

4.   For those of you who are already familiar with the concepts of attunement and relational connection circuits: yes, Emily was offering attunement. And as Miranda was able to receive this attunement, she regained access to her relational connection circuits, she was able to share Emily's capacity and maturity skills through the attunement connection, and she was then able to successfully process the pain associated with Charlotte and me leaving. For those of you who are not yet familiar with attunement and relational circuits, these concepts will be explained in parts 3 and 4 and then this example will be even more meaningful.

the onset of the illness and the immediate present, and also seems to be completely unaware of this huge lack of accurate contextual information. The person's VLE therefore constantly makes up "best guess" explanations based on the combination of painfully outdated information from his distant past and the information immediately in front of him.

In contrast to someone with Korsakov's syndrome, as you read this book *your* VLE is giving you *accurate* explanations with respect to what you are doing and why because *you remember* getting an e-mail from a close friend telling you about the book and urging you to check it out, *you remember* looking at the material on our website and then deciding to order a copy, *you remember* beginning chapter 1 when you finally got some free time this morning, and *you remember* continuing to read because you were impressed by the thought-provoking research and case studies presented in the first fifteen pages. Your VLE is working with this adequate, accurate contextual information and therefore comes up with accurate explanations.

However, if you had Korsakov's syndrome, the only contextual information you would have would be your observations and immediate memory from the last thirty seconds, and your memories from before you developed Korsakov's (which could easily have been fifteen years ago). Working with this profoundly inadequate contextual information your VLE would come up with dramatically erroneous explanations. For example, with observations of your immediate surroundings and memory of the content from the last several paragraphs as the only information regarding the past fifteen years, your VLE might explain to you that you are back in school, taking a course on neuropsychology as part of the pre-med program. Furthermore, your VLE might explain to you that you are in deep trouble and must now begin a frantic search for the syllabus, since you can't seem to remember much that has happened this semester, you can't remember whether or not you should be working on a term paper, and you can't remember whether or not there will be an exam tomorrow morning.

The following verbatim transcript from an interaction between Dr. Sacks and one of his patients with Korsakov's provides a painfully dramatic true example:

> "What'll it be today?" he says, rubbing his hands. "Half a pound of Virginia, a nice piece of Nova?" (Evidently he saw me as a customer—he would often pick up the phone on the ward and say "Thompson's Delicatessen".)
>
> "Oh Mr. Thompson!" I exclaim. "And who do you think I am?"

"Good heavens, the light's bad—I took you for a customer. As if it isn't my old friend Tom Pitkins . . . Me and Tom" (he whispers in an aside to the nurse) "was always going to the races together."

"Mr. Thompson, you are mistaken again."

"So I am," he rejoins, not put out for a moment. "Why would you be wearing a white coat if you were Tom? you're Hymie, the kosher butcher next door. No bloodstains on your coat though. Business bad today? You'll look like a slaughterhouse by the end of the week!"

Feeling a bit swept away myself in this whirlpool of identities, I finger the stethoscope dangling from my neck.

"A Stethoscope!" he exploded. "And you pretending to be Hymie! You mechanics are all starting to fancy yourselves to be doctors, what with your white coats and stethoscopes—as if you need a stethoscope to listen to a car! So, you're my old friend Manners from the Mobil station up the block, come in to get your boloney-and-rye . . ."

William Thompson rubbed his hands again, in his salesman-grocer's gesture, and looked for the counter. Not finding it, he looked at me strangely.

"Where am I?" he said, with a sudden scared look. "I thought I was in my shop, doctor. My mind must have wandered . . . You'll be wanting my shirt off, to sound me as usual?"

"No, not the usual. I'm *not* your usual doctor."

"Indeed you're not. I could see that straightaway! You're not my usual chest-thumping doctor. And, by God, you've a beard! You look like Sigmund Freud—have I gone bonkers, round the bend?"

"No, Mr. Thompson. Not round the bend. Just a little trouble with your memory—difficulties remembering and recognizing people."

"My memory has been playing me some tricks," he admitted. "Sometimes I make mistakes—I take somebody for somebody else . . . What'll it be now—Nova or Virginia?"

So it would happen, with variations, every time—with improvisations, always prompt, often funny, sometimes brilliant, and ultimately tragic. Mr. Thompson would identify me—misidentify me, pseudo-identify me—as a dozen different people in the course of five minutes. He would whirl, fluently, from one guess, one hypothesis, one belief, to the next, *without any appearance of uncertainty at any point* (emphasis mine).[5]

---

5.   Reprinted with permission from Oliver Sacks, *The Man Who Mistook His Wife for a Hat* (New York: HarperCollins, 1970), pages 108–109.

As is especially clear from this example, a person's VLE has an amazing ability to make things up, and this amazing ability to fabricate can be accompanied by an alarming absence of self-awareness.

VLE Confabulations Make It More Difficult to Spot Triggering

With respect to unresolved trauma and implicit memory, the relevant point is that your VLE will quickly and smoothly come up with an explanation for why and how your *current circumstances* are causing you to experience any triggered thoughts and emotions (thoughts and emotions that are actually content from unresolved trauma coming forward as implicit memory). And, unfortunately, the confabulated, flawed VLE explanations *feel* very much like valid VLE explanations. Without a lot of deliberate practice, most of us don't seem to perceive any difference between valid explanations and flawed, confabulated explanations.

Having an explanation that accounts for the triggered thoughts and emotions as being reasonable responses to events in the present makes it even more difficult to recognize the implicit memory content for what it is. When unresolved trauma, implicit memory, and VLE explanations come together in this way, you will try to resolve your painful thoughts and emotions by focusing your energy and attention on the triggers in the present, as if they are the true source of the implicit memory traumatic content; and if the trigger happens to be another person's behavior, you will try to resolve your painful thoughts and emotions by attempting to make her change this terrible behavior that is causing all your problems.

Let me give you an example. When I was a kid, our two-week family vacations each summer were hugely important. The rest of the year was hard. The news was filled with horrors from the Vietnam War; environmental activists were warning us about how the exploding population and pollution from modern industry would soon cause global ecological disaster; John Kennedy, Robert Kennedy, and Martin Luther King were all assassinated during my childhood; and everybody knew that we would all die in a nuclear holocaust if somebody pushed the wrong button. Closer to home, the crime and racial tensions in our neighborhood caused me to feel physically unsafe much of the time; I had difficulty in school because of my dyslexia; I didn't have any friends that really understood me; and I was skinny, slow, not good at any sports, and without musical or artistic talent. On top of all of this, it felt as if my parents were intensely absorbed in dealing with all the HUGE problems, and were therefore only marginally available to me.

But our family vacations each summer were different. For two weeks each year we escaped from the playground and the neighborhood where I felt physically unsafe, from the pollution that constantly reminded me of environmental destruction, from the crowding that reminded me of global population problems, and from the media full of disaster and death. And we escaped *to* rural environments that I loved. All my hobbies revolved around various aspects of nature study, so the plants and animals were familiar friends and I felt safe and comforted in their company. Furthermore, we escaped from the church leadership responsibilities and counseling emergencies that weighed on Dad so heavily. During our family vacations Dad was usually smiling and laughing as opposed to worrying and frowning. (My best childhood memories with Dad are all from family camping trips.)

This was the oasis I looked forward to all year, and it felt like I needed to obtain the absolute maximum benefit from each precious day, hour, and minute of this special time in order to make it through the rest of the year. Consequently, it was of utmost importance that we leave early enough to get out of Chicago before the onset of rush hour. If any combination of unexpected delays caused us to start too late, we could spend the first couple hours of precious vacation sitting in rush hour traffic instead of sailing down the interstate on the way to our campsite, and this was a disaster to be avoided at all costs.

Forty years later, Charlotte and I would have regular conflict around leaving for vacations. The plan would usually be to leave at 6:00 a.m., providing a barely adequate margin of time for slipping out of the city before the beginning of morning rush hour. And at 0600 hours (military time), I would be sitting in the car, looking at my watch, and waiting to pull away from the curb, while Charlotte would still be inside taking *much too long* to deal with last-minute details. At this point urgency about getting started before it's too late and anxiety that we might get stuck in traffic would start coming forward as implicit memory, and as each second went by they would become increasingly intense. If Charlotte was still in the house at 6:05 a.m., I was a very unhappy camper; and God have mercy if she should have forgotten to get money out of the bank the day before, forcing us to lose ten more minutes driving by the cash station.

This is where VLE confabulations and the invisibility of implicit memory would come in. The urgency and anxiety would *feel* true and valid, as if both their presence and the full extent of their intensity were reasonable in the present, and my VLE would come up with a variety of explanations justifying this perception: "*Of course* I want to get started on time! I work long hours at a very stressful job and I need *adequate* restoration. *Adequate* restoration means getting started on time, so that we have *enough* time to relax at our campsite instead of spending our vacation sitting in traffic. *Any reasonable person would feel the same way.* And besides, we *agreed* to leave at **6:00** a.m., so I'm expecting to leave at **6:00** a.m.—what's so unreasonable about expecting her to simply abide by something she has *already explicitly agreed to?! . . .*" In the years before I had insight regarding what was really going on, I would then try to resolve my painful thoughts and emotions *by focusing my energy and attention on the triggers in the present, as if they were the true source of the implicit memory traumatic content.* Instead of realizing, "Boy, I'm really triggered. This is stuff from *my* old memories, and it's really affecting the way I treat Charlotte—I can *feel* how I get impatient, unreasonable, and judgmental whenever this stuff gets stirred up," and then focusing on dealing with *my* old trauma so that I would stop dumping it on Charlotte, I would focus my energy and attention on Charlotte and her terrible behavior: "If I could just get *Charlotte* to prepare more thoroughly the night before, get up earlier, be less obsessive and more efficient, etc., so that she'd be in the car at 5:57 a.m.[6] and ready to pull away from the curb at 0600 hours, *everything would be fine.*"[7]

Another important part of this whole implicit memory and VLE confabulation picture is that when someone does something that stirs up an unresolved traumatic memory, it will feel intensely subjectively true that she should take responsibility for causing *all* my pain—I won't just want her to take responsibility for pain caused in the present by the behavior that *triggered* the underlying trauma, I will want her to confess, apologize, and make restitution as if she caused the full extent of the pain in the underlying traumatic memory. I didn't just want Charlotte to take responsibility for causing the small portion of distress that would have been reasonable in response to her being five minutes late, I wanted her to confess, apologize, and make restitution as if she were the true source and origin of all the frustration, disappointment, and anxiety that was really unresolved childhood

---

6. Providing the necessary *additional three minutes* for her to adjust the mirrors, adjust the seat, check her purse, look at the map, fiddle with the change so that it would be properly organized for easy access at toll booths, etc.

7. In the interest of truth and justice: implicit content from my childhood vacation memories also contributed to the fact that I was sitting in the car looking at my watch while Charlotte was still running around the house. When I was a child, my "morning of the trip" responsibilities had always included helping to pack the car, but after that was completed I sat impatiently in my seat waiting for the grown-ups to take care of all the other stuff (the stuff I always left to Charlotte after I finished packing the car), like making sure we had money for gas, directions to get to where we were going, and emergency phone numbers, making sure the lights were turned off and the doors were locked, etc. If I hadn't been thinking and behaving from inside the perspective of my childhood family vacation memories, I would have been *in the house helping Charlotte* instead of *sitting in the car judging her.*

pain. And I would not feel heard, understood, validated, safe, or ready for reconciliation until this had happened.

Smart criminals provide a good analogy. The really smart criminal does not just leave an unsolved crime, with a team of investigators that are still trying to find him. Instead, he is always careful to frame someone else, so that the case is closed. The really smart criminal wants to see someone else convicted for his crime, so that the detectives stop looking for clues. The combination of VLE confabulations and unresolved trauma coming forward as implicit memory is similar, in that the problem is not left as an "unsolved crime," where you're still looking for clues. The implicit memory content *feels* true in the present, and your VLE comes up with a confabulated explanation for why the triggers in the present should take full responsibility for the implicit memory content that has come forward. You are no longer looking for the clues that would point to underlying trauma, because someone has already been arrested and convicted. This analogy is particularly valid because an important part of the damage from this combination of trauma, implicit memory, and VLE confabulations is that people in the present get "framed" for content that is actually coming from underlying trauma.

For example, let's say Nancy had an alcoholic father who was emotionally and physically unsafe. Whenever he got angry he would threaten, bully, and intimidate, and this frightening behavior frequently escalated to actual physical violence, so Nancy knew he was not just bluffing. This scenario occurred over and over throughout Nancy's childhood, and she has many traumatic memories of these events. Now, twenty-five years later, Nancy is married to David, who occasionally gets angry *but never bullies, intimidates, threatens, or gets violent.* For example, David gets home from work as friends are showing up for a dinner party, and as he brings in the mail he notices a receipt for another thirty-five dollar parking ticket. Two minutes later, when he walks into the kitchen to help with last-minute preparations, Nancy notices his angry face and asks him "What's the matter?"

"We just got another parking ticket receipt in the mail today, that's what's the matter!" David retorts. "This is the *fourth* thirty-five dollar ticket you've gotten trying to save time by parking in one of the fifteen minute spaces right in front of the office, instead of going to the fifty-cent meters two blocks away. I thought we had talked about this, and agreed that it's unrealistic to think that you'll be able to take care of business and get back to the car in less than fifteen minutes." David looks irritated as he says this, and his frustrated voice is slightly raised, but he does not make any kind of threatening gesture toward Nancy, drop the slightest hint that there will be "consequences," or even glare at her. In fact, he makes these comments while still choosing to help by carrying one of the serving dishes to the table. Furthermore, fifteen minutes later he apologizes to Nancy and the guests for getting so upset about a "stupid little parking ticket," and then finishes with: "Considering how much we've paid for my speeding tickets, I really shouldn't be judging Nancy for her parking issues." And he is genuinely pleasant (even to Nancy) throughout the rest of the meal.

However, whenever David gets angry Nancy *feels* bullied, intimidated, and threatened because his anger triggers her unresolved memories, and the toxic content comes forward as "invisible" implicit memory *that feels true in the present*. Furthermore, her VLE looks at the information in front of her and comes up with an explanation along the lines of: "I *feel* bullied, intimidated, and threatened, and I'm having these feelings *because David is bullying, intimidating, and threatening me with his anger. He feels* dangerous when he's angry, and I know he'll escalate to violence if I don't do what he wants. . . ." She is vaguely aware that she has never seen David get violent, with her or anyone else, and also that she can't identify any actual specifics that would indicate bullying, intimidation, or threat; but she still accepts the combined implicit memory and VLE explanation package *because it feels so compellingly true.*

This combination of implicit memories and erroneous VLE explanations creates a point of unresolvable conflict (or an "irreconcilable difference" in the language of our divorce courts). Whenever this memory content is active, Nancy *feels* threatened, intimidated, and bullied; she demands that David take full responsibility for intimidating and bullying her by threatening violence; and she will only feel heard, validated, safe, and ready for reconciliation if he does this. This was all true *with respect to her father*, and her conditions for reconciliation and demands regarding taking responsibility would have been appropriate *with respect to her father*; but the combination of her implicit memories and VLE confabulated explanations also creates the subjectively compelling perception[8] that this same picture is true *in the present with respect to David*. However, since this picture is *not* actually true in the present, he cannot honestly own it. They are therefore stuck with an unresolvable conflict, in which she's demanding that he acknowledge what feels compellingly true to her and he's refusing to own what he knows is not his.

John and Sara provide another example. When John was a boy his father spent most of his time and energy building an increasingly successful business, and he ignored John's mother, who became increasingly lonely. John's mother eventually got a job outside the home in order to have more

---

8.   It is almost impossible to overstate the intensely compelling quality of the combined implicit memories and VLE explanations.

interaction with other adults, and her beauty and intelligence did not go unnoticed. Her boss appreciated her competence, perceived her as attractive, and genuinely enjoyed her company. Initially, this friendship seemed like a good thing. John noticed that his mother's boss was very kind to her, he often noticed his mother smiling as she talked to her boss, and she was generally much happier. Unfortunately, what began as a friendship developed into an affair, and John's mother eventually left the family in order to marry her boss. Now, twenty-five years later, John is married to Sara, who is outgoing and friendly to all her acquaintances (including men), *but never the least bit inappropriate.* For example, at the church Christmas party Sara might be in a circle of conversation that includes several of their men friends. She is telling jokes, laughing, and smiling at everyone, but she is not being flirtatious, dropping even the slightest sexual innuendos, or being inappropriate in any other way. Furthermore, John is in the circle of conversation right next to hers and it is clear that she is happy to have him nearby.

However, when he notices her talking to and smiling at other men, he *feels* vulnerable, fearful, betrayed, and rejected. When he sees Sara smiling at her male friends, his unresolved memories are triggered and the toxic content comes forward as "invisible" implicit memory *that feels true in the present.* It *feels true* that Sara is engaging in inappropriate intimacy. He admits he has absolutely no evidence indicating that she's had an actual *physical* affair (yet), but he fears that she may be having sex with these other men, and it *feels true* that Sara will eventually abandon him to run off with another man. Furthermore, his VLE looks at the information in front of him and comes up with an explanation along the lines of: "I feel anxious and betrayed, and I'm having these feelings *because Sara is being unfaithful.* I wouldn't feel this way if she weren't doing *something* inappropriate. . . ." He's vaguely aware of the reality that he can't explain exactly why Sara's friendly smiles are inappropriate, and that he has never observed any other inappropriate behavior, but he still accepts the combined implicit memory and VLE explanation package *because it feels so compellingly true.*

This combination of implicit memories and erroneous VLE explanations once again creates a point of unresolvable conflict. Whenever this memory content is active, it *feels true* to John that Sara is betraying him and that she will eventually abandon him. He admits that there's no proof of sexual unfaithfulness (yet), but he wants her to at least take responsibility for having an *emotional* affair with any male friend at whom she frequently smiles. At the *very* least he wants her to acknowledge that her smiling at other men is inappropriate, and he will only feel heard, validated, safe, and ready for reconciliation if she does this. *His mother's* friendship and smiles did become inappropriate, *his mother* did have an emotional affair that eventually lead to sexual unfaithfulness and abandoning the family, and his conditions for reconciliation and demands regarding taking responsibility would have been appropriate *with respect to his mother*; but the combination of his implicit memories and VLE explanations also create the subjectively compelling perception that this same picture is true *in the present with respect to Sara*. However, since this picture is *not* actually true in the present, she cannot honestly own it. They are therefore stuck with an irreconcilable difference, in which he's demanding that she acknowledge what feels compellingly true to him and she's refusing to own what she knows is not hers.

Returning to my dyslexia trauma provides a third example that is less dramatic but a lot closer to home. As described earlier, I had great difficulty in learning to read. In spite of my best efforts during the two years of kindergarten and first grade, I could not do something that all the other kids appeared to be handling easily. At this point I needed a lot of help from the adults in my life: I needed my teachers to recognize my learning disability and initiate special assistance so that I would not remain hopelessly stuck with a problem I could not solve; I needed my parents and teachers to help me navigate the painful experience of repeated failure, especially in a context where others were succeeding; and I needed my parents and teachers to help me correctly interpret the meaning of my reading difficulties.

Unfortunately, none of this happened. My teachers failed to recognize my dyslexia, concluding, instead, that I just wasn't trying, and my parents were unaware of the problem. Furthermore, my classmates would laugh at my dyslexic mistakes and make various comments implying that I was stupid. As a result of all this, I felt inadequate because I could not learn how to read, I felt inadequate because I was unable to successfully navigate the experience of failing at a task others could do easily, I came to the distorted conclusion that I was stupid, and I felt shame due to this distorted belief. Not surprisingly, with two years of daily practice I developed a very specific *inadequate—"I'm stupid"—shame* package, and this package would especially get triggered by any situation in which I was having difficulty but others were doing well.

Forty years later, Charlotte and I decided that playing Scrabble would be a fun thing to do for one of our date nights. Charlotte: "Oh, look at this, I can spell 'quiz'! Let's see . . . with ten points for the *q*, a triple-letter score for the ten-point *z*, and a double-word score for the whole word . . . that comes to ninety-six points!" Karl: "Well, I can spell trigger, with a triple-letter bonus on the two-point *g*, but all the other letters are just one-pointers. How come my word is longer than yours but I only get fifteen points?!" This went on, move after move, until we finished the game with Charlotte at 427 and Karl at 158. If this whole Scrabble episode had been filmed, and the tape analyzed by a group of objective observers, they would *all* agree that Charlotte had just been having a good time playing Scrabble and that she was particularly good at it. These same observers would also see that she had been smiling, glad to be with me, and not doing anything inappropriate or inconsiderate. Unfortunately, I was *not* able to see through the eyes of our theoretical observers. As Charlotte was doing so well and I was having so much difficulty, I began to feel increasingly inadequate, stupid, and humiliated because this particular scenario triggered my unresolved memories, *and the toxic content came forward as "invisible" implicit memory that **felt true in the present**.* And it *felt true* that her dramatic victory was the true source and origin of my painful thoughts and emotions.

Furthermore, Charlotte did not recognize or fix the problem. Our objective observers, once again carefully analyzing the video, would notice that I hadn't said anything and that I was doing a good job of hiding my growing unhappiness. Our helpful observers would probably also realize that it was *my* adult-maturity responsibility[9] to notice I was not doing well, that it was *my* adult-maturity responsibility to let Charlotte know there was a problem, that it was *my* adult-maturity responsibility to *ask*[10] for her assistance, and that it was *my* adult-maturity responsibility to retain ownership of *my* problems regardless of whether or not Charlotte gave me the help I asked for. Unfortunately, I was once again unable to perceive the situation from the perspective of our "oh-so-helpful" observers. As more traumatic content came forward as "invisible" implicit memory that *felt true in the present*, I became increasingly angry at Charlotte for not taking responsibility for my care. It *felt true* that I needed help from the adults in my life—it *felt true* that Charlotte should have noticed my distress, figured out what was wrong, and "initiated special assistance;" it *felt true* that *Charlotte* should have taken responsibility for helping me navigate failure in a situation in which others were succeeding; it *felt true* that *Charlotte* should have lead in the process

---

9. When I refer to "adult-maturity" responsibilities, I am specifically referring to the adult stage of psychological/spiritual maturity, and the responsibilities corresponding to this stage of maturity, as presented in James G. Friesen, et al., *The Life Model: Living from the Heart Jesus Gave You—The Essentials of Christian Living* revised 2000-R, (Van Nuys, CA: Shepherd's House Publishing, 2004) and E. James Wilder, *The Complete Guide to Living with Men* (Pasadena, CA: Shepherd's House Publishing, 2004).

10. Part of my adult-maturity responsibility is to make sure my *asking* is a "clean" request—a request that is free of entitlement or any implication that there will be consequences if the answer is 'no.' For an especially excellent discussion of "clean" requests, see Dallas Willard's discussion of "the dynamic of the request" (Dallas Willard, *The Divine Conspiracy: Rediscovering Our Hidden Life in God* [New York: Harper Collins, 1998], pages 231–244).

of helping me interpret the meaning of the experience; *and it felt true that Charlotte's failure to do these things made her responsible for my pain.*

To make matters even worse, Charlotte occasionally tried to be helpful by pointing out how I could have earned three times as many points if I had used the same letters to spell a different word, strategically placed at a spot on the board that would have made use of bonuses. Our objective, non-triggered observers, perceiving things correctly, would see that she was truly trying to help me become a better Scrabble player by offering coaching tips, and that she was offering her tips in a friendly, encouraging manner. Unfortunately, I was *still* not able to see the situation through the eyes of our objective, non-triggered, always-better-than-me observers (*thank you very much*). Charlotte's comments unconsciously reminded me of my classmates pointing out my failures, and this became yet another way in which the Scrabble scenario triggered my unresolved memories. Even more toxic content came forward as invisible implicit memory that *felt true in the present,* and it *felt true* that she was being hurtful by making comments that just highlighted my stupidity.

My VLE looked at all this and came up with an explanation along the lines of: "*She's* the one who keeps playing so hard even when she's way ahead, and *she's* the one who keeps pointing out how I could've made better moves. She should notice that she's beating me by such a wide margin, she should notice that this is bothering me, she should care for my distress by backing off, and she should realize that her 'tips' are just making things worse. It's *her* failure to be sensitive and considerate that is 'making' me feel so bad. *I* would be *fine* if she would just stop beating my pants off and then making insensitive remarks implying that I'm an idiot." At some vague level I realized that I couldn't explain exactly why her dramatic victory was making me feel *so* bad, and that I couldn't explain exactly why it should be *Charlotte's* responsibility to notice that I'm unhappy, figure out what's the matter, and initiate fixing the problem; but I still accepted the combined implicit memory and VLE package *because it felt so compellingly true.* At some level, my "bottom-line" internal response was: "I can't quite articulate all the reasons right now, *but I know I'm right.* She's got to be doing *something* wrong to make me feel so bad! I'll come back to it later and find more convincing arguments, but in the meantime I'll keep working with what I *know* is true: *She's responsible for my distress, and she ought to be doing a lot more to fix the problem!*"

To the extent that I was unable to recognize and own my triggering and VLE confabulations, this combination of implicit memories and confabulated explanations created a point of unresolvable conflict with respect to my Scrabble pain. I wanted Charlotte to admit that her behavior had been both hurtful and negligent—I wanted her to take responsibility for both causing my pain and for failing to care for me once I was in distress. And I would have felt heard, validated, safe, and ready for reconciliation only if/ when she had done this. These demands regarding taking responsibility and conditions for reconciliation would have been appropriate *with respect to my parents and teachers regarding my kindergarten and first-grade experience*. In kindergarten and first grade, it *was* appropriate for me to expect my teachers to care for me. It *was* appropriate for me to expect my teachers to figure out what was the matter and take responsibility for initiating assistance, and they *did* set me up for feeling inadequate by failing to recognize my learning disability or to initiate special assistance. It *was* appropriate to expect the adults in my life to take the initiative in helping me navigate the difficult situation of being unable to learn something other kids were mastering easily, it *was* appropriate to expect them to help me interpret the meaning of the experience, and they *did* contribute to my pain by failing to provide this care.

All this would have been appropriate and accurate when I was six years old with respect to my teachers and parents, but the combination of my implicit memories and VLE explanations created the subjectively compelling perception that this same picture was true *in the present with respect to Charlotte*. However, since this picture was not actually true in the present with respect to Charlotte, she could not honestly own it. We were therefore stuck with an irreconcilable difference, in which I was demanding that she acknowledge what felt compellingly true to me and she was refusing to own what she knew was not hers.

Note regarding examples: Before moving on, I want to take a moment to make sure you realize our examples are simplified so that it's easier to see the teaching points. In real life, you almost never see conflicts in which one person carries all the triggering and the other is essentially perfect. Real-life situations are messier and more difficult to sort out because there's almost always triggering and imperfection on both sides.

4

Central Nervous System Extrapolation, Denial, and Self-Deception

Even with all this information regarding invisible implicit memory, the Verbal Logical Explainer, and confabulated explanations, it's still hard to understand the incredibly compelling subjective experience of *totally believing* that the triggered thoughts and emotions are *true and valid in the present*—that they are being *fully caused* by events in the present. Another way to put this is: "Why do we believe our VLE confabulations with such conviction even when they have so many holes?"[1] For example, in the scenarios presented above, systematic evaluation by an outside observer would quickly reveal the weaknesses of Nancy's VLE explanations. If I were one of her close friends I could easily point out many flaws in her assessment:

> So you're saying that David was bullying and intimidating you by threatening violence when he got angry about you getting another parking ticket? I was there—remember? He was angry for a minute or two, but then he cooled down, and it seemed like he'd forgiven you completely by the end of dinner. Didn't you tell me once that he has never even *hinted* that he might hurt or punish you if you didn't do what he wanted? And didn't you tell me that he's never made any kind of threatening gesture, like raising his hand, or even leaning toward you in a menacing way?
>
> And here's another one I don't understand. I've known you guys for twenty years, and I've been around you a lot. My observation is that you get angry at David with pretty much the same frequency and intensity as he gets angry at you, but it never seems to occur to you that *you* are bullying or intimidating *him*. . . .

Similarly, systematic evaluation by an outside observer would quickly reveal the weaknesses of John's VLE explanations, and if I were one of his close friends I could point out just as many flaws in his assessment:

---

1. Note that we only seem to experience this profound gullibility with respect to *our own* VLE explanations. It is usually pretty easy to spot the irrational logic and missing evidence when other people's VLEs present us with confabulated explanations.

So, you're saying that Sara was flirting and trying to pursue some kind of inappropriate relationship because she was being friendly and smiling? John—your two sisters were standing right beside her, and she was talking to your friends! I was standing in the same circle of conversation, and I don't think she was doing anything different from the rest of us—we were *all* being friendly and smiling.

You told me once that you've never found the slightest shred of evidence indicating that she's been unfaithful—has that changed? And you always say that her friendly behavior and smiles are inappropriate, but, to be perfectly honest, I've never been able to understand you when you've tried to explain how you came to this conclusion.

And here's another one I don't understand. I've known you guys for twenty years, and I've been around you a lot. My observation is that *you* are friendly toward other women, and frequently smile at them, but it never seems to occur to you that *you* are pursuing inappropriate relationships. . . .

Systematic evaluation by an outside observer would also reveal the weaknesses of my VLE explanations. In fact, now that I'm no longer triggered, I can think back on the experience and point out a number of obvious flaws myself:

So, you're saying that Charlotte was hurting and humiliating you? Think about the details of her behavior—she was smiling, she was glad to be with you, and there wasn't even the slightest hint of taunting, gloating, or trying to prove she's better than you. In fact, she really wasn't focusing on the competition at all—if you think about it carefully, you'll remember that she was hardly even aware of your score. I was there, remember? "Humiliation" seems like a strong word for losing a board game to a friendly opponent, in the comfort of your own living room, with no spectators, no consequences, and a noncompetitive atmosphere. Unless there was something else getting stirred up, one would think you could just eat some humble pie, acknowledge that you have trouble with Scrabble, and then take pride in Charlotte's expertise.

And let's talk about your reaction to her coaching tips—think about her facial expressions and her voice tones—can you honestly tell me she was trying to be hurtful? She was very gentle as she offered her tips, and she was constantly encouraging you. I think it's pretty clear that she was just trying to help.

While we're at it, let's talk about your conviction that it was somehow Charlotte's responsibility to recognize and fix the problem. . . .

Central Nervous System Extrapolation

Another piece of the puzzle that helps to explain our gullibility with respect to VLE confabulated explanations is that the central nervous system extrapolates, or fills in, at a number of different levels.

Filling In at the Level of Explanation

VLE confabulations are what we get when the central nervous system fills in at the level of explanations. In the examples discussed above, such as with the split brain experiment when the research investigator asked, "Why did you pick the shovel?" and the hypnosis demonstration when the hypnotist asked, "Why did you open the window?" there were holes with respect to explanations. And instead of acknowledging "I don't know—there's just a big hole where an explanation should be," the central nervous system VLE fills in the hole with a confabulated explanation that is actually what mathematicians and scientists call an *extrapolation*—an *educated guess based on the information that **is** available.*

Filling In at the Level of Perceptual Interpretation

Central nervous system extrapolation is revealed at the level of perception when Gestalt principles, such as *closure*, produce perceptual illusions.[2] For example (figure 4.1), the open lines at the end of each segment in the left-hand figure lead your central nervous system extrapolator to complete the box in an attempt to obtain closure, and you therefore perceive the larger cube. In

Perceptual Interpretation

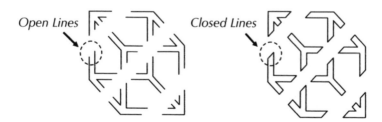

Figure 4.1   The open lines at the end of each segment in the left-hand figure prompt your central nervous system to fill in the missing segments of the larger cube, whereas the closed lines at the end of each segment in the right-hand figure do not prompt this perceptual extrapolation.

---

2.   Most psychology text books on perception will include discussion of central nervous system extrapolation at the level of perception. See, for example, the discussions of subjective/illusory contour figures and the Gestalt laws of perceptual organization presented in Stanley Coren, Lawrence M. Ward, and James T. Enns, *Sensation and Perception*, sixth edition (Hoboken, NJ: J. Wiley & Sons, 2004), pages 242–248.

contrast, the closed lines at the end of each segment in the right-hand figure do *not* prompt your central nervous system extrapolator to attempt closure, and your overall subjective experience is that you do *not* perceive the larger cube. The only actual, *physical* difference between these two figures is that the open lines at the end of each segment have been closed, but the difference in *subjective perception* is dramatic. Almost everyone immediately, spontaneously perceives the larger cube in the top figure, and almost no one perceives the larger cube in the bottom figure.[3]

FILLING IN AT THE LEVEL OF COGNITION

Central nervous system extrapolation is revealed at the level of cognition when we perceive illusory correlations.[4]

FILLING IN AT THE LEVEL OF SENSORY PROCESSING

An ingenious study published in 2005 reveals the central nervous system filling in with respect to auditory processing (see figure 4.2). The researchers created unique soundtracks for each of the study subjects, with the customized soundtracks consisting of a combination of songs that were familiar and songs that were unfamiliar to the particular subject. They then cut out *two- to five-second* sections from various points in the soundtracks and replaced the missing music with segments of silence. The subjects listened to these modified songs as they were having their brains scanned, but without any instructions regarding the music (no instructions to focus deliberately on the music or to watch for gaps), and then after the scans were completed they were questioned about their perceptions regarding the songs they had heard. *All* of the subjects reported *hearing the familiar songs play without interruption*; and in marked contrast, they *all* reported *hearing the gaps in the unfamiliar songs.* Yes, you read that correctly: *none* of the subjects perceived the gaps in the familiar songs, and *all* of the subjects noticed the gaps in the unfamiliar songs. Furthermore, the brain scans showed bursts of activity from certain areas of the auditory cortex as the recordings came to each

---

3.   We asked for a show of hands at the seminar in which we presented this material, and 99 percent of the audience immediately perceived the larger cube in the left-hand figure but *not* in the right-hand figure. Only one person, a design engineer who has spent her career focusing on three- dimensional structures, reported perceiving the larger cube in the right-hand figure.

4.   Many research studies have demonstrated central nervous system extrapolation in the form of illusory correlations. For the original demonstration and discussion of illusory correlations, see Loren J. Chapman, "Illusory Correlation in Observational Report," *Journal of Verbal Learning and Verbal Behavior* Vol. 6 (1967): pages 151–155. For more recent, corroborating research, see David L. Hamilton and Terrence L. Rose, "Illusory Correlation and the Maintenance of Stereotypic Beliefs," *Journal of Personality and Social Psychology* Vol. 39, No. 5 (1980): pages 832–845; and David M. Sanbonmatsu, Frank R. Kardes, and Paul M. Herr, "The Role of Prior Knowledge and Missing Information in Multiattribute Evaluation," *Organizational Behavior and Human Decision Processes* Vol. 51 (1992): pages 76–91.

silent segment in the familiar songs—*the researchers could actually observe the auditory cortex extrapolator working to fill in the holes.*[5]

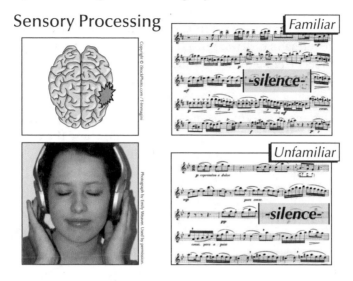

Figure 4.2   Two- to five-second sections are cut from various points in the customized sound tracks, and the missing music is replaced with segments of silence.

Another fascinating example of central nervous system extrapolation at the level of sensory processing is the filling in of the retinal blind spot. The retina lives at the back of the eye, and is like the sensor in a digital camera (figure 4.3). An image of what we are seeing is focused through the lens of

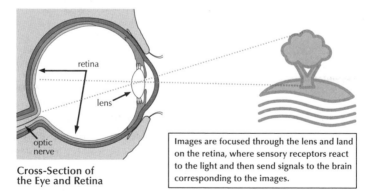

Figure 4.3   The retina is located at the back of the eye, and is like the sensor in a digital camera. Diagram of the eye © Charlotte Lehman and Karl Lehman. Used by permission.

---

5. David J. M. Kraemer et al., "Sound of Silence Activates Auditory Cortex," *Nature* Vol. 434 (March 10, 2005): page 158.

the eye and lands on the retina, where the sensory receptors (rods and cones) react to the light and then send signals that correspond to the image. As illustrated in figure 4.4, the nerve fibers from the rods and cones come out the *front* of these sensory receptors, so that they must then penetrate back through the retina in order to form the optic nerve that travels to the brain. The nerve fibers from all the rods and cones gather together into a bundle, and then penetrate through to the back of the eye in one place, called the optic disc. The point with respect to this discussion is that the area of this optic disc does not have any receptor cells. This means that there is *no input* from the part of the image falling on the optic disc, and the corresponding hole in the visual field is called the retinal blind spot.

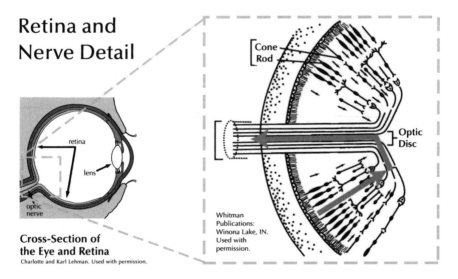

Retina and
Nerve Detail

Cone
Rod

Optic
Disc

retina

lens

optic
nerve

**Cross-Section of
the Eye and Retina**
Charlotte and Karl Lehman. Used with permission.

Whitman
Publications:
Winona Lake, IN.
Used with
permission.

Figure 4.4   Nerve fibers come out of the front of the sensory receptors, and therefore must penetrate back through the retina in order to travel to the brain. Diagram of the retina reprinted with permission from Jensen (1982, page 136).

If the retinal blind spot were directly represented in our visual perception, our view of the world would include a black hole corresponding to the lack of input from the optic disc, as illustrated in figure 4.5. However, as we all know, we *do not* perceive a black hole in our visual field, and this is because our central nervous system extrapolates to fill in the retinal blind spot. The central nervous system extrapolator in charge of this function samples the input from the edges of the hole, and then uses this information to make an educated guess regarding what should go in the hole. Charlotte using her graphics software to repair a damaged photograph provides a good analogy. She makes an *educated guess* that missing material from the damaged spot

Figure 4.5   If the retinal blind spot were directly represented in our visual perception, we would "see" a black hole corresponding to the lack of input from the optic disc.

probably looked a lot like parts of the picture immediately adjacent to the flaw, and therefore repairs the scene by filling in the hole with a sample from this nearby material (figure 4.6).

Figure 4.6   Missing material from damaged spot being filled in by samples taken from nearby grass. The effectiveness of this kind of extrapolation is dramatically demonstrated by how hard it is to find the "hole" in the third panel. (If you weren't deliberately looking for it, you would never see it.)

The usual filling in of the retinal blind spot is obviously quite subtle—after all, most people are never even aware of it. However, if damage to the retina enlarges the blind spot, the filling-in phenomena can become increasingly dramatic. In his most recent book, *The Mind's Eye*, Dr. Sacks describes his own, personal experience with the amazing/sobering abilities of the central nervous system extrapolator in the context of an enlarged blind spot. As the condition causing damage to his retina progressed, Dr. Sacks began to observe that his central nervous system was generating increasingly elaborate and detailed perceptions to fill in the steadily growing hole in his visual field. For example, if he looked at the sky, the half of his visual field that was initially covered by a dark blob would rapidly fill in with a pattern of blue sky and clouds. *And the totally fabricated sky and clouds were hard to distinguish from the scene visible to the healthy half of his retina.*[6]

The central nervous system extrapolation to fill in the retinal blind spot can be exposed by the simple exercise presented in figure 4.7. When the small image on the right side of the figure is completely covered by the blind spot, the central nervous system extrapolator fills in the hole with input from the surrounding white background. As you can observe, when the hole is filled in with input from the white background, the image of the butterfly *completely disappears!* [7]

CENTRAL NERVOUS SYSTEM EXTRAPOLATION
FILLS IN HOLES IN OUR VLE EXPLANATIONS

In light of the fact that central nervous system extrapolation fills in the holes at so many different levels, I am guessing that some kind of central nervous system extrapolator helps to fill in the holes that can sometimes make VLE confabulations appear so weak to outside observers.

Good Old Denial and Self-Deception

I think the last pieces of the puzzle are good old denial and self-deception. Most of us don't want to know just how dysfunctional we are: we don't want to see just how often we are triggered; we don't want to see just how many of our perceptions, thoughts, and emotions are implicit memories coming from unresolved trauma; and we don't want to see just how many of our explanations are actually VLE confabulations trying to justify our triggered reactions. So we look away from the clues that tell us something's missing. We look away from the evidence telling us, "Something's wrong with this picture." We look away from the data points that tell us something's wrong with the way we understand ourselves and the world around us. We

---

6.   For additional description of this dramatic extrapolation in the context of an enlarged blind spot, see "Persistence of Vision: A Journal" in Oliver Sacks, *The Mind's Eye*, large print edition (New York: Random House, 2010), pages 189–263.

7.   Note that this exercise does not simply demonstrate lack of input. As pointed out earlier, the expected result from simple lack of input would be the perception of a "hole" of blackness or darkness, corresponding to the "hole" in the retina produced by the optic disk. However, as you can easily prove to yourself, your central nervous system extrapolator fills in the hole with white. This point can be rigorously demonstrated by doing the exercise with a variety of different backgrounds. If the butterfly is placed on a pale blue background, your extrapolator will fill in the hole with pale blue; if the butterfly is placed on a bright red background, your extrapolator will fill in the hole with bright red; and if the butterfly is placed on pattern of wavy lines, your extrapolator will fill in the hole with wavy lines.

Seeing Your Blind Spot

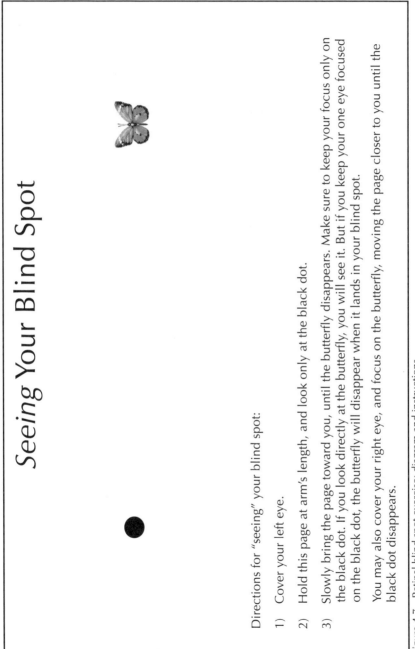

Directions for "seeing" your blind spot:

1) Cover your left eye.

2) Hold this page at arm's length, and look only at the black dot.

3) Slowly bring the page toward you, until the butterfly disappears. Make sure to keep your focus only on the black dot. If you look directly at the butterfly, you will see it. But if you keep your one eye focused on the black dot, the butterfly will disappear when it lands in your blind spot.

You may also cover your right eye, and focus on the butterfly, moving the page closer to you until the black dot disappears.

Figure 4.7   Retinal blind spot exercise: diagram and instructions

look away from the evidence pointing to the flaws in our VLE confabulated explanations (and if there are any holes that our central nervous system extrapolators don't get, we just ignore them).

It's pretty easy to maintain a blind spot when we don't want to see what's hiding in the blind spot and when we don't want to know that we have a blind spot. To put this another way: it's amazing how easy it is to be fooled when we're fooling ourselves and we want to be fooled.

The most generous formulation is that we just don't know what to do with the data points that don't seem to fit, so we ignore them.

5

Trauma, Implicit Memory, VLE Confabulations, and Our Relationship with the Lord

The most important impact from all these phenomena is that they can affect our relationship with the Lord in the same way they affect our relationships with others. If we are triggered by some aspect of our interactions with *the Lord*, then all of the above dynamics will result in traumatic implicit memory and VLE confabulations undermining our relationship with *him*.

An Example from My Own Experience (Two-Year-Old Separation Trauma)

My experience with memories of being separated from my parents at the age of two provides a good example. Mom had mononucleosis during her pregnancy with my younger sister. Between the pregnancy and the mono, she got to the point where she couldn't even get out of bed—Dad had to carry her across the hallway to the bathroom. She was certainly too ill to care for my four-year-old brother and myself, so we were sent to stay with friends in another city for three weeks while she was recovering. To put this in perspective: a two-year-old will experience a three-week separation from his parents in much the same way as he will experience his parents dying suddenly—they disappear suddenly, and stay away longer than any possible two-year-old ability to understand or cope with their absence. Furthermore, a two-year-old perceives his parents to be omnipotent—he believes nothing happens unless they allow it, and that nothing could make them do anything they don't want to do. This means he will believe he's separated from his parents because they *want* to be away from him, and he will believe that they can hear his calls and could come if they wanted to, but that they are *choosing* to ignore his cries for help.

An important part of trauma is that we come up with distorted interpretations regarding the meaning of the experience; and by the end of these three weeks of separation I had come up with many distorted interpretations, such as: "I've been abandoned and I'm on my own," "It's hopeless and I'm powerless—they aren't coming, and nothing I can do will make them come," "I can't trust their hearts toward me because there's no possible justi-fication for allowing this to happen," and "They won't help me when I'm overwhelmed and need their help." Along with these distorted, erroneous beliefs came a miserable morass of associated emotions—loneliness, rejec-tion, hopelessness, powerlessness, feeling overwhelmed, and confusion. And I was also very angry that they had left me, that they were allowing me to suffer so intensely, and that they wouldn't come when I called for them.

In the years that followed, this toxic content would often get activated and transferred onto the Lord. Any time I would become stuck in a situa-tion that felt overwhelming, and call out to the Lord for help but then not be able to perceive his presence or assistance, my interactions with the Lord in the present would match my interactions with my parents in the origi-nal memory closely enough to activate the beliefs and emotions from the two-year-old separation. The beliefs and emotions from the two-year-old separation trauma would then come forward as implicit memory and get transferred onto the Lord—it would feel intensely true that I couldn't trust God's heart toward me because he chooses to allow things for which there is no possible justification; it would feel intensely true that he's not with me now, and won't come even though I call and call for him; and it would feel intensely true that he won't do anything when I'm overwhelmed and need his help. The tangle of negative emotions would come forward as well, and since all of this would come forward as "invisible" implicit memory accom-panied by VLE confabulated explanations, I would have no awareness or insight regarding "Oh, these thoughts and emotions are coming from trau-matic childhood memories." Instead, I would perceive that the thoughts and emotions were *about the Lord*, and that they were true, valid, and reasonable *in the present*.

For example, our car got flooded so that the main wiring harness and the main circuit board for all the computerized electronics were *under water* for *several weeks* while we were away on an extended business/vacation trip. In case you're thinking that our car rolled into a pond while we were away, and that our friends and neighbors just left it there for three weeks, I'll explain how soberingly easy it is to flood the electrical system in a VW Passat. In our model of the Passat, if the moonroof leaks, the water runs into the frame so that it can be invisibly channeled into the handy three-inch air space underneath the carpet in the passenger compartment. And *why* do you think there are three inches of air space underneath the carpet? Well, I'll tell you: that's where the engineers decided to put the main wiring harness and the main computerized circuit board. Therefore, when our moonroof leaked, gallons of water ran through the frame to completely fill the air space under the carpet, and these key components of the electrical system quietly sat underwater for three weeks without anyone even noticing.

Not surprisingly, when we returned from our trip we found that the car wouldn't start. When we had it towed to the dealer their head mechanic said we would have to have the entire electrical system replaced, and that it would cost *seven thousand dollars*! So we asked for a second opinion from the non-dealer mechanic who usually cared for our car—a very bright guy with thirty-five years of experience and a fully equipped garage at his disposal. He said that he had never had good results trying to repair this particular scenario in the VW Passat, *and told us that he wouldn't touch it*!

Oh. Wow. Not what we wanted to hear.

So I decided to try to fix it myself and spent the next two weeks feeling constantly overwhelmed by the size and complexity of the project (figure 5.1). I repeatedly asked the Lord for help as I struggled with this daunting scenario, but I was usually *not* able to perceive his presence or assistance,

Figure 5.1   Passat electrical nightmare—I spent two weeks feeling constantly overwhelmed by the size and complexity of the project.

and each time this would happen the unresolved toxic content from my two-year-old trauma would come forward as "invisible" implicit memory: it would feel intensely true that the Lord was not with me and that he wouldn't come even if I called and called; it would feel intensely true that he wouldn't do anything even though I was overwhelmed and needed his help; it would feel intensely true that I couldn't trust his heart toward me because he chooses to allow things for which there's no possible justification; I would feel intensely powerless, discouraged, betrayed, abandoned, and angry; and because of the way "invisible" implicit memory works *it would feel intensely true that my pain and anger were really about the situation in the present, and especially about the Lord failing to respond to my calls for help.*

The real truth was that the Lord was with me, standing beside me, and offering to help, but I was unable to perceive his presence. I will provide more details in a minute, but the really short summary is that in the context of the two-year-old separation trauma, I had made choices to push him away, and these choices were still hindering me from perceiving his presence or receiving his help. However, I was initially unaware of this larger picture, and so instead of feeling hope, surrendering my VLE confabulations, recognizing my thoughts and emotions as traumatic content coming forward as implicit memory, and then turning to the Lord for healing, I would perceive the distorted conclusions to be true, I would perceive the implicit memory negative emotions to be valid in the present, *and I would focus my energy and attention on fighting with the triggers.* I would focus on the car's failure to start and on the Lord's failure to respond, with the intense subjective perception that the true source of my distress would be resolved if I could just get him to come, be with me, and help me fix the car. I would plead with the Lord, asking and asking and asking that he manifest more tangibly; I would argue with him, trying to convince him that his response was inadequate and that he should intervene more powerfully; I would have waves of the intense subjective perception that the Lord was deliberately refusing to be with me or help me; and then I would point my frustrated anger at *him*, trying to punish him with every hurtful accusation I could think of. After bouncing back and forth between these reactions for varying lengths of time (sometimes hours), I would eventually settle into a miserable confused discouragement, and then finally force myself to move on to some other task because I didn't know what else to do.

The good news is that this especially miserable incident with the car led to a breakthrough regarding my two-year-old separation trauma memories, enabling me to finally recognize and reverse the choices to push the Lord away that had hindered me from being able to perceive his presence or receive his help. Part of the breakthrough was that this whole ordeal with the car occurred as Charlotte and I were finishing with the first wave of developing our Immanuel teachings. As part of developing this material I had become *profoundly* convinced that if we could not perceive the Lord's presence it was because there was something in the way, and that the Lord always wanted to help us resolve these blockages. Another part of the breakthrough was that I had new information and insight regarding this particular triggered content and the time of separation from my parents. (I had never had any conscious memory of these events, since they occurred when I was so young. But shortly before the ordeal with the flooded car, I had learned about this history from conversations with my older brother and parents, and I was finally recognizing the connections between the two-year-old separation trauma and this particular toxic content that would get transferred onto the Lord. So even though these triggered thoughts and emotions felt so intensely true *in the present*, and even though they felt so intensely true *with respect to the Lord*, the conviction that they were actually implicit memory from this unresolved trauma was even more powerful.)

Therefore, as I sat in the car surrounded by tools, wires, and disassembled parts of the electrical system, I chose to surrender my bitter accusations that God was perversely withholding the help I needed, I chose to acknowledge that there must be something on my side that was in the way, and I chose to ask for help. I was still so angry that I could barely keep from screaming and swearing at the Lord, but I managed to choke out a prayer. (It is a testimony to God's mercy and grace that he honored my true heart, even though it was mixed in with a lot of triggered confusion and anger.) My "humble," "submitted," "open-hearted" (sarcasm intended) prayer was something along the lines of:

> Lord, I am *so* angry that you're not manifesting in some way that I can perceive and that you're not providing more tangible help. And it feels *intensely, excruciatingly* true that this is all *your* fault, and that *you* should apologize and then fix the problem. But I know you're here with me, I know there must be something in the way, and I am *so* tired of being stuck in this triggered place of blaming you. Oh, man, *it infuriates me to say this*! Grrrrrrr! (brief pause to fume silently) Okay: What am *I* doing that's hindering me from perceiving your presence? What choice do *I* need to make to take the next step forward?

The moment these words were out of my mouth I felt like I was inside the two-year-old separation memories. I could perceive Jesus' presence standing right beside me, and I had the sense that he was saying, "Karl, your mom isn't going to come back for a long time—let me comfort you." Furthermore, I realized that the response I had made at the time of the original trauma, and that I had stubbornly held onto for forty years, was something along the

lines of, "The only plans I'm interested in are ones that include you producing my mother *right now*. I can't believe you're even talking to me about
some other plan. If you don't have Mom with you, *then just get away from
me*—go jump off a cliff, *and I hope there are rocks at the bottom!*"

Not surprisingly, telling the Lord to jump off a cliff had kind of gotten in
the way of my being able to sense his presence or receive his help. However,
thanks to a number of new factors, including the ones just mentioned, I
was finally able to surrender my anger and my demand that the Lord make
things different, and I reversed the choice to refuse his help. As soon as I
chose to welcome Jesus instead of push him away I was able to connect with
him inside the two-year-old memories, and being able to feel his comfort
and receive his assistance inside the memories immediately lead to healing
for some of the most important aspects of the separation trauma. From that
point forward it no longer felt like God was refusing to be with me or help
me as I continued to struggle with the car, and over the next several days
(with some strategic guidance from God) I was able to completely restore the
electrical system for a total cost of $125. Furthermore, since this experience
I have noticed that the (now healed) two-year-old "traumatic memories" no
longer hinder my ability to connect with Jesus when I struggle with something difficult, ask for help, but then do not initially perceive his presence.[1]

I am very grateful that this story now has a happy ending, but for many
years prior to this breakthrough healing, the toxic content from these traumatic memories greatly hindered my relationship with the Lord. And this
is only one of many examples from my personal experience. The reader
will probably recognize that my experiences with trauma from maturity-
inappropriate sermon content and from overhearing small group discussions
provide two more examples of traumatic implicit memory undermining my
relationship with the Lord, and essays available from www.kclehman.com
provide several additional stories from my personal experience illustrating
this unfortunate phenomenon.[2]

An interesting story from an emotional healing session I facilitated
makes this same point about the importance of how unresolved trauma

---

1. For a much longer version of this story, including a more thorough discussion of the
new resources that contributed to the breakthrough, see "Immanuel, an Especially Pernicious
Blockage, and the Normal Belief Memory System," available in both essay and DVD format
from www.kclehman.com. Also, for full disclosure regarding this story, yet another part of the
breakthrough was that I was miserably triggered to this toxic content most of the time for two
weeks, and the intensity and persistence of this pain helped me realize that I was ready to try
something new.

2. See, for example, "Dad/God Isn't All-Knowing or All-Powerful: A Case Study and
Discussion," and "Unresolved Issues in the Therapist/Facilitator: One of the Most Important
Hindrances to Emotional Healing" (available as free downloads from www.kclehman.com).

affects our relationships with the Lord, but from a different direction. This particular person had been through many long, difficult sessions working through many horrible memories, and in this particular session (somewhat understandably) began to complain about how long the Lord was taking to relieve her pain. Fortunately, she was in a memory where she could clearly perceive Jesus' presence and where she felt a strong connection with him. So I encouraged her to engage directly with him regarding her concern.[3] She expressed her questions and unhappiness directly to Jesus, paused for a couple minutes, and then reported that the Lord had responded with the following comment:

> I love my children, and I'm glad to free them from suffering, but the primary, most important purpose of all this emotional healing stuff is to remove the blockages that are between your heart and me. *The primary, most important purpose of emotional healing is to remove the blockages that hinder your heart from coming to me.*[4]

And since this session, many others in similar situations have received essentially the same message.

Rocky and Maggie

The negative impact of unresolved trauma on our relationships with the Lord, and the corresponding need to take care of traumatic memories so that they stop hindering our relationships with the Lord, are so important that I want to further emphasize these points with video clips from a couple of live emotional healing sessions. I strongly encourage you to play the clips from the *Rocky: Father-Son Wounds* and *Maggie #3: Labor & Delivery Trauma* sessions at this point.[5] I have also included the following transcripts of the video clips for readers who do not have access to the *Outsmarting Yourself* website or a DVD player. However, while the written transcripts provide the same *cognitive* content, these very important points regarding the ways in which unresolved trauma affects our relationship with the Lord, and the importance of resolving these traumatic memories, will be communicated

---

3. I love it when the person has a clear perception of Jesus' presence and a strong connection with him because when a really tough issue comes up, I just coach the person to take it to Jesus.

4. He also talked with her about her discouragement regarding her ongoing suffering, but the comment about the primary purpose of emotional healing struck both me and the person as being especially profound.

5. The clips from the *Rocky: Father-Son Wounds* and *Maggie #3: Labor & Delivery Trauma* sessions can be viewed from either the *Outsmarting Yourself* website (www.outsmartingyourself.com), or from the optional *Outsmarting Yourself* companion DVD.

with much more *emotional* power if you view the live emotional healing sessions as opposed to just reading about them. So, again, I strongly encourage you to view the video clips.[6]

Clips from *Rocky: Father-Son Wounds*

We begin the session with an opening prayer, and then I coach Rocky to simply describe whatever comes into his awareness—any thoughts, feelings, images, memories, or physical sensations that come into his awareness.

ROCKY: I feel a kind of heaviness in my stomach, kind of a deep burden, a heavy sadness. Uhm, I'm just kind of vaguely thinking of how many times I felt that as a kid—I felt that over and over again. I felt very alone. . . .

I guess I feel apart from my family, I feel kind of alone in my practice in some ways. I feel like I'm so busy with the business of running the practice and kind of toiling alone in my prayer. . . . Not having done the training and stuff that some of you guys have done, I guess I feel out of pace even—even kind of left alone with this. It's almost like the lone ranger stuff, you know. . . .

(Sighing, shaking his head) It's like somehow Rocky ends up being alone. No matter what he does, no matter how hard he tries, even if he's doing right, he has to do it by himself—he ends up being alone.

DR. LEHMAN: There you go—stay with that Rocky, "Somehow Rocky always ends up being alone." . . . *(Rocky begins sobbing.)*

ROCKY: . . . I even feel like that with the Lord sometimes—it's like, it's like: "Lord, I don't know how to stay in touch." *(intense emotions, tears)*

DR. LEHMAN: *(Directly to the Lord)* Lord Jesus, what do you want Rocky to know, about that deep sadness, and the loneliness? About: "Even if I'm doing the right thing, no matter how hard I work—even if I'm doing the right thing, I gotta do it by myself. I'm on my own. I don't even feel that you're with me, Lord."?

---

6. Note that the complete, seventy-seven-minute and seventy-two-minute versions of these sessions have been edited down to nine minutes each for the clips presented here, so a lot of material is obviously missing. However, the content needed to reinforce the points we are discussing is still discernible if you don't get distracted by trying to follow the details of the process. For those who want to see more, intermediate condensed versions (sixteen minutes and fourteen minutes, respectively) are available from the store page of www.kclehman.com as parts of the *Live Emotional Healing Ministry ~ Four Condensed Sessions* (#8 in the Live Ministry Series DVDs) and *Live Emotional Healing Ministry ~ Condensed Sessions, 4th Set* (#20 in the Live Ministry Series DVDs), respectively. The complete seventy-seven minute and seventy-two minute versions are also available from the store page of www.kclehman.com.

ROCKY: You know, a part of me knows Jesus is with me, and then part of me thinks, (choked up) "I don't want to be disappointed."

It's like, "Leave me alone, I'll take care of it—just leave me alone—just don't make it worse."

. . . It's like there's a promise, and then it gets dashed.

. . . Inside, it's like I want to tell Jesus, "Just leave me alone."

(Skipping to a point later in the session: Dr. Lehman and Rocky have prayed, asking the Lord to reveal any underlying traumatic memories that contribute to Rocky's thoughts and emotions, and then Rocky reports.)

ROCKY: I think there were times when I was around my dad . . . I was little one time, I was really little, and he had some kind of thing at his work—he had a little restaurant or something, and it was some kind of cowboy thing and he had a cowboy hat and a gun. . . . I remember feeling, you know, like he brought that for me. And then I was standing with him, but I just felt so alone—there was no contact. *(intense emotions)*

I remember just glazing over—I was like, "Whoa, I don't understand this. Why would he bring these things for me and then not want to talk to me, not want to look at me. I don't understand."

When I was with my dad I used to feel invisible—I felt like he couldn't see me. There's a memory—we're in the basement and I have the hat on. The hat's too big for me, the gun's so heavy I could hardly lift it, and he's standing next to me but it's like he's in a trance—he's somewhere else. . . . And after a while I remember turning away—I wasn't even looking at him anymore—I just couldn't take it. . . .

(Skipping forward in the session)

ROCKY: You know, I think, Karl, that the Lord showed me my father *was* in a trance. I mean, he was really *gone*. And as I'm looking up, as I would've been as a little boy, it's like I see Jesus walking from behind him and kneeling down—just kinda holding out his arms, kinda holding out his hands, with a very knowing look on his face. It's like he really knows—how sad, how alone, how hurt, how invisible I felt.

It's like he understands—it's okay to feel those things.

It's as if he's showing me: "Your dad was in a trance because of him, not because of you." And that feels true.

But even as . . . I'm looking at Jesus, I'm partly turned away, you know what I mean? I remember I looked into this cabinet that was next to where my dad and I were standing and I just stared intently into the cabinet—I was just focusing on things in the cabinet. I just wanted to get away from all that [pain regarding my dad], and be over here instead. . . .

(Skipping forward in the session)

Well that's interesting. It's like Jesus—rather than waiting for me to turn—he has slipped in and he's sitting between me and the cupboard. And he's kind of like this *(Rocky demonstrates kneeling on one knee)*, down on the ground, resting on one . . . *(pause)*

DR. LEHMAN: One knee?

ROCKY: Yeah, and then he's like this *(Rocky demonstrates kneeling on one knee, leaning back a little bit, in a very relaxed posture, and looking down slightly, as if looking at a small child standing in front of him)*, and he's just looking and he's smiling. He's really, uhm—it's a very inviting smile, very calm.

It's very much a sense of being known and understood, and that it's really okay—it's okay to feel all these things, and that he understands.

DR. LEHMAN: Even the fear of disappointment?

ROCKY: Uhmm-hmm (yes). And why I didn't turn to him—I was too afraid. So he said, "Look, I'll sit where you can see me—I'll come to you."

(Skipping forward, to a point several minutes later in the session)

ROCKY: There was a series of other things that came through—times, memories, particular times in my childhood when I was—when I really suffered from not having a dad, and I feel the Lord's presence in those places. . . . I feel like there's an openness between Jesus and I. . . .

(Follow-up interview sixteen months after the initial session)

ROCKY: And since that time I have had much less fear and anxiety, much less self-soothing behavior. I don't know if people can necessarily tell, but I've lost between fifty and sixty pounds through just no longer eating to manage my emotional needs. And just feeling a freedom to care for myself, with exercise and doing recreational things, [and more balance with respect to] the way I handle myself relationally and the expectations I put on myself at work. So I think that [emotional healing session] was a compelling time when I was able to experience that . . . Jesus is really with us. . . .

I also describe to people the shift: [in the past] when things would go wrong in my life, my first, knee-jerk, heart response was, "Why are you allowing this? Why aren't you helping me? Lord, where are you—are you out golfing?" And now, when things go wrong, my initial response is, "This really stinks, I really don't like this, but I know that you're with me."

DR. LEHMAN: Wow!

ROCKY: And it's experiential.

DR. LEHMAN: Yes! So where that session started—feeling sad and lonely, "I'm on my own, it always ends up Rocky's alone," that feels different?

ROCKY: Absolutely!

DR. LEHMAN: That is so cool.

ROCKY: And it feels different *in the oven—in the furnace*, which is the true test.

CLIPS FROM *MAGGIE #3: LABOR AND DELIVERY TRAUMA*

This session begins with Maggie talking about her work with an especially complicated and difficult client, and about negative feelings toward the Lord that have been coming up in this context. The material presented here begins with the tail end of this initial discussion.

MAGGIE: I'm struggling with sometimes getting mad at Jesus. . . . It feels like that what he's asking me to do is—is just so hard. It's—it's just— it almost feels *mean*.

(*Additional initial comments, several minutes later in the session*)

MAGGIE: I've got my husband on one side, saying, "We need better boundaries. This is a major disruption." I find myself looking at him, saying, "Why are you so selfish?" And that is so inappropriate because he has gone—he has put up with so much. I mean, that's not right. And then I'm kinda frustrated at God because, you know, *he could make this a lot easier!*

(*Skipping forward to several minutes later in the session, with Maggie now talking directly to the Lord*)

MAGGIE: It just feels hard, God, from every side—it feels like my husband is hard, it feels like you're being hard, and it feels like my client is relentless.

It feels like it's just been going on so long, and I'm just—I'm tired. I'm just really tired.

(*Again skipping forward in the session: Dr. Lehman has coached Maggie to focus on Jesus and ask him for guidance regarding any underlying traumatic memories that might be contributing to her thoughts and feelings. She has just done this, and after a long pause she continues with the following.*)

MAGGIE: Hmm. Okay, I'm just going into a flash—just a flash—of my first labor and delivery. . . .

I'm just—I'm just thinking about how hard that labor and delivery was for me, because what the doctor did was—you know, near the end you start having the Braxton-Hicks contractions? I started having fairly regular ones and went to the hospital. They probably should've sent me home, but he went ahead and admitted me, hooked me up to Pitocin, gave me an epidural, and it was just the classic "knock down, drag out." . . .

I'm remembering that the doctor never even came in to see me. We waited a really long time—it was the middle of the night, and, uhm, . . . (long pause as Maggie becomes choked-up and tearful), I know that women have babies all the time, but this was my first one, and I was young, and I didn't know the drill for being in hospitals.

He never even came in until I had pushed for two hours, and then, when he was stitching me back up, I could feel it a little bit, and I said, "That hurts," and he was crabby.

He was hard. . . .

(Skipping to a point several minutes later in the session)

MAGGIE: So Lord, where are you?

DR. LEHMAN: *(To Maggie)* Let's make the explicit invitation. *(Then, speaking directly to the Lord)* Lord, we invite you. We invite you to be with Maggie in this place, and we ask that you would help her to perceive your presence.

(To Maggie again) And now just report whatever happens, because if you don't perceive his presence then we'll troubleshoot.

MAGGIE: *(Long pause)* Alright, I see him, right down there, by the doctor. *(pause)* And he was also there before the doctor got there. *(pause)* And he's filled with compassion. *(pause, emotions, tears)* And he knows that I've been so strong.

. . . I can—I can just really feel his compassion. *(quiet pause)* I feel like he's telling me that it's gonna be okay—that even though this wasn't his plan for what childbirth is supposed to be like, it's gonna be okay.

And just knowing that he's there—I mean, there's such a contrast between him and that doctor. . . .

(Skipping to several minutes later in the session)

MAGGIE: I don't know about most women, but I think childbirth is really the pits. I hated it. I thought it was such a rude experience, all the way. You know, everything from just your dignity and being exposed, to just the pain of it. I mean, it's just really hard.

DR. LEHMAN: Tell Jesus about all of that.

MAGGIE: Okay, *(pause, and then speaking directly to the Lord)* So Lord, I cannot relate to women who . . .

DR. LEHMAN: Gush about how beautiful it is?

MAGGIE: Yes! And they talk about how, the moment the baby comes, they just forget all their pain. Lord, I have **not** forgotten! And I'm grateful for the baby, but that was hard *(emotions, tears)*.

(Long pause, emotions, tears) He says he knows.

(Long pause, smile) It's the weirdest thing—just because he says he knows, it feels better. *(laughs)* Do you think he's attuning again?

DR. LEHMAN: What do you know about that? And that's step three in the healing pathway—he probably knows all that stuff too—that that's often the most important, strategic piece of emotional healing work.

MAGGIE: He's not—he's not telling me [anything complicated, surprising, or theologically profound], but . . .

DR. LEHMAN: But it *feels* true that he's with you and that he gets it, right?

MAGGIE: Uhm-hmm.

DR. LEHMAN: Isn't that amazing?

MAGGIE: Yeah. Yeah, it is. . . .

(Skipping to several minutes later in the session)

MAGGIE: Well you know, it's funny, because now I can embrace that whole thing that women say: "I can forget the pain, now that I see the baby." It's like, all of a sudden, that feels true.

DR. LEHMAN: . . . So with the trauma out of the way, you're actually experiencing that joy-childbirth thing that women talk about? . . .

MAGGIE: Uhm-hmm . . . Yeah. Yeah. Yeah, kind of wild isn't it?

DR. LEHMAN: That's pretty cool.

MAGGIE: It is!

(Many minutes later, as part of the debriefing at the end of the session)

DR. LEHMAN: One of the things you said at the beginning was, "Jesus feels hard—it feels like Brad is hard, Jesus is hard, and the client is relentless." It would be interesting to see [now] whether you can find any place where it feels like Jesus is hard.

MAGGIE: No, he doesn't feel hard at all right now. . . .

DR. LEHMAN: So, when you're thinking about the ways he could inter-vene, but he doesn't—he just sits there watching you—he doesn't feel hard?

MAGGIE: Hmm mm. No. . . .

DR. LEHMAN: Even when you poke around there, and you think about how tough it is and how much you'd like him to intervene—in the places you know he *could* intervene, but he just sits there watching and *doesn't* intervene—it doesn't feel like he's hard or mean?

MAGGIE: It feels like he's sovereign. . . . It feels like he's sovereign, and he's much smarter than I am, and he knows—he has a purpose for what he's doing, you know.

DR. LEHMAN: And that actually *feels* true?

MAGGIE: Yeah. Yeah, it does. Yeah.

TRAUMATIC IMPLICIT MEMORY GETTING TRANSFERRED ONTO THE LORD
There are lots of things we could talk about from these clips, but the point I want to make for this discussion is that we can see unresolved traumatic content coming forward as "invisible" implicit memory and getting trans-ferred onto the Lord. For example, at the beginning of Rocky's session it felt true to Rocky that *the Lord* was not with him or caring for him. However, as the session progressed it became clear that these thoughts and feelings were actually coming from memories—memories in which they *were* accurate, but with respect to *his father*—memories in which it was true that *his father* was not with him or caring for him. This unresolved content was coming forward as implicit memory that *felt true in the present*, Rocky's VLE was explaining to him that these thoughts and feelings were true and valid in the present *with respect to the Lord*, and then this all changed when the trauma with his father was resolved. As you probably noticed, Rocky even named this himself in the follow-up interview:

> [In the past], when things would go wrong in my life, my first, knee-jerk, heart response was: "Why are you allowing this? Why aren't you helping me? Lord, where are you—are you out golfing?" And now, when things go wrong, my initial response is: "This really stinks, I really don't like this, *but I know that you're with me.*"

Similarly, at the beginning of Maggie's session, it felt true that the difficulty of working with a certain client was becoming increasingly hard to endure, it felt true that the Lord should have been doing more to give her relief and ease her burden, and it felt true that he was "hard" and "mean" because he was present but chose not to provide more help. However, as the session progressed it became clear that these thoughts and feelings were actually coming from memories—memories of her first delivery, where the overall experience *was* more than she could handle,[7] and where these thoughts and feelings *were* accurate, but with respect to *her doctor*—memories in which it was true that *her doctor* was hard and mean, and it was true that *her doctor* should have provided understanding, encouragement, sensitivity, and other resources that would have given her relief and eased her burden. This unresolved content was coming forward as "invisible" implicit memory that *felt true in the present,* Maggie's VLE was explaining to her that these thoughts and emotions were true and valid in the present *with respect to the Lord,* and then this all changed when trauma from the difficult delivery and uncaring doctor was resolved.

It is important to note that, just as with trauma and the effects of trauma in general, trauma hindering our relationships with God can be caused by surprisingly minor painful experiences, trauma hindering our relationships with God is much more common than most people realize, and the negative effects of trauma on our relationships with God can be subtle.

---

7. We know that the overall experience was more than she was able to handle because it was stored as trauma—if she *had* been able to adequately process the experience, even though it would still have been very painful and difficult, *it would not have been traumatic.*

6

The Importance of Neutralizing Traumatic Implicit Memory and VLE Confabulations (Summary)

Let us summarize with respect to the strategic importance of neutralizing traumatic memories and VLE confabulations:

- Psychological trauma can be caused by painful events that may seem minor, and the effects of trauma can be very subtle, so traumatic memories are much more common than most people realize.

- When traumatic memories are activated, the toxic content they carry comes forward and powerfully affects our perceptions, thoughts, beliefs, emotions, abilities, and choices.

- This traumatic, toxic content comes forward as "invisible" implicit memory, so that it feels true in the present and is not recognized as coming from underlying unresolved trauma.

- Our VLEs come up with explanations that focus on the triggering stimuli in the present.

- Our central nervous system extrapolators fill in most of the holes in the VLE confabulated explanations, and good old denial and self-deception take care of anything that is left over.

- The end result is that we usually believe the VLE confabulated explanations, accept the implicit memory content as true in the present, and blame the triggers as if they are the original source of the implicit memory content from the underlying traumatic memories.

- If we perceive that a specific person is responsible for the triggering situation, we will only feel heard, validated, safe, and ready for reconciliation if he takes full responsibility for the implicit memory traumatic content. This creates an irreconcilable difference because he cannot honestly do this.

- Finally (and most important), if we are triggered by some aspect of our interactions with the Lord, then all of the above dynamics will result in traumatic implicit memory content and VLE confabulations undermining our relationship with him. Our perception is that traumatic implicit memories and VLE confabulations combine to create some of the most important blockages hindering people from perceiving the Lord's presence and from connecting with him more intimately.

Putting all this together, we can see how important it is to neutralize our traumatic memories and VLE confabulations.

One More Reason

As an interesting addendum to this part of the book, I want to mention one more reason why it's important to resolve our traumatic memories. As we age, the frontal lobes of our brains are especially affected, and the defenses we use to manage our unresolved issues are progressively weakened. As our coping mechanisms weaken, we become progressively more reactive and dysfunctional *unless we also heal and mature as we age to offset our weakening defenses.* This phenomena is currently being highlighted by aging veterans who are developing full-blown, disabling post-traumatic stress disorder (PTSD) after fifty-plus years of minimally impaired functioning. For example, Dr. Deirdre Johnston noticed a large number of combat veterans from WWII and the Korean War who had just recently developed PTSD in conjunction with progressing dementia. When she examined several of these cases more carefully, the information she gathered revealed that these men had displayed subtle evidence of unresolved trauma through the decades since their combat experiences, but that they had been able to raise families, maintain employment, participate in their communities, etc. with minimal functional impairment. Apparently, they had been able to effectively manage their unresolved traumatic memories for these many years since their combat experience. However, these men began to develop full-blown, disabling PTSD as age-related dementias eroded the strength of their psychological coping tools.[1]

The elderly who have spent their lives maturing and cleansing their minds and spirits are an inspiration. When these people experience dementia it reveals the beautiful truth that their grace, humility, maturity, courage,

---

1.   Dierdre Johnston, "A Series of Cases of Dementia Presenting with PTSD Symptoms in World War II Combat Veterans," *Journal of the American Geriatric Society* Vol. 48 (2000): pages 70–72. For additional evidence supporting this same point, see also Margriet E. van Achterberg, Robert M. Rohrbaugh, and Steven M. Southwick, "Emergence of PTSD in Trauma Survivors with Dementia," *The Journal of Clinical Psychiatry* Vol. 62, No. 3 (2001): pages 206–7.

gentleness, etc., go all the way to the core. In contrast, the elderly who have spent their lives clinging to their defenses and blaming others are a warning. When these people experience dementia their underlying immaturity, woundedness, and dysfunction are exposed. The short summary is this: as you age, you will increasingly walk around in your psychological and spiritual underwear. Do you want to wash that underwear before your family, friends, and neighbors have to see it?

At this point, you are hopefully asking: "So what do we do?! How do we expose and neutralize our traumatic memories and VLE confabulations so that they won't continue to disrupt our lives and relationships?" An excellent question! And fortunately, there are answers.

Part Two

Exposing and Neutralizing Traumatic Implicit Memory and VLE Confabulations

7

The First Half of the Basic Plan

Finding and Healing Underlying Traumatic Memories

As explained earlier in the section on psychological trauma, when we encounter pain our brain-mind-spirit system tries to process the painful experience, and there is a specific pathway that this processing follows (figure 7.1). When we *are* able to successfully complete this processing journey, we get through the painful experience without being traumatized—we emotionally and cognitively "metabolize" the experience in a healthy way, and instead of having any toxic power in our lives, the adequately processed

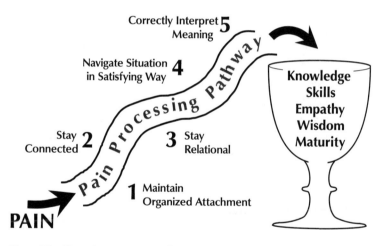

Figure 7.1   The pain-processing pathway

painful experience contributes to our knowledge, skills, empathy, wisdom, and maturity. As also mentioned earlier, various problems and/or limitations can block successful processing; and when we are *not* able to complete the processing journey, then the painful experience becomes a traumatic experience, and the memory for this experience will then carry unresolved traumatic content.

Healing for Psychological Trauma

The good news about the pain-processing pathway and traumatic memories is that each time a traumatic memory gets activated we get another chance to finish the processing.[1] If we haven't acquired any additional resources since the time of the original trauma, this actually isn't very good news—we just feel bad, get stuck in the same places once again, and eventually put the unresolved content back into the same old traumatic memory file. However, if things have changed in good ways (for example, our maturity skills have grown, we are surrounded by supportive community, and we can connect with the Lord), we *will* be able to successfully complete the processing tasks, the traumatic memory will be *permanently* resolved, *and it will no longer carry any toxic content that can cause trouble by coming forward as implicit memory.* Therefore, the first half of the basic plan for exposing and neutralizing traumatic implicit memory and VLE confabulations is the ongoing, long-term endeavor of finding and resolving the underlying memories (that are the source of the traumatic implicit content that comes forward when we get triggered).

The bad news is that traumatic memories can be difficult to access. However, the good news is that traumatic memories are consistently accessible under the right conditions. The bad news is that traumatic memories are difficult to modify. However, the good news is that traumatic memories are consistently open to modification under the right conditions. The bad news is that the processing tasks necessary to resolve the toxic content carried in traumatic memories cannot be successfully completed unless very specific conditions are in place and unless very specific resources are available. However, the good news is that toxic traumatic memory content can be consistently resolved when the right conditions are in place and the necessary resources are available.

This all leads to a very practical and very important bottom line. If we want to strategically design a psychotherapy or emotional healing ministry intervention that consistently accomplishes permanent resolution for traumatic memories, we need to:

- figure out, and then deliberately, systematically set up the conditions necessary for accessing traumatic memories;

- figure out, and then deliberately, systematically set up the conditions necessary for traumatic memories to be open to modification; and

---

1. Isn't this great? Instead of just failing the test we get to keep taking it until we pass! Thank you, Lord, for making this gracious provision by allowing unresolved memories to get triggered over and over and over again until we finally resolve them.

- figure out, and then deliberately, systematically set up the conditions and provide the resources necessary for the person to successfully complete unfinished processing tasks.

The Immanuel Approach

More good news is that God knows all this stuff, and he wants to help us get healed. If we are able to perceive God's presence, connect with him, and receive help from him, then *he* can lead the process, *he* can help us access traumatic memories, *he* can help us set up the conditions so that they can be modified, and *he* can help us successfully complete the remedial processing that will transform them into fully metabolized experiences that will then contribute to knowledge, skills, wisdom, maturity, and compassion. For people who are able to perceive the Lord's presence, connect with him, and receive help from him, this potentially complicated process can become very simple. *The Lord* can lead the process, help the person access the memories, help the person set up the conditions so that they can be modified, and help the person get through the processing pathway, without *us* needing to explicitly manage any of these details. With the basic version[2] of the Immanuel approach to emotional healing, all the facilitator needs to do is:

- establish the foundation for the session by helping the person to perceive the Lord's presence and establish an interactive connection with him;[3]

- coach the person to turn to Jesus, focus on Jesus, and engage with him directly at every point in the session;[4] and

---

2. Even with careful coaching, some people are not yet able to perceive the Lord's presence, establish an interactive connection with him, and receive help from him. When working with these people the facilitator needs to know more about traumatic memory and the processing pathway, and deliberately apply this information as she leads the session. A more advanced version of the Immanuel approach includes principles and tools that enable the facilitator to guide this more complicated process. These principles and tools for more advanced Immanuel approach emotional healing are presented in the "Brain Science, Psychological Trauma, and the God Who Is with Us" essay series (available as free downloads from www.kclehman.com).

3. I am experiencing an *interactive* connection with the Lord when I perceive his presence in some way and it *feels* true that we are having a living, real-time, mutual, contingent *interaction*. When I am experiencing an interactive connection, it feels true that the Lord sees, hears, and understands the emotions and thoughts I am experiencing and communicating, and it also feels true that he is offering contingent responses to my emotions and thoughts. See chapter 18, pages 165–167, for examples and additional explanation regarding interactive connection.

4. This includes coaching the person to turn to Jesus, focus on Jesus, and engage directly with Jesus regarding any difficulties that arise. In fact, coaching the person to focus on Jesus and engage directly with him regarding any points of difficulty is the most basic, most common, and most important form of Immanuel approach troubleshooting.

- watch carefully for any point where the person loses interactive connection with the Lord, and then help the person reestablish an interactive connection at any point we discover that she has lost this all-important foundation.[5]

Even more good news is that these principles and tools are more than just hopeful theory. We have been using the Immanuel approach for several years now, and the results have been *very* encouraging. Closest to home, we have found this approach to be wonderfully effective for our own, personal healing work. It has been effective for resolving major issues, such as the attachment trauma I experienced from the extended separation from my parents when I was two years old; and it has also been effective for resolving trauma from much smaller painful events, such as my experiences of childhood injustice when the bullies on my grade-school playground cut in line during batting practice.

We have found this approach to be wonderfully effective for our emotional healing work with clients, and people in our mentoring groups have consistently been experiencing powerful healing with the Immanuel approach. Some of these people have even been willing to release recordings of their sessions to provide encouragement and teaching resources for others.[6] Furthermore, we have observed that a number of private practice clients and mentoring group participants who had previously been stuck for many, many sessions have begun moving forward with the Immanuel approach. Charlotte and I have used a variety of emotional healing tools over the years, and in our experience the Immanuel approach has been the easiest to use, the safest, and the most effective.[7]

---

5. For examples of these simple sessions, in which all I do is help the person to perceive Jesus' presence, connect with him, synchronize with him, *stay* synchronized with him, ask him for guidance, and engage with him directly whenever they encounter problems, see *Renae: Healing Helps Parenting, Maggie #2: "If I leave, she could die," Maggie #3: Labor & Delivery Trauma, Rita #3: Jesus Is Better Than Candy*, and *Steve: "Just" Be with Jesus*. All of these live-session DVDs are available through the store page of www.kclehman.com.

6. At the time of this writing (winter 2013), we have twenty-one live emotional healing sessions available in both full-length and condensed versions. For detailed descriptions of these sessions, see the store page of www.kclehman.com.

7. Some of the stories of healing that Charlotte and I share in this book actually occurred through the use of these other healing tools, and some of our live ministry sessions portray healing facilitated by these other healing tools; however, the Immanuel approach shares many core principles and techniques with these other emotional healing tools, and our perception is that the Immanuel approach starts with the strongest parts of these earlier tools and then adds new pieces that make it easier, safer, and more effective. Our website, www.kclehman.com, provides a number of essays describing and discussing these other emotional healing tools, such as "traditional" prayer for emotional healing, Eye Movement Desensitization and Reprocessing (EMDR), and Theophostic®-based emotional healing. See especially chapter three, "More Introduction

Our friends and colleagues who are using the Immanuel approach are also seeing dramatically positive results. For example, Kim Campbell, recently the medical director for a well-known ministry that serves the persecuted church, used the Immanuel approach to provide emotional healing for traumatized/persecuted Christians in countries such as Pakistan, Nepal, Sri Lanka, Nigeria, the Philippines, Ethiopia, Iraq, Laos, Thailand, Myanmar, and Colombia. The following is one of the many amazing stories of healing that Kim has shared with us.

David[8] was born into a deeply religious Muslim family in a Muslim village in a Muslim country in southwest Asia, and his family members and neighbors became very upset when he and one of his uncles became Christians. Not surprisingly, his family and neighbors became even more upset when his uncle began openly telling others about his faith, when David began preaching, and when people were delivered and miraculously healed in response to David's prayers. David was twenty-six years old in July of 2006 when his uncle was abducted and executed by a group of enraged extremists, and a month and a half later two men with AK-47s came into the family sweet shop where David worked and emptied fifty rounds, leaving David lying in a pool of blood with eleven gunshot wounds. His survival is miraculous, since the doctors at the local hospital refused to treat him, and he therefore did not receive any medical care until he got to a hospital in a distant city eight hours later. But his left arm was so badly damaged that it had to be amputated.

The ministry mentioned earlier helped David with the cost of his medications and with a prosthesis for his left arm, and when Kim visited in October of 2007 to provide medical follow-up, he also asked David about the psychological aspect of the trauma. David stated that he was "all right," but his face and voice looked and sounded depressed, and with further probing Kim discovered that he had full blown post-traumatic stress disorder (PTSD), including flashbacks of the machine gun fire during the attack. Kim then led him through the Immanuel process, and Jesus showed David that he had always been with him, that he was with him throughout every moment of the attack, and that he would always be with him in the future. At the end of the ministry time, when Kim asked him to go back to the memory of being shot, David sat quietly, with a surprised-but-peaceful look on his face. He

---

(A Psychiatrist's Journey), in Karl Lehman, *The Immanuel Approach (to Emotional Healing and to Life)* (Libertyville, IL: This Joy! Books, in print), for a brief summary of the relationship between these other emotional healing tools and the Immanuel approach. Theophostic® *is a trademark of Dr. Ed Smith and New Creation Publishing.*

8. Names and other identifying information have been changed/disguised in order to care for the safety of certain participants in several of the following stories.

reported that he could still recall being startled by the shooting, but that he was now aware of Jesus' presence *with him, in the memory, even during the shooting,* and that the memory was no longer distressing.

We have heard more amazing stories of healing from Sarah Yoder, a woman serving with this same organization, and one of the women on a mission team that has been working with persecuted/traumatized women and children in Colombia. In certain areas of Colombia, Marxist guerillas and various other paramilitary groups have been attacking the church, and part of this attack has been to target pastors for assassination. There are now hundreds of women and children in Colombia whose husbands/fathers have been murdered because of their involvement in Christian ministry. An especially horrifying part of the story is that, in their efforts to intimidate the church, the assassins deliberately try to make the murders as traumatic as possible for the survivors. So they will routinely do things like going into the pastor's home and killing him in front of his wife and children. Not surprisingly, almost all of these women and children develop PTSD. Most of them also develop associated problems such as bitterness and depression, and many of them withdraw from involvement in church and ministry.

However, God's power to heal is even greater than the enemy's power to destroy. As I write this (March 2010), it has been just two weeks since Charlotte and I had the privilege of spending an evening with Sarah, hearing first-hand accounts of the redemptive healing the Lord has been providing for these women and children. In September of 2008, Kim, Sarah, and two other women went as a mission team to work with forty-eight of these widows. The mission team was able to lead the Colombian widows through the Immanuel process, and every single one of them appeared to receive profound healing. The team was able to go back for a second visit in July of 2009 and worked with sixty more widows, once again leading them through the Immanuel process, and once again observing that every single participant appeared to receive profound healing. Initially, almost all of the women described persistent despair as one of their heaviest burdens; but their healing encounters with the Lord have resulted in such dramatic transformations from despair to joy that acquaintances have made spontaneous comments about the participants being "changed women." The women participating in these Immanuel missions have also consistently reported resolution of the various signs and symptoms of PTSD.

When we met with Sarah two weeks ago, she said that all of the women they have been able to follow have continued to do well, with continued freedom from PTSD, continued freedom from depression, and continued restoration of joy. Furthermore, *most of these women now report that they have been able to use the Immanuel approach to facilitate emotional healing for their children.*

The following story is just one example of the kind of trauma the Lord has been working with and the kind of redemption he has been providing. Pastor Enrico, his wife, Rebecca, and their family lived on a small farm in an area where the Marxist guerillas and other paramilitary groups frequently skirmish for control. One day in 1995 soldiers came to the farm. Soldiers often came to the farm, usually demanding food or livestock, but on this day they decided to assassinate pastor Enrico. No questions. No comments. They just shot him, leaving Rebecca without a husband and their four small children without a father. Rebecca developed PTSD, became depressed, and withdrew from ministry. At the time of the mission team's visit in September of 2008 it had been fourteen years since she had lost her husband, but her pain seemed as fresh as if he had died the day before. And her children, in addition to developing PTSD and withdrawing from church, expressed intense and persistent hatred toward the perpetrators. The team was able to lead Rebecca through the Immanuel process, with the Lord providing profound healing for the trauma of her husband's murder; and not only has Rebecca remained free of PTSD and depression since this healing work, but she has also been able to use the Immanuel approach with her children, all of whom have experienced profound healing and are now free of PTSD and depression. In fact, the Lord's healing work has been so complete that the children have been able to forgive the men who killed their father, Rebecca has returned to ministry, starting a house church that is now bursting at the seams, and the children, on their own initiative, have started a youth group that is also now bursting at the seams.[9]

And then there are our young friends, Andy and Kristin Ross, who attend our church and live in our neighborhood here in Evanston, IL. Neither Andy nor Kristin have any mental health training,[10] but they have done a lot of reading about Christian emotional healing, they have watched a bunch of our videos, we helped them get started by facilitating a handful of Immanuel sessions for each of them, and Charlotte and I have given them an evening of coaching/mentoring on six or seven occasions over the last two years. They now do Immanuel healing with each other as a routine part of their ongoing

---

9. Both the house church (forty to fifty members) and the youth group (thirty to forty members) have outgrown Rebecca's home. Participants must now bring their own chairs so that they can meet in the street in front of the house.

10. As we make final preparations for the second edition to go to print (summer 2014), Andy has just finished a two year Masters of Pastoral Counseling program (on the way to becoming a Licsenced Professional Counselor), but at the time I wrote this text for the first edition (spring 2010), Andy had not yet started his mental health training.

personal growth, and using the Immanuel approach to deal with underlying trauma is a standard part of how they resolve conflict in their marriage.[11] They also volunteer some of their time each week to provide free Immanuel approach sessions for any in our community who wish to receive emotional healing, and they have seen many people blessed by the resolution of traumatic memories.

One of the most exciting things about the Immanuel approach is that several of the new components make it possible to design *group* Immanuel exercises that are both safe and effective.[12] I have worked closely with our colleague, Dr. E. James Wilder, in developing Immanuel approach group exercises, and we have seen dramatically positive results with these exercises. For example, during the winter of 2010 Dr. Wilder visited a country in Asia that is recovering from many years of civil war and from massive trauma associated with a recent natural disaster. Charlotte and I had the privilege of spending an evening with him less than a month after he returned from this trip, and his report was very encouraging. Dr. Wilder spent a week with a team of forty-five ministers, mental health professionals, and lay people, training them in the use of the Immanuel approach, and especially focusing on the Immanuel approach tools that can be used in group settings. The core of his teaching program was to repeatedly take the trainees through the group exercises themselves. From the very first day the participants began receiving healing in their own lives as they "practiced." By the middle of the week every single person was connecting with Jesus and receiving healing each time the group went through the exercises. And by the end of the week every participant had received healing for a number of different traumatic memories.

Here are a few examples:

- There was a group of participants from the war zone who had trouble trusting the rest of the trainees. At the beginning of the week they tried to avoid anybody from the larger group, and they would not participate in activities with the larger group. However, after receiving healing these people were able to participate joyfully with the rest of the group.

11.   When one or both marriage partner(s) is/are being triggered by something the other is doing, it is extremely difficult to facilitate emotional healing for each other. Andy and Kristin therefore have other prayer partners to help with Immanuel healing for these situations. (Charlotte and I have this same arrangement.)

12.   For a detailed discussion of these new components and how they make it possible to use the Immanuel approach in group settings, see chapter fourteen, "ImmanuelApproach Safety Nets," and chapter twenty-four, "Immanuel Approach Exercises for Groups and Beginners," in Karl Lehman, *The Immanuel Approach (to Emotional Healing and to Life)* (Libertyville, IL: This Joy! Books, in print).

- One of the pastors attending the training had been "executed," along with a number of other believers who had been rounded up by anti-Christian militants. After spraying the group of Christians with bullets, the militants thought they were all dead and buried the bodies in a shallow mass grave. Amazingly, this pastor revived from the initial shock of being shot, dug himself out of the shallow grave, made it back to his home, and eventually recovered from the physical injuries; but, not surprisingly, he had also been psychologically traumatized, and he displayed dysfunctional reactions to reminders of the trauma. By the end of the week these traumatic memories had been healed, and he appeared to be free of the PTSD symptoms associated with these events.

- Another pastor attending the training reported that he had been anxious for as long as he could remember, but that after the healing exercises he was feeling peace for the first time in his life.

Furthermore, by the end of Jim's visit the participants were confident that they would be able to take the Immanuel approach home with them—they were planning to go home and start using the Immanuel approach with their spouses, children, extended families, friends, neighbors, colleagues, parishioners, and clients.[13]

Another exciting thing we have observed with the Immanuel approach is that it sometimes works with non-Christians, and when it does, those who have thereby experienced Jesus' living, loving presence, and received healing from him, usually decide to follow him. For example, two of the people attending Dr. Wilder's recent training seminar in Asia started the week as non-Christians. (They had been required to attend by their employers, who figured that Dr. Wilder, as a Western Ph.D. psychologist, might provide valuable information regarding treatment for post-traumatic stress disorder.) However, even though they were not Christians, they were still willing to try the exercises, and by the end of the week both of them had experienced the Lord's living, personal, Immanuel presence, received healing from him, and decided to follow him. A similar scenario during our May 2009 seminar in Panama provides another example. A non-Christian mental health professional found one of the flyers for the seminar, and probably decided to attend because he thought my lectures on psychological trauma and implicit memory would be valuable, regardless of my explicitly Christian perspective. However, even though he was not a Christian, he was still willing to

---

13. As of January 2011, almost a year later, the leader of the group Jim worked with reports that they are still using the Immanuel approach, that it continues to be very effective, and that it has been especially helpful and effective in working with traumatized children.

participate in the Immanuel approach group exercise that we included at the end of the seminar. And he was astonished by the results—he experienced God as a loving father for the first time in his life, he went to several traumatic memories and received profound healing in each of them, and then he ended the exercise by deciding to follow the Lord.

Rhonda and Danny Calhoun, friends of ours and codirectors of Our Father's Farm ministry near Kansas City, have also observed this same phenomena. They routinely use the Immanuel approach, and recently shared with us about their experiences with Sarah and Claire.[14] Sarah came to them at the age of thirteen, almost totally disabled by post-traumatic stress disorder from the horrible abuse she had endured. Even though she had been rescued from the abusive environment of her early childhood at the age of six, and had received regular care from a team of mental health professionals for seven years, she was still unable to eat normally due to a variety of triggered reactions, she was unable to sleep normally due to regular nightmares and triggered reactions to being in bed, she was unable to participate in mainstream public schooling, and she could rarely get through the day without intrusive traumatic memories causing panic attacks.

Thankfully, she responds well to work with the Immanuel approach, and has received transformative healing through a series of beautiful, gentle interactions with Jesus. By the time she was fifteen she was thriving instead of barely surviving, and this is where the Immanuel approach and non-Christians come in. Her friend and next-door neighbor, twelve year-old Claire, was a deeply troubled non-Christian girl who regularly cut herself. One day Claire came to Sarah, intensely upset, asking for help, and saying that she was going to cut herself. Sarah didn't know what to do, so she invited Jesus to be with her. She was quickly able to perceive his living, interactive presence, and then she asked him for help. In response, she felt like the Lord said, "Bring Claire to me, like Rhonda does with you."

So fifteen year-old Sarah invited twelve year-old Claire to try Immanuel prayer, and even though Claire wasn't a Christian she was still willing to try it. She promptly experienced what she describes as "close encounters of the Jesus kind" —she had a mental image of Jesus standing in front of her, he told her that *he* had been cut so that *she* would not have to be cut, he showed her the marks on his body, and then he went on to say, "You've always wanted a family. . . . would you like to be part of my family?" She said yes. Sarah and Claire didn't take time to discuss theology, but I think this qualifies for becoming a Christian, since Claire has been talking to Jesus regularly and following him openly since this initial encounter. Furthermore, Claire

---

14. Not their real names.

hasn't cut herself, or had the urge to do so, since that day in the summer of 2009.[15]

Yet another exciting thing about the Immanuel approach is that it provides an especially gentle, safe, and effective tool for doing emotional healing work with children. As described above, the widows in Colombia have been using the Immanuel approach to facilitate healing for psychological trauma in their children, the people that Dr. Wilder trained in Asia have been using the Immanuel approach to facilitate emotional healing for traumatized children (see footnote #12), the Calhouns used the Immanuel approach to facilitate emotional healing for thirteen-year-old Sarah, and Sarah used the Immanuel approach to facilitate emotional healing for twelve-year-old Claire. Furthermore, we are getting a steady stream of very encouraging stories from many others who are using the Immanuel approach for emotional healing work with children.

For example, when Emme was nine years old, several girls in the suburb where her family lived reported men in a car pulling up beside them and offering to give them a ride. Furthermore, in one of these situations one of the men had actually gotten out of the car and chased the girl. Even though she wasn't personally harmed or threatened, and even though these worrisome events never developed into anything more dangerous, something about these frightening incidents got stuck in Emme's mind in a way that was traumatic. She became persistently fearful about being "stolen" by strange men, and began having recurrent nightmares in which she was kidnaped, kept in some kind of cage or jail, "and I never saw my family again." She became fearful of walking in the neighborhood (even with a group of friends), to the point that she insisted on being driven to and from school and to and from her friends' houses. She even felt unsafe in her own home if her parents stepped out of the house for as little as three to five minutes. On top of everything else, her fears about being kidnapped caused her to begin fearing that she might not truly be a believer: "If I'm not trusting God and experiencing peace, maybe I'm not really a Christian."

Cognitively, Emme realized that her persistent fears and frightening dreams were abnormal. (None of her friends, exposed to the same news about the same incidents, had these fears and dreams.) And she hated the way her fearful thoughts and dreams made her feel. But she couldn't get rid of them. She would experience partial, temporary relief when her parents and others would remind her of the promises in Scripture about the Lord being

---

15. See "Can the Immanuel Approach Be Used with Non-Christians?" in Chapter 29 (Frequently Asked Questions) for additional discussion regarding the Immanuel approach with non-Christians.

with her, reassure her regarding their presence to protect her, and reassure her about the reality of her safe neighborhood, but she would quickly slip back into fearfulness, with the frightening thoughts about being kidnapped feeling more true than the Bible verses or her parents' reassurances. And this unhappy state of affairs persisted for several years.

Fortunately, Emme's grandfather (a close friend of ours, who Emme calls "Grand") is an experienced Immanuel approach facilitator, and she heard her parents talking about how he would pray with people whenever he was in town. After hearing many stories about how these people experienced healing and freedom as a result of praying with her grandfather, she asked her mom and dad if she could be one of the people Grand prayed with the next time he came to visit. So when her grandparents came to visit just before Thanksgiving 2011, Emme was first in line. In the middle of the Immanuel prayer time, Emme began to think about being kidnapped and to feel the familiar fear associated with these thoughts. But then something different happened. As she describes it,

> Always before, I would get so overwhelmed by the fear that I wouldn't think about anything else. But during the prayer time, for the first time, other thoughts came into my mind while I was thinking about being stolen and feeling the fear. . . . I wasn't trying at all to find the answer myself—Grand had told me to just listen for what God's going to say to me—and these thoughts just came into my mind all by themselves.

When I asked Emme to describe the subjective quality of these thoughts, she said that they "felt different from my usual thoughts—somehow they just felt different," and then added, "It's hard to get words, but somehow I knew the thoughts were from God, and they felt true."

According to Emme, the Lord started out with the basics, resolving her fears about whether or not she was truly a believer: "God said, 'You are mine,' meaning, 'You are a Christian.'" And then the Lord reassured her with simple yet powerful truths, such as "Do not be afraid, for I am your God," and, "I will always be with you. Even if your mom and dad aren't with you, and you feel alone, you're not really alone. I will always be with you." Finally, God explained to her that "when we go through hard times, and bad things happen, God knows we're gonna get through it with his help. He's not going to let anything happen to me that I can't handle. And then he said, 'Do not fear. I will help you get through it—whatever happens.'"

One of the most important points is that these thoughts from the Lord felt true. Furthermore, follow-up reveals that they have continued to feel true, and that they had power to produce deep and lasting change. In the past when her mom, dad, and others reminded her of Bible verses and reassured her regarding the safety of her neighborhood, Emme would begin to struggle with doubts regarding the verses and reassurances within minutes to hours, and the frightening thoughts about being kidnapped, the associated fearful emotions, and the haunting nightmares would all return in full measure within days. In contrast, it has now been more than two months since her Immanuel prayer time with her grandfather, and she has remained completely free from doubts, frightening thoughts, fearful emotions, and scary dreams.[16] Now the truth consistently *feels* true. When I was talking to Emme on the phone a couple weeks ago, she spontaneously commented, "It's silly to be so scared. I live in a safe neighborhood, I'm with my friends, my parents are close by, the Lord is always with me—why should I be afraid of being kidnapped?" These realities now feel so true, and her old fears now feel so unreasonable, that she almost seems to forget that for several years her frightening thoughts about being kidnapped felt more true than verses from the Bible or reassurances from her parents. At the end of our conversation, she popped out with, "I'm for sure more joyful, more happy, now that I'm not scared all the time."[17]

You can see why we are excited about the Immanuel approach, and why we are confident that you can permanently resolve your traumatic memories if you earnestly pursue emotional healing.

Where/How Do I Get Training Regarding the Immanuel Approach?

It probably won't surprise anybody to hear that many people have been contacting us with questions along the lines of, "I would like to use the Immanuel approach to emotional healing in my _____ (psychotherapy practice, ministry, church, small group, family, marriage, etc). How/where do I get training that will enable me to do this?" Unfortunately, at this time we do not have any kind of training institute, we do not offer internships/apprenticeships,[18] and we are not providing regularly scheduled seminars

---

16. As we make final preparations for the second edition to go to print (winter 2014), it has now been more than two years since her Immanuel prayer time with her grandfather, and she continues to be completely free from doubts, frightening thoughts, fearful emotions, and scary dreams related to being kidnapped.

17. See "Can the Immanuel Approach Be Used with Children?" in Chapter 29 (Frequently Asked Questions) for additional discussion regarding the Immanuel approach with children.

18. Our essays occasionally mention "mentoring groups." These groups must be kept small for a variety of reasons, and due to our limited availability we are only able to provide two of

designed to train people to use the Immanuel approach. In the absence of this kind of Immanuel approach training package, appendix C offers a summary of the resources that *are* currently available, and then describes how to use these resources in putting together a do-it-yourself Immanuel approach training program. Also, although we are not currently providing a regular schedule of Immanuel seminars, we do, occasionally, provide training events related to the Immanuel approach. (All relevant information regarding these seminars will be posted in the "Events" section of the "Training" page of our Immanuel approach website, www.immanuel approach.com).[19] Furthermore, a number of others, such as pastor Patti Velotta and our friend, Mark, are now providing Immanuel approach training. As we become aware of trainers that we know personally, we will post brief descriptions of the individuals and ministries providing training, along with contact information, in the "Trainers" section on the "Training" page of this same website. Information regarding trainers will also be increasingly available through the Immanuel approach network directory (accessed from the "Referrals" page of this same website), as self-identified trainers post profiles.

Where/How Do I Find Someone to Facilitate Immanuel Approach Healing for Me?

It also probably won't surprise anybody to hear that we receive many, many requests along the lines of, "Can you help me find a therapist/emotional healing minister who can facilitate Immanuel approach emotional healing for me?" We are working hard to train Immanuel approach facilitators, to post information regarding these people on the "Referrals" page of our Immanuel approach website, and to build the Immanuel approach network directory, but the small number of facilitators we are aware of are profoundly unable to provide sessions for the large number of people who want them. At least for now, most people will need to find or recruit their own Immanuel approach facilitators. See appendix C, part III ("Finding/Recruiting Your Own Immanuel Approach Facilitator") for our thoughts regarding how one might pursue doing so.

---

them. Therefore, unfortunately, we are not able to offer this kind of mentoring to the general public.

19. We may be able to offer regular Immanuel approach training seminars at some point in the future, but at least for the next few years we will be focusing our time and energy on other projects, such as finishing a number of live-ministry DVDs that are currently in process, developing additional material for the Immanuel approach website, and writing several more books.

8

The Second Half of the Basic Plan

Recognizing and Acknowledging "Invisible" Implicit Memory and VLE Confabulations, and Then Choosing Behavior Based on Truth

Each specific traumatic memory that gets resolved is a step forward, but none of us will be finished with *all* of our traumatic memories any time soon. In the meantime, we need to embrace the challenge of at least partially neutralizing our traumatic implicit memory and VLE confabulations by recognizing and acknowledging them, and then once these previously "invisible" phenomena have been exposed, making behavioral choices based on the truth carried in our non-traumatic memory files.

The "time of departure" conflict described earlier provides a good example. There was a block of several years when I had figured out that I was being triggered, but I had not yet resolved the underlying memories. However, activation of traumatic implicit memory is not voluntary. That is, the way in which stimuli in the present activate old memories is a *nonconscious, involuntary* neurological phenomena—nobody asks us: "Do you want these little triggers to stir up nasty, disruptive toxic content from traumatic memories?"—there is no point in the process where Nancy gets to *choose* whether or not to allow triggering (by her husband's behavior) to open up the memory files from trauma with her alcoholic father. And since we don't choose whether or not to get triggered by a certain situation, I could not simply choose to block the implicit memory content from coming forward. Regardless of my new insights and self-awareness, I still got triggered—I still felt the intense urgency and anxiety, it still felt true that it was all about Charlotte not being ready to roll away from the curb at exactly 0600 hours, and intense frustration and judgment toward Charlotte would still well up spontaneously inside of me.

However, recognizing that I was triggered helped me to make other choices that dramatically reduced the cost of my traumatic implicit memories and VLE confabulations. Recognizing that I was triggered opened up the possibility of acknowledging that I was triggered, and that much of my urgency, anxiety, and frustration therefore belonged in the original memories as opposed to being appropriate in the present. Knowing that I was triggered (and understanding what this meant) helped me choose to remind myself that Charlotte's sense that we would still make it had always been accurate (in all the years of our marriage, we had never actually gotten stuck in rush-hour traffic). So when Charlotte was just getting into the car at seven minutes after six o'clock, I was all bent out of shape, and she would reassure me that we'd be okay, I would *choose* to challenge my triggered urgency, anxiety, and frustration by deliberately reminding myself that she was probably right. Realizing I was triggered helped me choose to remind myself of the times when Charlotte's slow and careful approach regarding last-minute details had prevented serious problems, and of the times when my "Stop-worrying-about-all-the-stupid-unnecessary-things-we-may-be-forgetting-and-just-get-in-the-car!" approach had resulted in costly omissions. Understanding that I was triggered helped me to recognize and acknowledge my judgments toward Charlotte, and then ask the Lord to help me release them. And finally, if our departure had gotten delayed past 6:05, I would usually feel intense temptation to punish Charlotte by being sullen and silent for the first several hours of the trip, and recognizing that I was triggered helped me choose away from this toxic behavior.

My experience with getting triggered to my two-year-old separation memories provides another good example. As you will remember, whenever I would feel stuck in an overwhelming situation and call to the Lord for help, but then not be able to perceive his presence or assistance, the painful thoughts and emotions from the two-year-old separation trauma would come forward as implicit memory. Before I understood implicit memory, triggering, VLE explanations, or the specific components of this particular traumatic memory package, when these memories would get triggered I would become intensely blended with the two-year-old implicit memory thoughts and emotions and I would swallow my VLE explanations "hook, line, and sinker," with absolutely no insight regarding what was really happening. "The Lord has abandoned me—he isn't here with me when I need him," "He won't come even though I call and call," "I can't trust his heart toward me because he allows things for which there's no possible justification," etc. would all *feel true, in the present*, and I would fully accept my VLE confabulated explanations that the triggers in the present were the true source and origin of my painful thoughts and emotions.

I would therefore focus my energy and attention on fighting with the triggers (the problem in the present causing me to feel stuck and overwhelmed, and my perception that the Lord was refusing to respond to my calls for help). I would plead with the Lord, asking and asking and asking that he manifest more tangibly; I would argue with him, trying to convince him that his response was inadequate and that he should intervene more powerfully; and I would experience waves of the intense subjective perception that the Lord was refusing to be with me or help me, and then I would point my frustrated anger at *him*, trying to punish him with every hurtful accusation I could think of. After bouncing back and forth between these reactions for varying lengths of time (sometimes hours), I would eventually settle into a miserable confused discouragement, and then finally force myself to move on to some other task because I didn't know what else to do.

Fortunately, by the time of the flooded-car disaster I finally had the benefit of insights regarding implicit memory, triggering, VLE confabulation, and the specific content from my two-year-old trauma. Furthermore, I had also become utterly convinced of the Immanuel truths that the Lord is always with us, that he always wants to help, and that if we are unable to perceive his presence or receive his help it's because there is something on *our* side of the equation that's in the way. Therefore, even though the underlying trauma had not yet been resolved, so that the triggered content still felt true in the present and the VLE explanations still felt valid, I was able to neutralize their damaging effects by recognizing them for what they were and then making behavioral choices based on the Immanuel truths regarding the Lord. Instead of following the old pattern of focusing on the triggers and then floundering in the swamp of begging, despair, anger, and confusion, I chose to surrender my confabulated explanations and then turn to the Lord for help, finally asking, "What am *I* doing that's hindering me from perceiving your presence? What choice do *I* need to make to take the next step forward?" And as you may remember, this is what opened the door for the healing breakthrough that finally dismantled the long-standing and very costly two-year-old separation trauma.

One last thought regarding recognizing our triggering and resolving underlying trauma in general: just as in the two-year-old separation trauma example, recognizing and acknowledging our traumatic implicit memory and VLE confabulations is a necessary prerequisite for exposing and resolving underlying trauma. If you think about it carefully, you will realize that we can't even ask the beginning question, "Am I ready to deal with the underlying traumatic memories?" until we surrender the VLE confabulations arguing for other explanations and acknowledge that we are triggered. We cannot receive healing for our unresolved traumas until we acknowledge that they exist.

Satellite Overview

Before jumping into the second half of the book, let's take a moment to orient ourselves by looking at another satellite overview picture. In part 1, I presented basic information about psychological trauma, and also discussed implicit memory, the Verbal Logical Explainer, and central nervous system extrapolation—related phenomena that are important to understand when working with psychological trauma. And in part 2, I presented an initial discussion of how to neutralize traumatic implicit memory and VLE confabulations.

In part 3, I will be talking about exacerbating factors that can make things much more difficult: maturity from the age of memory, memory-based negative reactions to the suggestion of possible triggering, and loss of access to our relational connection circuits. In part 4, I will describe additional resources and insights that are helpful for working with both straightforward and more difficult situations: the importance of taking responsibility for *our own* stuff, additional resources for recognizing when our traumatic memories are getting stirred up, and tools for reestablishing access to our relational connection circuits. And in part 5, I will talk about specific interventions for helping *others* who are triggered. The content in part 3 is the more advanced material I mentioned in the introduction—answers to questions that some of you may not yet be asking. Again, for those of you who are new to all of this, just try to catch enough of the main points so that you can know what's here and come back for it when you need it.

Now that we are oriented, let's move on to part 3.

Part Three

Additional Factors That Hinder Recognizing and Acknowledging Traumatic Implicit Memory and VLE Confabulations

9

Sometimes It's Easy;
Sometimes It's REALLY HARD

As described in part 2, the first half of the basic plan for neutralizing the negative effects of psychological trauma is to engage in the ongoing process of permanently resolving traumatic memories; and the second half of the basic plan is to recognize and acknowledge when we are being affected by traumatic memories, and then make behavioral choices based on truth. However, if you have already tried to apply these principles in your life you have already discovered this, and if you are just learning about implicit memory and VLE confabulations you will soon discover it: It can sometimes be REALLY HARD to recognize, and ESPECIALLY REALLY HARD to acknowledge, traumatic implicit memory and VLE confabulations. Charlotte, myself, and many of our close friends and colleagues have been deliberately pressing in to this challenge for a number of years now, and we have all been struck by how it can seem almost easy in some situations, but extremely difficult in others.

For example, a number of years ago I noticed the message light flashing on our business line as I was on my way to bed, and decided to check the voice mail before turning in for the night. One of our patients had been in crisis and I thought the message might provide an encouraging update regarding the situation. The message had been left at 11:00 p.m., and did provide an update, but unfortunately it was not encouraging. The patient's mother reported that she had been especially upset that evening, and after tearing up her room, yelling at the rest of the family, and talking about suicide, she had ridden off into the night on her bicycle and had been gone for several hours. The patient's father then got on the phone and demanded that I "do something." After listening to this message I felt vulnerable, powerless, helpless, and overwhelmed, I became increasingly anxious, and I was unable to calm myself down. As a psychiatrist I had been confronted with many intense, difficult, complicated situations, and these crisis scenarios had always made me anxious; but I had always eventually been able to accept the reality that I had done my best and that I was ultimately not the One in control, and then I would be able to calm down. However, this particular situation triggered a combination of especially difficult underlying memories so that I became unusually anxious and was not able to calm myself down.

At 2:00 a.m. I was still awake, pacing around our bedroom in the dark, and covered with sweat from head to toe as a result of my persistent intense anxiety. Charlotte woke up, realized that I was pacing around in the dark worrying, and gently offered: "I wonder if some of this anxiety might be coming from old memories—maybe we could try that emotional healing prayer thing." This was near the beginning of my personal healing journey, and it hadn't even occurred to me that my anxiety might be coming from underlying memories. Being miserable for hours had increased my open-mindedness, and the thought that my pain might be caused by something we could fix felt like good news. I was not consciously aware of any connection to underlying memories and it didn't feel like I was remembering past experiences, but the intensity of my reaction was so dramatic that triggering seemed quite plausible once she mentioned the possibility. Furthermore, the dynamics between Charlotte and me in this particular situation were not triggering me in any way, and she offered her thoughts with gentleness and compassion so she felt like a safe ally. All these positive factors resulted in my welcoming her suggestion, and then being able to recognize the clues and acknowledge my triggering without defensiveness.[1]

In contrast, there have been times when Charlotte has suggested that my negative thoughts and emotions might be coming from unresolved trauma, but I have *not* welcomed the suggestion, and found it to be *incredibly* difficult to recognize or acknowledge that I was triggered. In these messy, difficult situations it has felt like Charlotte was my enemy, and my spontaneous response has been to become defensive and adversarial. The clues indicating triggering have been much more difficult to spot, and from my defensive, adversarial attitude I fought the possibility, working to strengthen my VLE confabulations as part of protecting myself from Charlotte, as opposed to working with her in looking for the clues that would help me recognize that traumatic implicit memory had come forward. In these scenarios the initial trigger has always been something that Charlotte had said or done, and the subjective perception that the *whole* problem was being caused by Charlotte's behavior in the present has been almost irresistible: "This isn't about some stupid memory! I'm not *remembering*

---

1.   Just for the record, our perception regarding the presence of triggering was confirmed by the follow-up. As Charlotte prayed with me, traumatic memories eventually came forward, and the unresolved content in these memories matched both the triggers that had stirred things up and the negative thoughts and emotions I was experiencing. Furthermore, the unusual, persistent anxiety completely resolved as we worked with the Lord to finish processing the unresolved content.

anything—I'm upset because *you* are being unreasonable, inconsiderate, selfish, immature, and careless!" It has always felt like she was blaming me when she suggested that I might be triggered, and that if I acknowledged being triggered in any way she would use this against me to dismiss my valid concerns. In these messy, difficult situations the whole issue of whether or not I would acknowledge my triggering has always seemed huge and perilous—as if Charlotte were not only my adversary but also more powerful than myself, and that I couldn't afford to make any mistakes in my efforts to protect myself from her. And when I would try to remind myself that Charlotte is my friend and a trustworthy woman of integrity, it has been hard to find or hold onto any specific memories that would support these hopeful thoughts.

So why do we have such tremendous difficulty recognizing and acknowledging our traumatic implicit memory and VLE confabulations in certain situations? Our perception is that, in addition to traumatic content coming forward as "invisible" implicit memory that feels true in the present, VLE confabulations explaining why the traumatic implicit content is really about the triggers, central nervous system extrapolations filling in the holes, and our self-deception/denial choosing to look the other way, there are several additional factors that can sometimes make the overall challenge much more difficult. These exacerbating factors are discussed in chapters 10 through 13.

10

Fighting the Battle, but with Child Resources

Maturity and External Locus of Control Corresponding to Childhood Memories

Unfortunately, most traumatic memories are from childhood experiences, and these memories often carry more than just unresolved negative thoughts and emotions. The additional components sometimes carried in these childhood memory packages contribute several of the exacerbating factors mentioned in chapter 9.

Maturity from the Age of the Original Experience

One of the additional components often carried in memories from early trauma is the child or infant maturity[1] we were operating out of at the time of the original experience. Therefore, when these memories get triggered, to the extent that we blend with[2] the child perspective from inside the memory package *we regress to the maturity level from the time of the original childhood experience.*

For example, it is normal and appropriate for a child to assume it's somebody else's job to do most of the work, so that the task remaining will

---

1. This discussion regarding maturity will be best understood in the context of Dr. Wilder's teaching regarding the needs, skills, and responsibilities corresponding to each level of maturity. For an excellent summary of Dr. Wilder's teaching regarding the five stages of maturity (infant, child, adult, parent, and elder), see James G. Friesen et al., "Maturity," chapter 2 in *The Life Model: Living From the Heart Jesus Gave You—The Essentials of Christian Living,* Revised 2000-R (Van Nuys, CA: Shepherd's House Publishing, 2004), pages 29–58.

2. Psychological *blending* is when implicit memory content *blends together* with the mental content corresponding to our experiences in the present, so that we *do not perceive any subjective difference* between the implicit memory content and content corresponding to the present. For example, when I blend with childhood memories, instead of standing in my non-triggered, adult ego state and thinking about autobiographical memories from the childhood experiences as if they were part of my past history, I will experience the childhood implicit memory thoughts and emotions as *blended together* with the thoughts and emotions from my adult ego state. I will *not perceive any subjective difference* between the implicit memory content and the content corresponding to my current adult experience, and the implicit memory thoughts and emotions will *feel true in the present.*

be relatively easy (have a level of difficulty appropriate for a child). When we blend with the child perspective carried in a traumatic memory package it will therefore feel reasonable to expect *somebody else* to carry most of the load, and this will make things more difficult when it comes to exposing and neutralizing our traumatic implicit memory and VLE confabulations. Instead of embracing the reality that it is *our* adult-maturity responsibility to recognize, acknowledge, and resolve *our* traumatic memories, we will expect others to do most of the work. For example, instead of taking responsibility for learning how to recognize when we are triggered, proactively watching for clues that indicate trauma getting stirred up, and *challenging ourselves* to acknowledge our triggering, we might demand that somebody else must "prove it" before we acknowledge our triggering and VLE confabulations; and when we do finally acknowledge our traumatic implicit memories and the ways they are coming forward into our present lives, instead of taking adult-maturity responsibility for the practical logistics, we will expect *others* to provide the time, energy, and finances for the necessary emotional healing.

External Locus of Control from the Age of the Original Experience

There is a particular package of beliefs, emotions, and choices that are *developmentally appropriate for a very young child*, but that become an especially sneaky, immobilizing trap when they get triggered forward into our adult lives. When we were infants or very young children it was often true that the grown-ups had all the power and control—that what we call the *locus of control* in a given situation was *external* (residing with the grown-ups), as opposed to *internal* (residing within ourselves). For example, when I was an infant it was often true that the pain I was experiencing was caused by *somebody else's* failure (my babysitter forgot to change my diaper); it was usually true that it was *somebody else's* responsibility to fix the problem (I'm certainly not going to change my own diaper); and it was usually true that *my* only responsibility was to express my unhappiness (start crying) and then wait for *somebody else* to do something. Furthermore, it was understandable and expected that I would become increasingly upset if *somebody else* did not fix the problem in a timely fashion (I would escalate to persistent screaming if the babysitter was talking to her boyfriend on the phone, ignored my initial distress, and left me in my painful wet diaper).

These perceptions, emotions, and choices were accurate and appropriate when I was an infant. The problem comes when I am forty-eight years old, this content gets triggered forward as implicit memory, and these infant-maturity external-locus-of-control perceptions, emotions, and choices feel accurate and appropriate *in the present.* When a situation in the present includes an interaction with the Lord that triggers this external-locus-of-control package, it will *feel intensely subjectively true* that it is the Lord's fault that I'm in pain,[3] it will *feel intensely subjectively true* that I should be allowed to signal my distress by simply being increasingly unpleasant, it will *feel intensely subjectively true* that it is his responsibility to figure out and fix the problem, it will *feel intensely subjectively true* that it is reasonable for me to simply wait for him to do his job, and it will *feel intensely subjectively true* that it is reasonable for me to become increasingly upset with him if the problem is not solved in a timely fashion. And when a situation in the present includes an interaction with any other person that triggers these beliefs, emotions, and choices, the same kind of scenario unfolds. When this happens with Charlotte, it will *feel intensely subjectively true* that it is Charlotte's fault that I'm in pain, that I should be allowed to signal my distress by simply being increasingly unpleasant, that it is *her* responsibility to figure out and fix the problem, that it is reasonable for me to simply wait for *her* to do her job, and that it is reasonable for me to become increasingly upset with her if the problem is not solved in a timely fashion.

This external-locus-of-control package can even be applied to the Lord and others at the same time. For example, as described earlier in the story about traumatic memories from my two-year-old separation trauma, when I would encounter a situation that felt overwhelming, ask the Lord for help, but then be unable to perceive his presence or help, the unresolved content from the separation trauma would get activated. This unresolved content would then come forward as implicit memory, and it would feel true in the present that the Lord was choosing to ignore my calls for help, it would feel true in the present that I couldn't trust his heart for me, etc. And since my two-year-old trauma memories also included this small-child external-locus-of-control package, when this material would come forward it would also feel true in the present that it was *the Lord's* fault I was in pain, it would feel reasonable that I should be allowed to signal my distress by simply becoming increasingly unpleasant, it would feel true that it was *his* responsibility to figure out and fix the problem, and it would feel reasonable to become increasingly upset with him if he did not resolve the problem in a timely fashion.

And then Charlotte would walk into the room, and being a nearby grown-up that might reasonably be expected to help, I would promptly apply the two-year-old external-locus-of-control package onto her as well.

---

3. Any time our interactions with the Lord (or any other person) are part of a triggering situation, our VLE will explain to us that it's his fault that we are in pain. When the triggered memory content also includes this external-locus-of-control package, it will usually get applied to the nearest grown-up, and the subjective sense that "it's his fault" will be doubly intense.

Somehow, even *from inside the* two-year-old memories, I would realize that I shouldn't blame Charlotte for the Lord choosing to ignore my calls for help, so it would *not* feel true that it was her fault, but the rest of the external-locus-of-control implicit memory package *would* get applied to her. It would feel reasonable that I should be allowed to signal my distress by simply becoming increasingly unpleasant, it would feel reasonable that it was *Charlotte's* responsibility to figure out what was wrong, it would feel reasonable that it was *her* responsibility to do whatever was necessary to fix it, and it would feel reasonable to become increasingly upset with her if she failed to resolve the problem in a timely fashion. So instead of asking for her help, and appreciating anything she was able to give me, I would simply become increasingly unpleasant, and then judge her and point more unpleasantness in her direction if she didn't figure out what was the matter and do whatever was necessary to fix the problem.

Charlotte and I went through the first ten years of our marriage before we began learning all this stuff about trauma, implicit memory, and the Verbal Logical Explainer; so during the first decade of our married life, whenever my two-year-old separation trauma got stirred up I became intensely blended with the child implicit memory content and had *no* insight regarding how my hurtful, entitled, external-locus-of-control thoughts, emotions, and behavior were coming from the underlying memories. In fact, my triggered thoughts and emotions would feel *so true* in the present, and my inappropriate, hurtful behavior toward Charlotte would feel *so reasonable* in the present that I would defend them instead of apologizing for them. Not surprisingly, my triggered thoughts and emotions, my hurtful and inappropriate behavior, my lack of insight, my entitlement, and my lack of apology would usually trigger and alienate my number one ally; and then, instead of getting help in exposing and resolving the underlying trauma, I would get a miserable conflict in which Charlotte and I would both become increasingly triggered.[4]

As illustrated by this example, this external-locus-of-control package is especially problematic because it will inherently hinder me from owning responsibility *now, in the present, as an adult,* for exposing and resolving the underlying traumatic memories. That is, if I believe it's the Lord's fault that I'm in pain, that he and Charlotte need to take responsibility for fixing the problem, and that it's reasonable for me to simply wait for them to take care of it, then I will not consider the possibility that *my* triggering might be contributing to the problem, I will not look for the clues that would confirm

---

4.   As I have learned about trauma, implicit memory, and triggering, as I have learned to quickly recognize external-locus-of-control implicit memory content for what it is, and as I have become able to quickly acknowledge this triggering to Charlotte, now I can ask her for help in an appropriate fashion and I am much more likely to get assistance.

this, and I will not take responsibility for finding and resolving the under-lying trauma.

There is also a partial version of this external-locus-of-control package that comes from beliefs, emotions, and choices that are developmentally appropriate for an older child. When we were older children, it was often true that the problem in front of us was too big for us—even after doing everything we were able to do for ourselves, we were still unable to resolve the problem. In these situations it was appropriate for *us*, as older children, to take responsibility for asking grown-ups for help. However, it was the *grown-ups'* responsibility to figure out what kind of help we needed, and it was the *grown-ups'* responsibility to give us this help in a way that we could use. If there were blockages hindering us from being able to receive the help they were offering, it was the *grown-ups'* responsibility to identify and resolve these problems. As older children, it was *developmentally normal and appropriate* to ask for help, but then to *believe* that the next move belonged to the grown-ups, to *feel* dependent, and to *choose* to wait for them to figure out what we needed and deliver it in a way that we could receive. And it was developmentally normal and appropriate for us to become increasingly upset with them if the grown-ups did not provide usable help in a timely fashion. These are accurate and appropriate beliefs, emotions, and behaviors for the developmental stage of *child* maturity. And, once again, the problem comes when I am an adult, this content gets triggered forward as implicit memory, and these child-maturity external-locus-of-control beliefs, emotions, and choices feel accurate and appropriate *in the present*.

When a situation in the present includes an interaction with the Lord or our community that triggers these beliefs and emotions, it will feel intensely subjectively true that we have done everything we are able to do for ourselves, that the problem is too big for us, that we have asked for help, and that now it is the Lord's/our community's job to give us appropriate help. And, to this point, these beliefs may even be true. However, it will also feel intensely subjectively true that if we have not yet been able to understand and/or use the help that has been given, it's because *the Lord/our community* are not giving us the right kind of help; it will also feel intensely subjectively true that it is *the Lord's/our community's* responsibility to identify and resolve any problems preventing us from being able to receive the help they are offering; it will also feel intensely subjectively true that it is reasonable and appropriate for us to wait for *the Lord/our community* to figure all of this out and do whatever is necessary to get us help we can use; and it will also feel intensely subjectively true that it is reasonable for us to become increasingly upset with them if they do not solve the problem in a timely fashion.

For example, when I had dyslexia and could not learn to read like the other kids in my class, it was my responsibility to tell the teacher that I needed more help. But it was the grown-ups' responsibility to figure out that simply repeating the usual methods over and over again was not working, it was the grown-ups' responsibility to figure out that I had dyslexia, and it was the grown-ups' responsibility to develop a customized teaching plan that took my special needs into account. When I was in first grade, it was *developmentally normal and appropriate* for me to ask for help, but then to *believe* that the grown-ups needed to solve the problem, to *feel* dependent, and to *choose* to wait for them to figure out what kind of help I needed and deliver it in a way that I could receive. The problem comes forty years later when I ask the Lord to help me with a stuck point in an emotional healing session, this first grade content gets triggered forward as implicit memory, and these older-child-maturity beliefs, emotions, and choices feel reasonable and appropriate *in the present*: "I've asked for help but I'm still stuck, so obviously the Lord has failed to provide help in a way that I can understand and use. It's *his* job to figure out what's in the way and come up with a plan that takes care of the problem, and there's nothing I can do about it except wait for *him* to do *his* job. Furthermore, it's reasonable for me to become increasingly upset with him if he hesitates in providing this care!"

Just as with the infant-maturity external-locus-of-control package, these older-child external-locus-of-control beliefs, emotions, and choices can profoundly hinder our ability to participate in the healing process. If we get stuck, this older-child external-locus-of-control package will hinder us from owning responsibility, *now, in the present, as adults*, for persistently pushing forward with the troubleshooting process. It may be true that we are still stuck even though we have already asked for help, but it is *our* adult-maturity responsibility to keep engaging with the Lord and others to obtain additional help and/or to figure out what's hindering us from using the help we have already received. However, if we *believe* we are stuck because the Lord and our community are not giving us help that we can understand and receive, and that it's *their responsibility* to identify and resolve the problems preventing us from being able to receive the help they're offering; if we *feel* dependent and helpless; and if we *choose* to wait passively for them to deal with these problems, then we will not own responsibility, *now, in the present, as adults*, for troubleshooting regarding the problems hindering our healing journey. We will not ask the Lord to show us what **we** need to do differently in order to cooperate more effectively with his plan to expose and resolve the traumatic memories that are getting stirred up—we will not ask the Lord to show us what **we** need to do differently in order to take the next step forward.

11

No, I'm **NOT** Triggered!

Memory-Based Negative Reactions to the Suggestion of Possible Triggering

As has been discussed, trauma coming forward as "invisible" implicit memory, our VLEs explaining that our pain is really being caused by triggers in the present, central nervous system extrapolations filling in the holes, self-deception and denial looking the other way, infant/child maturity expecting others to do most of the work, and infant/child external-locus-of-control waiting passively for someone else to take care of the problem all contribute to why it is sometimes very difficult to recognize and acknowledge triggered traumatic memories and VLE confabulations. In addition to these factors, most of us also have specific, memory-based negative reactions to the suggestion that we might be triggered.

Absence of Attunement

Let me begin discussion of this point with a brief introduction regarding the especially important form of interpersonal emotional connection called attunement (figure 11.1). I am successfully *offering* attunement if I see you,

Attunement Offered	. . . Received
❏ I see you	. . . You feel seen
❏ I hear you	. . . You feel heard
❏ I correctly understand your internal experience	. . . You feel understood
❏ I join you in your emotions	. . . You feel I am with you
❏ I genuinely care about you	. . . You feel that I care about you
❏ I am glad to be with you	. . . You feel that I am glad to be with you

Figure 11.1   Offering and receiving attunement

hear you, correctly understand your internal experience, *join* you in the emotions you're experiencing, genuinely care about you, and am glad to be with you; and you are successfully *receiving* my attunement if you *feel* seen, heard, and understood, if you *feel* that I am *with* you in your experience, and if you *feel* that I care about you and that I am glad to be with you. The many and powerful benefits of attunement are discussed at length in the "Brain Science, Psychological Trauma, and the God Who Is with Us" essays,[1] but for the point being made here, the very short summary regarding one of these benefits is that when there is an attunement connection between them, *vulnerable individuals,* such as children, *can temporarily share the neurological, emotional, and spiritual resources of stronger individuals.*

Now let's put this together with our discussion from part 1 regarding how a painful experience only becomes psychological trauma if the person is not able to successfully process the painful experience. If any person going through a painful experience has safe, strong friends or family who are attuning to him—people who are truly *with* him in the experience, who are seeing him, hearing him, and understanding him, who are empathizing with him, who genuinely care for him, and who are glad to be with him— *he will almost always[2] be able to receive tremendous assistance from their attuned presence, this will almost always[3] enable him to successfully process the painful experience, and he will therefore almost never be traumatized.* An important implication of this is that *most traumatic memories will therefore include the absence of attunement.* That is, if the presence of attunement almost always prevents trauma, then the absence of attunement will necessarily be part of most painful situations that do become traumatic.

Unfortunately, this almost universal aspect of trauma can create a *second level* of difficulty when it comes forward as part of the traumatic implicit memory. Since implicit memory feels true in the present, when trauma that includes this component gets triggered, "I'm still waiting for someone to see me, hear me, understand me, be *with* me in my pain. . . ." will *feel true in the present.* This is certainly the case for myself—when I'm triggered, what feels true is that I want someone (for me, this is usually Charlotte) to see me, hear me, understand me, empathize with me, care about me, and be glad to be

---

1. For additional discussion of attunement, see especially the pre-introduction to "Brain Science, Psychological Trauma, and the God Who Is with Us ~ Part II" (available as a free download from www.kclehman.com).

2. We are not always able to *receive* attunement. For example, choosing to turn away in bitterness, self-pity, or rebellion can prevent us from receiving attunement.

3. Some painful situations are so overwhelmingly intense and complicated that the person will be traumatized even in spite of additional resources received through attuned connection to others.

with me. Now, if she notices that I'm triggered and immediately starts trying to point this out *without first providing the attunement that I'm still waiting for,* the "absence of attunement" aspect of the original trauma gets activated. When this happens, all the implicit memory pain associated with *not* receiving attunement in the context of the original trauma—the pain associated with *not* having others who were with me and relationally connected to me as I went through the painful experience; the pain of *not* having others who heard me, understood me, and empathized with me; the pain of *not* having others who genuinely cared about me and were glad to be with me—promptly comes forward into the present. I may not even have any conscious awareness or insight regarding my need and longing for attunement, but I will still feel all this pain from lack of attunement, and my disappointment, frustration, and associated VLE confabulations will be pointed at the person suggesting that I might be triggered.

Desire for Validation and Agreement

In the original painful situation, we want others to validate the difficulty of the situation we are in, and to agree with our assessment of the situation. As this desire for validation and agreement is included as part of the implicit memory content that comes forward *into the present*, it means that we will want others to validate our perception regarding the size of our pain *in the present*—we will want them to validate our perception that the implicit memory pain is real and valid *in the present*, and that the size and intensity of our reactions are therefore reasonable *in the present*. We will also want them to agree with our VLE confabulated explanations about how triggers in the present are the true source of the implicit memory pain. However, others cannot offer this validation and agreement with integrity, since our confabulated explanations are not true and our triggered perceptions, thoughts, and emotions are not accurate, and when they withhold the desired validation and agreement we will usually feel disappointed, frustrated, invalidated, disbelieved, and misunderstood.

Furthermore, when someone suggests that we are triggered, inherently implying that our implicit memory perceptions, thoughts, and emotions are unreasonable (*in the present*), to the extent that we are blended with the implicit memory content *it will feel as if they are invalidating our perceptions, thoughts, and emotions **in the original experience.***

Feeling Blamed, Accused, and Invalidated

Many traumatic experiences include being actively blamed, accused, and invalidated, as opposed to being heard, understood, validated, attuned to, and believed. For example, when a child is molested by a close family member, the rest of the family is often unable/unwilling to deal with the many painful consequences of acknowledging this horrible reality, and so they attack and blame the child instead. Sadly, we've heard many stories along the lines of: "When I told Mom that grandpa molested me, she called me a liar, washed my mouth out with soap, and told me I'd get a good spanking if I ever said anything like that again," or "When I told Dad that my brother made me have sex with him, he said it was my fault for wearing the wrong clothes."

This sadly common component of trauma can cause even more "second-level" trouble when it comes forward as part of the traumatic implicit memory package. When we have already been triggered, so that parts of the underlying traumatic memory have already come forward as implicit memory that feels true in the present; and when we have been triggered by interactions with people, so that our VLE confabulated explanations are already focusing on people in the present; someone suggesting that we might be triggered can feel like the problem is being blamed on us, and this will activate any blamed-accused-invalidated components of the original experience. When this happens, the subjective sense of being blamed, accused, and invalidated in the context of the original trauma will immediately come forward as implicit memory that *feels true in the present*, corresponding confabulated explanations will focus on whoever is suggesting the possibility of triggering, and we will become very defensive and adversarial.

A closely related dynamic comes from experiences where we were involved in a conflict, we acknowledged responsibility for some aspect of the problem, and then the other people involved focused only on our part of the problem and used our admission as grounds to disqualify everything we had to say, *including valid concerns*. Once again, this specific component can create a second level of difficulty when it comes forward as part of the traumatic implicit memory package. When we have already been triggered, so that parts of the underlying traumatic memory have already come forward as implicit memory that feels true in the present; and when we have been triggered by interactions with people, so that our VLE confabulated explanations are already focusing on people in the present; someone suggesting that we might be triggered can activate this acknowledging-responsibility-leads-to-valid-concerns-being-dismissed component of the original trauma. When this happens, the subjective sense that our admission of responsibility will be used as grounds for dismissing valid concerns will immediately come forward as implicit memory that *feels true in the present*, corresponding confabulated explanations will focus on whoever is suggesting the possibility of triggering, and we will become defensive and adversarial.

When I'm triggered to memories with these second-level components and Charlotte suggests the possibility that old trauma might be getting stirred up, it usually *feels compellingly true* that she is blaming, accusing, and invalidating me, and that if I admit I'm triggered she will use this to disqualify anything else I might say: "Oh, yeah, right! Everybody else is innocent, and the real problem is that I'm triggered—if it wasn't for all my triggering and dysfunction everything would be just fine! And, of course, since I'm triggered, *nothing* I have to say has any merit. If we just blame and invalidate Karl, *everybody else* can go on ignoring *their* stuff. . . ." (heavy sarcasm intended).

Feeling It Is Unsafe to Acknowledge Responsibility

Furthermore, many of us have had experiences in which it was not safe to acknowledge doing something wrong. Even good and loving parents can get intensely triggered, and have episodes in which they overreact to something their child has done. For example, a small child might disobey some household rule, and as a result break something that is especially precious to the parent. When Dad discovers the broken treasure and asks, "Who did this?" the child honestly acknowledges, "I did," and then Dad grabs the child, shakes her, and screams at her for being careless. If the person had experiences in which it was not safe to honestly acknowledge her faults, then suggesting the possibility that she might be triggered (indirectly asking her to acknowledge that her woundedness is contributing to the problem) can activate this traumatic content. To the extent that this is happening, she will feel defensive and unsafe, even when the suggestion is made carefully and gently.

12

Loss of Access to Relational Connection Circuits

We have been created to be relational beings—we have been created to be in relationship with God and with each other. Our minds and spirits have been created to desire relationship and to function best in relationship, and the Lord has actually designed specific circuits in our biological brains to serve this longing and need for connection. When these brain circuits are

Relational Connection Circuits

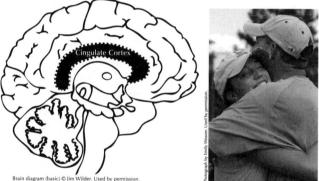

Brain diagram (basic) © Jim Wilder. Used by permission.

Photograph by Emily Weaver. Used by permission.

Figure 12.1   We have been created to be relational beings, and the Lord has actually designed specific circuits in our biological brains to serve our longing and need for connection.

functioning as designed, our spontaneous, normal experience will be to feel relationally connected and to feel the desire for connection. We will experience others as relational beings, we will be aware of others' true hearts, we will feel compassionate concern regarding what others are thinking and feeling, we will perceive the presence of others as a source of joy, and we will be glad to be with them. We will both *want* to offer attunement and *be able* to offer attunement, we will be flexible and creative even when unexpected circumstances require that we change our plans at the last minute, little things won't "get under our skins," and we will perceive the relationships involved to be more important than any problems we might be trying to solve. When these brain circuits are functioning as designed, our spontaneous, normal experience will be to perceive others as allies, *even in difficult interpersonal situations*; and as part of this allied attitude we will want to *join* with them in the *collaborative* process of exploring the situation together, we will want to understand their perspectives, and we will want to *join* with them in the *collaborative* process of working together to find a mutually satisfying solution. Charlotte refers to this way of living as "operating in *relational mode.*"

Unfortunately, there are certain problems and conditions that can cause us to temporarily lose access to these brain circuits. When this happens we operate in *non-relational mode.* Our spontaneous experience in non-relational mode will include the *absence* of feeling relationally connected, and we won't even *want* to be connected. We will *not* perceive others as relational beings, we will *not* be aware of others' true hearts, we will *not* feel compassionate concern regarding what others are thinking and feeling, and we will *not* be glad to be with them or experience their presence as a source of joy. We will *not* want to offer attunement or be able to offer attunement, we will be rigid and unable to think outside the box, we will find little problems to be much more irritating, and the problems we are trying to solve will feel more important than the relationships involved. When we are operating in non-relational mode and we encounter difficult interpersonal situations, instead of perceiving others as allies we perceive them as adversaries, and instead of wanting to join, explore, understand and collaborate we will tend toward judging, interrogating, and focusing on trying to "fix" the situation. Furthermore, when we lose access to our relational connection circuits in the context of being upset with a specific friend or family member, instead of perceiving that person's presence as an emotional resource, we will perceive him as the problem and as an adversary.

EVERYTHING with respect to relationships will turn out better and flow more easily when you are in relational mode, and operating in relational mode is *especially* important when dealing with conflict.

Another piece of fascinating brain science provides further understanding of why it is *so* costly to lose access to these circuits and *so* important to get them back online. In another one of his intriguing case studies, Dr. Sacks, the neurologist and author mentioned earlier, describes a patient who developed a particularly interesting form of color blindness. After an injury to the part of his brain responsible for processing color, this patient not only lost the ability to see color in the present, he also lost the ability to think in color, he lost the ability to dream in color, and he even lost the ability to remember in color. In contrast to this patient with brain-based color blindness, if *you* close your eyes you can't see color in the present; but if I ask you to remember, think about, and imagine a yellow banana, you will generate an internal image of a banana that *looks* yellow. The subjective experience may not be as vivid or as intense as actually seeing a banana with your eyes open, but even generating a mental image of a banana will include the subjective experience of *perceiving yellow*. This gentleman with brain-based color blindness could remember the *fact* that bananas are yellow, but he could no longer generate an internal image of a yellow banana or recall the subjective experience of actually *seeing* yellow in any context. In fact, he could no longer recall the subjective experience of actually seeing any color, so that even his memories came forward completely in black and white. *When he lost the part of his brain responsible for processing color, the subjective experience of color was removed from every aspect of his life.*[1]

My perception is that a similar phenomena occurs with our relational connection circuits. *When we lose access to the parts of our brains responsible for processing relational connection, we temporarily lose the relational aspect of every area of our lives.* We not only lose the ability to be relationally connected to those around us in the present, we also lose the ability to think relationally, and we even lose the relational connection components of our memories.

One of the most important consequences of this loss has to do with attune -ment. As described earlier, attunement is an especially powerful form of relational connection, and when we are connected to others through attune -ment we can temporarily share their neurological, emotional, and spiritual resources. For example, if we are in a painful situation that is beyond our capacity and/or maturity skills, *but we are linked to the Lord and/or others in our community through attunement*, we can still successfully complete all processing tasks by "borrowing" capacity and maturity skills from the Lord or any others who are stronger and more mature. However, when we lose access to our relational circuits we temporarily lose this special attunement bridge, and for as long as we remain in non-relational mode we are no longer able to receive this capacity and maturity skill augmentation from others.[2]

The memory aspect of this picture is also strategically important. This is discussed in much greater detail in the "Brain Science, Psychological Trauma, and the God Who Is with Us" essays, but a very short summary is that positive relational experiences accumulate in our memory banks, and

---

1. Oliver Sacks, *An Anthropologist on Mars* (New York: Vintage Books, 1995), pages 3–41.

2. For the purposes of this discussion all you need to know about capacity and maturity skills is that they are both *really* important in being able to successfully complete your journey through the processing pathway. For a detailed discussion of capacity, maturity skills, and how they relate to our ability to successfully process painful experiences, see part 2 of the "Brain Science, Psychological Trauma, and the God Who Is with Us" essay series.

the positive relational memories that accumulate in these accounts play a vitally important role in our psychological and spiritual development. For example, we develop *secure attachment* as we accumulate a large pile of memories for experiences in which our care providers are emotionally available, correctly understand our needs, empathize with any distress we might be feeling, and respond appropriately to the unique problems we bring them. A second example is *relational connection joy*. We develop a strong, stable baseline of relational connection joy as we accumulate a large pile of memories for experiences in which our care providers are glad to be with us. If you are not familiar with the terms "secure attachment" and "relational connection joy," for the purposes of this discussion all you need to know is that these are really important, really valuable ideal foundations for all aspects of life.[3]

And the point with respect to memory is that *we carry our secure attachment and relational connection joy with us,* even into difficult situations, *because they are anchored in the positive relational memories that we carry with us.* If I have the emotional foundation of secure attachment and a baseline of relational connection joy, both being deeply anchored in memories from a lifetime of positive relational experiences with family, friends, and the Lord, I can stand on this foundation of emotional security and relational joy even when I'm surrounded by people who are upset with me and attacking me. Just as traumatic content can come forward as implicit memory, positive content from these positive relational memories can also come forward as implicit memory. Even as the people in front of me are criticizing me and accusing me, the content from my positive relational memories can come forward as implicit memory, and it will *feel* true in the present: "Yes, but my family and friends love me, understand me, and are glad to be with me, and the Lord loves me, understands me, and is glad to be with me."[4]

However, when we lose access to our relational connection circuits and drop into non-relational mode, *we temporarily lose access to the resources in all of our relational connection memory bank accounts.* It's as if the banks are closed and all the ATM machines are temporarily out of service. To the extent that our relational connection circuits are off-line, we can't *feel* the relational connection memories that are the source of secure attachment, we can't *feel* the glad-to-be-with-you relational connection memories that

---

3.   Even if you have never heard of them before, just the names "secure attachment" and "relational connection joy" sound valuable and important, don't they? For additional discussion of secure attachment and relational connection joy, see the corresponding entries in the glossary, and also "Brain Science, Psychological Trauma, and the God Who Is with Us ~ Part II."

4.   The other key phenomenon that enables us to carry joy and secure attachment into difficult situations is a living connection with the Lord in the present.

accumulate to build the foundation of joy we ideally stand on as we address every other aspect of our lives, we can't *feel* the relational connection memories that accumulate as the subjective, intuitive sense of trust and safety in our relationships with our spouses, family, and friends, and we can't *feel* the relational connection memories of perceiving the Lord's presence as a person. Just as the man with cortical color blindness could remember the *fact* that bananas are yellow but could not recall the subjective experience of actually *seeing* yellow, the left sides of our brains will be able to remember these past experiences as *information,* but the subjective, intuitive, emotional right sides of our brains will not be able to *feel* any of the resources in these relational connection memory accounts.

And this is all relevant to traumatic implicit memory and VLE confabulation because the package that comes forward with traumatic memories being activated *usually also includes loss of access to our relational connection circuits.* Remember the pain-processing pathway from the beginning of

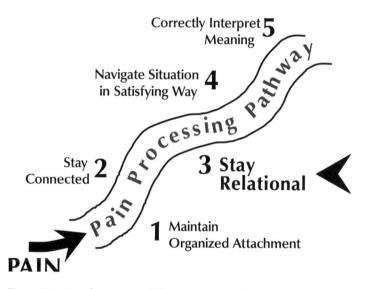

Figure 12.2 In order to successfully process a painful experience we need to stay in relational mode.

our discussion? Well, in order to successfully process a painful experience we need to *stay* in relational mode as we feel the negative emotions associated with the experience (figure 12.2). In fact, providing this necessary condition by maintaining access to our relational circuits is one of the most important processing tasks, and being unable to stay in relational mode is one of the most common and most important processing failures that causes painful experiences to become traumatic. This means that one of the most common and most important pieces of unresolved content carried in traumatic memories is loss of access to our relational connection circuits. And if the unresolved content carried in a particular traumatic memory includes loss of access to your relational connection circuits, then *these circuits will go*

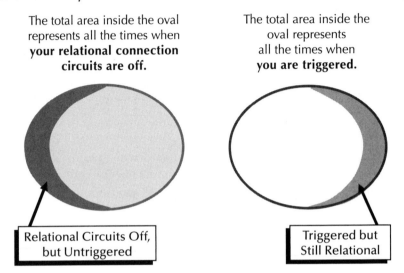

Figure 12.3   There are a few situations in which your relational circuits are off even though you are not triggered, and there are a few situations in which you are triggered but still relational.

off line every time this particular memory gets activated. Not every traumatic memory carries this problem, so being triggered does not always cause this temporary loss of relational mode (figure 12.3); but my perception is that most traumatic memories do carry loss of relational connection (figure 12.4).

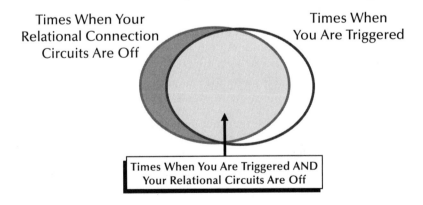

Figure 12.4   However, most traumatic memories carry loss of relational mode.

Therefore, in most situations where you are triggered you have *also* fallen into non-relational mode, and you are confronted with the challenge of recognizing and acknowledging your traumatic implicit memory and VLE confabulations *without access to your relational circuits in the present,* and *without access to any of your memory-anchored relational resources.*[5]

---

5. See "Brain Science, Psychological Trauma, and the God Who Is with Us—Part II" for additional discussion regarding how maintaining access to our relational circuits is one of the most important processing tasks in the pain-processing pathway.

13

Summary Regarding the Additional Factors That Can Make Things Especially Difficult

To fully appreciate the additional factors that can sometimes make it so difficult to recognize and acknowledge our triggering and confabulations, let's look at the whole pile in one place:

- To start with, we are trying to deal with the toxic content that has come forward due to the initial trigger stirring up unresolved traumatic memories. Dealing with this toxic content is challenging all by itself, and the trauma coming forward as "invisible" implicit memory, our VLEs explaining that our pain is really being caused by triggers in the present, central nervous system extrapolations filling in the holes, and self-deception and denial looking the other way all make it difficult to recognize and acknowledge our triggering.

- To make things even more difficult, we must work out of the infant or child maturity from the time of the original traumatic experience. The external-locus-of-control package (a normal part of our maturity package when we are infants/children), especially gets in the way.

- Specific, memory-based negative reactions to the suggestion of possible triggering—pain from lack of attunement, feeling blamed and accused, pain from lack of validation or agreement, and the feeling that it's not safe to acknowledge responsibility—result in defensive, adversarial reactions toward the people we are interacting with in the present.

- And we are facing all this without access to our relational circuits in the present and without access to any of our memory-anchored relational resources.

When we are triggered, others try to point this out to us, and all these pieces are present, we get *exceptionally* challenging situations like the messy, difficult scenarios between Charlotte and me described earlier.

Part Four

Additional Resources and Insights

As described in part 3, there are situations in which it is extremely difficult to recognize, acknowledge, and neutralize our triggered traumatic memories and VLE confabulations. Traumatic toxic content getting activated so that it comes forward into the present, this toxic content coming forward as "invisible" implicit memory, our VLEs explaining that our pain is really being caused by triggers in the present, central nervous system extrapolations filling in the holes, self-deception and denial looking the other way, infant/child maturity expecting others to do most of the work, infant/child external locus of control waiting passively for someone else to take care of the problem, specific memory-based negative reactions causing us to become defensive and adversarial, and losing access to our relational circuits are all exacerbating factors that contribute to these especially difficult scenarios. Thankfully, there are additional resources and insights that can help us with these especially difficult situations.

14

I Need to Take Responsibility for *My* Triggered Traumatic Content and VLE Confabulations

One strategic point in this whole endeavor is for each of us to take responsibility for exposing and neutralizing *our own stuff*—our own triggered traumatic content and VLE confabulations.

One of the most valuable aspects of embracing responsibility for exposing and neutralizing our own stuff is that this sidesteps the complicated hornet's nest of having to receive this difficult truth from others. As just described above, when we are triggered and someone else tries to point this out to us, we often respond by taking a defensive, adversarial stance and the situation usually does not turn out well. In contrast to this "does not turn out well" approach, where we wait for others to suggest that we might be triggered and then respond with adversarial defensiveness, we can deliberately, aggressively, and proactively *embrace* the responsibility and *take the initiative* with respect to the life-giving challenge of exposing and neutralizing our triggered traumatic content and VLE confabulations. Instead of demanding that others "prove it" before we even acknowledge our triggering, and then fighting them every step of the way, *we* can take responsibility for *our own stuff.*

Another valuable aspect of embracing responsibility for exposing and neutralizing our own stuff is that this is an *adult-maturity attitude* that inherently challenges the *infant/child-maturity attitude* of expecting others to carry most of the load, and that inherently challenges the external-locus-of-control package that is the *opposite* of taking responsibility for our own stuff. As just described in part 3, when we are triggered to infant or child memories we often end up operating out of the infant or child maturity from the time of the original trauma. In my own experience, I know that when I'm in an early memory and recognize infant or child thoughts and attitudes, remembering my adult-maturity commitment to take responsibility for my own stuff helps me push toward adult maturity, even from the *inside* of the infant/child memory; and remembering my adult maturity commitment to take responsibility for my own stuff especially helps me expose and challenge the external-locus-of-control package.

Furthermore, embracing responsibility for exposing and neutralizing our own stuff helps us respond constructively when *others* suggest that we might be triggered. No matter how vigorously you take responsibility for exposing and resolving your traumatic implicit memory and VLE confabulations, I can promise you that there will still be situations in which others are asking (or maybe even challenging) you to recognize and acknowledge your triggering. I know from my own experience that repeated, deep resolutions to vigorously pursue exposing and neutralizing my triggering and VLE confabulations have helped—when Charlotte suggests that I might be triggered, and the negative reactions described in part 3 are welling up inside of me (urging a variety of non-relational responses), I can feel that my commitment to taking responsibility for my own stuff helps me choose to listen to her and consider the probability that she is right.

15

Additional Resources for Recognizing Triggering

Due to all the factors discussed earlier—traumatic content coming forward as "invisible" implicit memory, VLE confabulations explaining why the traumatic implicit content is really about the triggers, central nervous system extrapolations filling in the holes, and our self-deception and denial choosing to look the other way—it is usually quite difficult to just directly recognize our traumatic implicit memory and confabulated explanations. *After* the underlying memories have been resolved, so that there is no longer active toxic content coming forward as implicit memory, it can be surprisingly easy to retrospectively spot the clues that pointed to triggering and to the holes in the no-longer-necessary VLE confabulations. But *before* the memories have been resolved, so that the distorted content is still living, active, and coming forward as "invisible" implicit memory that *feels true in the present,* it is usually soberingly difficult to recognize our triggering.

The retinal blind spot provides a good analogy. As each of us have experienced, it is extremely difficult to perceive our retinal blind spots without the help of the special technique for exposing them.[1] Triggering and VLE confabulations are similar, in that it is usually very difficult to perceive them directly. Just as with the retinal blind spot, they usually remain undetected unless we use special tools and/or special skills to expose them.

The good news is that, as we have been wrestling with this challenge over the last several years, we've discovered certain clues that consistently indicate triggering, and it has become less and less difficult to recognize when we're triggered as we have grown in the skill of spotting these clues.[2] For example, with memories for experiences that included thoughts formulated as words, the vocabulary of the words coming forward with the memory has always matched the age of the original trauma. Childish words from early experiences have usually gotten edited into adult vocabulary before we actually spoke them out loud, but with a little practice we have learned to spot the internal thoughts that first come forward in the vocabulary of our childhoods.

---

1. So far, we have never encountered anyone who discovered her retinal blind spot without the help of the special tool presented in figure 4.7.

2. The "we" here includes Charlotte, myself, and a number of our close friends and colleagues.

When I have thoughts that include, "You're just a poo-poo head!" I can be pretty sure I'm dealing with implicit memory from kindergarten or first grade. Another common indicator of triggering is what we call "small infraction, big reaction." That is, if I encounter a small problem/frustration/disappointment, but respond with a reaction that is much more intense than would normally be expected, I am almost certainly triggered.

Unfortunately, we have also noticed that for most of these clues it takes a lot of practice to learn to recognize them, and even when we do learn to recognize them, most of us still experience intense resistance to acknowledging the truth they are pointing toward. For example, the "small infraction, big reaction" clue tends to be very effective in helping us recognize when *others* are triggered, but tends to be much less effective in helping us recognize when *we ourselves* are triggered. As described above, when we are triggered, the traumatic content coming forward as implicit memory feels true in the present, we react to this implicit memory content as if it were true in the present, and we tend to accept our VLE's explanations for why the intensity of our reaction is reasonable and appropriate in the present. Later, after we have calmed down and the underlying trauma is no longer active, we will sometimes be able to recognize that the intensity of our reaction has been inappropriate; but this ability to recognize our exaggerated reactions usually occurs only in situations where the exaggerated intensity has been very dramatic, and even in these situations we will usually feel resistance (due to second-level triggering) and persist in clinging to the VLE confabulations justifying our reactivity.

Fortunately, there is one particular set of clues that most people find to be especially valuable, easy to learn to spot, and even relatively easy to acknowledge. In fact, most people find this one set of clues to be adequate for almost all of the work they need to do with respect to recognizing and acknowledging their triggers. If you are one of the people who have difficulty with this particular set of clues,[3] or if you are ready for the advanced course focusing on the 15 percent of your triggers that are the most difficult to recognize and acknowledge, then you can refer to the additional discussion of clues that indicate triggering provided in appendix D.

Watch for Loss of Access to Relational Connection Circuits

As mentioned earlier, the Lord has designed specific circuits in our biological brains to serve our longing and need for connection, and when these brain

---

3. For example, people with severe dismissive attachment will have difficulty with the clues discussed below, since these clues are organized around awareness with respect to attachment circuit activity.

circuits are functioning as designed, we are in relational mode. Our spontaneous, normal experience will be to feel relationally connected and to feel the desire for connection. We will experience others as relational beings, we will be aware of others' true hearts, we will feel compassionate concern regarding what others are thinking and feeling, we will perceive the presence of others as a source of joy, and we will be glad to be with them. We will both want to offer attunement and be able to offer attunement, we will be flexible and creative even when unexpected circumstances require that we change our plans at the last minute, little things won't "get under our skins," and we will perceive the relationships involved to be more important than any problems we might be trying to solve. We will perceive others as allies, even in difficult interpersonal situations, and we will want to join with them in the collaborative process of exploring the situation together, we will want to understand their perspectives, and we will want to join with them in the collaborative process of working together to find a mutually satisfying solution. When these brain circuits are functioning as designed, our spontaneous, normal experience will be to feel the resources carried in our relational memory files, and we will be able to share capacity and maturity skills with those to whom we are connected.

Furthermore, when we temporarily lose access to these brain circuits and fall into non-relational mode, our spontaneous, normal experience will include the absence of feeling relationally connected, and we won't even want to be connected. We will not perceive others as relational beings, we will not be aware of others' true hearts, and we will not feel compassionate concern regarding what others are thinking and feeling. Instead of experiencing others' presence as a source of joy, we will experience their presence as either a problem to be solved or a resource to be used, and we will not be glad to be with them. We will not want to offer attunement or be able to offer attunement, we will be rigid and unable to think outside the box, we will find little problems to be much more irritating, and the problems we are trying to solve will feel more important than the relationships involved. When we encounter difficult interpersonal situations, instead of perceiving others as allies we perceive them as adversaries, and instead of wanting to join, explore, understand, and collaborate we will tend toward judging, interrogating, and focusing on trying to "fix" the situation. When we are in non-relational mode we will not be able to feel the resources carried in our relational memory files, and we will not be able to share capacity and maturity skills with those to whom we are connected.

As also mentioned earlier, the package of unresolved content that comes forward with traumatic memories being activated usually includes loss of

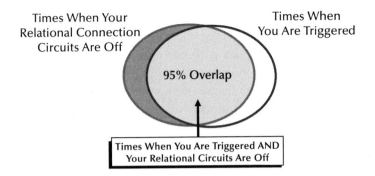

Figure 15.1   If I'm triggered I'm almost always in non-relational mode, and if I'm in non-relational mode I'm almost always triggered.

access to our relational connection circuits. Not every traumatic memory carries this problem, so being triggered does not always cause this temporary loss of relational mode; and there are other causes for loss of access to these circuits, so loss of relational mode does not always mean you are triggered,[4] but in my personal experience the overlap is about 95 percent (see fig. 15.1). In the vast majority of cases, if I'm triggered, my relational circuits are off-line, and if I've lost access to my relational circuits, I'm triggered.

Furthermore, I've found it to be much easier to recognize and acknowledge that I've lost access to my relational circuits than to recognize and acknowledge that I'm triggered. Even after years of practice, I still find it especially difficult to *acknowledge* that I'm triggered. In fact, even when I'm just talking to myself, I often still experience intense resistance to acknowledging my triggering and confabulated explanations. There's nobody accusing me of being triggered, there's nobody challenging me to admit that I'm triggered, there's not even anybody gently suggesting that I *might* be triggered—I'm just sitting by myself, stewing about something that's upsetting me, and when I have the thought, "This feels like triggering—many of these thoughts and feelings are probably coming from old trauma," my spontaneous internal response (to *myself*) is something along the lines of: "Rrrrrrr! Why don't you go find

---

4.   One of the other causes for loss of access to our relational connection brain circuits is dismissive attachment. A large part of dismissive attachment is learning to live without access to one's relational connection circuits, and to the extent that a person has dismissive attachment he will be going through life with these circuits off-line. Experiencing painful emotions that directly overwhelm our emotional maturity skills in the present is another problem that can cause us to lose access to our relational connection circuits. For example, if you are in an earthquake and your house is collapsing around you, you can lose access to your relational connection circuits if your fear becomes so intense that it overwhelms your adult maturity skills in the present. However, our perception is that traumatic memories being activated is the most common cause of losing access to our relational connection circuits.

somebody else to invalidate!"[5] In striking contrast, I have been pleasantly surprised to discover that this resistance has been almost entirely absent when it comes to recognizing and acknowledging that I have lost access to my relational connection circuits.

Therefore, I would encourage you to evaluate, with respect to your own experience, the overlap between loss of access to your relational circuits and triggering; and if you are one of the people with a very strong correspondence (like myself), then learning to recognize the clues indicating that your relational circuits have gone off-line can be your most valuable tool for recognizing when you're triggered.

RELATIONAL CONNECTION CIRCUIT CHECKLIST
Whenever you are upset, ask yourself the following questions:

1. Do I feel connected to _____ (fill in names of the people involved in the problem)?

2. Do I feel desire to be connected to _____ (again, fill in names of the people involved)?

3. Do I experience them as unique, valuable, relational beings?

4. Am I aware of their true hearts?

5. Do I feel compassionate concern regarding what they are thinking and feeling?

6. Do I *want* to offer attunement?

7. Am I *able* to offer attunement?

8. Am I free of judgment?

9. Do I experience their presence as a source of joy (as opposed to a problem to be solved or a resource to be used)?

10. Am I glad to be with them?

11. Am I comfortable making eye contact (other than angry glaring)?

12. Am I flexible and creative (as opposed to rigid and unable to think outside the box) with respect to thoughts and behavioral options?

13. Am I patient and tolerant (as opposed to impatient, intolerant, and irritable)?

---

5.   As I have carefully observed this phenomena, I have noticed that when I think about the possibility that I might be triggered, I am often subtly (or not so subtly) judgmental, blaming, invalidating, and non-relational in other ways *toward myself*. My perception is that the resistance and angry reactions to my own thoughts that I might be triggered come from *internally* failing to attune to my child-memory self as I suggest the possibility of triggering.

14. Do I perceive the relationships involved in the situation to be more important than the problems I am trying to solve (as opposed to the problems feeling more important than the relationships)?

15. Do I perceive others as allies, and want to join, explore, understand, and collaborate (as opposed to perceiving others as adversaries, and tending toward judging, interrogating, and focusing on trying to "fix" the situation)?

16. Can I easily recall past positive experiences with the person, and do I feel the positive emotions that should be associated with these good memories?

17. Can I easily think of things I appreciate about the person, and do I feel gratitude as I think about these specific appreciations?

If the answers to these questions are "no," then your relational connection circuits are off; and if these circuits are off, you are probably triggered. At the very least, noticing that you have lost access to your relational connection circuits should prompt you to ask, "Am I triggered?" *with the assumed answer being "yes" until proven otherwise.*

Note: As you review these questions, it's important to understand that they are not asking whether you know what you *ought* to think and feel, whether you know how you *ought* to act, or whether you are aware of the kind of consequences that might ensue should you act on your hurtful, non-relational thoughts, feelings, and impulses. These protective left-hemisphere brain functions often remain at least partially intact when you are in non-relational mode, and to the extent they remain intact they will enable you to make better choices regarding your *outward behavior*; but these cognitive-awareness-of-truth and outward-behavior issues are not the focus of the relational connection checklist. Rather, these relational circuit checklist questions are asking about the thoughts, emotions, attitudes, and impulses that come forward *spontaneously* and *involuntarily*, and that *feel* true

Loss of Access to Relational Circuits, Expanded Discussion

As we have been presenting this material in various settings, many have asked for examples and additional explanations regarding the checklist questions. We have prepared these additional examples and explanations, but we have also noticed that the need for this additional discussion and the points at which it will be helpful can vary dramatically from one person to the next. For example, if a person spends most of his time with strong access to his relational circuits, prioritizes relationships,[1] knows the difference between true relational joy and feeling good from other sources, and is already aware of the pain he causes his family and friends when he goes into non-relational mode and treats them like problems or resources—this person will immediately understand the meaning and implications of the question, "Do I experience their presence as a source of joy? (as opposed to a problem to be solved or a resource to be used)."

In contrast, if a person has dismissive attachment and has learned to live with his relational circuits off most of the time, he will tend to think that non-relational mode is the normal, logical, efficient, appropriate way to do things. He might look at this same checklist question and respond with something like:

> I'm not being non-relational, I'm just trying to get the job done. Some people are difficult and unhelpful, and I'm just trying to get those people out of the way. On the other hand, there are people who help and contribute. I don't "use" them—I just try to include them in my plan for getting the job done. And as far as joy is concerned, of course the difficult people are *not* a source of joy—*they're a pain in the neck!* And of course the helpful people *are* a source of joy—they help me get the job done and then I feel good.

---

1. If a person is truly spending *most* of his time with *strong* access to his relational circuits, he will inherently, necessarily, automatically, unconsciously prioritize relationships. Give yourself an extra point if you had this thought before looking at the footnote.

Examples and additional explanation will be required just to convince this person that another, better way of relating to people even exists.[2]

If you feel like most of this additional discussion is unnecessary, be *really* grateful for what it means that these checklist questions already make so much sense to you. If you feel like these examples and explanations are just right, then be grateful that you are now making sense out of these checklist questions. And if you feel like this additional material is inadequate, and all of this stuff about relational connection, relational joy, relational mode, and non-relational mode is still confusing, I would encourage you to look at the much more detailed discussion of these subjects provided in "Brain Science, Psychological Trauma, and the God Who Is with Us ~ Part II."

Expanded Discussion Regarding Specific Checklist Questions

DO I FEEL CONNECTION? DO I FEEL DESIRE FOR CONNECTION?
When I am in non-relational mode I don't feel emotionally connected to the people around me; however, I am usually not even aware of this lack of connection because when I lose access to my relational circuits I also lose the *desire* for connection. I don't notice the lack of connection because I don't miss it. Food and hunger provide a helpful analogy. If the parts of your brain that create the subjective experience of hunger are damaged, you can miss meals and have a very empty stomach, but you won't be aware of your lack of food because you don't feel hungry.[3] Similarly, if your relational circuits are off-line you can be starving for lack of connection but not be aware of it because you don't feel "hungry" for relationship.[4] In contrast, if *my* relational circuits are on, but *Charlotte* is triggered and non-relational, so that she does not want to be with me, then I am acutely aware of the loss of

---

2.   A person who is *temporarily* really stuck in non-relational mode at the time he first reads the question might initially respond much like the guy with dismissive attachment, but his response will change when he eventually gets back into relational mode.

3.   Research since the initial studies of hypothalamus lesions indicates that hunger and feeding behavior are actually quite complex, with a number of different factors contributing, but the early studies showing that hunger/feeding dramatically decrease after certain brain lesions are still adequate for the purposes of this analogy. See, for example, the study by Anand and Brobeck, in which rats with certain specific brain injuries decreased spontaneous feeding behavior even to the point of starvation. Bal K. Anand and John R. Brobeck, "Localization of a 'Feeding Center' in the Hypothalamus of the Rat," *Proceedings of the Society for Experimental Biology and Medicine*, vol. 77 (1951): pages 323–324.

4.   If you go for long periods with your relational circuits off most of the time, you will experience lack of joy, you may feel an odd emptiness or restlessness, and you might go looking on the Internet or in the refrigerator for something to make yourself feel better, but you won't directly feel desire for connection.

emotional connection. I feel an ache, a sadness, and a painful loss until our connection is reestablished.

My experience with chronic anxiety triggering provides a good example of how lack of connection and lack of desire for connection can manifest in subtle ways. As described earlier, I spent much of my childhood feeling anxious about the many ways in which the world seemed to be falling apart. I was not able to maintain access to my relational circuits when I felt anxious and overwhelmed in this way, so slipping into non-relational mode is therefore part of the package that comes forward when these memories of childhood anxiety get triggered forward. Unfortunately, the world we live in seems to provide a steady supply of triggers for these memories, and I have spent much of my adult life with this non-relational anxiety package triggered forward to some degree. I have also spent a large portion of my life energy developing a hundred different tools for coping with this anxiety, so the observable distress in the present is usually subdued, but it's almost always there—often with smouldering anxiety noticeable only as noise in the background.

My Verbal Logical Explainer works hard to convince me that the problems in front of me in the present are the true source of my distress, so I focus my attention and energy on the triggers in the present, with the perception that I will finally get free of the anxiety that haunts me if I can just work hard enough and solve enough problems. In this place of subtle triggering I am intensely problem-focused, solution-focused, and task-focused. And as I am focusing so intensely on problems, and the tasks at hand that will contribute to solving the problems, I am usually unaware of the fact that I am also subtly non-relational. I don't have any active animosity toward the people around me (unless they are contributing to the problems), I'm just not emotionally connected, I don't feel the lack of connection, and the thought of trying to be more connected doesn't enter my mind. In fact, if someone mentions the need for more connection my spontaneous internal response is usually something along the lines of: "Taking time for relational activities would be very nice if we could afford it, but right now we have more important things to take care of."

The good news is that I have become more and more aware of both loss of connection and loss of desire for connection as I have learned to deliberately observe the status of my relational circuits. Whenever I suspect that I might have slipped into non-relational mode I go over the checklist, and when I explicitly ask these specific questions regarding connection it's usually pretty easy to tell whether or not I feel emotionally connected and whether or not I feel the desire for connection.

The loss of desire for connection associated with loss of access to our relational circuits also has special implications for when we are in conflict. When I'm triggered toward Charlotte and I'm in non-relational mode, working to get my relational circuits back on so that I can be connected to her feels like cleaning the toilets so that I can have the privilege of washing the dishes. When I don't feel any desire for connection, the motivation to do the work to get my relational circuits back on must come from truth, commitment to Charlotte, and obedience to the Lord that are deeper than, and not dependent on, my immediate feelings. This is a place where I need to recognize that I'm triggered, where I need to recognize that I'm in non-relational mode and that *my lack of desire for connection is part of the problem,*[5] and where I then need to make behavioral choices based on the truth carried in my non-traumatic memory files. And when I stand on truth, commitment, and obedience, and choose to use the calming exercises and other tools described below, I will start to feel the ache and sadness from loss of connection, and the subjective desire to restore connection, as my relational circuits come back on line.

Do I Experience Them as Unique, Valuable, Relational Beings?

When I am in relational mode I perceive others as unique individuals who are inherently valuable, and it feels true that relationship with them is more important than any benefit they might provide or any contribution they might make. When I am in relational mode I even value those who can't contribute and those who actively make things worse. Even though they don't contribute anything of practical value, and may even be significant liabilities from a utilitarian perspective, I still perceive them as inherently valuable because they are unique, relational beings—children of God, created in the Lord's image, and capable of true, free-will relationship.

In contrast, when I have lost access to my relational circuits and am running in non-relational mode, the value of a person is based on how that person affects me. When I am in non-relational mode I still perceive some people as valuable, but when I look closely I realize that I only value those who are honest, considerate, intelligent, conscientious, loyal, strong, and hard working, and that I only value them because of the benefits they can contribute. When I look closely I realize that I do not perceive them as inherently valuable relational beings. And

---

5. In my personal experience with conflict between Charlotte and me, it has been very helpful to recognize that my lack of desire for connection is part of the problem, and to know that choosing to get my relational circuits back on line is the best long-term plan, *even though I can't feel these truths at the point I am applying them.* That is, even though this knowledge is almost totally cognitive at the time I am applying it, having these truths deeply embedded in my non-traumatic memory files still helps me to chose behavior that is *constructive* as opposed to *destructive*.

when I am in non-relational mode I do not value people who don't contribute or who actively make things worse. When I am in non-relational mode I perceive these people as liabilities to be avoided (or eliminated).

Also, note that even when I am in non-relational mode my cognitive left hemisphere still knows the "correct" answers—I still know, *cognitively*, that all other people are unique, valuable, relational beings.[6] I can still remember what I *ought* to think and feel, and from forty-plus years of practice as a Christian I will often give myself these answers as an automatic reflex, without even checking to see what actually feels true. But if I carefully examine what actually *feels* true, I discover that I perceive the weak and the bad to be burdens on society, and that I wish there were some acceptable way to get rid of them. People who are selfish, lazy, greedy, wasteful, hurtful, dishonest, destructive, entitled, criminal, or even just disabled, take more than they contribute, and therefore threaten *my* survival by pushing the whole world closer to the edge of social and ecological collapse. When I am in non-relational mode, and I deliberately check regarding what actually feels true, I catch myself having thoughts like: "Lord, if you love these people so much, why don't you just take them to heaven where you can take care of them? Then they could finally get what they need without depleting and overwhelming the rest of us."

Am I Aware of Their True Hearts?

Our use of "true heart" in this context is something we learned from Dr. Wilder, and it may be a concept unfamiliar to many of you. Our true hearts are the hearts that Jesus gives us when we choose to follow Him. Our false selves will wander into the bushes on many different occasions and for many different reasons, but our true hearts perceive the Lord's will and desire to cooperate with it.[7]

So what do we mean when we ask: "Are you aware of a person's true heart?" Let me provide a functional explanation by way of an example. Charlotte has recently felt both a calling and a longing to serve our church as one of the part-time pastoral staff. Something felt right about the whole idea from the moment she first mentioned it, and I loved seeing her excitement as she thought about the fulfillment and satisfaction she anticipated with this new position; but moving so much of her time away from our private practice and emotional healing ministry would require many changes with

---

6. I realize that this point has already been mentioned. I am bringing it up again because it is so important.

7. For additional discussion of this understanding of our true hearts, see James G. Friesen et al., *The Life Model: Living from the Heart Jesus Gave You—The Essentials of Christian Living* Revised 2000-R (Van Nuys, CA: Shepherd's House Publishing, 2004), pages 107–126.

respect to how we organized our lives, and my perception was that most of these changes would make *my* life more difficult. As we discussed all these possible changes and challenges there were times when my relational circuits were *on* and I *could* perceive her true heart, and there were times when I got triggered, lost access to my relational connection circuits, and was *not* able to perceive her true heart.

When my relational circuits were *on* and I *was* able to perceive Charlotte's true heart, thoughts such as the following would feel true:

> Even though I can't figure out how we'll get everything done, I know Charlotte's true heart desire is to do what's right in caring for our business, our emotional healing ministry, our marriage, and each of our individual needs.

> Charlotte loves me, she cares about how all this will affect me, and she wants to hear me. If some part of this new plan doesn't work for me and I'm not okay, I can tell her and she'll listen to me.

And finally,

> Charlotte is a woman of integrity, I know she's committed to knowing and doing the Lord's will above all else, and we can work together in continuing to discern regarding this new plan. If other important needs aren't getting cared for, Charlotte will be able to acknowledge that and make any necessary adjustments; and if it turns out that this plan isn't from the Lord at all, we'll be able to discern this together and Charlotte will be able to surrender it.

In contrast, when my relational circuits were *off* and I was *not* able to perceive Charlotte's true heart, very different thoughts would feel true, such as:

> This new thing's gonna be easier and more fun, and Charlotte's gonna run off after it, abandoning both me and our important emotional healing ministry work.

> She's just immature and selfish. As long as she gets what she wants she doesn't really care about how this is gonna affect me—she doesn't really care that her spending more time doing things she finds more rewarding is gonna force me to spend more time doing things I find less rewarding—she doesn't care that I'm gonna be trapped in the salt mines while she's off having fun.

And,

> There's nothing I can do about it because she doesn't want to hear what I have to say. If I tell her I don't like how things are turning out, she'll just blame me and say it's because I'm triggered.

These negative thoughts may be accurate to varying degrees regarding Charlotte when she is triggered and non-relational, but her thoughts, feelings, and behaviors when she is triggered and non-relational do *not* reflect her true heart. Furthermore, when I'm operating in relational mode I can hold onto the truth about her true heart even if, at the moment, this truth is being obscured by her displaying triggered, distorted, non-relational thoughts, feelings, and behaviors.

Do I Feel Compassionate Concern Regarding What They Are Thinking and Feeling?

The key here is *compassionate* concern. When I am in relational mode I feel *compassionate* concern for the thoughts and feelings of those around me—I want to know what they are thinking and feeling *so that I can be with them and help them*, and I feel sad if they are in pain. When I am in relational mode my concern for the thoughts and feelings of others is not contaminated by dynamics of self-protection or secondary gain (subtle or otherwise).

In contrast, when I have lost access to my relational circuits and am operating in non-relational mode I may feel concern, but it is *not* truly compassionate. For example, when I am in non-relational mode I may feel concerned that a homeless person is in distress, but this is because I'm concerned that he might ask me for money. I may feel concerned that a colleague is struggling in his marriage, but this is because I'm concerned that he might call me on Saturday afternoon wanting to talk about the situation. And I may feel concerned that a client is in distress, but this is because I'm concerned that he may blame me and want to sue me. Or I may feel intense interest and concern regarding whether or not an important colleague thinks I'm competent, but this is because I'm hoping she will endorse our training seminars. Similarly, a non-relational politician may feel intense interest and concern regarding voters' perceptions with respect to his trustworthiness, but this is because he wants their votes.

In fact, when I'm in non-relational mode I sometimes feel concern regarding what others are thinking and feeling that is actually the *opposite* of compassionate. For example, if one of the "juvenile delinquents" in our neighborhood is being punished for stealing my bicycle, my concern regarding his thoughts and feelings might look something like: "I hope the punishment causes him to feel enough pain to really teach him a lesson, and I hope he's thinking 'I'll *never* do that again!'" You might think that this would be pretty easy to spot, but actually you may be surprised. When you are *really* non-relational your judgmental, punitive thoughts will feel amazingly reasonable and appropriate, and your VLE will work diligently in finding explanations to cognitively justify your conclusions. "I'm not being non-relational, I'm just making sure that he experiences appropriate consequences so that he will be motivated to change! *It's for his own good—*in the long run he'll be as miserable as the rest of us if we enable him to continue this dysfunctional behavior!"[8]

When I'm in non-relational mode, any concern I feel regarding what others are thinking and feeling will always be tainted by dynamics of self-protection and/or secondary gain.

And when I am in non-relational mode I may simply feel *no* concern regarding the thoughts and feelings of others. My observation is that when I am in non-relational mode I am only concerned about another's thoughts and feelings if I believe that person has the power to affect me in some way. If I am *truly* convinced that he cannot affect me in any way—that his fear and pain will not be able to burden me, that his anger will not be able to threaten me, and that his approval will not be able to benefit me—then his thoughts and feelings will simply seem irrelevant. I might still know, *cognitively*, that I *ought* to be concerned, but if I check carefully regarding what *feels* true I discover that I do not actually feel concern regarding his thoughts and feelings.

DO I WANT TO OFFER ATTUNEMENT? AM I ABLE TO OFFER ATTUNEMENT?
When we are in relational mode and we encounter someone in distress, our spontaneous response is to *want* to offer attunement. It feels natural, right, and satisfying to offer attunement, and it is especially satisfying if the person is able to receive the attunement we offer and then experiences relief. In contrast, when we are in non-relational mode and we encounter someone in distress, our spontaneous response is to be anxious that the need to care for him will place a burden on us, and/or to be irritated that he is in our way, and/or to be disgusted by his pathetic neediness. We may still know, cognitively, that we *ought* to feel compassion and offer attunement, but if we carefully observe what actually feels true we will find some combination of anxiety, irritation, and disgust.

Furthermore, when we are in relational mode we are *able* to offer attunement. Our relational circuits are necessary for every aspect of

---

8.   Note that when you are in relational mode you can still administer appropriate consequences, but *you will feel truly compassionate concern even as you do this*, and "appropriate" will tend to be less severe.

attunement—our relational circuits are necessary for genuinely caring about the person and being glad to be with her, and our relational circuits are necessary for the empathic resonance that makes it possible for us to truly[9] see and hear the other person, for us to fully[10] understand her internal experience, and for us to join her in the emotions she is feeling. Therefore, when we are in relational mode, *and have access to our relational circuits*, if we choose to offer attunement we are *neurologically capable* of doing so. In contrast, when we are in non-relational mode, and have *lost* access to our relational circuits, we are neurologically *incapable* of offering attunement (regardless of whether or not we choose to try). When we are in non-relational mode we simply don't have access to the necessary neurological equipment.

In fact, trying to offer attunement and discovering that I am unable to do so is sometimes the first relational circuits checklist clue that I recognize. For example, there have been times when both Charlotte and I have been upset about something, I correctly perceived that she had fallen into non-relational mode, and I knew, cognitively, that one of the best things I could do was to help her regain access to her relational circuits by offering attunement. However, I was so focused on trying to fix *her* distress that I didn't notice that *I* had also fallen into non-relational mode. When I tried to offer attunement I was surprised to discover that I didn't seem able to do it; and as soon as I noticed this and started asking "why?" I realized that I did *not* have the empathic resonance necessary for truly seeing, truly hearing, fully understanding, and joining, and I realized that I did *not* genuinely care and that I was *not* glad to be with her. Finally, I glanced at the other checklist questions and realized that I had also fallen into non-relational mode.[11]

---

9.   We can make objective observations and receive cognitive, utilitarian information while in non-relational mode, but we cannot *truly* see and hear another person without the empathic resonance that contributes so centrally to attunement.

10.   We can understand objective, cognitive, utilitarian aspects of a person's experience while in non-relational mode, and we can even gather an intuitive, gut-level understanding of the non-relational aspects of her experience while in non-relational mode, but we cannot fully understand her internal experience without the empathic resonance that contributes so centrally to attunement.

11.   In these situations I'm making the *behavioral choice* to try to help, but when I stop and carefully examine what feels true, I notice that I *don't* genuinely care and that I am *not* glad to be with her. My choice to help comes not from spontaneously feeling desire to offer attunement, but rather from some combination of 1) anxiety regarding ways in which her distress may affect me, 2) the desire to manage unpleasant emotions in *me* that are being directly triggered by *her* distress, 3) cognitive truth that helping her get back into relational mode is truly a good plan, 4) commitment to Charlotte, and 5) obedience to the Lord.

Aᴍ I Fʀᴇᴇ ᴏғ Jᴜᴅɢᴍᴇɴᴛ?

When I judge I make negative assumptions about the person's heart/motives (note that this is the opposite of seeing her true heart). When I judge I perceive that I am fundamentally better than the other person, and that I would have done things differently (better) *even if I had to deal with all of the same challenges she has had to face.* When I judge I perceive that the other person is just plain "bad" in some way, and that negative consequences should be applied "to teach her a lesson" (note that this is the opposite of compassionate concern). In our experience, judgment and relational mode have been *absolutely, totally, completely, 100 percent* incompatible. That is, when we have found ourselves to be judging and then checked our relation circuits, we have *always* found them to be offline.[12]

Dᴏ I Exᴘᴇʀɪᴇɴᴄᴇ ᴛʜᴇ Pʀᴇsᴇɴᴄᴇ ᴏғ Oᴛʜᴇʀs ᴀs ᴀ Sᴏᴜʀᴄᴇ ᴏғ Jᴏʏ?
Aᴍ I Gʟᴀᴅ ᴛᴏ Bᴇ ᴡɪᴛʜ Tʜᴇᴍ?

These two questions go together because relational mode being-glad-to-be-with-others is inherently connected to perceiving their presence as a source of joy. You might say that the being-glad-to-be-with-others associated with relational mode is *caused* by experiencing their presence as a source of joy. Or you might even say that relational mode being-glad-to-be-with-others is a *manifestation* of experiencing their presence as a source of joy.

Falling in love is one of the clearest, most intense examples of the kind of "source of joy" and "glad to be with" that we are talking about here. If you are in love with someone you will *always* be glad to be with her, being with her will always bring you great joy, and nothing else seems to matter. You may have to get up at 6:30 a.m. on Saturday morning and go to a dingy church basement kitchen to wash dirty dishes left over from a late-night ministry event, but if the person you're in love with is also present you will be joyfully glad to be with her. The feelings parents have for their newborn children is another especially clear, intense example of these relational connection experiencing-others-as-a-source-of-joy/glad-to-be-with-them phenomena.

It is important to note that relational connection joy is not the same thing as simple pleasure,[13] and that relational connection glad-to-be-with never depends on receiving practical benefits. Even in non-relational mode there are situations in which we feel better when others are with us, but this

---

12. For additional discussion of judgment, see "Judgments and Bitterness as Clutter that Hinders Emotional Healing," available as free download from www.kclehman.com.

13. People who have spent many years trying to compensate for lack of true relational joy by pursuing pleasure may even have a hard time telling the difference between the two. One way to learn to recognize relational connection joy is to watch for times when all of the other checklist questions indicate that you are in relational mode, and then carefully observe and ponder the subjective quality of the good feelings you get when you notice that others are glad to be with you.

is different than the source-of-joy/glad-to-be-with package we experience when in relational mode. For example, Charlotte is a tremendous ally. She is intelligent, knowledgeable, skillful regarding many specific strategic tasks, strong, loyal, honest, conscientious, and discerning. Unless she is the source of the triggers that are upsetting me, when I am in non-relational mode I always feel better if Charlotte is nearby. If Charlotte is with me I feel less anxious, less vulnerable, and more secure—I feel like more resources are available and that I will be more able to handle any challenges that might come forward. But, again, this is not the same as the experiencing-others-as-a-source-of-joy/glad-to-be-with-them phenomena that we experience when in relational mode. When I am in non-relational mode, if a person has assets that would benefit me in some way, I think of her as a resource to be used; if a person won't affect me or my plans, then her presence or absence seem irrelevant; and if a person is opposing me or uses more resources than she contributes, then I think of her as a problem to be solved.

Note also that perceiving others' presence as a source of joy and being glad to be with them is clearest, strongest, and easiest to notice when the others are glad to be with us; but when access to our relational circuits is especially strong, we can be glad to be with others and perceive their presence as a source of joy even when they are *not* glad to be with us. For additional discussion of super-relational mode, see "Variable Intensity and Clarity with Respect to Relational Circuit Phenomena" on page 144 of this chapter.

AM I COMFORTABLE MAKING EYE CONTACT?

When we are in relational mode, making direct eye contact feels normal and comfortable. In fact, when we are in relational mode direct eye contact in most day-to-day interactions feels so natural and happens so spontaneously that it hardly even enters our conscious awareness. We usually don't think about it until we encounter someone who avoids eye contact, and then we realize that something doesn't feel quite right when we interact with others without making eye contact. Comfort with direct eye contact is easiest to notice when we are in positive relationships of special intensity, such as being in love or the euphoric connection parents often experience with their infants. As everybody knows, lovers spend a lot of time gazing into each other's eyes,[14] and parents can spend hours smiling at and making direct eye contact with their babies.

---

14. The Google search engine came up with 3,910,000 hits for "lovers gazing into eyes," so it appears that a lot of people are aware of this phenomenon (Google search, April 27, 2010). There is even a research study documenting careful empirical observations and thorough statistical analyses regarding eye contact between people who claim to be in love, all of which verifies that lovers do, indeed, spend an unusual amount of time gazing into each other's eyes. Zick Rubin,

In contrast, when we are in *non*-relational mode *avoiding* sustained eye contact feels normal and comfortable. In fact, when we are in non-relational mode avoiding direct eye contact in most day-to-day interactions feels so natural and happens so spontaneously that it hardly even enters our conscious awareness. This has certainly been the case in my own experience. When my childhood anxiety package is triggered forward, and I am in my (subtly non-relational) problem-focused, solution-focused, task-focused mode, I consistently avoid sustained eye contact; *but I was totally unaware of this until Charlotte pointed it out to me.* After Charlotte commented on my minimal eye contact during a number of different interactions, I began to observe myself more carefully with respect to this. I noticed that there were many situations in which I would frequently glance very briefly at the other person's face and eyes, but almost never sustain eye contact for more than a moment. Furthermore, I decided to watch for these episodes of avoidance and then counteract the spontaneous avoidance by deliberately trying to make more eye contact, and I was surprised to discover how difficult this turned out to be—when I tried to sustain eye contact I would feel distracted, off balance, and unable to concentrate on the problem-focused, solution-focused, task-focused thoughts I had previously been pursuing.

However, at the time Charlotte and I were first making these observations I had no insight with respect to being in non-relational mode, and avoiding eye contact in these situations felt so compellingly natural, spontaneous, and necessary that my VLE was still working to come up with explanations for why my avoidance of eye contact was normal and appropriate: "Of course I minimize eye contact when I'm focusing on an important task—eye contact is an intense and complicated interpersonal interaction, and it drains too much cognitive energy. I need all my mental resources to formulate the thoughts I'm trying to communicate, . . ." I focused on the *accurate* observation that trying to sustain eye contact impaired my ability to think clearly, but was completely unaware of the more important point that sustaining eye contact would *not* have impaired my ability to function if I had not lost access to my relational circuits. I did not understand this at the time, but my perception now is that sustained eye contact brings the truly, inherently relational aspects of the situation[15] to the foreground in a way that makes them much harder to ignore. With my relational circuits

"Measurement of Romantic Love," *Journal of Personality and Social Psychology*, vol. 16, no. 2 (1970): pages 265–273.

15. I am not referring to communication in order to transfer cognitive information or synchronize tasks, but rather to the truly, inherently relational aspects of the situation, such as whether or not the other person is okay, whether she feels relationally connected, whether she is glad to be with you, whether you are glad to be with her, etc.

off-line I would feel confused and unsure regarding these relational aspects of the situation, and trying to deal with them would distract me and throw me off balance.

Finally, I decided to carefully observe my pattern of eye contact during conversations when I was in relational mode and compare this to my pattern of eye contact during similar conversations when I was in non-relational mode. What I found was that when I was in relational mode I could discuss the same subject with the same person, but comfortably sustain longer blocks of eye contact without any of the uncomfortable feelings of being distracted, off balance, confused, overburdened, or unsure. When I was in relational mode, and therefore had access to my relational circuits, I could navigate the relational tasks related to sustained eye contact so smoothly and easily that I didn't even notice them. And prior to these deliberate observations, *making* eye contact felt so natural when in relational mode, and *avoiding* eye contact felt so natural when in non-relational mode, that I had been completely unaware of the fact that I would go back and forth between maintaining or avoiding eye contact depending on whether or not my relational circuits were on line.

Discomfort and avoidance with respect to sustained eye contact are much easier to notice when we are intensely triggered and non-relational. For example, when I am intensely triggered and non-relational during especially painful conflicts with Charlotte, sustained eye contact is acutely uncomfortable and avoidance of sustained eye contact is much more noticeable. I make the briefest possible glances toward her face in order to monitor her reactions, but otherwise I avoid eye contact completely. Furthermore, trying to force myself to sustain eye contact during one of these conflicts is immediately and intensely distressing. A very reliable indicator that we have fully resolved a conflict, and that I am back in relational mode, is that sustained eye contact once again feels comfortable and enjoyable.[16]

Since becoming convinced that discomfort and/or avoidance with respect to eye contact is an indicator of non-relational mode I have become much more aware of these phenomena. Now there are times when discomfort /avoidance with respect to eye contact is the first checklist clue I become consciously aware of, and then I glance at the other checklist questions to confirm that, yes, I have indeed lost access to my relational circuits. Charlotte and I have also noticed that my tendency to avoid eye contact has been steadily decreasing as I have been getting more healing and applying

---

16. Even with the phenomenon being much more dramatic during these painful conflicts, I still did not become consciously aware of this discomfort and avoidance with respect to sustained eye contact until I began to deliberately monitor the status of my relational circuits.

the tools described below, both of which have contributed to spending more and more of my time in relational mode.

Note: Sometimes when I am triggered, non-relational, and angry, I feel the desire to make direct eye contact, but for the purpose of glaring at the other person as part of expressing my anger. Being comfortable with making eye contact does *not* include this desire to glare angrily at your opponents during a fight. Being comfortable with making eye contact also does not include the non-relational satisfaction one gets after successfully intimidating others with an angry glare.

Am I Flexible and Creative, As Opposed to Rigid and Unable to Think outside the Box?

When we are in relational mode we are flexible and creative with respect to thoughts and behavioral options. This is easiest to see when unexpected circumstances force us to make last-minute changes, but even in routine situations this same profile is still present (although more subtle) as a general baseline disposition. Part of the reason for this is that there are higher-level brain centers directly responsible for flexibility and creativity, and these neurological systems that provide flexibility and creativity work much more effectively when we are operating in relational mode.[17]

Another part of the reason for the flexibility and creativity that we enjoy when operating in relational mode is that more resources are available. We feel connected to the Lord and others, we experience the presence of the Lord and others as sources of joy, we can feel the relational connection joy and secure attachment carried in relational memories, and we can share the capacity and maturity skills of those to whom we are connected through attunement. When we have access to all of these resources associated with operating in relational mode we feel like we can afford to be flexible and creative. When we feel like we have plenty of resources, when we feel strong and safe, and when we feel like there's a wide safety margin, then we feel comfortable trying new ideas, considering alternatives with uncertain outcomes, and taking chances with new and different ways of doing things—we feel like we have room for errors and surprises, both of which occur much more frequently when we are being flexible and experimenting with new, creative ideas.

In contrast, when we are in *non*-relational mode we are rigid and unable to think outside the box as opposed to flexible and creative. This is easiest to

---

17. These higher-level brain centers responsible for flexibility and creativity are the same as the level 4 neurological systems responsible for the fourth step of processing on the pain-processing pathway. See part 2 of the "Brain Science, Psychological Trauma, and the God Who Is with Us" essay series for additional discussion regarding why access to our relational circuits is necessary for these level 4 neurological systems to be able to function well.

see when unexpected circumstances force us to make last-minute changes, but even in routine situations this same profile is still present (although more subtle) as a general baseline disposition. Part of the reason for this is that loss of access to our relational circuits seriously impairs the function of the higher-level brain centers that provide flexibility and creativity with respect to our thoughts and behavioral options.

Another part of the reason we lose flexibility and creativity when we fall into non-relational mode is that fewer resources are available. When we are operating in non-relational mode we *don't* feel connected to the Lord and others, we *don't* experience the presence of the Lord and others as sources of joy, we *can't* feel the relational connection joy and secure attachment carried in relational memories, and we *can't* share the capacity and maturity skills of those to whom we are connected through attunement. When losing access to our relational circuits causes us to lose access to all of these associated resources we feel like we *cannot* afford to be flexible or creative. We feel like we are working "close to the edge"—like we are driving on a narrow mountain road with no safety rails instead of practicing in an empty parking lot—and in these situations we feel like we need a lot more control in order to be safe. In these situations we want to stay with the familiar, with the "tried and true," where we can be more confident with respect to the outcome.

My experience during a recent trip to California provides a good example of the flexibility and creativity we enjoy when operating in relational mode. At one point during this trip forty people had gathered in the living room of my hosts for a presentation about the Immanuel approach. This presentation was organized around PowerPoint slides and segments from our live session DVDs, and one of their friends was bringing the video projector. However, fifteen minutes before I was supposed to start we discovered that there had been a miscommunication and that the video projector might be as much as thirty minutes late. Fortunately, various aspects of the situation resulted in my being much less triggered and having much better access to my relational circuits than is usually the case when I do presentations, so that I was able to remain calm, flexible, and creative in exploring alternatives instead of rigidly locking onto my need for the not-yet-available projector.[18]

There was a large-screen entertainment center set into one of the walls, but we had made plans for the video projector because the entertainment center was not set up to interface with my laptop for the PowerPoint slides. I paused, thought for a few moments, and then realized I could rearrange my

---

18. For example, I could have insisted on waiting for the projector, and then gotten increasingly anxious, frustrated, and judgmental as the long delay became increasingly uncomfortable.

presentation to start with the live session clips that we *could* play directly from the entertainment center, and hopefully the projector would arrive by the time we had finished with the session clips. So, as a few late arrivals were getting settled we made last minute readjustments to accommodate this new plan, I put my DVD into the player, the menu came up on the screen, and we were ready to start. After brief introductions I selected the clip I intended to use and pushed the "play" button. Nothing happened. We quickly discovered that the first clip on the menu—the one I had tested to make sure the DVD player worked but that was *not* actually part of this particular presentation—was the only one that would play.

Once again I paused, thought for a few moments, and then realized that I could rearrange the presentation to start with the live demonstration we had originally planned for the end of the afternoon. The live demonstration went beautifully, and the projector arrived as we were finishing, but when we set it up we realized that our original plan to project onto the wall wasn't going to work after all. So once again I paused, thought for a moment, and then realized that I could rearrange the presentation so that I could share our Immanuel healing stories from Columbia, Pakistan, Kenya, and Panama while several guys improvised a projection screen. Once the screen was set up we were finally able to play the session clips and PowerPoint slides from my laptop, and despite all the drama and last-minute changes the overall presentation went amazingly well.

One of the most interesting things about this experience is that I was consciously aware of my mental and emotional states as all these pieces were unfolding. I was acutely aware of feeling calm and thinking clearly (as opposed to feeling frantic and experiencing muddled thinking, as would have been the case if the last-minute changes had triggered me into unresolved trauma), and I was acutely aware of feeling creative and flexible. This may sound strange, but the flexibility and creativity were so dramatic (and so unusual for me in this kind of situation), that I was consciously aware of them and could actually feel them—I could subjectively *feel* the effects of my flexibility and creativity brain centers being able to function optimally. I was also consciously aware of feeling resourceful, relationally connected, and emotionally strong, so that I felt like I could afford to be flexible and creative—I felt like I had enough space to be able to explore creative alternatives to the original plans.[19]

---

19.   Some of you may be wondering, "So what happens when you're doing a seminar and last-minute changes *do* trigger you into unresolved trauma and push you into non-relational mode?" The humbling truth is that I feel frantic, my thinking gets muddled, I am not flexible or creative, and I turn to Charlotte for help. She stays calm, thinks clearly, remains flexible and creative, and comes up with the solutions.

AM I PATIENT AND TOLERANT, AS OPPOSED TO IMPATIENT, INTOLERANT, AND IRRITABLE?

When we are in relational mode we tend to be patient and tolerant. In contrast, when we lose access to our relational circuits we tend to be impatient, intolerant, and irritable. This is certainly true for me. When I'm in relational mode I can tolerate an amazing amount of discomfort, obstruction, harassment, nonsense, discourtesy, delay, incompetence, difficulty, and inconvenience without getting frustrated or judgmental; but when I'm in non-relational mode my psychological/emotional "skin" is thin, I am easily frustrated, and I am quick to criticize and judge everything and everybody.

For example, I often drive in the left lane because it tends to move more quickly *as long as you don't get stuck behind somebody trying to make a left turn.* In order to avoid this I watch the cars ahead of me very carefully, and if somebody starts signaling for a left turn I quickly move into the right lane in order to slide around the potential obstruction. This plan usually works quite well. However, occasionally I come up to cars stopped at an intersection and stay in the left lane because there's only one car in front of me and he's *not* signaling for a turn. But then he puts on his left-turn signal *after* I've come to a complete stop with cars beside me in the right lane. If I'm in relational mode when this happens I feel a little wave of disappointment, but *not* frustration, impatience, or judgment. I feel merciful toward the driver in front of me, and have spontaneous thoughts along the lines of: "Hey, give him a break. I'm sure poor driving skills are not the most important thing about this person. He may be a wonderful father and husband, but just never learned to use his turn signals as part of courtesy to the drivers behind him. Or maybe he's just learning to drive—I can remember my first practice drives in city traffic! Dad was trying to teach me advanced stuff like these details with respect to turn-signal courtesy, but I was just trying to stay on the road and not hit anybody!"

In contrast, if I'm in non-relational mode when this happens my spontaneous reaction is to feel waves of frustration, impatience, and judgment. I do *not* feel merciful toward the driver in front of me, and my spontaneous thoughts are more along the lines of: "Oh, great! Now I'm gonna have to sit behind this idiot for who knows how long. And he's probably on his cell phone, too absorbed in his own stuff to be courteous to others. What an inconsiderate, selfish, immature, jerk!" I'm not yelling, swearing, or making obscene gestures. I don't even say any of this out loud. But these are the thoughts that come spontaneously into my mind and they are laced with frustration, impatience, and judgment.

The grocery store checkout lines provide another generous source of opportunities for me to observe my reactions to hassles and inconveniences. One of my favorites is waiting in line until there is only one person left in front of me, and then discovering that the person at the cash register is new and that she has just made an error that can only be fixed by the busy manager (who takes five minutes to get to the station). If I'm in relational mode when this happens I feel a little wave of disappointment, but *not* frustration, impatience, or judgment. I have grace for the stressed-out teenage checkout clerk, and the thoughts that come to me are something like: "Poor girl—I would hate to be in her shoes. She looks like she's trying hard. I wish I could do something to help. Hey, there is something I can do! 'Lord, bless this young lady. Help her to stay calm and know that you love her.'" However, if I'm in non-relational mode when this happens my spontaneous reaction is to feel a combination of frustration, impatience, and judgment. I do *not* have grace for the checkout clerk, and the thoughts that come to me are more like: "Come *on* girl, focus! You make some careless mistake, and now I have to wait an extra five minutes for the manager to come and fix the problem. And who designed this stupid system anyway? If you're gonna have teenagers at the cash register you should at least set things up so that they can't make errors that require a five-minute wait and manager assistance."

Then there are our godsons, now six and eight years old. Between the two of them they can create an amazing amount of obstruction, nonsense, difficulty, delay, and inconvenience. For example, for some reason they decide to take off their shoes *and socks* every Sunday morning—sometimes before the service starts while their dad is practicing with the praise band, sometimes during the service while I'm watching them for their father as he leads worship, sometimes while they are at Sunday school, sometimes during the fellowship time after the service, and sometimes several times in several locations in a single morning. And they often leave each sock and shoe in a different location. Then there are the bathroom breaks. *Every* Sunday, ten minutes into the service, they ask to go to the bathroom. After very brief visits to the urinals they take five minutes to wash their hands (with lots of splashing, and multiple applications of liquid soap from the dispensers they like to play with), and then they grab eight paper towels before I can stop them. Fifteen minutes later they claim they need to go to the bathroom again, fussing and threatening to pee in their pants when I persist with "No." Apparently they think I'm too slow to realize that they just want another chance to run down the hallways at the back of the church and then play at the sinks. And there are *many* more where these two examples came from.

When I'm in relational mode my spontaneous emotional response is usually some combination of disappointment, compassion, and humor, and I have thoughts like: "Of course they're immature and irresponsible—they're grade-school boys," "How do they even come up with this stuff? I don't want to reinforce it by laughing, but what a kick in the pants!" "They're not hurting anybody, and this is how they learn that I love them even when they're difficult," or even, "They need a lot of grace right now, since their mom's been out of town for the last two weeks on a business trip." In contrast, when I'm in non-relational mode my spontaneous emotional response is a combination of frustration, impatience, and judgment, and I have thoughts like: "What's the matter with these guys? Why don't they just behave!" "Can't they focus on what I asked them to do for a single minute?" "I *just* told them not to do that!" and one of my favorites, "I was much better behaved when I was their age." When I'm in relational mode I still set limits and administer consequences, but as I'm doing this I'm feeling various combinations of disappointment, humor, and compassion. In contrast, when I'm setting limits and administering consequences in non-relational mode I'm feeling frustration, impatience, and judgment.

And there are a host of other examples, large and small: We're at a restaurant and the waitress forgets to bring us water, or the entrees take a long time getting to the table. I drop my toothbrush on the bathroom floor. The driver in front of me is talking on his cell phone and doesn't notice when the traffic signal turns green. I'm in a hurry and Charlotte is driving too slowly. I spill a glass of milk. We have just embarked on an out-of-town trip, but when we are three blocks from home we realize that we have to go back for an important item that has been forgotten.[20] An internet page takes fifteen seconds to load instead of the usual seven. I'm trying to get to the sink (refrigerator, stove, microwave), but Charlotte's in my way and I have to stand there for several seconds while waiting for her to move. Four traffic signals in a row, the light turns red just as I get to the intersection. I can't find my glasses. I can't find my keys. I can't find my pen. I can't find my clipboard. I buy and load a new software package, but when I try to use it all I get is a little window with the message, "An unspecified error has occurred."

When I'm in tolerant relational mode many of these small hassles don't even get on the screen—I just pick up the toothbrush without even thinking about it. And when I encounter hassles too big to escape notice I'm able to deal with them with patience, grace, and humor. However, when I'm in irritable

---

20. This one is particularly interesting. In relational mode I'm spontaneously thankful that we remembered so quickly, so that we can easily return and get it, but in non-relational mode my only response is to be intensely irritated that we forgot it in the first place.

non-relational mode even the smallest hassles are surprisingly bothersome—even the incredibly minor toothbrush inconvenience triggers a flash of frustration. And no matter what kind of difficulty I encounter, I almost always end up criticizing and judging something and/or somebody.

When I'm in relational mode others in relational mode seem reasonable, whereas those who are non-relational seem picky, fussy, and judgmental.[21] In contrast, when I'm in non-relational mode others in non-relational mode seem reasonable, whereas those who are still relational seem naive, imprudent, and enabling.[22] Also, when we talk about being patient and tolerant we are not talking about being lazy, careless, and irresponsible, so that nothing bothers you because you let other people clean up all the messes.

Noticing that little things are bothering me is another one of my "first alert" clues—sometimes this is the first checklist clue that I become consciously aware of, and then glancing at the other checklist questions confirms that I have, indeed, fallen into non-relational mode.

Do I Perceive the Relationships Involved to Be More Important than any Problems I Might Be Trying to Solve?

When I'm in relational mode, my spontaneous response in situations in which there are problems that involve people is to perceive that the relationships are more important than the problems. Without any deliberate thought or choice to "be relational," I spontaneously organize my thinking and behavior around the people and relationships involved, with the "practical" problems (such as getting the car repaired, getting adequate service at a restaurant, straightening out errors with respect to hotel reservations, sorting out logistical details regarding visits to family, or getting a neighbor to pick up after his dog) being secondary concerns. In contrast, when I'm in non-relational mode, I know that I ought to care about the people and relationships, and that the people and relationships ought to feel more important than the practical problems, but in truth, trying to care for the people and relationships just feel like complications that make the problems more difficult. When I'm in non-relational mode, I spontaneously organize my thinking around trying to fix the practical problems, with people and relationships being secondary concerns. And if I'm totally honest with myself, my spontaneous response is that I would be happy to cut off the relationships and/or eliminate the people if it would help make the problems go away.

---

21. Note that when I'm in relational mode, those who are in non-relational mode seem picky, fussy, and judgmental, *but I'm still able to be patient with them.*

22. When I'm in relational mode there are still people that I perceive to be naive, imprudent, and enabling, but there's much more space for healthy patience and tolerance. That is, the criteria for discerning between healthy patience and dysfunctional enabling become much more generous.

Do I Join-Explore-Understand-Collaborate, As Opposed to Interrogate-Judge-Fix?

When we are in non-relational mode, our spontaneous response in difficult interpersonal situations will be the adversarial approach of interrogating,[23] judging, and focusing on trying to "fix" the situation.[24] In fact, when I'm really triggered and non-relational I *start* with judging the person, which is followed by interrogation with the objective of confirming my judgments. After the interrogation phase I judge some more, move on to trying to fix the situation, and then finish with a final round of judgment just for good measure. In contrast, when we are in relational mode, instead of interrogating, judging, and then trying to fix the situation, we will be able to *join* with the other person in the *collaborative* process of exploring the situation *together*, we will be able to understand her perspective, and then we will be able to *join* with her in the *collaborative* process of working *together* to find a mutually satisfying solution.

Can I Easily Recall Positive Memories? Do I Feel Appreciation?[25]

When I'm in relational mode I can easily recall past positive experiences with Charlotte, and I feel the positive emotions that should be associated with these good memories. Furthermore, I can easily think of things I appreciate about her, and I feel gratitude as I think about these specific appreciations. For example, a couple weeks ago Charlotte and I participated in a THRIVE marriage retreat, where we spent the weekend away from our usual triggers and repeatedly engaging in exercises designed to help us get in/stay in relational mode. By the end of the retreat we were struck by how easy it was to remember the many good times we have had together—laughing, crying, and snuggling on our sofa as we watched one of our favorite G-rated movies for the fifth time, bicycling along the country roads around the family cabin in Massachusetts, an air boat ride in the Florida everglades as part of our tenth anniversary "Big Trip," Charlotte reading C.S. Lewis'

---

23.   "Interrogation involves the aggressive questioning of another with presumptions about what the other person may be experiencing and with ulterior motives in seeking out particular responses." Daniel J. Siegel and M. Hartzell, *Parenting from the Inside Out* (New York: Jeremy P. Tarcher/Putnam, 2003), page 91.

24.   These thoughts regarding relational circuits and join-explore-understand-collaborate vs judge-interrogate-fix were prompted by insights regarding the relational response of explore-understand-join vs the non-relational response of interrogate-judge-fix presented in *Parenting from the Inside Out*. For the original discussion of explore-understand-join vs interrogate-judge-fix, see Daniel J. Siegel and M. Hartzell, *Parenting from the Inside Out* (New York: Jeremy P. Tarcher/Putnam, 2003), pages 89–92.

25.   In his work with third-world cultures, Dr. Wilder has found that checking whether a person can feel appreciation when thinking about positive memories is one of the simplest, most straight-forward ways to monitor whether or not she is in relational mode.

Narnia Chronicles out loud as I worked on various home improvement projects, a recent anniversary dinner at the Outback Steakhouse, enjoying our vast collection of nature documentaries together, many hours of fellowship and sharing during the road trips to visit the Tsuyuki parents in New York and the Lehman parents in Kansas, watching a family of river otters playing around us as we canoed with friends in the Minnesota boundary waters, and more. And as I recalled these good memories, I could *feel* the happiness, affection, excitement, gratitude, enjoyment, hope, and wonder originally associated with the experiences.

Furthermore, at several points during the weekend we were instructed to name things we appreciated about each other, and we were also struck by how easy it was to think of these—I appreciate Charlotte's mature relationship with the Lord, her intelligence, her spiritual discernment, and her deep understanding of Scripture; I appreciate that she does most of the grocery shopping, runs our office, and takes care of the laundry; I appreciate her conscientiousness, her integrity, her willingness to own her triggering, and her commitment to pursuing her own healing and growth; I appreciate that she's such a good sport regarding nature documentaries; I appreciate her beauty, her grace, and that she can run a marathon; I appreciate that she can read a map, that she's a skillful driver, that she loves my family, and that she's truly the best friend I've ever had. And I could *feel* profound gratitude as I was thinking about these specific appreciations.

In contrast, when I'm in *non*-relational mode it is strangely difficult to find memories for past positive experiences with Charlotte, and if I am able to find positive memories I'm strikingly *unable* to feel any of the positive emotions that would be expected to be associated with them. Furthermore, it is strangely difficult to think of things I appreciate about her, and if I am able to name things I should theoretically appreciate I'm strikingly *unable* to feel the gratitude that ought to be associated with these specific appreciations. For example, Charlotte and I recently got into a miserable non-relational tangle when she came to pick me up at the airport. Due to an unfortunate misunderstanding, she circled outside in heavy traffic for thirty minutes while I sat inside waiting for the time I thought we had agreed on for my pick up. I can't remember the details regarding our interactions when we finally connected, but the short summary is that we ended up triggering each other intensely and both falling into non-relational mode. After driving for a while in unhappy silence, Charlotte finally suggested: "Maybe thinking about positive memories and naming specific appreciations would help us get back into relational mode."

The first problem was that I didn't *want* to remember past positive experiences. My spontaneous internal response to her suggestion was something along the lines of, "I don't like you, I don't want to be with you, and I certainly don't want to remember past positive experiences with you!" After wrestling with this humbling internal response for a few minutes I eventually made the behavioral choice to try to recall previous times of positive connection, and I remember being struck by how difficult it was. At first I couldn't find anything—when I asked myself the direct question, "What about good times with Charlotte?" *no* memories came forward spontaneously. Eventually I decided to try logical, systematic techniques for scanning through factual information. For example, I thought about special nature moments (always positive experiences for me), and then systematically scanned through these memories for special nature moments in which Charlotte had also been present. This approach eventually came up with a few memories, but they seemed like fuzzy, far away experiences with no emotional power. I knew, factually, that they had happened, and I could even get a few faint images, but I did not feel even the slightest hint of the positive emotions that should have been associated with them.

And then, purely as an act of discipline and obedience to the Lord, I chose to name specific things I appreciate about Charlotte. I was again struck by the fact that nothing came forward spontaneously, and I again eventually decided to try logical, systematic scanning techniques. Charlotte and I often do deliberate appreciation exercises, so I went right to, "Let's see, what have I said in the past when we've done this?" This approach resulted in a number of things I knew I *ought* to appreciate, and I could force myself to name them, but they were lifeless facts. For example, I could acknowledge the fact that Charlotte takes care of our laundry, and I knew, logically, that I should appreciate this, but I did not actually *feel* any gratitude.[26]

Make a Short List of Your Favorites

When you are first learning to recognize the places where you fall into non-relational mode, and you encounter situations in which you are unsure regarding the status of your relational circuits, the complete set of checklist questions along with the explanatory examples will provide many helpful reference points. (If you tend toward dismissive attachment and spend much of your time quietly working in non-relational mode, we are also hoping that

---

26. As described below (discussed at length in chapter 19), choosing to engage in deliberate appreciation is an intervention that can bring your relational circuits back on line. So I gradually became able to feel appropriate associated positive emotions as I continued with this discipline, and thereby began to regain access to my relational circuits. Initially, however, I was not able to feel *any* gratitude or other positive emotions.

the many examples in the expanded discussion will help convince you that spending more time in relational mode is a goal worth pursuing.) However, this twenty-one-page package of material is a bit cumbersome, especially since our hope is that you will learn to watch the status of your relational circuits as an easy, natural, routine part of everyday life. When you are angry or anxious, when you are in any kind of conflict, when you find yourself feeling judgmental, when you notice irritability, when you realize that you lack joy, or when you are feeling bad for any reason, our hope is that one of your first responses will be to check to see whether a slide into non-relational mode (and probable associated triggering) are contributing to the problem. But the average person isn't going to carry this book around so that she can go over all sixteen questions and refer to the explanatory examples every time she suspects she might be losing access to her relational circuits.

Therefore, I encourage you to make a more convenient "short list" of your favorite checklist questions. After you have gone over the complete checklist several times, pick your seven favorites—the ones that you find to be especially clear and easy to use—and write these on a three-by-five-inch card that you can keep in your wallet, purse, or pocket. Then, whenever you suspect non-relational mode, pull out the card for a quick check. I did this when I was first learning to recognize the places where I was falling into non-relational mode and found it to be very helpful. (I used my card practically everyday, and sometimes several times per day.)[27] If you are still unsure after checking your short list you can always refer back to the complete checklist and explanatory examples.

Desire for Attunement Is an Exception

An interesting phenomenon with respect to our relational connection circuits is that the need and desire for someone to attune to me—the need and desire for someone to see me, hear me, understand me, empathize with me, care about me, and be glad to be with me—is the one relational aspect of my being *that still remains even when I have lost access to my relational connection circuits.* So if I'm asking, "Do I feel desire to be connected to Charlotte? Do I experience her presence as a source of joy? Am I glad to be with her?" *in the context of imagining Charlotte attuning to me,* I can get "yes" answers even though I have actually lost access to my relational connection circuits. Therefore, when using the relational connection circuits checklist it is important to answer the questions while either experiencing or imagining the person doing things other than attuning to you.

---

27.   After several weeks of practice, if something prompted me to check my relational circuits I could pause for a few moments and go over my short list of favorite questions without even looking at the card.

Variable Intensity and Clarity with Respect to Relational Circuit Phenomena

As you observe your own experience and hear from others regarding their experiences, you will probably notice that the intensity and clarity of relational circuit phenomena can vary from situation to situation and from person to person. Almost everybody can identify times when they are clearly in relational mode (the answers to all the questions are clearly "yes") and times when they are clearly in non-relational mode (the answers to all the questions are clearly "no"), and for most people these are both quite common. However, the intensity can vary, with some situations in which you will answer "YES" or "NO" with great intensity, and other situations in which the answers will still be clear but there will be much less intensity.

For example, when you are especially overwhelmed by negative emotions and have essentially lost all access to your relational circuits, you think of solutions like "Just shoot all the people who are causing the problem." Scrooge's famous line from *A Christmas Carol*, "If they would rather die [than go to the poor house], they had better do it, and decrease the surplus population,"[28] provides an excellent example. I also have some good examples from my own life. When I am feeling especially overwhelmed by fear and hopelessness and my relational circuits are 99+ percent off-line, I fantasize about being able to push a big red button that would make all the "bad" people disappear. This isn't about bitterness or the desire for revenge (in which cases I would want to see my enemies suffer),[29] but rather just a profoundly non-relational way to solve the problem of feeling overwhelmed by things that make me feel frightened and hopeless. Corrupt, short-sighted politicians who make decisions that cause me to feel frightened, powerless, out of control, and hopeless about the future? Just press the big red button and they magically disappear! Self-serving, short-sighted businessmen who plunder their companies and manipulate the financial markets in ways that undermine the economy of the entire nation, causing me to feel frightened, powerless, out of control, and hopeless about the future? Just press the big red button and they magically disappear! Terrorists who massacre innocent women and children, causing me to feel frightened, powerless, out of

---

28. Charles Dickens, *A Christmas Carol* (New York: New American Library, 1984), pages 38–39.

29. Bitterness and desire for revenge are separate issues from the status of your relational circuits. They will always be *associated* with your relational circuits being way dim, since you can't feel bitterness and desire for revenge and be relational at the same time, but they are not the *same thing* as having your relational circuits turned way down. The clearest data point supporting this distinction is that it is possible to be profoundly non-relational, as in the examples I describe, while *not* feeling bitterness or desire for revenge.

control, and hopeless about the future? Just press the big red button and they magically disappear! No pain, no mess, no fuss, no lawyers or court costs—just clean, convenient, instantaneous vaporization.

The most miserable conflicts between Charlotte and me provide another example. In the middle of several of our most miserable conflicts, when I felt overwhelmed by frustration and disappointment and could not imagine how we would ever resolve the problem, access to my relational circuits went down to essentially zero and I found myself wishing that I could magically escape from the relationship. I knew that I would never actually divorce Charlotte, but I wished that I could somehow go back in time and never have married her in the first place, or that maybe she could just die in a convenient plane crash. I didn't want her to suffer, but rather just to go away and never come back. My rocket-launcher solution for construction-zone cheaters provides yet another example of the kind of thoughts and feelings we experience when our relational circuits are essentially off-line.

Fortunately, being in non-relational mode to this degree of starkness and extremity is rare. Most of us spend most of our time either moderately non-relational or moderately relational. For example, most of the time when I am in non-relational mode, access to my relational circuits is weak but they are not completely off-line—the answers to all of the relational circuit checklist questions are clearly no, but I'm not fantasizing about rocket launchers or big red "Vaporize!" buttons.

On the other end of the spectrum, where you are especially free of triggering, access to your relational circuits is especially strong, and your relational circuits are active with special intensity, you enter a super-relational zone where you experience strange things like *feeling* love for your enemies. Thankfully, I also have some personal examples from this end of the spectrum. For several years now I have been working very deliberately to stay in relational mode as much as possible—by continuing work to resolve every traumatic memory I can find, by cultivating a baseline attitude of gratefulness, and by using all of the other tools described below (chapters 17 through 22). The result of all this is that I have been generally less triggered and more relational, and that occasionally all the conditions are present to put me in the super-relational zone. I can still remember the first time I thought to go through the checklist questions while in the super-relational zone. It was actually a bit strange. As I went through the checklist, I realized that I not only felt compassionate concern for my family and friends, but that I actually felt compassionate concern *even for my enemies*—even for people who had hurt me badly. I realized that I felt glad to be with the people I am usually glad to be with when I'm in relational mode (Charlotte, my friends, my family), and this of course did not surprise me; but then I thought about the most difficult people in my life, and was a bit startled to realize that I would even be glad to be with *them*—that their presence in the room with me would bring me genuine joy. During these times in the super-relational zone I have been so blessed by Charlotte's presence that when she asks, "What should we do this evening?" my response is, "I don't care what we do, as long as we do it together," *and it's actually true*—we can spend the whole evening doing household chores and I'm thoroughly happy as long as she's with me.

Unfortunately, relational mode with compassion and joy of this intensity is rare. Again, most of us spend most of our time either moderately relational or moderately non-relational. For example, most of the time when I am in relational mode, access to my relational circuits is strong but not SPECTACULAR—the answers to all of the relational circuit checklist questions are clearly yes, but I'm not feeling euphoric joy, feeling like I would be glad to be with the most difficult people in my life, or feeling love for my enemies. And most people will occasionally notice situations in which access to their relational circuits (and corresponding relational mode status) is at an intermediate point that is much less clear. The answers to some of the questions may be a hesitant yes, the answers to other questions may be a hesitant no, and the answers to some of the questions may be even more unclear.

Again, I want to alert readers to the variability that can sometimes occur with respect to the intensity and clarity of relational connection circuits phenomena. I hope that being aware of this variability will prevent unnecessary confusion as you observe relational circuit phenomena and use the checklist.

Two Significant Patterns Regarding Triggered Traumatic Implicit Memory and VLE Confabulations

As I have carefully studied triggered traumatic implicit memory content and the VLE confabulations we come up with to explain it, I have observed two significant patterns.

It's easy to spot the big ones, but most of us miss the little ones
It's easy to spot the most glaring examples, but most of us don't even stop to ask the question with respect to the many, many less dramatic cases of triggered traumatic implicit memory and VLE confabulations.

It's easy to spot if you know about it and look for it
It's easy to spot these phenomena if you look for them, know how to recognize them when you see them, and think systematically and logically about your VLE explanations. However, most of us don't even know these phenomena

exist. We don't see what we don't know exists, don't look for, and don't know how to recognize. A common experience among medical personnel provides a good analogy. When medical professionals learn about a new illness, they suddenly see it everywhere. Sometimes this is just the product of overactive imaginations, but often the truth is that people with the illness in question had been walking around in front of them for years, but they missed these cases because they hadn't known the illness was there, hadn't known how to recognize it, and hadn't been looking for it.

My own experience provides a good example. When I was in medical school one of our professors briefly described Tourette's syndrome, but then said that it was extremely rare and that most of us would probably never see a case. Not surprisingly, I went on my way believing that I would never meet a person with Tourette's, I never looked for it, and I never saw it. Then, many years later, I read an article that refreshed my memory regarding the details of Tourette's, and that also claimed it was many times more common than we had previously believed. During the next two weeks I was astonished to notice that a man sitting on a bench in a nearby park had Tourette's, that one of the kids riding his bicycle through our neighborhood had Tourette's, and that one of the checkout clerks at our local Jewel grocery store had Tourette's. I had been walking past these people for years, but hadn't noticed their Tourette's because I didn't expect it to be there, had forgotten how to recognize it, and wasn't looking for it.

Not All Pain Is from Triggered Traumatic Memories

It is important to remember that painful thoughts and emotions sometimes actually *are* caused by problems in the present. As discussed in much more detail in chapter 29, a common scenario is for real problems in the present to cause painful thoughts and emotions that are valid and appropriate in the present; but then these thoughts and emotions resonate with unresolved trauma, so that traumatic memory content gets activated and comes forward as well. The end result is a situation in which "invisible" traumatic implicit memory is *contributing* to the person's painful thoughts and emotions, and the person is *also* experiencing some pain that is fully legitimate and appropriate in the present.

The Reality Regarding Triggering Can Be Overwhelming and Hard to Accept

One common stumbling block that can hinder people from accepting and using these principles and tools is that the reality revealed with respect to triggering, traumatic implicit memory, and VLE confabulation can be overwhelming. The truth can be painfully hard to accept. As Charlotte and I have carefully observed ourselves and those around us, our observation is that subtle, low-grade triggering is especially pervasive and chronic. Our perception is that most people are triggered a lot of the time, and that a soberingly high percentage of people are triggered most of the time. This may be hard for many to accept. We encourage you to make your own observations, and to ask God for help in perceiving (and accepting) whatever truth the evidence reveals.

As Charlotte and I have pressed into this with respect to ourselves, we have found the reality regarding how often we are impaired by triggering to be painfully humbling. However, once we got over the initial bump of severe narcissistic mortification, we have found these insights and tools to be TREMENDOUSLY valuable. We have also discovered the truths revealed to be ultimately hopeful, in that every place where we are impaired by triggering is a place where we will experience dramatic improvement as we expose and neutralize our triggered implicit memory and VLE confabulations.

Advanced topics warning: I encourage you to skip the remainder of this chapter (for now) if many of the concepts presented in *Outsmarting Yourself* are new to you and you are reading through the book for the first time, trying to get the big picture. At this point in your learning journey, slowing down to study these advanced topics will hinder you from getting the more important overview understanding of how all the pieces fit together. Come back to this material after you have been through the whole book at least once, you feel that you have a good understanding of the basic principles and tools, you have developed some skill with respect to recognizing when you are triggered and/or when you have lost access to your relational circuits, and you want to fine-tune your ability to identify episodes of triggering and non-relational mode. Feel especially free to skip the section on the neurology corresponding to relational circuit variability. (I included this material as and extra for those with a particular interest in psychoneurology.)

Specific, Memory-Anchored Responses to Checklist Questions (Advanced Topic)

As we become more skillful with respect to noticing when we fall into non-relational mode and/or when we are triggered, it is helpful to understand that some of our responses to checklist questions are caused by specific traumatic memories, and that it can cause problems to think of these *specific, memory-anchored* responses as equivalent to responses that are *inherently part of being in non-relational mode*. For example, in addition to the discomfort with eye contact that is inherently part of being in non-relational mode I also have very specific traumatic memories that affect my responses to direct eye contact. On my grade-school playground, direct eye contact was often interpreted as a challenge, and sometimes just making direct eye contact with one of the angry bullies was enough to get yourself beaten up. Therefore, when encountering a person who is both powerful and angry, in addition to the discomfort that is inherently part of being in non-relational mode I also have a very specific, memory-anchored, *fearful* avoidance of making eye contact. Traumatic memories that include shame provide another example, since the subjective experience of shame always includes a distinctive, universally recognized desire to avoid eye contact. Therefore, when something triggers traumatic memories that include unresolved shame, in addition to the discomfort that is inherently part of being in non-relational mode I also have a very specific, memory-anchored, *shameful* avoidance of making eye contact.

In some situations it will not be a problem to think of these specific, memory-anchored negative reactions to eye contact as being in the same category with the discomfort that is inherently part of being in non-relational mode. For example, if an encounter with an angry, powerful person stirs up my playground memories, and I erroneously conclude that my specific, memory-anchored fearful avoidance of eye contact is actually one of the universal checklist clues indicating loss of access to relational circuits, I will still end up *correctly* concluding that I am triggered and in non-relational mode. Similarly, if something stirs up shameful traumatic memories, and I erroneously conclude that my specific, memory-anchored shameful avoidance of eye contact is actually one of the universal checklist clues indicating loss of access to relational circuits, I will still end up *correctly* concluding that I am triggered and in non-relational mode.

However, what happens if I notice that these fearful and shameful avoidances of eye contact are especially dramatic and easy to recognize, and then get in the habit of relying more and more heavily on these reactions as the clues that tell me whether or not I'm in relational mode? The answer is that it will become easier and easier for me to miss situations in which my triggering and non-relational mode are subtle. Since these specific, memory-anchored reactions to eye contact are *not* inherently associated with non-relational mode, it is possible for other triggers to push me into non-relational mode packages that do not include either the fearful or shameful discomfort with respect to eye contact. For example, what happens if I get triggered to my subtle, background childhood anxiety, with its subtle, low-profile non-relational mode? In this situation, I might think to check my relational circuits, glance briefly at the eye contact question, notice that I am not experiencing either the fearful or shameful avoidance of eye contact, and then *erroneously* conclude that I must still be in relational mode.

Thinking of specific memory-anchored responses to checklist questions as being in the same category as responses that are inherently part of being in non-relational mode can also lead to confusion when we are communicating with others regarding these phenomena. Responses tied to specific memories can be extremely variable from one person to the next, whereas responses that are inherently a part of being in non-relational mode will be much more universal. If people present their *specific, personal,* memory-anchored responses as if *all* people sliding into non-relational mode should be having these same experiences, then anyone who does not have similar specific, memory-anchored responses will be confused. Therefore, if you are discussing the checklist questions as a group or teaching this material to others, it is helpful to make the distinction between responses to checklist questions that are due to specific memory content getting triggered forward vs responses that are inherently a part of being in non-relational mode.

Note again: If this material is new to you and the content in this section seems too technical, don't worry about the distinction between specific, memory-anchored responses and responses that are inherently part of being in non-relational mode. *Just focus on watching for situations in which the answers to **all** of the checklist questions are no.* If the answers to all the questions are no you can be 99.9 percent certain that you have lost access to your relational circuits.[30] This basic approach will miss some of the situations in which you are subtly triggered and non-relational, but learning to recognize any of the situations in which you lose access to your relational circuits is a big step forward. You can come back to this section when you master the basics, start to suspect that you are missing episodes of subtle triggering and/or non-relational mode, and want to take your relational circuits game to the next level.[31]

---

30.   In the language of statistics, you will have very, very few false positives.

31.   You can also come back to this section if you are a part of discussions about triggering, non-relational mode, and the relational circuits checklist, and you (and/or others) are experiencing confusion due to people describing very different subjective experiences associated with losing access to their relational circuits.

Neurology Corresponding to Variable Clarity and Intensity (Advanced Topic)

For readers interested in the neurology corresponding to the variable clarity and intensity of relational circuit phenomena, here is a very, very condensed summary: The degree to which a person is able to maintain access to her relational connection circuits depends on the strength of the negative emotions she is feeling relative to the strength of the neurological connections that have been developed between her relational circuits and the circuits responsible for the negative emotions in question. The strength of these neurological connections grows as we practice the maturity skill of staying relational while feeling negative emotions, and this practice/development must be accomplished separately for each of the six key negative emotions.[32] Therefore, the degree to which you maintain or lose access to your relational connection circuits will vary from one painful experience to the next, depending on which negative emotions are present, depending on the relationship between the strength of the emotions and the strength of the relational circuit connections for the specific emotions in question, and depending on these same variables from the time of the original experience for any traumatic memories getting stirred up by the painful experience.[33] For a MUCH more detailed discussion, see part 2 in the "Brain Science, Psychological Trauma, and the God Who Is with Us" essay series, especially the sections toward the beginning of the document addressing negative emotions, attunement, maturity skills, and relational circuits.

---

32.   According to Dr. E. James Wilder, the six primary negative emotions are fear, anger, disgust, sadness, shame, and hopeless despair. See, for example, E. James Wilder, *The Complete Guide to Living with Men* (Pasadena, CA: Shepherd's House Publishing, 2004), page 302.

33.   These same variables from the time of the original experience for any traumatic memories getting stirred up will determine the extent to which non-relational mode will be part of the implicit memory coming forward with the traumatic memory packages.

17

Regaining Access to Our
Relational Connection Circuits

As described above, one of the most damaging effects of getting triggered is loss of our relational connection circuits. Conversely, if we are in any kind of difficult situation and triggered traumatic memories have caused us to lose access to our relational circuits, one of the most helpful things we can do to limit the negative impact of our traumatic implicit memory and VLE confabulations is get these circuits back on line. Regaining access to our relational circuits will have very direct positive effects on how we relate to all those around us; and regaining access to our relational circuits will indirectly increase our ability to cope with any difficulty by restoring access to the strategic resources that depend on these circuits—both the resources depending on relational memory, such as secure attachment and memory-anchored relational connection joy, and the resources depending on relational connection in the present, such as relational connection joy in the present and being able to share the capacity and maturity skills of those to whom we are connected through attunement. Regaining access to these circuits will actually enable our brains to function more effectively. As mentioned earlier, EVERYTHING with respect to relationships will turn out better and flow more easily when we are in relational mode, and having our relational circuits on line is especially important when dealing with conflict.

The especially messy, difficult scenarios described earlier, in which it is incredibly hard for me to recognize and acknowledge my triggering, provide a specific example that is particularly relevant to our current discussion. As discussed above, one of the most important factors contributing to these messy, difficult situations is that I drop into non-relational mode, and when I am operating in non-relational mode I am unable to feel my relational connection joy memories or the relational memories that anchor my secure attachment, I am unable to experience relational connection joy in the present, I am unable to receive capacity and maturity skill augmentation from the Lord or others in my community, and the loss of these resources contributes[1] to my feeling small, weak, insecure, alone, and vulnerable. And this,

---

1. Other factors, such as being inside a childhood memory that includes aspects of feeling small, weak, insecure, alone, and vulnerable can also contribute to this overall subjective perception.

in turn, contributes to the messy, difficult scenarios described earlier—to my perception that Charlotte is bigger and more powerful than I am, to my perception that I can't afford to make any mistakes in my efforts to protect myself from her, and to my perception that acknowledging my triggering is therefore huge and perilous. When I'm really triggered and my relational circuits are really off-line, I feel unable to protect myself from my huge and powerful opponent, and it feels like I will be unable to handle the invalidation and injustice she will inflict upon me if I acknowledge that I'm triggered.

However, this all changes dramatically when I get back into relational mode. At the front end of these messy, difficult scenarios, when my relational circuits are off-line, I am immersed in the intense negative perceptions just described and the challenge of acknowledging my triggering seems incredibly, unreasonably difficult; but then I regain access to my relational circuits (using the interventions described below), and this all changes. I come back to the same conflict, often with Charlotte's perceptions, attitudes, and behavior unchanged, but now with my relational circuits and relational resources back on line *my* perceptions and subjective experience are completely different. Instead of feeling alone, I perceive the presence of the Lord and feel the memory-anchored presence of my community. And although acknowledging my triggering still feels vulnerable, I feel secure enough, large enough, and strong enough to be able to care for myself. Acknowledging my triggering feels *moderately challenging* as opposed to *incredibly, unreasonably, excruciatingly difficult/nearly impossible*, and I am always then able to take this humbling but life-giving step that helps our conflict resolution move forward.

A closely related phenomenon provides another example of how everything with respect to relationships turns out better when we are operating in relational mode. When I have lost access to my relational circuits and all the resources that go with them, I feel small, weak, insecure, alone, vulnerable, unable to care for myself, and ultimately unsafe.[2] In these situations I end up *fighting to protect myself,* like a cornered animal, instead of *engaging in constructive dialogues,* like a civilized human being. However, this all changes dramatically when I get back into relational mode. When I have regained access to my relational circuits, and all the resources associated with my relational circuits are once again available, I perceive the presence of the Lord and of my community instead of feeling alone, and I feel large, strong, secure, able to care for myself, and safe. In these situations, instead of fighting to protect

---

2. Many of us learn to defend ourselves from these unpleasant vulnerable/unsafe emotions by "powering up" and going into attack mode, and some people have learned to do this so quickly that they are no longer even consciously aware of the initial perceptions of being alone, small, weak, vulnerable, unable to care for themselves, and unsafe.

myself I am able to engage in constructive dialogues in which I can be attuning, open-minded, compassionate, generous, patient, and flexible.

This point is so important that I want to describe yet another example of how everything with respect to relationships turns out better when we are operating in relational mode. In my description of the especially messy, difficult interactions with Charlotte, I mentioned that when I try to remind myself that she is my friend and a trustworthy woman of integrity it is hard to find or hold onto any specific memories that support these hopeful thoughts. There are other memory phenomena that also contribute, but dropping into non-relational mode, so that I can't *feel* these positive relational memories regarding Charlotte, is probably the biggest reason I have trouble finding and holding onto them. And, once again, this all changes dramatically when I get back into relational mode. Over and over again, I have been amazed at how hard it is to find, feel, and hold onto positive relational memories when I am struggling in non-relational mode; and in these same situations I have been equally amazed at how it becomes so much easier to find, feel, and hold onto memories for positive past experiences with Charlotte as soon as I return to relational mode.

Fortunately, the Lord knows that EVERYTHING with respect to relationships works better when our relational circuits are functioning properly, he knows that our relational circuits are especially crucial in dealing with conflicts, he knows that we frequently lose access to these circuits, *and he has provided a plan for getting them back on line.* In fact, the Lord has provided several resources that we can use to regain access to our relational circuits: receiving attunement, deliberate appreciation, calming, and humor.

18

Regaining Access—
Receiving Attunement

This is discussed in much more detail in part 2 of the "Brain Science, Psychological Trauma, and the God Who Is with Us" essays, but the short summary is that the Lord has designed our brains so that receiving attunement is uniquely effective for helping us regain access to our relational circuits. He has designed our brains so that perceiving someone with us in our pain; perceiving that this person is glad to be with us; feeling that this person hears, understands, and empathizes with us in our pain; and choosing to receive this attunement[1] *will smoothly, quickly, and consistently bring our relational connection circuits back online* (see figure 18.1). If there are people in our community who are able to hear us and be with us in this way, then sharing our upset thoughts and emotions with one of these friends can do the job.

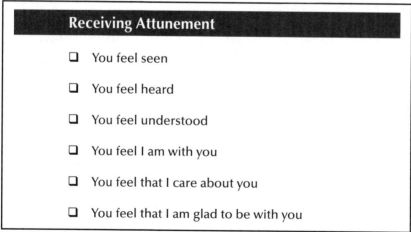

Figure 18.1   Receiving attunement

Unfortunately, friends with the capacity and maturity skills necessary for being with us in our pain and offering attunement are often not conveniently available when we are most in need of this kind of help. For example,

---

1.   As discussed in more detail below, we can choose to turn away from the attunement others offer us by choosing to indulge in bitterness and/or self-pity and/or rebellion.

Charlotte and I sometimes encounter days when we are juggling intense client sessions, meetings to sort out difficult church situations, urgent phone calls, and time sensitive e-mails; and we are trying to coordinate our efforts so that we can also find space for making a bank deposit, picking something up from the grocery store, returning a book to the library, and eating supper before our evening meetings and client sessions. Occasionally, as we try to navigate one of these special days, we mis-communicate in some way that causes frustrating, costly complications; and when this happens I usually get triggered, fall into non-relational mode, perceive the miscommunication to be Charlotte's fault, and then judge her for causing the additional complications. Furthermore, my triggering and judgment usually trigger her into non-relational mode. In these unfortunate situations we are not able to provide attunement for each other, since we are both triggered and non-relational, and we also do not have the time or space to find friends who can offer attunement.

And then there are the times when Charlotte and I have an argument right before we go to bed. I can usually fall asleep after one of these arguments because I'm so tired at the end of a long day, but then I wake up in the middle of the night and can't get back to sleep because I trigger myself by thinking about the unresolved conflict. I don't think my friends want to get "Can you please offer me attunement?" phone calls at three o'clock in the morning.

Receive-Attunement-from-the-Lord Intervention

Fortunately, those of us who experience the Lord as a personal presence can regain access to our relational circuits by receiving attunement from the Lord. And this is especially good news, since the Lord is always with us, and glad to be with us, even in our pain, he always cares, and he always hears, understands, and empathizes with us in our pain—the Lord is *always* with us and offering attunement, even at three o'clock in the morning. Furthermore, it is often surprisingly easy to receive attunement from the Lord. For example, I have found that the simple intervention described below usually enables me to quickly and smoothly receive attunement from the Lord and thereby regain access to my relational circuits. Some people are initially unable to use this tool,[2] and many of those who are able to use it require a bit of coaching and/or practice to get to the point where it flows

---

2. For example, people who are not yet able to establish an interactive connection with the Lord are not able to use this intervention, this intervention will not work if the person is not yet able to talk about his pain (the person can't feel heard and understood if he's not accurately articulating the painful thoughts and emotions that are upsetting him), and the person will not be able to receive attunement if bitterness and/or self-pity and/or rebellion are causing him to turn away from relational connection.

smoothly and is consistently effective, but it's worth trying because it has the potential to be the most accessible, easiest to use, and most effective intervention for getting back into relational mode.

I have been using this tool on a regular basis for a number of months, and it now flows so smoothly that I never think about separate components. However, for the purposes of teaching/learning I find it helpful to break the intervention into the following six steps:

- Initial prayer

- Recall memory of previous interactive connection

- Re-enter memory

- Transition to living, real time, interactive connection in the present

- Stop trying to stop the pain; instead, stand straight in the pain and talk to the Lord about it

- Receive the Lord's attunement.

INITIAL PRAYER
It's always good to start with prayer. When I receive attunement from the Lord I take a few moments for something along the lines of, "Thank you, Lord, for the Immanuel truth that you are with me, even in the middle of my pain. Please help me to re-establish an interactive connection."

RECALL MEMORY OF PREVIOUS INTERACTIVE CONNECTION
The next step is to recall a memory of a previous interactive connection with the Lord. As described earlier (chapter 7, footnote #3), I am experiencing an *interactive* connection with the Lord when I perceive his presence in some way and it feels true that we are having a living, real time, mutual, contingent[3] *interaction*. When I am experiencing an interactive connection, it feels true that the Lord sees, hears, and understands the emotions and thoughts I am experiencing and communicating, and it also feels true that he is offering contingent responses to my emotions and thoughts.

---

3.   *Contingent* interaction means that our responses are directly related to (*contingent* upon) what the other is experiencing and communicating. For example, if I meet my godson in the park and he comes running to me with a big smile, a contingent interaction would be to greet him with "Hey! It's good to see you! It looks like you're having a good day." And if I'm walking through the park and I see him standing by himself and crying, a contingent interaction would be to kneel down beside him and quietly ask "What's the matter? Tell me what happened." In contrast, if I see him alone and crying, a *non*-contingent interaction would be to ignore his distress and greet him with "Hey! It's good to see you! Isn't this a beautiful day?"

An experience I had several years ago provides a good example of an interactive connection with the Lord. My friend Thomas died in his sleep after fighting through 35 years of severe chronic mental illness. He never did anything important in the eyes of the world, but I think he was a hero. In my assessment, few people have done so well carrying such a heavy load. In spite of 35 years of suffering with severe mental illness that medication was only partially able to control, he remained faithful to the Lord. Most people with chronic mental illness use alcohol and/or street drugs to numb the pain, but Thomas never did this. In fact, not only did he not spend his money on pain numbing substances, but he intentionally lived extremely simply, so that he could have money left over from his welfare income to give to the church. This is just one of the ways in which he was quietly heroic. Several months before he died, I asked him: "Thomas, how do you cope with all the suffering in your life?" And his reply was, "I focus on Jesus—every day, all day long. If it wasn't for Jesus, I couldn't do it."

Several days after Thomas died I was out on my exercise walk. I had learned that I could use the simple prayers from the beginning of our Immanuel interventions[4] to connect with Jesus during my exercise time, so I invited the Lord to be with me and asked him to help me perceive his presence. The moment I finished the prayer a spontaneous mental image came into my awareness, and in this image Jesus was walking beside me, enjoying the weather, with the kind of smile you see on the face of someone who's walking with a good friend on a beautiful day. The image was very faint (as is usually the case when I perceive the Lord's presence); but even though the image was so subtle, somehow it also felt 100 percent true and real. After walking along for a while, just enjoying Jesus' quiet, smiling, friendship presence, I commented (in my thoughts): "Lord, I'm so glad that Thomas is with you now." This is hard to describe, but I was facing forward as I was walking, and my mental image of Jesus was that he was in my peripheral vision, just as would be the case if a friend were walking beside me in the "real" world. Immediately—the moment I had finished making this comment about Thomas—I "saw" Jesus' head turn toward me, this big grin broke out on his face, and I sensed the clear response, "So am I!" And then, "He has fought the good fight, and has finished the race. He is here with me now—his suffering has ended, and he is being rewarded for his heroic faithfulness."

All readers will probably recognize that the conversation between Jesus and me about Thomas was an interactive connection, but some may miss that

---

4. For additional description and discussion regarding these simple prayers and Immanuel interventions, see "Brain Science, Psychological Trauma, and the God Who Is with Us ~ Part V."

an interactive connection was present even before the verbal communication. From the moment I became able to perceive his presence, an interactive connection was established as *non*-verbal communication began flowing back and forth between us—just as is normally the case when two friends walk side by side without *talking*, but communicating in many subtle, *non-verbal* ways that they are aware of each other and glad to be together. For example, every so often I would turn my head towards him, just the slightest bit, and a quick smile would flash onto my face spontaneously and involuntarily, indicating that I was aware of his presence and that it was giving me great joy to have him walking beside me. And before I was even finished with my quick, subtle gesture, his head would flick just the slightest bit towards me and he would flash his own smile, indicating that he was also aware of my presence, that he noticed my smile, and that he was also glad to be with me.

From the first moment that I perceived his presence until after our conversation regarding Thomas had ended, this was an interactive connection where it felt true that Jesus and I were having a living, real time, mutual, contingent interaction—where it felt true that he saw, heard, and understood my emotions and thoughts, and where it felt true that he was offering contingent responses to the emotions and thoughts that I was experiencing and communicating. (The point here is that the interactions in an interactive connection can be *subtle,* and often occur without any explicit verbal exchange. I don't want you to miss interactive connections with the Lord just because they don't include communication with words.)

Getting back to "recalling a memory of a previous interactive connection" as step two in the receive-attunement-from-the-Lord intervention, an obvious question is "How do I find/choose the memory?" One approach is to ask the Lord to bring forward the memory he wants you to work with, and then wait for a minute or two, paying careful attention to whatever comes into your awareness. Another approach is to make a list of the times you have had interactive connections with the Lord that have been especially clear and meaningful, and then experiment with using each of these memories for the purpose of the receive-attunement-from-the-Lord intervention. After a bit of experimentation and practice you should find one or two memories that are consistently effective, and once this has been established you can quickly go to one of these memories whenever you need to receive the Lord's attunement.

Re-enter Memory

After finding/choosing a memory of a previous interactive connection, spend a minute or two thinking about the memory and recalling the original experience as vividly as possible. The goal is to *re-enter* the memory—to recreate, as much as possible, the brain-mind-spirit state of being *inside* the original interactive connection with the Lord. For example, I often use the memory described above, in which I perceived the Lord walking beside me and talking to me about my friend, Thomas. When I re-enter this memory I try to recreate the whole situation in my mind—I picture myself (first person, from the *inside* of the experience) carrying my exercise weights and walking toward the lake on Kedzie Boulevard; I recreate the same mental image of the Lord walking beside me as a friend, smiling and appearing to enjoy the weather; I repeat the comment, "Lord, I'm so glad that Thomas is with you now;" I recreate the mental image of the Lord suddenly turning to me, with his big smile; I remember the sense that he heard me, that he understood me, and that he responded contingently to what I was thinking and feeling; and I remember his specific response, "So am I! He has fought the good fight, and has finished the race. He is here with me now—his suffering has ended, and he is being rewarded for his heroic faithfulness."

If you are having trouble re-entering your memories for previous interactive connections, detailed written accounts can sometimes help you connect more powerfully. For example, I am very familiar with my story of talking to the Lord about Thomas, I have reviewed the written account many times, and I am able to re-enter this memory even without looking at the written account. But I experience a stronger connection when I take the time to read through the detailed account. Even though I am so familiar with the story, I still consistently leave out (or skim over) emotionally important details when I think about it without the benefit of my written notes. Putting together a detailed written account, and then reading it when you're triggered, do take a bit of time and effort, but I would encourage you to try this if you're having trouble re-entering your positive memories and re-establishing an interactive connection.

The reason we re-enter the memory of a previous interactive connection is that this seems to provide an especially good context for establishing an interactive connection in the present. And this makes sense neurologically, psychologically, and spiritually. The brain, mind, spirit conditions in the original experience were obviously "just right" for establishing an interactive connection (since it happened), and re-entering the memory recreates, to a large extent, these "just right" brain, mind, spirit conditions.

TRANSITION TO LIVING, REAL TIME, INTERACTIVE CONNECTION IN THE PRESENT

From what Dr. Wilder and I have observed, it seems to be a very small step from being inside the *memory* of a previous interactive connection to establishing an interactive connection *in the present*. In fact, our observation is that when people re-enter memories of previous interactive connections, with the desire and intention of establishing an interactive connection in the present, they are always able to make the transition from their memories to living, real time, interactive connections in the present unless there is a specific problem blocking the process.[5] Furthermore, this transition seems to take place spontaneously, without us having to do anything other than shift the focus of our attention to our relationship with the Lord in the present.

For example, when I want to receive attunement from the Lord I think about and re-enter the Thomas memory, as just described. When I get to the place where I'm inside the memory and have reconnected with the original experience, I stay with the mental images from the memory but change the focus of my attention to my relationship with the Lord in the present, specifically checking to see what feels true with respect to the Lord *in the present.* That is, I stay inside the mental imagery of walking toward the lake with the Lord walking beside me, but I ask "Does his presence in this imagery feel like it's only a memory, or does it feel like he's with me in the present, as a living presence?" And when I do this I always discover that it feels true that the Lord is with me in the present, and that he has re-established an interactive connection.

An important practical point with respect to the transition from memory to a living interactive connection in the present is that the connection in the present is often much more subtle than the connection in the experience you are remembering. For example, when I'm upset and use the Thomas memory as the starting point for receiving attunement, my perception of the Lord's presence when I transition to the present is usually just a faint, single frame from the memory images of the Lord's face, accompanied by a subtle knowing that he's aware of my experience, that he's listening, that he understands, that he cares, that he's empathizing with me in my pain, and that he's not upset with me for being messy. I usually do *not* perceive the kind of dramatically spontaneous and contingent responses that were part of the interactions about Thomas, like when the Lord surprised me by suddenly turning toward me, flashing a big smile, and making comments that I had not been expecting.[6]

---

5. For example, I have worked with people who have dissociated internal parts that understand how this works, and realize that establishing an interactive connection often leads to working with painful memories. These parts therefore often allow the initial steps of recalling and re-entering the memory of previous interactive connection, but then shut things down when it comes to the step of transitioning to a living, interactive connection in the present. Another example is people who have an intense triggered fear that they won't be able to connect with the Lord, and this intense fear derails the process at the point they would otherwise be transitioning to an interactive connection in the present.

6. I think it is valid to think about the Lord seeing us, hearing us, understanding us, caring for us, and empathizing with us in our pain as subtle forms of contingent response. Therefore, I am experiencing a subtle form of interactive connection with the Lord if I am talking to him

However, even though the interactive connection in the present is usually much more subtle, it still works as a foundation for receiving attunement.

For the purposes of receiving attunement from the Lord, the key with respect to your interactive connection is that it feels true that he sees you, that he hears you, that he understands you, that he cares, and that he is empathizing with you in your pain. Your perception of the Lord's presence may be very faint, and you may not experience dramatic contingent responses, but if these key pieces *feel* true then your interactive connection with the Lord will provide a perfectly adequate foundation for receiving attunement.

As already mentioned, we don't have to do anything to *produce* the transition from memory to refreshed interactive connection in the present, but in my experience there are several things that have been helpful with respect to cooperating with the process. I have been learning to recognize what the refreshed connection in the present looks like for me, I have been learning to recognize that it is real even though it is often very subtle, and I have been growing in faith with respect to the whole process. Growing/learning with respect to these points has enabled me to spend less time and energy worrying about whether my interactive connection with the Lord is real, so that I can more easily move on to the next steps of talking to the Lord about my pain and receiving attunement.

Some have asked for more explanation regarding how it works. The first comment I want to make along these lines is that this memory-based technique for establishing a living, real-time, in-the-present interactive connection with the Lord is **not** simply a combination of autobiographical memory and guided imagination. Thinking about interactions with one of your friends can be helpful in making this point. I think we can all see that actually talking to your friend is not the same as remembering a previous conversation, nor is it the same as thinking up an imaginary conversation. When you remember a past conversation you are simply replaying memory for known events that have already happened—the characters in your memory don't start coming up with new and unexpected responses. And when you think up an imaginary conversation, *you* are generating both sides of the interaction and you aren't surprised by anything your imaginary friend says or does. In contrast, when you are actually having a living, interactive connection with your friend in the present, *she* will come up with spontaneous, original, contingent responses that you don't anticipate and that are not under your control. Furthermore, no combination of re-entering memories for past conversations and thinking up imaginary new conversations will

---

about my pain (as described below), and it feels true that he sees, hears, and understands me, that he cares about me, and that he is empathizing with me in my pain.

cause your friend to suddenly appear in front of you and establish an inter-active connection in the present.

I have also come up with a second friendship analogy to help present what I think *is* happening with this memory-based technique for establish-ing interactive connection with the Lord. Let's say a close friend is waiting in your living room, wanting to connect with you. Let's also say that you are in an emotional space where you would be happy to connect with your friend, but you enter the room blindfolded so that you are not initially aware of her presence. Finally, let's say that you spend several minutes thinking about and re-entering a memory for a previous positive interactive connec-tion with this person, and then you take off your blindfold to discover that your friend is sitting in front of you. I think we can all see that unless some specific problem gets in the way, you will flow naturally into an interactive connection with your friend in the present. For example, you would prob-ably blurt out something like, "Oh, wow! I was just thinking about you. I'm so glad to see you!" And things would flow pretty easily from there.

Now let's apply this analogy to the Lord. In our Immanuel emotional healing sessions people regularly meet the Lord as a living presence, and establish contingent, interactive connections with him, in the context of being "inside" of memories for past experiences. I also believe that the Lord can wait for you in your memories just as the friend in my hypothetical anal-ogy can wait for you in your living room. Furthermore, we can assume that the Lord wants to connect with you as he waits for you in your memories, since he always wants to connect with you. So, the Lord wants to connect with you and is waiting for you in your memories for past experiences of interac-tive connection, and you go into one of these memories wanting to connect with him. After spending a minute or two thinking about and re-entering the memory, especially focusing on and appreciating Jesus' presence in the memory, you stay with the content from the memory but change the focus of your attention from the historical connection in the memory to the question of whether the Lord is with you in the present. Changing the focus of your attention to the question of whether the Lord is with you as a living presence in the present is like taking off the blindfold. Unless there is some specific problem in the way, you will perceive the Lord's living presence and flow naturally into a living, contingent, interactive connection in the present.[7]

---

7. Note that there is still something mysterious/unexplained here, since the Lord is waiting for us in the present as well as in *all* of our memories, but most of us can not just perceive his presence and connect with him in the present and/or the average memory in the same way we can perceive his presence and connect with him in the context of memories for previous interactive connection. Somehow the context of memories for previous interactive connections provides an especially effective context/bridge for establishing an interactive connection in the present.

STOP TRYING TO STOP THE PAIN, TALK TO THE LORD ABOUT IT

One of the key ingredients for receiving attunement is feeling that the Lord is *with* us in our pain, and focusing our attention on trying to avoid the pain/ manage the pain/make the pain stop seems to get in the way of this aspect of the attunement connection. For example, several weeks ago our car failed its biannual emission control test, and the failure report said that one of the oxygen sensors needed to be replaced. I have a software package designed to help with do-it-yourself car repair, and when I ran the scan for the emission control system it reported that, in addition to the oxygen sensor, the catalytic converter adjacent to the oxygen sensor was also malfunctioning. I thought I would do a little reading before spending the $1200 that it would cost to replace both of these parts, and with several hours of looking through my repair manuals and searching on the internet I discovered that an upstream leak in the exhaust system could cause perfectly functional catalytic converters and oxygen sensors to produce faulty readings. I didn't want to spend twelve hundred dollars only to discover that I had replaced perfectly good parts and not fixed the real problem, so I crawled under the car to check the exhaust pipes. And what do you think I found? There was a leak immediately upstream from both of the supposedly faulty parts! I took the car to our garage where they replaced the leaking exhaust pipe segment, and when they hooked up their diagnostic computer after finishing the job the catalytic converter and oxygen sensor were working without the slightest malfunction. *Hurray!* I waited a week so that the emission numbers stored in the car's computer would be from driving cycles performed after the repairs, and then I was finally ready get this hassle behind me.

So, yesterday I took the car back to the testing station. After stepping into the little waiting booth, I watched the technician plug the cable from the testing station computer into the access port under the dashboard and then go back to his monitor. I expected him to look at his monitor screen for about 60 seconds, motion me back to my car, and then hand me the certificate indicating that our car had passed. But instead he punched some buttons and kept watching the screen. And then he went back to the car, fiddled with the cable, and returned to his monitor. And then he went back to the car, fiddled with the cable, and returned to his monitor, now with a furrowed brow. And then he went back to the car, turned the ignition off and then on again, fiddled with the cable, and returned to his monitor. And then he went back to the car, worked the ignition *again*, fiddled with the cable *again*, and returned to his monitor. And then he called his supervisor over, and they repeated the whole process, together. He was clearly frustrated by the time he had finished with all of this (instead of the usual 90 second procedure), and brusquely motioned me back to my car. Finally, he came to my window, thrust the paperwork at me, and with an angry, adversarial edge to his voice stated, "You failed. Your computer won't connect, so you fail automatically. Take it back to your mechanic."

Wow. Not what I was hoping for or expecting. As I drove away from the testing station my mind was spinning: "They had no trouble accessing the car computer at the garage—what on earth could prevent this computer from connecting? I don't even know where to start! . . . It's probably some mysterious software glitch that *nobody* will be able to find or fix . . . The mechanics at the garage will probably say 'Our system connects just fine—there's nothing to fix,' but the guy at the testing station will just keep sending me back to the garage with 'You fail automatically because your computer won't connect!' *And there won't be anything we can do about it*—we'll have to junk our perfectly functional car, with only 75,000 miles on it, just because their stinking computer can't *verify* the reality that there are no emission problems!"

This whole scenario triggered me intensely, and the package of unresolved childhood stuff that came forward definitely included falling into non-relational mode. Fortunately I realized that I was triggered, that I was in non-relational mode, and that I would be able to handle every aspect of the problem more effectively if I could get back into relational mode, so I tried to use the receive-attunement-from-the-Lord intervention. But my mind kept going back to fixing the car:

> "This is so unfair—this is outrageous! There must be something we can do about it. . . . Maybe I can find something on the internet about failure to connect with testing station computers. . . . Maybe I can call the garage and see if they've encountered this problem before. . . . Maybe I can talk to the supervisor at the testing station, so that I can at least get a printout of the error codes—that might provide some clues about where to start. . . . If we can't fix the computer interface problem, I wonder if there's any way the testing station could actually just test the emissions, like they used to do. . . . And if we *can't* find any way to pass the emissions test, what do we do about the trip we're planning to take in two weeks? Could we get a rental car that would be compatible with our custom fit roof-top bike racks? . . ."

And on and on and on. Unfortunately, it was very difficult (it didn't work) to receive the Lord's attunement while I was focusing my attention on trying to resolve my distress by fixing the car.

To be able to let the Lord be *with* me in my pain, I had to temporarily let go of trying to fix the car and just let myself feel the frustration, helplessness, discouragement, anxiety, etc. When I was eventually able to do this I was then also able to let the Lord be with me *in* my pain, I was able to talk to him about my pain, and I was able to receive his attunement. This principle is especially important when you're intensely triggered and most of the pain is implicit memory from underlying trauma; but even when you are only minimally triggered and most of your distress is truth-based pain from problems in the present, *in order to receive the Lord's attunement you have to temporarily let go of trying to stop the pain and just let yourself feel it.*

Another key ingredient for receiving attunement is feeling that the Lord truly understands our situation, and this happens much more easily if we are able to accurately describe our pain. Occasionally people will have the poignant experience of perceiving that the Lord understands their pain even though they have *not* been able to find words to describe their distress; however, in most situations it seems that being able to accurately describe our pain dramatically facilitates the process of receiving attunement. Therefore, once we have established an interactive connection, the next step in receiving attunement is to feel the pain and talk to the Lord about it instead of focusing on fixing the problem. That is, temporarily let go of trying to avoid the pain/manage the pain/make the pain stop, get words for what feels true with respect to the pain, and then share this with the Lord as clearly, honestly, thoroughly, and vulnerably as possible.[8]

I have spent a lot of time during the last several years experimenting/practicing with the receive-attunement-from-the-Lord intervention in my own life, and I have also spent a lot of time coaching others through the process of receiving attunement from the Lord. I would like to offer a number of observations from my experience in both of these settings with the "stop trying to stop the pain, talk to the Lord about it" step. Hopefully these practical points from my many hours of beta-testing will be helpful for others.

- When talking to the Lord about our pain it is important to focus on *ourselves*, especially focusing on the painful thoughts that feel true and the negative emotions we're experiencing. In contrast, focusing on the person(s) we're upset with, describing to the Lord all the reasons why they are bad and wrong, and thinking about how to fix the problem by making *them* change always seem to be counterproductive.

  For example, in the scenario with the car I would find myself talking to the Lord about all the ways in which the guy at the testing station

---

8.   My perception is that focusing on trying to make the pain stop and being unable to accurately describe our pain are two of the most common reasons for being unable to receive the Lord's attunement.

was bad and wrong: "He had no business being so angry and mean—it's not like I already knew about the problem when I came in, or that I was intentionally blocking his computer access just to ruin his day . . . The whole situation wouldn't have felt so bad if he had been considerate and helpful instead of unfriendly and intimidating, and I would have been able to ask for more details regarding the computer connection problem, . . ." etc. I would find myself talking to the Lord about all the ways in which the people at the garage were bad and wrong: "The computer connection worked just fine when I went in for the first test, but now, *after the garage messed with it*, it's broken—something they did probably caused the problem, but I doubt they'll take responsibility for fixing it, . . ." etc. I would find myself talking to the Lord about all the ways in which the people in charge of the whole system were bad and wrong: "This setup is bad! It's not right that my car is running beautifully, my actual emissions are fine, but I fail the test just because *their* computer can't read the numbers stored in the *car's* computer, . . ." etc. And I would find myself thinking about ways to fix the problem by making all of these other people be different.

Many of my thoughts about what others were doing wrong and what they should do differently may even have been correct, but focusing on these issues (instead of on myself and my pain) still interfered with the process of receiving attunement. In fact, nothing really happened with respect to receiving attunement until I let myself just feel the pain associated with whole failed test mess, and then focused on myself and my pain as I talked to the Lord:

> "Lord, when I think about interacting with the guy at the testing station I feel vulnerable, intimidated, off balance, small, and confused. . . . If I think about trying to be assertive and persistent in asking for more information I feel unsafe—what *feels* true is that he'll retaliate by punishing me or hurting me in some way. . . . When I think about the possibility that the garage caused the problem, but won't take responsibility for it, I feel angry and helpless—like I'm trapped in an unfair situation where the other people have all the power and there's nothing I can do. . . . And when I think about the overall scenario I feel powerless, helpless, and hopeless—the problem with the computer feels overwhelmingly complicated, and I don't even know where to start. . . . It feels like people out there somewhere are making decisions that affect me, but I have no voice or recourse—it feels like the people with the power are worrying about their own concerns, and don't really care about what happens to me, . . ." etc.

And as I was able to focus on *myself* and talk to the Lord about my *pain*, I began to feel that he heard me, that he understood the situation I was in, and that he was empathizing with me in my pain, I was able to receive his attunement, and I came back into relational mode.[9]

- It is sometimes important to tell the Lord about our anger, as part of feeling that we're getting to express all our negative emotions and feeling that the Lord is hearing us. And in almost all of these situations it is also important to then move from talking about our anger to talking about our pain. There are some exceptions, but my perception is that in most situations we use feeling anger and talking about anger as defenses to protect ourselves from feeling more painful negative emotions, such as shame, fear, powerlessness, sadness, and despair.

- When using this receive-attunement-from-the-Lord intervention, it is helpful to keep reminding ourselves that our goal in this exercise is to establish an interactive connection, feel our pain (instead of trying to make it stop), talk to the Lord about it, and receive his attunement. Our goal is *not* to fix the problem in the present that is upsetting (triggering?) us, and our goal is *not* to find and resolve an underlying trauma that might be present. Our goal with this exercise is to establish an interactive connection with the Lord, feel our pain, talk to him about it, *and then receive his attunement so that we can get our relational circuits back online.*

- Even though our goal with receiving attunement is *not* to do the whole job of working through underlying memories, it is still helpful to be aware of the possibility that triggered underlying trauma may be contributing to our upset. This understanding helps with finding the right words to express ourselves to the Lord. If we are trying to make sure that our thoughts and emotions make sense *with respect to the situation in the present*, and if we are trying to make sure that we are being balanced, reasonable, constructive, and fair *with respect to the situation in the present*, but some portion of the upset is coming from *old memories*, we will resist the words that most accurately express the painful thoughts

---

9. It is significant to note that I was able to handle every aspect of the problem more effectively after regaining access to my relational circuits: I was able to think much more clearly, and found helpful information on the internet; I had a productive conversation with the garage manager—he did say "Our system connects just fine—there's nothing to fix," but he also mentioned that he has seen this problem before, that sometimes it just goes away as mysteriously as it shows up, and that I should just try testing it again before doing anything more complicated; and, finally, I went back to the same testing station where the same technician was still on duty, I was able to calmly explain the situation and the mechanic's recommendations, their computer was able to connect without any difficulty, and our car passed. *Thank you, Jesus!*

and emotions that are feeling true. And my experience is that we are most likely to *feel* that the Lord hears us, understands us, and is with us in our difficult situation when we get the words that most accurately express our pain. If we are insisting on words that make sense with respect to the present, and that are balanced, reasonable, constructive, and fair with respect to the present, we will also inherently be resisting the words that actually feel true, and this will hinder our ability to receive the Lord's attunement. Even when we are not trying to do the whole job of working through the underlying trauma, if we are aware that the upset could be coming from old memories then we are much more able to recognize and accept words even when they don't seem to be balanced, reasonable, constructive, fair, or make sense in our present situation.

This point particularly makes sense if we formulate the situation as "We need to feel and receive the Lord's attunement from *inside* any memories that are being triggered." If some significant portion of the upset is coming from old memories, *but we're resisting the words that feel true from inside the memories,* then to the extent that we're blended with the experience of being inside the memories we will not feel heard or understood, and this will directly interfere with feeling and receiving the Lord's attunement.

For example, as I was talking to the Lord about my thoughts and feelings regarding the failed emissions test mess, internal noise about being balanced, reasonable, constructive, fair, and making sense kept getting in the way. Even though my complaints against the testing station guy *felt* true, the logical, adult part of my mind could see that I was exaggerating his negative behavior—he had been a bit grumpy and gruff, but not really angry, mean, or threatening. And even though they all felt intensely valid, my logical mind could see that my reactions of feeling vulnerable, intimidated, off balance, small, and confused were not fully reasonable. I could also see that there was something that didn't quite fit regarding my sense that I was unsafe and that he would hurt me in some way if I persisted in asking for more information.

Even though it felt intensely true, my logical mind knew that it wasn't fair to accuse the garage of causing the problem without additional evidence. I realized that it wasn't reasonable to accuse them of refusing to take responsibility when I hadn't even talked to them about it. I could see that my perception of being powerless, helpless, and without recourse with respect to the whole situation wasn't fully accurate. Finally, my adult, logical mind could see that all of my reactions were much more intense than was warranted by the reality in the present. And these concerns about being balanced, reasonable, constructive, fair, and making sense made it very difficult to simply own and articulate the spontaneous internal reactions that actually felt true.

As you probably already realize, the whole point here is that the thoughts I was having and the emotions I was feeling were *not* really coming from the situation in the present. When I was able to recognize this—to recognize that I was triggered—I was able to let go of trying to make sure that my thoughts and emotions made sense, and that they were reasonable, balanced, constructive, and fair.[10] This made it easier to get the right words for what *felt* true (the thoughts and feelings associated with the underlying memories), and this, in turn, made it easier to perceive that the Lord really heard and understood my pain.

- Closely related to the point just made: when we're talking to the Lord about our pain, we should try to get the most accurate words for what *feels* true. NOT the thoughts and emotions we know we *ought* to have, and not the thoughts and emotions that make the most sense, but the thoughts and emotions that are actually there. That is, we should try not to worry about whether our thoughts and emotions make sense, whether they're "right," whether they're consistent with Biblical truths, whether they're sinful, etc., but rather just try to get words for what *feels* true.

- If memory connections come up spontaneously, embrace the memories and talk to the Lord about them (as opposed to trying to push the memories away).[11] If an important part of our pain is actually coming from memories, connecting with them and then talking to the Lord from the perspective of being inside the memories is an especially powerful and especially effective way to talk to the Lord about our pain. Furthermore, receiving the Lord's attunement from inside the memories will actually contribute to permanent healing for the memory trauma.

- Working with a therapist to help us feel our pain and talk to the Lord about it may be a good plan if we have persistent difficulty with receiving attunement (I often help people with these pieces of the process when

---

10. It's still very important to challenge yourself to be reasonable, balanced, constructive, fair and to make sense when actually interacting with the other people involved in the situation (this is part of moderating the impact of triggered implicit memory and VLE confabulations), but you need to *temporarily* let go of these concerns when you are trying to receive attunement.

11. This is for people who have the capacity and maturity skills necessary to do this without getting into trouble. If you are *not* able to safely work independently with your own traumatic memories, then if you are using the receive-attunement-from-the-Lord intervention and memory connections come up spontaneously: 1) ask the Lord to carry the memory content, 2) focus on his presence with you in the present, and 3) go back and forth between using the calming exercises described below (chapter 20) and talking to the Lord about your pain in the present.

I'm facilitating Immanuel emotional healing sessions). We should also remember to ask the Lord to help us feel our pain and to help us talk about it more effectively.

RECEIVE THE LORD'S ATTUNEMENT

In most situations, once we establish an interactive connection with the Lord, we are able to talk to the Lord about our pain, it feels true that he is with us in our pain, and it feels true that he hears us, understands us, cares about us, and empathizes with us in our pain, then we will spontaneously receive his attunement without having to do anything specific or deliberate. The key point I want to make in this section is that on some occasions when the Lord offers attunement *we will make choices that block our ability to receive it.*[12] In my experience, choosing to persist in bitterness and/or self-pity and/or rebellion are choices to turn away from relationship, and choosing to turn away from relationship makes it impossible to receive attunement. My two-year-old separation trauma provides a good example. The Lord was with me, offering comfort and attunement, but I was not able to receive his comfort or attunement because I was turning away from relationship by persisting in my choices to indulge in bitterness and self-pity.[13]

If you are talking to the Lord about your pain, and you perceive that he is offering attunement, but you are *not* able to receive his attunement and return to relational mode, then check for these potential blockages. For additional discussion, and also interventions for exposing and removing bitterness, see: "Judgments and Bitterness as Clutter that Hinders Emotional Healing," and "Judgments and Bitterness Toward the Lord." For additional discussion, and also interventions for exposing and removing self-pity, see: "Deadly Perils of the Victim Swamp: Bitterness, Self-Pity, Entitlement, and Embellishment." Additional discussion, and also interventions for exposing and removing rebellion, would also be helpful, but this essay has not yet been completed.[14]

---

12. Note that this point (along with many of the other points made with respect to receiving attunement from the Lord) also applies to receiving attunement from family, friends, and others in our community.

13. Note also that the memories for this trauma remained stuck until I chose to release my bitterness, surrender my self-pity, and turn back to relationship; and when I finally did make these choices I was immediately, spontaneously able to receive the Lord's comfort and attunement, I regained access to my relational circuits, and I was finally able to move forward with respect to healing for this trauma.

14. The essays on bitterness and self-pity are available as free downloads from www.kclehman.com, and the essay on rebellion will also be posted for free download as soon as it is completed.

Putting All of This Together with Respect to Receiving Attunement
from the Lord and Regaining Access to Your Relational Circuits

To the extent you perceive that the Lord is empathetically with you in your negative thoughts and emotions, to the extent it feels true that he hears you, understands you, cares about you, and is glad to be with you, and to the extent you are able to receive the Lord's attunement, *you will regain access to your relational circuits and come back into relational mode.*

Receiving Attunement from the Lord Becomes Easier and Increasingly Effective with Practice

When I first started using this intervention for receiving attunement from the Lord I found it a bit awkward, it took a lot of time, and it was occasionally only marginally effective. However, with ongoing practice I have grown in skill with respect to recognizing the Lord's presence and his interactive responses *even when they are **very** subtle*, I have grown in faith with respect to these phenomena being real *even when they are **very** subtle*, I have become more skillful with respect to keeping my focus on myself, feeling my pain, and talking to the Lord about my pain, and I have gotten better at both avoiding and resolving the problems that get in the way of receiving attunement. After maybe a year of regular practice, receiving attunement from the Lord now usually flows smoothly and easily, I am often able to receive attunement and get back into relational mode within five to fifteen minutes, and the intervention is almost always effective.[15] Therefore, if you find the receive-attunement-from-the-Lord intervention to be inconsistently effective, difficult, and slow when you first try it, I strongly encourage you to persist through a season of practice before deciding that this tool does not work for you.[16]

Spiritual Disciplines That Facilitate Receiving Attunement

One of the essays on our website, "Spiritual Disciplines and Emotional Healing Ministry: Choosing Healing," describes spiritual disciplines that can prepare us for participating most effectively in the Immanuel approach

---

15.   I still sometimes have difficulty with establishing an interactive connection with the Lord, I still sometimes have difficulty with letting go of trying to stop the pain (so that I can stand straight in the pain and let the Lord be with me there), I still sometimes have difficulty with getting words for my distress, and I still sometimes have difficulty with actually receiving the Lord's attunement, but I persist in practicing with each of these because receiving attunement from the Lord is such a *tremendous* resource.

16.   Receiving attunement from your family, friends, and others in your community also becomes easier with practice.

for emotional healing. Our perception is that practicing these same disciplines can also make it easier for us to acknowledge our pain, feel our pain, talk to the Lord about our pain, and receive his attunement, all of which prepare us for using the receive-attunement-from-the-Lord intervention most effectively. These disciplines therefore provide an additional resource for those who are having difficulty.[17]

What about Those Who Are Not Able to Establish an Interactive Connection with the Lord?

Unfortunately, many people are not able to perceive the Lord's presence or establish an interactive connection, and our receive-attunement-from-the-Lord intervention obviously depends heavily on being able to establish an interactive connection with him. Fortunately, there are still a number of things these people can do in order to regain access to their relational circuits.

Expose and Resolve Blockages That Prevent Interactive Connection

Our experience is that when a person is unable to perceive the Lord's presence or establish an interactive connection, the problem is almost always (always?) caused by specific blockages. Furthermore, our experience is that almost all (all?) of these people become able to perceive the Lord's presence and establish an interactive connection when these blockages are identified and resolved. Exposing and resolving these blockages almost always involves exposing and resolving traumatic implicit memory content that is getting transferred onto the Lord, but it can also involve exposing and resolving other issues that can hinder a positive connection with the Lord.[18]

My experience with the two-year-old separation trauma provides an excellent example. I was unable to establish an interactive connection with the Lord in the original experience because I was turning away from him in bitterness and self-pity (and telling him to jump off a cliff). For the next forty years I was unable to perceive the Lord's presence or establish an interactive connection in any situation where the separation trauma would get triggered because these same unresolved blockages would come forward and get in the way. And when I finally resolved these blockages in the context of the flooded car crisis, I was immediately able to perceive the Lord's presence and establish an interactive connection in this place.

---

17. These spiritual disciplines will also prepare you for receiving attunement from your family, friends, and others in your community.

18. For example, bitterness, self-pity, self-protective vows, rebellion, and demonic interference.

An emotional healing session in which I was working on fear of rejection provides another example. A lot of things happened in this session, but the most important was that I remembered a number of experiences in which I did not do what I knew was right because I was afraid of being ridiculed and rejected by my friends. The leader of the little group of four boys with whom I spent the most time often came up with ideas that involved breaking parental/neighborhood rules in one way or another, and he would, of course, want the rest of us to join him in his schemes. Another friend was a shoplifter. He also liked company, and would occasionally ask me to go with him on his stealing expeditions. And this friend's older brother liked to play with explosives, and he would sometimes ask me to go with him when it was time to set off his home-made bombs. Between these three scenarios there were a lot of memories in which I went along with things I knew were wrong. I knew they were wrong, I did not want to participate, I was miserable the whole time we were engaged in these activities, and I felt persistently guilty afterwards, but when I made objections the others would call me a sissy, coward, goody-goody, etc, and then I would go along in order to avoid further ridicule or rejection.

The last memory that came forward was my earliest experience of stealing. The memory began with my three closest friends describing how easy it was to steal candy from the neighborhood convenience store, and trying to coax me to join them. "Come on!" "You can do it," "Watch us," "We never get caught" they encouraged. Our leader's older brother, an especially experienced thief, was also with us, and he eventually lead the way by boldly walking into the store, strolling to the candy section, picking up a candy bar and eating it, putting other candy in his pockets, and then going to the cash register to buy one inexpensive item. Watching others steal was one thing, but actually taking something myself was another matter entirely, and I *really* did not want to do this. I made a series of excuses, but they continued to encourage/ridicule me with "What's the matter? Are you scared? Are you a sissy? We do it all the time." After a few more minutes of this I finally went into the store, picked up one of those long sticks of bubble gum (sour cherry, if I remember correctly), and walked out with it.[19]

And as I looked at all of these memories, I knew that my persistent resistance to these activities had been a manifestation of the Lord's presence in my heart. I had always been aware of how the stealing and disobedience were wrong because they hurt others and betrayed my parent's trust, but in this session I finally realized how my choices to participate in these activities

---

19.   James Henry Leigh Hunt claims that "Stolen sweets are always sweeter," but I could hardly taste my stolen gum, and felt terrible after finishing it. In fact, I suffered from such persistent guilt that I eventually told my parents, told the store owner, and paid for the stolen gum. From "Song of Fairies Robbing an Orchard," by James Henry Leigh Hunt (1784–1859).

had been choices to turn away from the Lord—I realized how I had turned away from his presence in my heart as part of my attempts to avoid ridicule and rejection.

As part of this session I also looked at experiences in which others had stolen from me. Angry thoughts welled up inside of me as I connected with how powerless to protect myself, vulnerable, and violated I felt when others had stolen from me: "You people who steal make it harder for the rest of us—we work hard for what we have. . . . Get a job and pay your own way!" And I wanted to apprehend and severely punish all those who had ever stolen from me in the past, or who would ever steal from me in the future. It was pretty obvious that I still had judgment and bitterness toward those who had stolen from me.

I spent more than an hour working through these memories, confessing and receiving forgiveness for stealing and disobedience, releasing judgment and bitterness toward those who had stolen from me, and especially dealing with my choices to turn away from the Lord as part of my attempts to avoid ridicule and rejection. After working through all of this, and also several other issues that might be expected to get in the way of connecting with the Lord, images from the candy stealing memory spontaneously came back into my mind. I was viewing the scene from inside the perspective of my five-year-old self, standing in front of the cash register at the convenience store and trying to figure out whether or not to walk out with the 5 cents worth of soon-to-be-stolen bubble gum. And then all of a sudden Jesus was beside me.

As I write these words, I can still picture his visible-but-invisible presence (I could see him, but nobody else could see him). He was about two feet away, to my right, and just a little behind me—between the cash register counter and the pastry rack—and he was squatting down with his elbows on his knees, so that his face was just slightly above the level of my own. He was all white, but opaque like a cloud as opposed to translucent like a ghost, and he was smiling and looking toward me. In addition to the visible image, I also had a tangible, subjective sense of the Lord's gentle friendship presence—I could *feel* his friendship, relational presence as a *person*. Furthermore, I somehow knew that he had always been there, but that all of the unresolved garbage carried in this network of memories had formed blockages that kept me from perceiving his presence.[20]

---

20. For a much more detailed (ten pages) description of this emotional healing session, see "Emotional Healing and Personal Spiritual Growth: A Case Study and Discussion" (available as a free download from www.kclehman.com).

The *Doug: "Immanuel Intervention" (intermediate)* and *Eileen: "Immanuel Intervention" (intermediate)* live ministry session DVDs provide two more examples of how specific issues can get in the way, and of how identifying and resolving these blockages can enable the person to perceive the Lord's tangible presence and establish an interactive connection. For extensive additional discussion regarding how psychological and spiritual issues can hinder a person from perceiving and establishing an interactive connection with the Lord, and for descriptions of techniques for exposing and resolving these blockages, see "Immanuel, an Especially Pernicious Blockage, & the Normal Belief Memory System," the "Discussion" section of "Emotional Healing and Personal Spiritual Growth: A Case Study and Discussion," and also the "Immanuel Intervention" section of part 5 in the "Brain Science, Psychological Trauma, and the God Who Is with Us" series.[21]

RECEIVING THE LORD'S ATTUNEMENT EVEN WITHOUT AN INTERACTIVE CONNECTION
Some people have such strong faith in the Lord's living, Immanuel presence that they are able to receive attunement from him even though they are not able to establish an interactive connection. And I am certain this is possible because I have experienced it myself. There were several years during which I did not yet experience interactive connections or perceive the Lord's presence in any tangible way, but my faith had become tremendously strong from witnessing so many others receiving healing (with observable, lasting fruit) through interactions with the Lord's living, Immanuel presence. And due to the strength of my faith I could talk to the Lord about my pain, and it *felt* true that he heard me, that he understood me, that he cared, and that he was empathizing with me in my pain *even without an interactive connection or perceiving his presence in any tangible way*—I was able to talk to the Lord about my pain and receive his attunement *based solely on faith*. This is not easy, but I would encourage you to try it if your faith is exceptionally strong and you are not yet perceiving the Lord's tangible presence or experiencing interactive connections.

ALTERNATIVE INTERVENTIONS FOR GETTING BACK INTO RELATIONAL MODE
For those of you who are not yet able to receive attunement from the Lord, it is important to remember that receiving attunement from others in your community, deliberate appreciation (as described in the next chapter), and calming (as described in chapter 20) remain available as effective interventions for regaining access to your relational circuits.

---

21.   All three of the essays mentioned are available as free downloads from www.kclehman.com, and the *Doug: "Immanuel Intervention" (intermediate)* and *Eileen: "Immanuel Intervention" (intermediate)* live ministry session DVDs can be obtained through the store page of www.kclehman.com.

19

Regaining Access—
Deliberate Appreciation

As described earlier (chapter 16) in the expanded discussion of the last checklist question, being able to remember past positive experiences and being able to feel the expected corresponding appreciation are *indicators* of being in relational mode. Interestingly, appreciation can also be a *resource* for moving from non-relational mode back into relational mode.

Evidence Supporting Deliberate Appreciation as a Relational Circuit Intervention

Fascinating research by Dr. John Gottman, discoveries regarding oxytocin, observations from cognitive therapy, work with our clients, and our own personal experience have all contributed to the discovery that *deliberately engaging in appreciation will consistently help you regain access to your relational circuits.*

John Gottman, Observable Behavior, and Bottom-Line Sociological Outcome

Some of the most original, intriguing research regarding marriage relationships has been carried out by John M. Gottman, Ph.D. He set up an apartment wired with video cameras and microphones, recorded randomly selected couples spending weekends together,[1] and then followed these couples for years into the future, monitoring bottom-line sociological outcome, such as whether a given couple reported being happily married ten years later or whether they were divorced. Dr. Gottman then subjected this large pile of carefully gathered information to rigorous statistical analysis, and thereby identified which observable behaviors corresponded to which bottom-line sociological outcomes. For example, did the couples who spent time watching Walt Disney movies together have a better chance of staying happily married? Or were the couples who never washed the dishes more likely to end up in divorce court?

---

1. Of course the couples were aware of being filmed and were willing to be a part of the study. Also, to preserve a certain necessary level of privacy, the couples were monitored only from 9:00 a.m. to 9:00 p.m., and never in the bathroom.

Since 1986 Dr. Gottman has filmed thousands of couples, he has recorded tens of thousands of hours of observable behavior, he has followed some of these couples for as many as fourteen years, and he has taken the resulting mountain of data and run it through a vast array of high-powered statistical analyses. One of the clearest conclusions from all of this research is that appreciation is good for relationships—the observable behavior of deliberately focusing on things you appreciate about your spouse leads to the bottom-line good sociological outcome of staying married, *and being happy with your marriage.* Couples that were already doing this did very well, and deliberately learning to do this proved to be a powerful positive force in salvaging even deeply troubled marriages.[2]

Gottman's research does not provide direct evidence proving my belief that deliberate appreciation pulls a person back into relational mode, but his fascinating studies are certainly consistent with my conclusions about appreciation and relational circuits. In fact, my hypothesis regarding Gottman's research is that helping people stay in relational mode, and helping them regain access to their relational circuits when they fall into non-relational mode, are two of the mechanisms through which appreciation produces benefit in these marriages.

NEUROBIOLOGY

One study has directly demonstrated that, at least in some people, appreciation releases oxytocin;[3] and a variety of other studies provides a growing pile of indirect evidence indicating that positive social interactions (such as appreciation) stimulate the release of oxytocin.[4] Furthermore, an extensive body of research demonstrates that oxytocin prepares your brain for emotional bonding and positive relational connection.[5] This research regarding oxytocin

2.   For additional discussion of Dr. Gottman's research, see John M. Gottman and Nan Silver, *The Seven Principles for Making Marriage Work* (New York: Three Rivers Press, 1999); and John M. Gottman and Clifford I. Notarius, "Decade Review: Observing Marital Interaction," *Journal of Marriage & the Family*, vol. 62, no. 3 (November 2000): pages 927–947. The Gottman Institute website (www.Gottman.com) also provides a vast array of additional information regarding Dr. Gottman and his research work with marriages and relationships.

3.   Rebecca A. Turner, Margaret Altemus, Teresa Enos, Bruce Cooper, and Teresa McGuinness, "Preliminary Research on Plasma Oxytocin Levels in Healthy, Normal Cycling Women: Investigating Emotional States and Interpersonal Distress," *Psychiatry*, vol. 62, no. 2 (summer 1999): pages 97–113.

4.   For a summary discussion of this point, see Kerstin Uvnas-Moberg, "Oxytocin May Mediate the Benefits of Positive Social Interaction and Emotions," *Psychoneuroendocrinology*, vol. 23, no. 8 (1998): pages 819–835.

5.   See, for example: Thomas R. Insel, James T. Winslow, Zouxin Wang, and Larry J. Young, "Oxytocin, Vasopressin, and the Neuroendocrine Basis of Pair Bond Formation," *Advances in Experimental Medicine and Biology*, vol. 449 (1998): pages 215–24; E.B. Keverne and K. M. Kendrick, "Oxytocin Facilitation of Maternal Behavior in Sheep," *Annals of the New York*

does not prove my belief that deliberate appreciation pulls a person back into relational mode, but the demonstrated connections between appreciation, oxytocin, emotional bonding, and positive relational connection are certainly consistent with my conclusions about appreciation and relational circuits.

COGNITIVE THERAPY

Both empirical research with cognitive therapy and cognitive therapy case studies demonstrate that our thoughts powerfully and predictably influence our emotions.[6] For example, deliberately focusing our attention on things we appreciate will consistently generate the corresponding positive emotion of gratitude. Furthermore, cognitive therapy research and case studies demonstrate that learning to think more positively with respect to another person, and the corresponding increased positive emotions toward the person, produce observable benefits for the relationship.[7]

The research and case study evidence regarding cognitive therapy does not prove my claim that deliberate appreciation pulls a person back into relational mode, but it is certainly consistent with my conclusions about appreciation and relational circuits. In fact, my hypothesis is that helping people stay in relational mode, and helping them regain access to their relational circuits when they fall into non-relational mode, are two of the mechanisms through which cognitive therapy for couples produces its benefits.

OUR CLINICAL OBSERVATIONS AND PERSONAL EXPERIENCE

The first step in the process for the Immanuel approach to emotional healing is to help the person establish an interactive connection with the Lord. Starting the session in the context of a positive, interactive connection with the Lord makes sure that the person begins her healing work with optimal resources in place, and it also provides a safe place for the person to come back to if she gets into trouble at any point later in the session. As Dr. Wilder

---

Academy of Science, vol. 652 (1997): pages 83–101; and C. Sue Carter, "Biological Perspectives on Social Attachment and Bonding," in *Attachment and Bonding*, eds. C. S. Carter et al., (Cambridge, MA: MIT Press, 2005), pages 85–100.

6. For recent, careful summaries of the extensive research evidence supporting these foundational principles of cognitive therapy, see David A. Clark and Aaron T. Beck, *Cognitive Therapy of Anxiety Disorders: Science and Practice* (New York: The Guilford Press, 2010), especially chapters 3 and 4; and Aaron T. Beck and Brad A. Alford, *Depression: Causes and Treatment,* second edition. (Philadelphia, PA: University of Pennsylvania Press, 2009), especially chapter 16.

7. For a recent, thorough discussion of the use of cognitive therapy for relationship difficulties, including discussion of research and case study evidence supporting the validity of these basic principles of cognitive therapy in the context of relationships, see Frank M. Dattilio, *Cognitive-Behavioral Therapy with Couples and Families: A Comprehensive Guide for Clinicians* (New York: The Guilford Press, 2010).

and I were working to refine the Immanuel approach, and especially as we were working to adapt it for use with groups, he suggested that deliberate appreciation could be included at the beginning of the session in order to prepare the person for connecting with the Lord. Even though we had not yet realized that appreciation is so directly effective for bringing a person back into relational mode, we were thinking about the research and case studies described above, and realized that appreciation does something that prepares the person's brain for positive relational connection. So we thought: "Let's start the Immanuel approach with thinking about past positive experiences with the Lord, and deliberately focusing on the aspects of these past experiences that we especially appreciate. This deliberate appreciation should make it easier to establish the positive interactive connection that we want to have in place as the foundation for the rest of the emotional healing session."[8]

And then later, when I was first developing our material about receiving attunement as a tool for regaining access to our relational circuits, I included deliberate appreciation as part of establishing the initial interactive connection, just as we had included deliberate appreciation in the initial steps for the Immanuel process for emotional healing. I had not yet discovered that establishing an interactive connection and receiving attunement from the Lord can be done without initial deliberate appreciation.[9] So, when I was first developing receiving attunement as a tool for getting back into relational mode, I would start with deliberately focusing on things I especially appreciated before moving on to establishing an interactive connection, talking to the Lord about my pain, and then receiving his attunement. It was very difficult, but I would force myself to push through the deliberate appreciation so that I could eventually get to the attunement that I knew would be effective.

The discovery that deliberate appreciation, *by itself*, could be so effective in pulling a person back into relational mode was actually an accident. On several occasions when I had gotten triggered into non-relational mode and was applying the early version of the receive-attunement-from-the-Lord intervention, I accidentally got carried away with the deliberate appreciation step. As is usually the case when starting from non-relational mode, deliberate

---

8.   For additional discussion regarding deliberate appreciation as part of the Immanuel approach to emotional healing, see "Brain Science, Psychological Trauma, and the God Who Is with Us ~ Part I: A Psychiatrist's Journey—A Brief Introduction to the Immanuel Approach," and "Brain Science, Psychological Trauma, and the God Who Is with Us ~ Part V: The Immanuel Approach, Revisited," both available as free downloads from www.kclehman.com.

9.   In fact, not only can we establish an interactive connection and receive attunement from the Lord without initial appreciation, but establishing an interactive connection and receiving attunement, *as tools for regaining access to our relational circuits*, are usually easier if we do *not* start with deliberate appreciation because deliberate appreciation is so difficult when we are intensely upset and non-relational.

appreciation was intensely difficult at first; but as I persisted with it and started to feel better, it got so much easier that I just continued. I kept focusing on things that I appreciated to the point that I felt a strong subjective sense of gratitude. And then, on one of these occasions, I noticed something strange: "Wait a minute! I'm just getting ready to establish an interactive connection, but I'm already back in relational mode. That's not supposed to happen until I perceive his presence, talk to him about my pain, and then receive his attunement!" After this interesting observation I began to both deliberately experiment and to observe more carefully with respect to this point, and quickly noticed that whenever I persisted with appreciation to the point of robust gratitude, I would *always* be back in relational mode *even though I had not even started with the steps of connecting with the Lord and receiving his attunement.* That is, if I persisted with it long enough, deliberate appreciation *alone* would eventually bring me back into relational mode.

And these observations regarding the ability of persistent, deliberate appreciation to bring a person back into relational mode have been repeatedly confirmed as Charlotte and I, Dr. Wilder, and several other teams we work with have experimented with this intervention in a wide variety of situations.[10]

PUTTING ALL OF THIS TOGETHER WITH RESPECT TO DELIBERATE APPRECIATION
AND REGAINING ACCESS TO YOUR RELATIONAL CIRCUITS
To the extent you are able to persist with the discipline of deliberate appreciation, and get to the point where you can feel gratitude, *you will regain access to your relational circuits.* Furthermore (as will be discussed shortly), if you start with receiving attunement and/or calming, and then engage in deliberate appreciation after you have already regained access to your relational circuits, this additional intervention will increase the strength with which you are established in relational mode.

Deliberate Appreciation Is Most Effective in the Context of Specific Memories

When we use deliberate appreciation as an intervention to help us get back into relational mode, the size/intensity of the positive effect will usually be

---

10. For example, as Dr. Wilder has used Immanuel emotional healing group exercises to work with people who have survived catastrophic trauma in third-world countries, he has encountered situations in which a number of people have gotten triggered into non-relational mode at the same time, but the participants were still relatively untrained and inexperienced with respect to receiving attunement from the Lord. In these situations, group exercises helping the participants to engage in persistent, deliberate appreciation have been consistently effective in getting everybody back into relational mode.

much larger if we think about things we appreciate in the context of specific memories and relationships, as opposed to thinking about things we appreciate only as abstract, theoretical concepts. For example, when I present this material as a seminar, I demonstrate this difference by doing two different versions of deliberate appreciation for emergency room security officers. When I appreciate emergency room security personnel in the context of abstract, theoretical information, I take thirty to forty seconds to make the following statements:

- I appreciate that the security officers take on the awkward (and sometimes very tense) task of searching patients as they come into the emergency room.

- I appreciate that they work all hours of the day and night.

- I appreciate that emergency room security officers intervene when patients become dangerous, risking their personal safety to protect others.

- I appreciate that their job can be very messy and unpleasant, sometimes requiring exposure to blood, saliva, vomit, urine, and feces.

I truly believe each of these statements, but when I simply summarize them as abstract, theoretical concepts I feel only a very slight sense of subjective gratitude.[11]

In contrast, when I appreciate security officers in the context of specific memories, I start by telling stories about my experiences with security officers during my psychiatric training. When I was working as a psychiatric resident I served in two different emergency rooms. At the VA hospital, the special security room for evaluating potentially dangerous patients had been converted into a part-time office, so that we had to work with aggressive, agitated, belligerent, mentally ill, and often intoxicated combat veterans in a room fully equipped with potential weapons, such as lightweight steel chairs and heavy metal lamps. But even more important than the inadequate physical facilities were the inadequate security personnel.

The security personnel were mostly older men, who were overweight, out of shape, and inadequately trained. The security officers were also all veterans themselves, and therefore had understandable loyalty and sympathy toward the veteran patients. Unfortunately, their loyalty and sympathy toward other

---

11.   This first part of the demonstration has occasionally generated more intense gratitude, but when I observed myself carefully I noticed that this only happened when the abstract, theoretical statements started prompting brief flashes of specific memory examples.

veterans was sometimes stronger than their concern for the safety of the psychiatric residents. For example, the official policy was that all psychiatric patients must be searched before being evaluated, but the security officers felt that it would be offensive to insist, and they therefore skipped the search if the patient was unhappy with the idea. The officers also wanted to avoid confronting their veteran colleagues in any way that might escalate to the point of needing to use physical restraints, so they would sometimes back down instead of stepping forward when patients would cross physical safety boundaries.

Furthermore, there were usually only two security officers on duty for the whole, huge, seven-story hospital, so there were often no officers in the emergency room. At these times we would have to send out a page for security staff if we felt a patient might be dangerous, and sometimes there would be long delays before anyone would arrive. The intense work flow pressure would usually push toward just going ahead without them. And there were also times when they would make an independent assessment that their presence was no longer needed, and then walk away in the middle of an evaluation without asking for my input.

Putting all of these factors together lead to some pretty scary situations. For example, there was the summer afternoon during my first year when I was sent in to see an extremely intoxicated Vietnam veteran with post-traumatic stress disorder (PTSD). The security staff were not present, but I was busy and tired, and decided to go ahead and get started instead of taking the time to page them and wait for them to get to the ER. I have often thought about and prayed for this veteran, and I understand why he had PTSD. He had been deployed in an area where the Vietcong would get children to wear hand grenades under their clothing, and then walk up to groups of soldiers as suicide bombers. After a number of these disastrous encounters, my patient's commanding officer had ordered him to go into a village they were approaching and shoot all the children. Needless to say, these memories haunted him terribly.

Nevertheless, it was still frightening to work with an agitated, aggressive, belligerent, thoroughly intoxicated soldier who was transferring all of his anger about these experiences onto me. After I had entered the room and shut the door, he came to within six inches of my face and proceeded to yell at me, with LOTS of swearing and spit spraying onto my glasses, for five minutes (that felt like two hours). Nobody even knocked on the door to check whether I was okay. At the time he was actually yelling at me I was mostly in shock, but afterward I realized that I would have been in serious trouble if he had decided to physically attack me. If the patient had really wanted to hurt me, he could easily have busted my lip (or beaten me to death with one of the heavy metal lamps) before effective intervention could have come to my aid. Even if the security officers had been in the room, their intervention would probably have been very conservative, such as asking him to sit down—if he had actually wanted to hurt me, their reluctance to precipitate confrontation would have resulted in intervention that was too tentative and too slow.[12]

On another occasion, an extremely angry and agitated veteran came into the emergency room asking for psychiatric care. He was six feet four inches tall and extremely muscular, probably weighing 270 pounds, and as he told the lady at the front desk that he needed to see a psychiatrist, he also mentioned that he would kill any police officers that he ran into. He was wearing combat fatigues, with large cargo pockets bulging with unknown contents, and he was carrying a large backpack, also bulging with unknown contents. Two security staff were in the emergency room, but they decided that it would be a bad idea to ask him to submit to being searched. They also decided that it might upset him if he mistook them for police officers, so they went into another office where they would not be visible. I was sent into the non-security room, alone, to do the psychiatric evaluation.

As I entered the room I knew that he had not been searched, and realized that he could be carrying any number of weapons in his bulging pockets and backpack. But then I also realized that he could easily attack me with the steel chair he was sitting on or the lamp on my desk, and if this weren't enough, I realized that a 270 pound extremely muscular combat veteran trained to kill enemy soldiers in hand-to-hand combat probably wouldn't need any weapons in order to inflict serious bodily damage.

It did not take long for things to get worse. After responding to my first several questions with angry outbursts, he jumped up from his chair and rushed across the room toward me. Fortunately, instead of attacking me he decided to barge out of the office, barge out of the emergency room, and commandeer the public transportation bus that had just stopped in front of the hospital. I think he was so upset that he didn't even know what he wanted, but his threats to kill anyone who didn't cooperate resulted in frantic calls to the police. Minutes later, a fully equipped SWAT team arrived.

It took the SWAT team several hours to get him off the bus, and when they did finally get him off the bus it took six men to restrain him. Physically out of control psychiatric patients can usually be safely restrained by securing their wrists and ankles, but this patient was thrashing and lunging so violently that

---

12.   This is not just an ungenerous speculation, since one of my colleagues had his nose broken by a patient before security stopped the assault, and on another occasion a patient attacked one of my colleagues and broke several of his ribs before the security officers intervened.

he required additional straps across his chest and forehead. Once he was in restraints it was my job to finish the admission evaluation, and as I did this he continued thrashing violently and yelling at the top of his lungs (swearing and threatening to kill me), with his eyes wild, his face purple red, and the bulging veins running across his forehead and along his neck looking as if they were about to burst.

I felt physically unsafe so consistently in the VA emergency room that I just tried not to think about it, so that fear would not get in the way of my efficiency.

My experience working in the University Hospital emergency room, on the other hand, was completely different. First of all, the special security room reserved for psychiatric evaluation had *not* been converted into a part-time office, and contained nothing that could possibly be used as a weapon.[13] But more important than the security *room* was the security *staff*, and especially one particular security officer. His name was Andre, and he was an African-American man who had briefly played professional football for the Seattle Seahawks. When wearing his thick-soled uniform shoes he was almost seven feet tall, and he probably weighed 280 pounds *before* putting on the body armor that he wore whenever he was on duty. I called him Andre the Giant, and I felt safe whenever he was on duty.

If there was a psychiatric patient to be evaluated, I never had to worry about finding the security guard. The nurses would page me to come and see the patient, and Andre would always already be there, waiting for me, when I arrived. And there was never tension regarding whether he would decide that his presence was no longer necessary, and therefore walk away in the middle of the evaluation. In fact, even when I told him that I didn't think I needed security protection for a particular patient, he would stay in the area and keep an eye on me.

In contrast to the security officers at the VA, Andre never neglected to search patients, and he would not allow anything that could possibly be used as a weapon. Not pocket knives, not box openers, not nail files. He would even ask people to put their pencils and car keys in the security box.

Andre would escort the person to the security room, and then stand in the doorway as I began the evaluation. If he sensed the *slightest hint* of danger, he would come into the room and stand beside me. And if he sensed more than the slightest hint of danger, he would step forward and motion me toward the door, so that he could easily block any attempt the patient might make to attack me. In contrast to the security officers at the VA, Andre had zero tolerance for threatening, or even marginally intimidating behavior.

---

13. The *only* thing in the security room was a large cushioned chair that was bolted to the floor.

If an angry patient even got out of the chair, Andre would quickly step into the room and give quiet but firm directions: "Sir, you need to go back to the chair and sit down. Now." If someone made a threatening gesture, or even an angry statement directed toward me, Andre would lean into the room and ask, "Dr. Lehman, is there a problem?" And even these quiet, simple interventions were amazingly effective when coming from a six-feet-ten-inch 280-pound security officer wearing body armor.

Andre would never avoid necessary, appropriate physical contact. If someone was extremely intoxicated and/or psychotic, and needed physical redirection, Andre was right there. And if someone was totally out of control and/or assaultive, so that physical restraint was necessary to keep everyone safe, Andre was right there. This was dangerous, and could also be very messy and unpleasant (extremely intoxicated accident victims could come in covered in vomit, saliva, urine, feces, and blood), but Andre never showed even the least sign of hesitation when physical contact was needed in order to keep everybody safe.

In addition to all of this, Andre knew more about physical safety in the emergency room than I did, and took measures to ensure my safety that I hadn't even thought of. For example, he would gently but firmly remind patients to remain seated, and to lean slightly back in the chair—a position that made it extremely difficult for the person to come at me suddenly. He would remind me regarding the safest way to position myself in the room, so that I could exit and close the door quickly and easily. And with especially agitated patients, he would remind me that we could offer appropriate medications, and then wait for them to produce calming benefit before continuing the evaluation.

After sharing these stories, I name specific things I especially appreciate about Andre:

- I appreciate that Andre was willing to deal with the unpleasant reactions that might be caused by his insisting on a careful, thorough search before allowing the person into the assessment area.

- I appreciate that Andre never avoided necessary physical contact, even though it was dangerous, and sometimes also very messy and unpleasant.

- I appreciate that he was always present.

- I appreciate that he was well trained regarding the many details that would contribute to my safety, and that he consistently took the initiative in making sure that these were in place.

- I appreciate that he went out of his way, at the cost of personal risk, in order to make it *easy* for me to be safe.

- I appreciate that he was HUGE, and that he was willing to wear heavy, uncomfortable body armor in order to be able to provide a physical presence that could actually handle dangerous, out of control patients.

- And I appreciate that *I actually felt safe* whenever Andre was on duty.

When I think about the abstract, theoretical reasons to appreciate security officers, I feel a mild, vague sense of appreciation; but when I think about Andre the Giant, and how much it meant to me to be able to work without having to risk serious physical injury, I feel appreciation at an entirely different level.[14]

Doing deliberate appreciation regarding the Lord provides another example. When I appreciate the Lord in the context of abstract, theoretical information, such as the attributes of God found in Scripture, I take thirty to forty seconds to make the following statements:

- Lord, I appreciate that you are perfect.

- I appreciate that you are omnipresent.

- I appreciate that you are powerful.

- I appreciate that you are just.

- I appreciate that you are merciful.

- I appreciate that you are righteous.

- I appreciate that you heal.

- I appreciate that you forgive.

I believe each of these statements, and I appreciate these truths about the Lord, but when I simply summarize them as abstract, theoretical concepts I feel only a very slight sense of subjective gratitude.

---

14. Note that the contrast between these two ways of doing the appreciation exercise is much more dramatic when I present this example live. Observable emotions come forward spontaneously when I do the exercise in the context of specific memories about Andre the Giant, but the reader cannot perceive this, since the written text does not include my facial expressions, voice tones, and other nonverbal communication.

In contrast, when I appreciate the Lord in the context of specific memories, I start with taking several minutes to think about, reconnect with, and reenter specific memories of previous positive connections with the Lord. For example, I think about my experience of interacting with the Lord regarding Thomas and his heroic faithfulness. I picture myself carrying my exercise weights and walking toward the lake on Kedzie Boulevard. I re-create the mental image of the Lord walking beside me as a friend, smiling and appearing to enjoy the weather. I repeat the comment, "Lord, I'm so glad that Thomas is with you now," and I re-create the mental image of the Lord suddenly turning to me with his big smile. I remember the sense that he heard me and understood me, and I remember the poignant specifics of his response: "So am I! He has fought the good fight, and has finished the race. He is here with me now—his suffering has ended, and he is being rewarded for his heroic faithfulness."

And then, after I have reconnected with the thoughts and emotions and re-entered the memory, I talk directly to the Lord about specifics that I especially appreciate:

- Lord, somehow many subtle things about the way you were walking beside me—your smile, the way you were strolling, your overall attitude—tell me that you were enjoying yourself—that you *like* being with me—that you think of me as a friend. This means so much to me.

- Lord, I feel like I can't even get words to fully express the vibrancy and vitality of your presence and smile. I appreciate how I knew that I was perceiving your living presence by the way your responses surprised me and felt so *alive*—so different from the internal perceptions that I initiate in my own mind.

- Lord, you know that I sometimes struggle with the fear that there will never be true justice—that people like Thomas will never be adequately compensated. I feel such deep reassurance from your striking, immediate, vivid, energized, detailed, emphatic response to my thought regarding Thomas. I appreciate that you recognize how hard his life was, that you're aware of how faithfully he followed you through the difficulties he lived with every day, and that you honor his quiet heroism. I appreciate that the magnitude of his struggle, of his obedience, and of his courage have not been lost on you; and that, even as we speak, he is in your presence, receiving his reward.

When I think about the abstract, theoretical reasons to appreciate the Lord, I feel a mild, vague sense of appreciation. In contrast, when I think about my experience of interacting with Jesus regarding Thomas, reconnect with the thoughts and emotions, reenter the memory, and then talk to the Lord about specific aspects of the experience I especially appreciated, I feel gratitude at a whole new level.[15]

RECONNECTING WITH A POSITIVE MEMORY REACTIVATES ORIGINAL APPRECIATION

Part of the reason specific memories are especially effective as the context for deliberate appreciation is that reconnecting with the memory for a previous positive experience will reactivate the original appreciation. As far as the internal states of our brains, minds, and spirits are concerned, reconnecting with/reentering the memory of an autobiographical event will re-create, to some extent, the conditions present in the original experience. For example, when I reconnect with the memory for a painful experience in which I felt sadness, such as when my pet squirrel died from thirst because the water dispenser broke while we were away on vacation, I reactivate the neurological circuits associated with the sadness from the original events, and to some degree I reexperience this sadness. Similarly, when I reenter the memory for a positive experience in which I felt appreciation, such as when the Lord spoke to me about Thomas, I reactivate the neurological circuits associated with the appreciation from the original events, and to some degree I reexperience this appreciation.

Advanced topics warning: Feel free to skip the next paragraph if you are not particularly interested in neuropsychology.

WORKING WITH THE RIGHT HEMISPHERE INCREASES
EMOTIONAL INTENSITY (ADVANCED TOPIC)

Another factor that contributes to the increased effect when we do deliberate appreciation in the context of specific memories has to do with the differences between the right and left hemispheres. The right hemisphere is the primary location for emotional processing, so that processing through the right hemisphere will generally produce a more intense emotional response. The right hemisphere is also the primary location for *experiential* knowing anchored in specific autobiographical memories, so that doing deliberate appreciation in the context of specific autobiographical memories will cause the right hemisphere to be much more involved. Therefore, doing the appreciation exercise in the context of specific autobiographical memories will

---

15. Again, the contrast between these two ways of doing the deliberate appreciation exercise is much more noticeable when I present this material live, with my facial expressions, voice tones, and other forms of nonverbal communication helping to convey the dramatic difference in emotional intensity.

cause the material to be processed through the right hemisphere, and will thereby produce the increased emotional intensity associated with right-hemisphere involvement.

Practical Tips Regarding Deliberate Appreciation

I have spent a lot of time during the last several years experimenting/practicing with deliberate appreciation as a resource for regaining access to my relational circuits, and I have also spent a lot of time coaching others through the process of deliberate appreciation. I would like to offer a number of observations from my experience. Hopefully these practical pointers from my many hours of beta testing will be helpful for others.

- Naming anything I appreciate—even simple things like "I appreciate that I don't have to go to bed hungry"—provides some benefit. It has to be true, but as long as it's honest, naming even the smallest details that you are grateful for will contribute to the overall appreciation momentum.

- As described above, naming appreciations in the context of specific memories is especially powerful.

- With practice, we can increase the power of many "simple" appreciations by moving them into the context of specific memories. For example, when I think about Charlotte doing the laundry, I can increase the appreciation benefit by thinking about specific memories. Instead of taking just a moment for the one-sentence thought, "I appreciate that Charlotte does the laundry," and then moving on, I can pause to remember the many, many times I have seen her carrying the baskets to the basement, the many, many times I have seen her standing by the washing machine sorting the piles, the many, many times I have seen her getting up from the desk in her home office in order to go move things from the washer to the dryer, and the many, many times I have seen her folding the clean laundry and putting it away.

  When I'm appreciating the fact that I'm not homeless, instead of taking just a moment for the brief, one-sentence thought, "I'm grateful that I have a warm, dry, comfortable, safe place to live," and then moving on, I can pause to remember camping trips that were especially cold and wet, and how it was so good to come home to a warm shower. I can think about camping trips where getting up to go to the bathroom at night meant going through mosquito-infested woods to an outhouse, and how it was so good to come back to a home with indoor plumbing. And I can think about January blizzards, with temperatures fifteen to twenty degrees below zero, and how it was so good to look out the windows at the blowing snow as we sat in front of our cozy wood stove with cups of hot chocolate.

When I'm appreciating the fact that I don't have to go to bed hungry, instead of taking just a moment for the brief, one-sentence thought, "I'm grateful that I have good food and food when I want it," I can pause to remember specific entrees that I have especially enjoyed (Panang curry at a local Thai restaurant, grilled salmon with Charlotte's special sauce, Mom Lehman's apple pie, and Dad Tsuyuki's marinated chicken). I can think about being intensely hungry after hours of baling hay with Grandpa and my brother, John Jr., and how good it was to come back to the farmhouse and find one of Grandma's huge, delicious, home-cooked meals waiting for us. And I can think about how I felt after missing meals for thirty-six hours as part of a college fund-raising project, and how grateful I am that I only feel that kind of hunger when I choose to fast.

- You may already be assuming this after reading the "Reconnecting with a Positive Memory Reactivates Original Appreciation" section, above; but just in case it's not already clear, deliberate appreciation in the context of a specific positive experience should include *reentering* the memory for the experience. Recalling the experience, thinking about it, and deliberately naming and focusing on specific things you appreciate are all good, but sometimes we can do all of this from an external, left-hemisphere, analytical perspective. This left-hemisphere perspective is beneficial, and it does contribute to appreciation, but it often lacks emotional power. It is therefore important to deliberately reconnect with/reenter[16] the memory. In fact, reentering the memory should be the primary mode, with the option to also include the left-hemisphere perspective as a complementary component that can augment the emotional power of reconnecting/reentering. As mentioned above, reentering the memory of a previous positive experience will automatically reproduce (to some degree) the gratitude you felt at the time of the original events.

  Many people spontaneously include reentering the memory when they recall a previous positive experience, and these folks probably think this point is silly and unnecessary. However, this point is not so obvious to everybody. When I first began experimenting with deliberate appreciation, I came at it almost exclusively from the external, left-hemisphere, analytical perspective. I had to *learn* to deliberately include

---

16. The goal is to *reenter* the memory – to re-create, as much as possible, the brain-mind-spirit state of being inside the original events.

reconnecting with/reentering the memories when I recalled previous positive experiences that I had appreciated.[17]

- If I'm upset with Charlotte, then thinking about positive memories *with Charlotte* and naming specific things I appreciate *about Charlotte* is both especially difficult and especially helpful in regaining access to my relational circuits.

- When naming appreciations in the context of specific memories, working with a number of memories in succession can be necessary in order to end up with robust gratitude. For example, I can think about the time when Charlotte was especially considerate and nurturing while I was messy and miserable with a particularly terrible case of the flu, and as I remember specific details regarding how she cared for me during this time my subjective feeling of appreciation goes from zero to three (on a scale of one to ten). Then I can think about the time Charlotte went to great lengths to get me a Christmas gift that I really liked and that was a complete surprise, and as I recall the care she took to do something she knows is especially meaningful to me, the intensity of my subjective feeling of appreciation goes from three to five. Then I can think about Charlotte doing most of the administrative work for our seminars, and as I remember the hours she has spent dealing with hundreds of logistical details so that our seminars run smoothly, my appreciation goes from five to seven. And then I think about the time Charlotte spent many, many hours caring for members of my family who were in crisis, and as I meditate on the ways she poured out her heart and time in caring for *my* family I can feel my appreciation go from seven to ten.

- It is important to remember, and meditate on, the dramatic events for which we are grateful (like those just mentioned above); but Charlotte and I have noticed that small acts of kindness, service, and generosity are also important, and especially as they add up with thousands of repetitions over time. For example, Charlotte makes me a cup of special coffee each morning (Starbucks Dark Sumatra, brewed with freshly ground beans). One cup of special coffee would not be a big deal, but when I think about how she has blessed me with this small kindness *every morning for years*, I can feel some serious gratitude.

---

17.   Another point that may seem obvious to some, but be helpful for others: When I reenter memories as part of deliberate appreciation, I go in with the clear objective of stirring up gratitude. I find that this helps me avoid wandering and/or getting distracted as I reconnect with the memory.

- It's okay to appreciate the same thing more than once. This may seem funny to some, but when I first started to practice with deliberate appreciation I felt like I was writing an essay for English class, where it is considered poor form to use the exact same adjective over and over again. If you're talking about something really large and it comes into the story more than once, you can refer to it as "huge" the first time you mention it, but then you need to find a variety of synonyms, such as "gigantic," "immense," "titanic," and "enormous" for subsequent appearances. Similarly, I felt like I had to come up with new things to appreciate each time I practiced with deliberate appreciation. It *is* a fun part of the challenge to see how many different things you can find to appreciate, but the point here is not to impress our high-school English teachers. As long as you are still truly grateful for it, you can appreciate a given blessing over and over and over again. For example, I was practicing appreciation while out walking recently, and about every five minutes I realized that I was still truly grateful for the bright, sunny day (a nontrivial blessing in January in Chicago). So every five minutes I named this (again), and thanked the Lord for the sunshine (again). The laundry mentioned above provides another example. Every week I realize that I still appreciate Charlotte doing the laundry. So I name this (again), thank her for it (again), and feel a subjective sense of gratitude (again).

- The subjective feeling of gratitude provides a simple indicator with respect to the effectiveness of deliberate appreciation. When deliberate appreciation is successful we feel gratitude, the more effectively we succeed in deliberate appreciation the more robust our subjective feeling of gratitude will be, and the more robust our gratitude the more solid our return to relational mode will be.

- In my experience, the biggest problem with appreciation is that it is really hard to do when you are in a foul mood, and the worse you feel the harder it is.[18] For example, when I'm really triggered, non-relational, and it feels like Charlotte is my enemy, it's hard to think of anything I appreciate about her, and even when I think of something I *know* is true I don't want to acknowledge it. The only kind of appreciations I feel like acknowledging are things like, "I appreciate that she's not a selfish, immature poo-poo head all the time," and even this comes out grudgingly. Even so, if I am able to discipline myself to persist in thinking

---

18. This is why we recommend starting with receiving attunement. As will be described in chapter 22, the ideal intervention for regaining access to our relational circuits is to start with receiving attunement, and then once we have gotten back into relational mode we can use deliberate appreciation to increase the strength with which we are established in relational mode.

204 Part Four: Additional Resources and Insights

about positive memories with Charlotte and naming specific things I appreciate about her, *regardless of my initial lack of enthusiasm*, my relational circuits always eventually come back on line.

- During times when I have been strongly in relational mode and feeling intense appreciation toward Charlotte, I have made a long list of positive past experiences with her and specific things I appreciate about her. And then, when I am upset, I have lost access to my relational circuits, my triggering is focused on Charlotte, I am trying to do the extra difficult task of appreciating her, and it is *very* hard to think of positive memories or specifics to appreciate, I pull out this list and it helps me get started.

- Just as with reentering positive connection memories as part of receiving attunement from the Lord, detailed written accounts can increase the emotional power when we are remembering previous positive experiences as part of deliberate appreciation. For example, I am very familiar with the stories of my experiences with emergency room security officers, I have reviewed the written account many times, and just thinking about Andre, even without the benefit of the written account, still produces feelings of gratitude. But when I take the time to read through the detailed account I consistently experience much stronger feelings of gratitude. Even though I am so familiar with the story, I still consistently leave out (or skim over) emotionally important details when I think about it without the benefit of my written notes. Putting together a detailed written account and then reading it when you're triggered does take a bit of time and effort, but I would encourage you to try this if you're having trouble with using deliberate appreciation to get back into relational mode.

- Deliberate appreciation is very difficult in situations where we are being repeatedly triggered to unresolved trauma, and the likelihood of ending up in these situations is directly proportional to the amount of unresolved trauma we carry. Therefore, deliberate appreciation will become progressively easier as we continue with the ongoing task of exposing and resolving our traumatic memories.[19] Charlotte and I have certainly observed this positive and encouraging trend as we have worked steadily during the past ten years to resolve our own traumas.

---

19.   It is interesting to note that there is a two-way interaction between deliberate appreciation and resolution of trauma. In one direction, deliberate appreciation as an intervention for pulling us back into relational mode will reduce the negative impact of triggered traumatic memories; and in the other direction, resolving trauma will make it easier to recall past positive experiences and to generate subjective gratitude as we focus on specifics that we appreciate.

Deliberate Appreciation Becomes Easier and Increasingly Effective with Practice

Just as with receiving attunement from the Lord, deliberate appreciation is a skill that we can learn. As Charlotte and I persist in practicing with deliberate appreciation we are definitely getting better at it—the whole process is flowing more and more easily, subjective feelings of gratitude are coming more and more quickly, and the end result is getting more and more robust.

Deliberate Appreciation Is Very Biblical

Deliberate appreciation is not just good clinical practice, it is also very biblical. The Old Testament contains many passages encouraging us to deliberately remember, and be grateful for, what the Lord has done for us:

> This is a day you are to commemorate; for the generations to come you shall celebrate it as a festival to the LORD—a lasting ordinance. . . . And when your children ask you, "What does this ceremony mean to you?" then tell them, "It is the Passover sacrifice to the LORD who passed over the houses of the Israelites. (Ex. 12:14, 26–27)[20]

> Remember that you were slaves in Egypt and that the LORD your God brought you out of there with a mighty hand and an outstretched arm. (Deut. 5:15)

> Remember how the LORD your God led you all the way in the desert these forty years. (Deut. 8:2)

> When you have eaten and are satisfied, praise the LORD your God for the good land he has given you. (Deut. 8:10)

> Remember that you were slaves in Egypt and the LORD your God redeemed you from there. (Deut. 24:18)

> When the whole nation had finished crossing the Jordan, the LORD said to Joshua, "Choose twelve men from among the people, one from each tribe, and tell them to take up twelve stones from the middle of the Jordan from right where the priests stood and to carry them over with you and put them down at the place where you stay tonight. . . . In the future, when your children ask you, 'What do these stones mean?' tell them that the flow of the Jordan was cut off before the ark of the covenant of the LORD. When it crossed the Jordan, the waters of the Jordan were cut off." (Josh. 4:1–7)

---

20. Unless otherwise specified, Scripture quotes are from *The Holy Bible: New International Version.* (Grand Rapids: Zondervan, 1984).

The Psalms are especially full of exhortations to deliberately remember and appreciate the Lord's goodness:

Sing praises to the LORD, enthroned in Zion; proclaim among the nations what he has done. For he who avenges blood remembers; he does not ignore the cry of the afflicted. (Ps. 9:11–12)

You who fear the LORD, praise him! All you descendants of Jacob, honor him! Revere him, all you descendants of Israel! For he has not despised or disdained the suffering of the afflicted one; he has not hidden his face from him but has listened to his cry for help. (Ps. 22:23–24)

Sing to the LORD, you saints of his; praise his holy name. For his anger lasts only a moment, but his favor lasts a lifetime; weeping may remain for a night, but rejoicing comes in the morning. (Ps. 30:4–5)

Sing joyfully to the LORD, you righteous; it is fitting for the upright to praise him. Praise the LORD with the harp; make music to him on the ten-stringed lyre. Sing to him a new song; play skillfully, and shout for joy. For the word of the LORD is right and true; he is faithful in all he does. The LORD loves righteousness and justice; the earth is full of his unfailing love. (Ps. 33:1–5)

Shout with joy to God, all the earth! Sing the glory of his name; make his praise glorious! . . . Come and see what God has done, how awesome his works in man's behalf! He turned the sea into dry land, they passed through the waters on foot—come, let us rejoice in him. . . . Praise our God, O peoples, let the sound of his praise be heard; he has preserved our lives and kept our feet from slipping. (Ps. 66:1–9)

Shout for joy to the LORD, all the earth. Worship the LORD with gladness; come before him with joyful songs. Know that the LORD is God. It is he who made us, and we are his; we are his people, the sheep of his pasture. Enter his gates with thanksgiving and his courts with praise; give thanks to him and praise his name. For the LORD is good and his love endures forever; his faithfulness continues through all generations. (Ps. 100:1–5)

Give thanks to the LORD, call on his name; make known among the nations what he has done. Sing to him, sing praise to him; tell of all his wonderful acts. . . . Remember the wonders he has done, his miracles, and the judgments he pronounced. (Ps. 105:1–2, 5)

See also: Ps. 68:4–6; 95:1–7; 96:1–13; 98:1–9; 103:1–22; 107:1, 2, 43; 117:1–2; 118:1–29; 134:1–2; 135:1–3, 19–21; 136:1–26; 147:1–20; 148:1–14; 149:1–9; 150:1–6.

And many of the Psalms model deliberately remembering and appreciating the Lord's goodness:

> I will give thanks to the LORD because of his righteousness and will sing praise to the name of the LORD most high. (Ps. 7:17)

> I will praise you, O LORD, with all my heart; I will tell of all your wonders. I will be glad and rejoice in you; I will sing praise to your name, O Most High. . . . *(ten more verses of specific appreciations)*. (Ps. 9:1–18)

> I love you, O LORD, my strength. The LORD is my rock, my fortress and my deliverer; my God is my rock, in whom I take refuge. He is my shield and the horn of my salvation, my stronghold. I call to the LORD Lord, who is worthy of praise, and I am saved from my enemies. . . . *(forty-six more verses of specific appreciations)*. (Ps. 18:1–50)

> Praise be to the LORD, for he has heard my cry for mercy. The LORD is my strength and my shield; my heart trusts in him, and I am helped. My heart leaps for joy and I will give thanks to him in song. The LORD is the strength of his people, a fortress of salvation for his anointed one. (Ps. 28:6–8)

> I will extol the LORD at all times; his praise will always be on my lips. My soul will boast in the LORD; let the afflicted hear and rejoice. Glorify the LORD with me; let us exalt his name together. . . . *(nineteen more verses of specific appreciations)*. (Ps. 34:1–22)

See also: Ps. 3:3–6; 5:4–12; 8:1–9; 12:5–7; 13:5–6; 16:1–11; 19:1–11; 21:1–13; 22:3–5, 9, 10, 22–31; 23:1–6; 25:8–15; 30:1–12; 31:19–24; 33:1–22; 36:5–12; 40:1–10; 48:1–14; 54:4–7; 57:1–11; 63:1–11; 65:1–13; 66:1–20; 67:3–4; 71:14–24; 73:1–28; 75:1–10; 76:1–12; 77:10–20; 89:1–18; 92:1–15; 95:1–7; 96:1–13; 98:1–9; 99:1–9; 100:1–5; 103:1–22; 104:1–35; 105:1–45; 106:1–48; 107:1–43; 108:1–5; 111:1–10; 113:1–9; 116:1–19; 118:1–29; 124:1–8; 126: 1–3; 134:1–3; 135:1–21; 136:1–26; 138:1–8; 139:1–18; 144:1–2; 145:1–21; 146:1–10; 147:1–20; 148:1–14; 149:1–9; 150:1–6.

The apostle Paul repeatedly encourages us to be grateful and to thank the Lord for his goodness:

> Do not get drunk on wine, which leads to debauchery. Instead, be filled with the Spirit. Speak to one another with psalms, hymns and spiritual songs. Sing and make music in your heart to the Lord,

always giving thanks to God the Father for everything, in the name of our Lord Jesus Christ. (Eph. 5:18–20)

Let the peace of Christ rule in your hearts, since as members of one body you were called to peace. And be thankful. Let the word of Christ dwell in you richly as you teach and admonish one another with all wisdom, and as you sing psalms, hymns, and spiritual songs with gratitude in your hearts to God. And whatever you do, whether in word or deed, do it all in the name of the Lord Jesus, giving thanks to God the Father through him. (Col. 3:15–17)

Devote yourselves to prayer, being watchful and thankful. (Col. 4:2)

Be joyful always; pray continually; give thanks in all circumstances, for this is God's will for you in Christ Jesus. (1 Thess. 5:16–18)

And Jesus models appreciation and gratitude, as he thanks the Father for many things:

Taking the five loaves and the two fish and looking up to heaven, he gave thanks and broke the loaves. (Mark. 6:41)

When he had taken the seven loaves and given thanks, he broke them and gave them to his disciples to set before the people. (Mk 8:6)

They had a few small fish as well; he gave thanks for them also and told the disciples to distribute them. (Mark. 8:7)

After taking the cup, he gave thanks and said, 'Take this and divide it among you. For I tell you I will not drink again of the fruit of the vine until the kingdom of God comes. (Luke. 22:17)

When he was at the table with them, he took bread, gave thanks, broke it and began to give it to them. (Luke. 24:30)

Then Jesus looked up and said, "Father, I thank you that you have heard me." (John. 11:41)

20

Regaining Access — Calming

Fortunately, we have been designed so that our brains and minds prefer to be in relational mode—we have been designed so that running in relational mode is the normal, optimal, most comfortable way for our brains and minds to function. In fact, the Lord has designed us so that our brains and minds will automatically find the way back to relational mode as we calm down. That is, if we get upset to the point that we drop into non-relational mode, our brains and minds will find the way back to relational mode if we can sufficiently calm the negative emotions that caused us to drop into non-relational mode in the first place.[1] To put this another way: negative emotions, and especially fear and/or anger, make it increasingly difficult to stay in relational mode as they become increasingly intense; and, conversely, to the extent we are able to calm intense negative emotions our brains will more easily cooperate with interventions for regaining access to our relational circuits. In many situations calming alone will be sufficient to enable us to get back into relational mode. Therefore, any intervention that will help us to calm down can be a resource for helping us get back into relational mode.

For those who want to pursue calming techniques more vigorously, an overwhelming pile of research and practical resources is easily available (the Google search I just did for "relaxation techniques" yielded 7,210,000 links); however, for the purposes of this book I am including only a brief description of a few techniques I find to be particularly easy to use and/or effective.

Especially Simple Calming Interventions

Some people find that very simple interventions can produce enough calming to allow them to regain access to their relational circuits. Interventions as simple as reading familiar, comforting, encouraging Scripture (such as Psalm 23), listening to calming music, or aerobic exercise. A very simple intervention suggested by Dr. Wilder is to repeat an affirmation based on Psalm 56:3, "Whenever I am afraid, I will trust in you, oh Lord," while taking a short walk (or even while walking back and forth across your living room).

---

1. When testing to see whether these statements are consistent with our personal experience, it's important to realize that people with dismissive attachment can learn to operate out of non-relational mode, even while calm, and that people with dissociative defenses can operate out of non-relational mode while disconnected (and appearing to be calm).

Shalom for My Body

Dr. E. James Wilder and Pastor Ed Khouri have developed a set of calming techniques that they call "Shalom My Body," since applying these techniques brings peace (shalom) to your body.[2]

The reader may notice that components focusing on the physical body are prominent in the shalom-for-my-body exercises. This has been done very deliberately. The physical body interventions have been designed to be as simple and concrete as possible, so that we can apply them even when we are intensely upset and our brains are significantly impaired by being in non-relational mode. Furthermore, interventions focusing on the physical body can produce surprisingly dramatic benefits for the whole body-mind-spirit system. Our bodies, minds, and spirits are so intimately connected that calming one will usually also produce powerful calming effects for the others.

The physical components of these techniques may seem a little odd, but this is because they have been designed to produce very specific patterns of stimulation to the sympathetic and parasympathetic nervous systems.[3] The end result is to produce a physiological "relaxation response" that helps to calm intense emotions by calming the physical reactions associated with the emotions.[4] This relaxation response is especially relevant to our discussion since it is especially effective in calming the fear and anger at the center of the fight-or-flight reaction (and these are the negative emotions that most powerfully push us into non-relational mode). See appendix E for additional discussion of the theory behind the shalom-for-my-body exercises, and also for information regarding additional resources by Wilder and Khouri.

---

2. Note that we have slightly modified the name of these calming exercises, from "Shalom My Body" to "Shalom for My Body."

3. The *sympathetic* nervous system is responsible for *activating* the many aspects of physical arousal associated with intense emotions. For example, when we encounter danger, the sympathetic nervous system activates the physiological changes associated with the fear and anger of the fight-or-flight response—the increased alertness, the increased muscle tension, the increased blood flow, and a variety of other physical reactions that prepare our bodies to either fight or flee. As the direct counterpart of the sympathetic nervous system, the *parasympathetic* nervous system is responsible for *calming* the many aspects of physical arousal associated with intense emotions.

4. The "relaxation response" is essentially the opposite of the sympathetic stimulation associated with the fight-or-flight response. Measurable physiologic changes associated with the relaxation response include decreased blood pressure, decreased heart rate, decreased respiration rate, decreased lactate levels in the blood, and EEG changes indicative of a calming effect with respect to brain activity. For a very understandable discussion of Dr. Benson and colleagues' extensive work with the relaxation response, see H. Benson, and M. Z. Klipper, *The Relaxation Response,* updated and expanded edition (New York: Harper Collins, 2000).

One advantage of the shalom-for-my-body techniques is that they can usually be used effectively in two to three minutes, whereas the additional interventions for calming described in appendix F often require ten to twenty minutes. And there are some crisis situations in which an intervention that can be applied in a couple minutes will actually get used, whereas a calming technique that requires ten to twenty minutes will not be realistically feasible. A second advantage of the shalom-for-my-body techniques is that they are usually effective even without initial practice sessions. In contrast, most people find that they need to invest in a number of practice sessions before the meditative prayer, deep breathing, and progressive muscle relaxation described in appendix F become effective as calming resources. The shalom-for-my-body techniques, however, become effective as soon as you do them correctly, and most people can learn them in a matter of minutes. The only need for practice is to repeat them a few times when you first learn them, so that you will remember how to do them when you need them. And effectiveness without the need for initial practice sessions is especially valuable in this particular context, since many of the people who have the most trouble with falling into non-relational mode also have trouble with the time, structure, planning, and discipline required to complete a series of practice sessions. And finally, the shalom-for-my-body techniques are uniquely effective for calming people whose non-relational upset includes disorganized attachment.[5]

In my experience, the shalom-for-my-body exercises are especially effective for rapidly reducing the intensity of fear and/or anger when I am experiencing fear and/or anger in response to feeling threatened in some way, and reducing the intensity of fight-or-flight fear and/or anger makes it much easier for me to then use the receiving attunement intervention and deliberate appreciation in order to fully regain access to my relational circuits.

INSTRUCTIONS FOR THE SHALOM-FOR-MY-BODY EXERCISES[6]
(Note: Your learning experience will be greatly enhanced if you study these written instructions in combination with viewing the video clips of Dr. Wilder and me demonstrating the exercises. These clips can be accessed from either the *Outsmarting Yourself* website, www.outsmartingyourself.com, or from the *Outsmarting Yourself* companion DVD.)

---

5. See appendix E for a brief discussion of disorganized attachment, and for discussion regarding how the shalom-for-my-body calming techniques are uniquely effective for people whose non-relational upset includes disorganized attachment.

6. Adapted from material received in personal e-mails (August 2010) from Dr. E. James Wilder and Pastor Ed Khouri. Used with permission.

1. Make sure that you have enough space around you so you can extend your arms and lean back in your chair without hitting anybody or anything.

2. The first part of this exercise has two variations, one for anger and one for fear. If you are feeling angry, begin the *Part One: Hands Up* exercises with your nostrils flared, an angry expression on your face, and inhaling through your nose. If you are feeling fearful, begin the *Part One: Hands Up* exercises with your eyes wide open, a frightened expression on your face, and inhaling through your mouth.

Part One: Hands Up

3. Choose the expression you will use for this part (angry, with nostrils flared; or fearful, with eyes wide open), and then do the following three things simultaneously:

    a) Inhale sharply.

    b) Throw your head back.

    c) Throw your arms up and to the sides, as if in response to someone saying "Stick 'em up!"

4. Now do the following four things simultaneously:

    a) Slowly bring your head forward (return to normal position).

    b) Breathe out slowly.

    c) Say out loud, "Whenever I am afraid, I will trust in you, oh Lord."

    d) Slowly lower your hands to your lap.

5. Repeat the *Part One: Hands Up* exercises four to six times.

Part Two: Yawn Left and Right

6. Turn your head to the left.

7. Yawn and inhale slowly (sometimes wiggling your jaw as you yawn triggers a real yawn).

8. Slowly bring your head back to facing forward, and as you turn your head forward say, "Whenever I am afraid, I will trust in you, oh Lord."

9. Turn your head to the right.

10. Yawn and inhale slowly (again, wiggling your jaw may trigger a real yawn).

11. Slowly bring your head back to facing forward, and as you turn your head forward say, "Whenever I am afraid, I will trust in you, oh Lord."

12. Repeat the *Part Two* exerices three or four times.

Part Three: Chest Tap and Rub

13. Rest your fingertips near the top of your chest, with your fingers slightly curved and each hand about two inches out from the center of your chest.

14. Start tapping alternating hands on your chest at about the speed of your heartbeat (you can get a feel for the speed of your heartbeat by placing the fingers of one hand on the large artery in your neck, immediately below your jaw and to the side of your windpipe).

15. As you inhale, do the following two things simultaneously:

    a) Breathe in deeply, smoothly, and a bit faster than normal.

    b) Steadily increase the speed you are tapping.

16. As you exhale, do the following three things simultaneously:

    a) Breathe out slowly and smoothly.

    b) Use your fingertips to gently massage the place on your chest where you were tapping.

    c) Say out loud, "Whenever I am afraid, I will trust in you, oh Lord."

17. Repeat the *Part Three* exercises three or four times.

Additional Interventions for Calming

As described above, I find the shalom-for-my-body exercises to be especially effective for rapidly reducing the intense fear and/or anger of the fight-or-flight reaction. In contrast, I find the meditative prayer, deep breathing, and progressive muscle relaxation described in appendix F to be more effective for moving from moderate/mild negative emotions to complete calm. For example, if I have been smoldering along for hours with subtle, ongoing triggering about something that is upsetting me, and this has caused me to also be smoldering along for hours in subtle non-relational mode, I find that the shalom-for-my-body interventions are not very effective. However, if I take five to fifteen minutes to use one of the calming techniques described in appendix F, I find that I can consistently calm down to the point that I come back into relational mode.

Furthermore, if you continue regular practice with the calming techniques described in appendix F, the benefits that you initially experience only during the relaxation exercises will eventually generalize to the rest of your life. Extensive case study evidence and biofeedback research demonstrates that consistent practice with these techniques can actually decrease a person's *baseline* sympathetic nervous stimulation, with measurable changes such as decreased esophageal spasm and stable reduction in resting blood pressure.[7] And this decrease in your baseline sympathetic nervous stimulation will enable you to be a calmer, less irritable, more stable person *in general*,[8] so that you will be less vulnerable to getting triggered into non-relational mode in the first place.

Calming Interventions Become Easier and Increasingly Effective with Practice

Just as with receiving attunement and deliberate appreciation, calming is a skill that we can learn. As I have persisted in practicing with the different calming interventions, I have found that they are taking less time and that they are increasingly effective. With respect to meditative prayer, deep breathing, and progressive muscle relaxation, there is also case study evidence and extensive biofeedback research demonstrating that, *with regular practice so that the person develops more skill*, these techniques can be still be effective resources for calming even in messy, difficult situations where you are upset, triggered, and non-relational, where you have less time, and where the environment is distracting and uncomfortable.[9]

---

7. Edmund Jacobson, *Progressive Relaxation: A Physiological and Clinical Investigation of Muscular States and Their Significance in Psychology and Medical Practice*, second edition, Midway Reprint (Chicago: University of Chicago Press, 1974), pages 357–381, 422–423; Edmund Jacobson, *You Must Relax: Practical Methods for Reducing the Tensions of Modern Living*, fifth edition (New York: McGraw-Hill, 1976), pages 145–146; Herbert Benson and Miriam Z. Klipper, *The Relaxation Response*, updated and expanded (New York: Harper Collins, 2000); and Herbert Benson and William Proctor, *Beyond the Relaxation Response* (New York: Berkley Books, 1984).

8. Observations described on pages 292–300 of Edmund Jacobson, *Progressive Relaxation: A Physiological and Clinical Investigation of Muscular States and Their Significance in Psychology and Medical Practice*, second edition, Midway Reprint (Chicago: University of Chicago Press, 1974) strongly support this point.

9. See, for example, Herbert Benson and Miriam Z. Klipper, *The Relaxation Response*, updated and expanded (New York: Harper Collins, 2000), especially pages xix, xxii, and 132–133; Herbert Benson and William Proctor, *Beyond the Relaxation Response* (New York: Berkley Books, 1984), especially pages 127, 129, 131, and 136–140; and Edmund Jacobson, *You Must Relax: Practical Methods for Reducing the Tensions of Modern Living*, fifth edition (New York: McGraw-Hill, 1976), especially pages 59–60, 147, and 197–216.

21

Regaining Access—Humor

Since the publication of the first edition of *Outsmarting Yourself,* we have come to recognize humor as yet another resource that the Lord has provided for bringing our relational circuits back on line. Our observation is that good clean humor, *free of sarcasm,* can often bring relational circuits on line as effectively as deliberate appreciation or calming. And if your relational circuits are already on line, humor can quickly and dramatically strengthen their activity. Most of us can easily demonstrate this effect in our own experience by simply reading a few particularly good jokes.

For example, observe your relational status as you go through the following jokes. Psychiatrist's secretary: "Doctor, there's a patient in the waiting room who thinks he's invisible." Psychiatrist: "Tell him I can't see him." (Pause for a few moments to let it sink in.) How many psychiatrists does it take to change a lightbulb? Only one, but the lightbulb has to want to change. (Pause for a few moments to let it sink in.) Why can't you hear a pterodactyl in the bathroom? Because it has a silent pee. (Again, pause for a few moments to let it sink in.) What did the Zen Buddhist say to the hot dog vendor? Make me one with everything. (Pause) Did you hear about the yogi who had his wisdom teeth extracted without anesthetic? He wanted to transcend dental medication. (Pause) What's brown and sticky? A stick. (Pause) I have enough money to last me the rest of my life . . . unless I buy something. (Pause) I was watching the Chicago marathon and saw one runner dressed as a chicken and another runner dressed as an egg. I thought, this could be interesting. (Pause) What's the last thing that goes through a bug's mind as he hits the windshield? His butt. (Pause) What do you get when you cross a little white mouse with a famous home decorator? Martha Stewart Little! (Pause) Why was Tigger looking in the toilet? He was looking for Pooh! (Pause) A computer once beat me at chess, but it was no match for me at kickboxing. (Pause) What's red and invisible? No tomatoes. (Pause) What's big and gray and writes gloomy poetry? T.S. Elephant. (Pause) What's invisible and smells like worms? Bird farts. (Pause) Everybody has a photographic memory . . . some people just don't have any film. (Pause) What do you get when you cross an insomniac, an agnostic, and a dyslexic? Someone who lies awake at night wondering if there really is a dog. (Pause) What do Alexander the Great and Winnie the Pooh have in common? They both have the same middle name. (Pause) I used to have a handle on life, but it broke.

And here are a couple of longer, story jokes, just for good measure. A man has to get to an early business meeting, so he's in the hotel lobby at six in the morning, and there's nobody else there. As he sits down with his doughnut and coffee, he hears a voice that says, "Nice tie." "Thanks," he replies, but when he looks around he can't find anybody who might have made the comment. A few moments later, the same voice says, "You're looking trim—have you been working out?" "Thanks," he replies again, but again he can't find the source of the voice. A couple minutes later, when the same disembodied voice comments that his goatee makes him look very distinguished, he gets up quickly and goes to the front desk. "Excuse me, but I've been having the strangest experience. I keep hearing a voice, but I can't figure out where it's coming from." "Oh, that," says the woman at the desk, "That's the continental breakfast. It's complimentary."

There once was a rich man who was near death. He was very grieved because he had worked so hard for his money and he wanted to be able to take it with him to heaven. So he began to pray that he might be able to take some of his wealth with him. An angel hears his plea and appears to him. "Sorry, but you can't take your wealth with you." The man implores the angel to speak to God to see if he might bend the rules. The man continues to pray that his wealth could follow him. The angel reappears and informs the man that God has decided to grant him an exception—he may bring one suitcase of his worldly wealth. Overjoyed, the man gathers his largest suitcase, fills it with pure gold bars, and places it beside his bed. Soon afterward the man dies and shows up at the gates of heaven to greet St. Peter. St. Peter seeing the suitcase says, "Hold on, you can't bring that in here!" But the man explains to St. Peter that he has been granted an exception and asks him to verify his story with the Lord. Sure enough, St. Peter checks and comes back saying, "You're right. You are allowed one carry-on bag, but I'm supposed to check its contents before letting it through." So St. Peter opens the suitcase to inspect the worldly items that the man found too precious to leave behind, and exclaims, "You brought *pavement*?!!!"

If you found these jokes to be funny (and especially if they made you laugh out loud), you should be able to feel an increase in the activity of your relational circuits.[1] If you were initially in non-relational mode, you should be able to notice a clear shift into relational mode, and if you were initially

---

1.   In my own experience, when I am *really* triggered, my relational circuits are *completely* off, and I am in *deep* non-relational mode, attempts at humor feel irritating instead of funny (and this includes jokes that usually make me laugh enthusiastically).

already in relational mode, but just barely, you should now feel more strongly relational.

The most common application of this reality is that many speakers intuitively use humor at the beginning of their presentations to "get the audience warmed up." What these speakers are doing, whether they realize it or not, is helping the audience to get their relational circuits on line (and/or to get their relational circuits more strongly on line). And an audience solidly established in relational mode will be a much more receptive audience—less critical, less fearful/guarded (more open to new ideas), less impatient regarding presentation quirks or flaws (like taking too long to tell a story or getting distracted by irrelevant details), more responsive, and more likely to give the speaker the benefit of the doubt at points where an unclear comment might be interpreted in either a positive or negative way.

Practical applications for day-to-day interpersonal relationships are a little less obvious. For example, Charlotte and I have never tried to crack jokes or taken a break to read *The Far Side* cartoons when we've lost access to our relational circuits as part of some interpersonal tangle.[2] However, there have been a number of situations in which we have both been triggered into non-relational mode, and then one of us spontaneously perceives some aspect of the situation that could be seen as funny. If this potential humor is presented in a way that is friendly,[3] and the other is willing to cooperate with the "humor intervention,"[4] we will both suddenly smile, and then laugh briefly as we both pop back into relational mode.

So what might this look like, in terms of concrete specifics? "Hypothetically," let's say Charlotte and I have been arguing, and I turn to her and give her the angry look that says, "You're *wrong*, this is *your fault*, and I'm *really* unhappy with you." But instead of showing me the unhappy face that tells me that my angry look has been successful in producing the intended distress, she cracks a little smile, hesitates for a moment, and then says, "I'm sorry sweetheart, but your angry look just isn't as effective when there's a big booger hanging out of your nose." At this point, if (underneath my anger) I'm really wanting to get back into relational mode so that Charlotte and I can reconnect, I will intuitively welcome this opportunity. I pause for the briefest moment, as I choose at some level to let go of my angry, adversarial attitude, and then I crack a little smile, we both break out laughing, I give Charlotte a hug and say, "I don't know why this makes me

---

2. Maybe the *Far Side* idea would be worth trying?

3. Again, be careful to avoid sarcasm, which is inherently adversarial and non-relational.

4. As opposed to deliberately resisting the humor in a misguided attempt to punish the "enemy" by stubbornly hanging onto non-relational mode.

so angry, but I want to be on the same team with you," and she returns the hug with a quiet, "me too."[5]

We have not actually done any work with trying to use humor as a deliberate intervention for helping us move from a triggered, non-relational place back into relational mode. Rather, as described in the "hypothetical" example, it has happened spontaneously in the context of interactions between Charlotte and me. Regarding the use of humor as a deliberate intervention, I would offer the caution that an attempt at humor during a conflict might be experienced by the other as mis-attuning, especially in more difficult situations in which the participants are really stuck in a non-relational, polarized, adversarial stance. However, the kind of spontaneous, friendly, subtle humor described in the above example can be a refreshing additional resource in relationships that are already in a moderately good place. In Charlotte's and my experience, our sense is that we cooperate with it when it shows up, as opposed to bringing it in as a deliberate intervention. We also perceive that it has been helpful for us to be aware of how humor can be a relational circuit resource, and that it helps to realize that this is okay (as opposed to worrying that it might be inappropriate in some vague way). In our experience, being aware of humor as a potential relational circuit resource, and realizing that it's okay, makes it easier to recognize what's happening and then cooperate with it when it shows up spontaneously.

One last piece regarding humor is that we have started to deliberately include it in our fun/play time. We have found that sharing particulary good jokes that one or the other of us has recently discovered always strengthens our relational circuit activity and increases our enjoyment in being together.[6]

We would be glad to hear from any readers who have found other creative ways in which to use humor as a relational circuit resource.

---

5.   I definitely take care of the booger before giving her a kiss.

6.   It's also just plain fun.

22

The Best Ways to Use These Resources (Advanced Topics)

> **Advanced topics warning:** If many of the concepts presented in *Outsmarting Yourself* are new to you, and you are reading through the book for the first time, trying to get the big picture, I encourage you to skip this chapter for now. Taking time at this point in your learning journey to go through these practical, nuts-and-bolts details will hinder you from getting the more important overview understanding of how all the pieces fit together. Come back to this material when you are ready to actually start using receiving attunement, deliberate appreciation, calming, and humor as tools for getting your relational circuits back on line.

As just described, the Lord has provided receiving attunement, deliberate appreciation, calming, and humor as resources that we can use to help ourselves move from non-relational mode back into relational mode. Now I would like to talk about the most effective ways to use these resources.

Receiving Attunement

As mentioned earlier, receiving attunement is the *ideal* intervention for helping us regain access to our relational circuits—the Lord seems to have designed our brains and minds so that attunement is able to reach us, even when we are stuck in the miserable place of being triggered and non-relational; and if we are then able to receive the attunement, it smoothly and efficiently brings us back into relational mode.[1] In most situations, receiving attunement is the most effective intervention for helping us get back into relational mode. In most situations, receiving attunement is also the intervention that is easiest to accept. When we are triggered and non-relational, deliberate appreciation is just plain hard to do; and when we are intensely triggered and non–relational, going directly to deliberate appreciation feels like the *opposite* of what comes naturally. When we are triggered

---

1. For additional discussion of the way in which attunement has been designed to be the ideal resource for helping us get back into relational mode, see "Brain Science, Psychological Trauma, and the God Who Is with Us ~ Part II" (available as free download from www.kclehman.com).

and non-relational, there are also often times when we will not welcome the idea that we should use calming interventions.[2] And when we are *really* triggered and our relational circuits are *really* off-line, humor can feel irritating instead of helpful. In contrast, when we are stuck in the miserable place of being triggered and non-relational, the only intervention that consistently[3] feels good and comes naturally is receiving attunement—it *feels good* for someone to see us, hear us, understand us, care about us, and be empathetically with us in our pain. Even when triggered and non-relational, we still want attunement and receive it gladly.[4]

And not only is receiving attunement usually the most efficient and the easiest-to-accept intervention for getting us back into relational mode, but it also provides several important additional benefits:

- **Contributes to permanently healing the underlying traumas:** Receiving attunement will directly contribute to the process of resolving the underlying traumas. As mentioned in the earlier discussion of trauma and relational circuits, in order to successfully process a painful experience we need to stay in relational mode as we feel the negative emotions associated with the experience; and providing this necessary condition for successful processing by keeping our relational circuits on line while connected to the painful experience and feeling the negative emotions is one of the most important tasks on the pain-processing pathway. As also mentioned in the earlier discussion, being unable to maintain access to our relational circuits is one of the most common and most important processing failures that causes painful experiences to become traumatic; and one of the most common and most important pieces of unresolved content carried in traumatic memories is loss of access to our relational

---

2.   The idea that we can use calming tools to reduce the intensity of our negative emotions will usually feel like good news if we are fearful/anxious as part of being triggered; but if we are angry and feeling blamed as part of being triggered, the idea of using calming interventions might meet with a response along the lines of: "Why should *I* calm down? My anger is justified—I'm just mad because I'm getting a raw deal here! And why are we suggesting that *I* should have to do more work so that the situation is easier for everybody else? What about some of the *others* involved here taking responsibility for *their* stuff? What about the *others* working to make changes so that the situation is easier for *me*? . . ." Also, if we are experiencing *low energy* negative emotions, such as sadness or hopeless despair, we will not feel either the need or desire for calming, whereas the thought of receiving attunement will still be appealing.

3.   As mentioned above, we can resist receiving attunement if we are choosing to persist in bitterness and/or self-pity and/or rebellion.

4.   In fact, when I am triggered and in non-relational mode, attunement is one of the few *constructive* things that I want and welcome. There may be many *unhealthy* things that I feel desire for—like revenge, power, and control so that I can "fix" the problem, or something that will make the pain go away by providing intense immediate gratification—but attunement is one of the few *constructive* things that I want and welcome.

circuits. Therefore, regaining access to our relational circuits, while feeling the pain associated with the underlying traumatic memories, is often one of the first things we need to do in order to resume successful processing; and receiving attunement while triggered and connected to the negative emotions enables us to do this.

Furthermore, in addition to helping us regain access to our relational circuits (*return* to relational mode), receiving attunement also augments our capacity and maturity skills, and this helps us successfully complete the important processing task of *staying* in relational mode as we experience the painful emotions associated with the memories. Even if this is the only place on the processing pathway where something moves forward, any progress with respect to this especially important processing task will *permanently* decrease the overall toxic power of the traumatic memories.[5]

- **Increases our ability to remain in relational mode as we re-enter the original triggering situations:** And it gets even better. Since receiving attunement also helps us with the processing task of *staying* in relational mode *while connected to the traumatic memories and toxic content*, to the extent that receiving attunement helps us to successfully complete this task, we will be able to *remain* in relational mode *even if we go back into the original situation and reengage with the same triggers that sent us into non-relational mode in the first place.* So when I go back to Charlotte and reengage regarding the conflict that started all the trouble, and the same triggers stir up the same unresolved trauma, I will be more able to *hold onto* my relational circuits instead of falling right back into non-relational mode.[6]

- **Builds psychological maturity skills:** Being able to successfully complete the processing task of staying in relational mode while feeling the negative emotions associated with a painful experience is a *skill* that can be *learned*. This is discussed in much greater detail in "Brain Science, Psychological Trauma, and the God Who Is with Us ~ Part II," but the very short summary is that we practice and learn this psychological maturity skill by repeatedly losing access to our relational connection circuits, and then receiving attunement and returning to relational mode *while still connected to the painful experiences/traumatic memories and feeling the negative emotions.* Another way to say this is that the experience of receiving attunement (and

---

5. See "Brain Science, Psychological Trauma, and the God Who Is with Us ~ Part II" for a greatly expanded discussion of these important points.

6. This will enable me to *persist* in being constructive, even if the conflict resolution process is difficult and lengthy.

thereby regaining access to our relational circuits) *while still feeling the negative emotions* is what strengthens the connections that provide the neurological basis for *learning* and *remembering* the *skill* of being able to stay in relational mode even while experiencing painful emotions.

The receiving attunement intervention therefore gives us a four-for-the-price-of-one super bonus deal—in addition to helping us get back into relational mode, we also receive these three additional benefits. In fact, if I have the time and emotional energy, and I'm not having trouble with triggered implicit memory getting transferred onto the Lord (see below), I intentionally avoid calming or appreciation before receiving attunement *so that I will still be feeling the negative emotions as I receive the Lord's attunement,* and thereby harvest these additional benefits. If I'm especially in the mood for personal growth, I go back and forth between receiving attunement from the Lord and deliberately stirring up the traumatic implicit memory by thinking about the triggers, so as to maximize these additional benefits of permanent healing, increased ability to stay relational when returning to the original triggering situation, and strengthened maturity skills. When I've had enough personal growth for the day (or I'm running out of time), I receive attunement until I'm back in relational mode, and then follow this with deliberate appreciation in order to make sure I've strongly reestablished myself in relational mode before reengaging with the original triggering situation.

Humor, calming, and deliberate appreciation will, indeed, enable us to return to relational mode, but in contrast to receiving attunement, when we use these alternative tools for reestablishing access to our relational circuits, *we will no longer be connected to the traumatic memories or feeling the associated negative emotions by the time we have returned to relational mode.* And regaining access to our relational circuits *while still connected to the pain and feeling the negative emotions* is a necessary ingredient for each of the additional benefits associated with receiving attunement. What this means is that when we use humor and/or calming and/or deliberate appreciation instead of receiving attunement, we will receive the many benefits of getting back into relational mode, but we will not contribute to permanently healing the underlying traumas, we will not increase our ability to remain in relational mode as we reengage with the original triggering situations, and we will not build psychological maturity skills.[7]

---

7.   It would actually be more accurate to say "we will not build *these particular* psychological maturity skills," since being able to deliberately calm ourselves (using deep breathing, muscle relaxation, appreciation, humor, or any other techniques) is itself a psychological maturity skill. For any who have not yet learned to do this, then practicing deliberate calming by any method will build this important, basic skill.

Therefore, a person should always include receiving attunement as part of the plan for getting back into relational mode unless: 1) she does not have people in her community who are able to offer attunement (and who are available at the time she needs it), and she is not yet able to receive attunement from the Lord; and/or 2) she simply does not have the time or energy needed to engage in receiving attunement.[8] Fortunately, deliberate appreciation, calming, and humor are available as alternative resources for these situations in which we are not able to use receiving attunement.

Deliberate Appreciation

When you are *already* in relational mode, it is easy to engage in deliberate appreciation. For example, if you get triggered into non-relational mode and then use calming and/or receiving attunement to regain access to your relational circuits, it is easy to use deliberate appreciation to *strengthen* your foundation in relational mode; or if you are already in relational mode and want to use the Immanuel approach to emotional healing, it is easy to use deliberate appreciation as part of establishing an optimal interactive connection with the Lord as the foundation for the session.[9] However (as mentioned earlier), when we are triggered and non-relational, deliberate appreciation is difficult; and when we are intensely triggered and non–relational, deliberate appreciation is *really* difficult. Therefore (as described below), we usually use deliberate appreciation as part of various combination packages. You can use deliberate appreciation as a stand-alone intervention if you have to,[10] and it will consistently bring you back into relational mode if you persist with it long enough, but this can be very difficult if you are intensely triggered.

In our experience, the primary place for deliberate appreciation as a stand-alone intervention is group situations in which most of the participants have not yet had teaching or experience with respect to receiving attunement or calming interventions, and a number of people have fallen

---

8. As we grow in skill with respect to establishing an interactive connection with the Lord, feeling our pain instead of trying to stop it, getting words for our distress, and talking to the Lord about our pain, it will become easier and easier to turn to the Lord for attunement whenever we are in distress. However, especially when we are first learning, this process can sometimes take a considerable amount of time and energy.

9. Again, for additional discussion regarding deliberate appreciation as part of the Immanuel approach to emotional healing, see parts I and V in the "Brain Science, Psychological Trauma, and the God Who Is with Us" essay series, both available as free downloads from www .kclehman.com.

10. For example, if you have fallen into non-relational mode because of a low-energy negative emotion (such as hopeless despair), so that calming will not produce much benefit, you are not able to receive attunement from the Lord, and there is no one in your community available to offer attunement, then you are left with deliberate appreciation as a stand-alone intervention.

into non-relational mode at the same time. For example, persistent, deliberate appreciation can be the easiest resource to use in church meetings where a number of people get triggered into non-relational mode, but where most of the participants have not yet learned about the shalom-for-my-body techniques and have not yet developed skill with receiving attunement from the Lord. Even though most of the people at the meeting have never even heard of relational circuits, receiving attunement, or calming techniques, you can take a break and coach the group to engage in deliberate appreciation until those in non-relational mode regain access to their relational circuits.

Dr. Wilder's recent experience with the Immanuel emotional healing seminar for the group in Asia provides another example. Almost all of the participants had survived very similar catastrophic traumas, so it was very easy for certain triggers to stir up a bunch of people at the same time. Early in the seminar, while the participants were still relatively untrained and inexperienced with respect to both receiving attunement from the Lord and the shalom-for-my-body techniques, there were situations in which a number of people got triggered into non-relational mode simultaneously. And in each of these situations, stand-alone appreciation interventions (group exercises helping the participants to engage in persistent, deliberate appreciation) were consistently effective in getting everybody back into relational mode.

Calming

Calming is especially valuable, either alone or in combination with other interventions, when we are experiencing intense fear and/or anger.

In my own experience, the only time I use calming as a stand-alone intervention is when I am in the middle of a complex, messy situation and there is no time for receiving attunement or deliberate appreciation. For example, if I'm in the middle of a difficult meeting and realize that I'm sliding into non-relational mode (or that I have already fallen into non-relational mode), I can take a few moments to close my eyes, relax my muscles (especially the muscles of facial expression), take a few deep breaths, and quietly go through several cycles of my relaxation prayer. With the increased skill and positive conditioned responses associated with regular practice, I can do all of this in less than a minute, while sitting at the table in the middle of an unresolved conflict, and still receive significant benefit. I can also use these same interventions in a very similar way if I'm in the middle of a difficult phone conversation. If I'm in a situation in which it's possible to take a short break, I find a place where I can go through the shalom-for-my-body exercises. Even if I only have two minutes, this can dramatically decrease the intensity of anger and/or anxiety, and thereby make it much easier to hold onto my relational circuits (or to regain access to my relational circuits if I have already lost them).

There are also times when I *initially* have trouble with receiving attunement, engaging in deliberate appreciation, or appreciating humor, and in these situations I'm glad to have calming exercises as an additional resource. For example, I still occasionally get triggered into an especially miserable place in which my implicit memory thoughts and emotions are pointed at the Lord; and it feels as if his choice to allow me to fall into a particularly unpleasant situation proves that he is both incompetent and uncaring, I am intensely angry at him, and the idea of turning to him for attunement feels almost offensive. When I am in this especially miserable place, focusing on things I appreciate is also extremely difficult, and jokes seem stupid and irritating instead of amusing. Fortunately, I find that I am still able to use calming interventions in these situations. Furthermore, I find that an initial round of calming always enables me to regain my ability to receive attunement, my ability to engage in deliberate appreciation, and my ability to appreciate humor; and I then apply these interventions as well, because the complete package is ideal and because calming as a stand-alone intervention seems to provide poor protection against relapse. That is, if I use calming to get myself back into relational mode, but then do not use receiving attunement and/or deliberate appreciation and/or humor in order to establish myself *more firmly* in relational mode, I often fall right back into non-relational mode when I re-enter the situation that triggered me into non-relational mode in the first place. Therefore, other than calming intervention practice sessions and the situations in which there is simply no time or space to engage in receiving attunement or deliberate appreciation, when I use calming it is always as the first step in a combination package (as described below).

Regular practice with meditative prayer, deep breathing, or progressive muscle relaxation can also be a resource for helping us *avoid* falling into non-relational mode. As mentioned in chapter 20, regular use of these calming techniques results in an increasingly stable reduction in the *baseline* stimulation of your sympathetic nervous system, so that you are generally more calm and less vulnerable to being triggered into intense negative emotions. Therefore, if you frequently fall into non-relational mode, and if you have a lot of trouble getting back out of non-relational mode, I encourage you to include regular practice with one or more of these calming techniques as part of your overall plan for caring for yourself and for those around you.

Finally, calming as a stand-alone intervention can be a blessing for those who are not yet able to utilize any of the other resources for regaining access to their relational circuits. Reading familiar, comforting, encouraging Scripture, listening to calming music, aerobic exercise, the shalom-for-my-body exercises, meditative prayer, deep breathing, and progressive muscle relaxation are all concrete, simple interventions that are still accessible even if a person is in a *really* bad mood, has not yet developed enough skill with respect to deliberate appreciation, is not yet able to establish an interactive connection or receive attunement from the Lord, is not with a friend who can attune to her, and is not able to apprciate humor due to her intense triggering. Furthermore, there are probably people who would not understand or be interested in receiving attunement from the Lord, deliberate appreciation, or trying to read jokes as relational-circuit interventions, but who might be willing to learn about very simple, concrete interventions for helping themselves calm down.

Humor

As mentioned above, Charlotte and I have not tried to deliberately use humor as an intervention for helping ourselves move from non-relational mode back into relational mode. Rather, as described in the "hypothetical" example, humor has volunteered itself as a resource in spontaneous situations, and we have been trying to learn to recognize and cooperate with it. As also mentioned above, we perceive that it has been helpful for us to be aware of how humor can be a relational circuit resource, and it helps to realize that using humor in this way is okay (as opposed to worrying that it might be inappropriate in some vague way). In our experience, being aware of humor as a potential relational circuit resource, and realizing that it's okay, makes it easier to recognize what's happening and then cooperate with it when it shows up spontaneously.

As also mentioned above, when we are intensely triggered and deep in non-relational mode, humor can feel irritating as opposed to helpful. When a person is intensely triggered, and stuck in a polarized, adversarial place, it is especially easy for him to feel painful mis-attunement if someone else tries to use humor in an attempt to get him back into relational mode.

Combination Packages

First, let me summarize several helpful points that we should keep in mind as we think about how to put together the best combination packages.

- **Include receiving attunement whenever possible:** As discussed earlier, receiving attunement is the *ideal* intervention, and whenever possible it should be included as part of any plan for getting back into relational mode.

- *Start* **with receiving attunement whenever possible:** As discussed earlier, we only receive the four-for-one additional benefits package when we are able to receive attunement and regain access to our relational circuits *while still connected to the traumatic memories and feeling the negative emotions.* Furthermore, you will receive the most benefit if you receive attunement and regain access to your relational circuits while still feeling the most intense negative emotions associated with the traumatic memories. Therefore, you get the most out of the four-for-the-price-of-one bargain if you receive attunement before applying any other interventions that might lessen the intensity of your negative emotions.

- **Especially avoid starting with deliberate appreciation:** Many, including myself, find it very difficult to go directly from being intensely triggered and non-relational to deliberate appreciation. It's possible, and it works, but it's *really* hard to do. (It usually feels painfully mis-attuning.)[11] Therefore, I especially avoid starting with deliberate appreciation whenever I put together a combination of interventions for getting back into relational mode.

- **Try to avoid calming as a stand-alone intervention:** As mentioned above, when I use calming to get myself back into relational mode, *without any additional interventions to prevent relapse*, I find that I am especially liable to fall back into non-relational mode when I return to the situation that caused me to lose access to my relational circuits in the first place. I therefore try to use calming in combination with other interventions, as opposed to using it as a stand-alone intervention.

- **Welcome humor when it shows up spontaneously, but be cautious about using it as a deliberate intervention:** As mentioned above, we have been trying to learn to recognize and cooperate with humor when it shows up spontaneously, but we are cautious about trying to use it as a deliberate intervention for helping someone else get back into relational mode. You can also experiment with adding humor to other packages as an additional resource for establishing yourself more strongly in relational mode. For example, after you have used one or more of the other tools to get yourself back into reational mode, take ten minutes to read

---

11. Trying to go directly from triggered non-relational mode to deliberate appreciation can feel like having a friend see you in distress, but instead of understanding your situation and being empathetically with you in your pain, he says, "Don't feel bad—just think happy thoughts!" When we are in distress, and a friend misses attunement in this way, we feel what I call mis-attunement pain. Similarly, this unpleasant experience could be described as being *painfully mis-attuning.*

a couple of pages of good jokes in order to further increase the activity of your relational circuits and thereby anchor yourself more solidly in relational mode.

With these points in mind, let me share about my experience with combination packages.

My Favorite—Receiving Attunement Followed by Deliberate Appreciation (and/or Humor)

My favorite intervention for regaining access to my relational circuits is receiving attunement followed by deliberate appreciation (and/or humor), and the reasons for this bring together many of the points that have been made earlier in this section. First and foremost, I am convinced that the Lord designed receiving attunement to be the most effective, four-for-the-price-of-one super bonus, *ideal* intervention for helping us get back into relational mode, so it makes sense that receiving attunement is at the center of my preferred intervention. Second (as just mentioned), we only receive the four-for-one super bonus benefits if we receive attunement and regain access to our relational circuits while still feeling the negative emotions, and the degree to which a person receives these additional benefits increases with the intensity of the negative emotions. So it makes sense to go straight to receiving attunement, without initial calming to eliminate negative emotions or decrease their intensity.[12]

Third, I find that receiving attunement provides the easiest, most gentle emotional transition from the miserable place of being triggered and non-relational. When I'm miserably triggered and non-relational, it *feels good* for someone to see me, hear me, understand me, care about me, and be empathetically with me in my pain—I *want* attunement and receive it gladly. So it makes even more sense to start with receiving attunement. And finally, although going *directly* from non-relational mode to deliberate appreciation is usually painfully difficult, once receiving attunement has helped me get my relational circuits back on line, it's easy to transition to appreciation (and/or humor) *as the second part of the plan*. Deliberate appreciation, specifically including any person(s) contributing to my upset, then establishes me much more strongly in relational mode, providing an ideal foundation for

---

12.   When I say, "The degree to which a person receives these additional benefits increases with the intensity of the negative emotions," I should add, "as long as the negative emotions don't overwhelm him to the point that he's unable to use the receiving attunement intervention." And if the negative emotions *are* too overwhelming, then he *should* start with calming (as described below).

reengaging constructively and protecting me from relapse.[13] So the intervention that *really* makes sense is to include both receiving attunement and deliberate appreciation (and/or humor), starting with receiving attunement to reestablish access to my relational circuits and then applying deliberate appreciation (and/or humor) to increase the strength of my relational mode foundation.

Receiving attunement followed by deliberate appreciation (and/or humor) is the intervention I use for regaining access to my relational circuits, unless an overriding concern requires switching to one of the alternatives described below.

Calming, Receiving Attunement, and Then Deliberate Appreciation (and/or Humor)

As described earlier, there are times when I *initially* have trouble with receiving attunement, engaging in deliberate appreciation, or appreciating humor. For example, when I get triggered into the place in which my implicit memory thoughts and emotions are pointed at the Lord, it feels like his choice to allow me to fall into a particularly unpleasant situation proves that he is both incompetent and uncaring, I am intensely angry at him, and the idea of turning to him for attunement feels almost offensive; or when I am deep in non-relational mode, and focusing on things I appreciate seems extremely difficult; or when I am intensely triggered, and humor feels more irritating than funny. As also described earlier, fortunately I am still able to use calming interventions in these situations, and I find that an initial round of calming always enables me to regain my ability to receive attunement, to engage in deliberate appreciation, and to appreciate humor. Whenever possible (when time, emotional energy, and social space are not problematic), I move from calming to receiving attunement, and then finish with deliberate appreciation (and/or humor). Reducing the intensity of the negative emotions reduces the *size* of the four-for-one benefits, but I do still receive some additional benefits, and going through the whole package protects against falling back into non-relational mode when I return to the situation that initially triggered me.

Also, if a person is experiencing overwhelming negative emotions, such as extremely intense fear or anger, he will sometimes find it difficult to think clearly enough to engage in receiving attunement, to focus enough to persist with deliberate appreciation, or to appreciate humor. In these

---

13. Note that deliberate appreciation focusing on any persons contributing to my upset will provide a stronger protection against relapse than humor. It also seems that deliberate appreciation has more inherent value as a behavior to get in the habit of practicing. However, using humor once in a while instead of deliberate appreciation can provide a bit of fun variety, and humor can also be used as an additional resource in combination with deliberate appreciation.

situations, the person might still be able to use one of the simple, concrete calming interventions, and this could reduce the intensity of his negative emotions to the point that he would be able to receive attunement, engage in deliberate appreciation, and appreciate humor. This would obviously be another place for the calming—receive attunement—deliberate appreciation (and/or humor) combination.[14]

BRIEF CALMING COMBINED WITH EITHER RECEIVING ATTUNEMENT OR DELIBERATE APPRECIATION (FOR SITUATIONS WITH LIMITED TIME, EMOTIONAL ENERGY, OR SOCIAL SPACE)

As mentioned above, I can use calming in situations in which time, emotional energy, and social space are all severely limited—with even a brief pause in the middle of a difficult meeting, I can take a few moments to close my eyes, relax my muscles, take a few deep breaths, and quietly go through several cycles of my relaxation prayer. However, as also mentioned above, when I use calming as a stand-alone intervention, without any additional interventions to prevent relapse, I find that I am especially liable to fall back into non-relational mode when I return to the situation that caused me to lose access to my relational circuits in the first place. Therefore, even in situations in which time and/or emotional energy and/or social space are limited, I try to combine calming with either receiving attunement or deliberate appreciation. I use calming to quickly reduce the intensity of any high-energy negative emotions, and with the intensity of the negative emotions reduced, it's much easier and takes much less time to use either receiving attunement or deliberate appreciation to establish myself more solidly in relational mode.

As described above, if time, emotional energy, and social space are *not* problematic, I go straight to receiving attunement because this has so many additional benefits, and then finish with deliberate appreciation to establish myself more firmly in relational mode. But if there's something I need to do, I really need to be in relational mode for the task at hand, and there isn't much time, then I start with a brief round of calming and finish with *either* receiving attunement *or* deliberate appreciation. For example, if Charlotte and I have gotten into a tangle that has triggered me into non-relational mode, we're supposed to be working as a team to facilitate an emotional healing workshop for our church in thirty minutes, and we're still working on last-minute preparations, I'll first take two to three minutes for the shalom-for-my-body exercises. And then, after this has reduced the intensity of my anxiety and frustration, I'll deliberately think about things I appreciate as I

---

14. Again, deliberate appreciation may have more inherent value than humor, and may provide stronger protection against relapse, but humor can provide fun variety and can also be used in combination with deliberate appreciation, as an additional resource.

continue with carrying supplies and arranging chairs. As mentioned earlier, the deliberate appreciation will be especially helpful if I focus on Charlotte for at least part[15] of this intervention.

CALMING AND DELIBERATE APPRECIATION (AND/OR HUMOR) FOR SITUATIONS IN WHICH RECEIVING ATTUNEMENT IS NOT AVAILABLE

If you are not yet able to receive attunement from the Lord, you do not have a friend able and available to offer attunement, and your triggered upset includes high-energy negative emotions such as fear and/or anger, then use the combination of calming and deliberate appreciation (and/or humor). Start with one or more of the calming interventions and persist with this until you have gotten back into relational mode. Once you have regained access to your relational circuits, it will be easy (as opposed to painfully mis-attuning) to transition to deliberate appreciation, and you can then continue deliberate appreciation until you are strongly established in relational mode. You can also experiment with including humor as an additional resource for establishing yourself more strongly in relational mode. And, once again, if interpersonal conflict is part of the picture it will be especially helpful to focus at least some of your deliberate appreciation on the person(s) who contributed to the original non-relational upset.[16]

It's Okay to Switch in the Middle

This may already be obvious, but I want to state it explicitly: it's okay to change the plan if you get into the middle of a situation and realize that your initial strategy isn't working. My own experience provides a good example. Years of combined healing work, maturity growth, and practice with receiving attunement have brought me to the place where I can *usually* receive attunement from the Lord with ease and efficiency; and when I lose access to my relational circuits, and I'm thinking about how to get back into relational mode, I make my judgment call with respect to strategy based on this usual scenario. That is, when I'm asking myself, "Do I have enough time and emotional energy to start with receiving attunement?" I make the decision based on my *usual* easy and efficient experience. However, occasionally I decide to start with receiving attunement and then discover that I'm having

---

15. If there are non-Charlotte things that seem easy to appreciate at this particular moment, I will spend some time focusing on these as an especially efficient way to get my relational circuits more solidly on line, and then deliberate appreciation focusing on Charlotte will flow more easily.

16. If interpersonal conflict is part of the picture, you want to make sure to include humor *in addition* to appreciation specifically focusing on the other people involved, as opposed to *substituting* humor for this appreciation intervention (which is especially helpful in preventing relapse when you go back into the initial difficult situation).

difficulty. Maybe something is hindering me from being able to establish the interactive connection, maybe I'm having trouble with letting go of trying to fix the problem so that I can just feel the pain, or maybe I'm having trouble with getting words for my distress—but the bottom line is that it's taking a lot more time and energy than expected. When I realize this, I feel free to switch to an option that will be more efficient with respect to time and emotional energy, such as quick calming and then appreciation.[17]

If you're just beginning to practice with receiving attunement from the Lord, you can approach most situations with, "I'll try starting with receiving attunement and see what happens." If this moves forward easily and quickly enough to work within a given situation, great. But if it seems like it's taking too long and/or requiring too much emotional energy, feel free to switch.

Experiment with What Works Best for You

I am hoping that the above thoughts and observations from my experience will be helpful, but you should also experiment with respect to what works best for you. The Lord knows your particular strengths and weaknesses, and also the unique aspects of the challenges you face. Ask him to help you find the best ways to use these interventions in the specific situations that you encounter.

---

17. My decision-making process regarding what strategy to use is usually not this explicit—at this point in my personal experience, it's usually a rapid, barely conscious, intuitive flow. But the discernment process described here is what we would see if I slowed things down, focused much more deliberately on the process, and took the time to articulate the details.

23

Summarizing with Respect to Regaining Access

As discussed in the last five chapters, to the extent we are able to implement an effective combination of calming, receiving attunement, and deliberately appreciating, we will regain access to our relational circuits and reestablish ourselves solidly in relational mode. And when we are able to feel the positive memories anchoring secure attachment, relational connection joy, and trust; when we are able to receive capacity and maturity skill augmentation from the Lord and/or others in our community; when we feel connected to the other people involved in the situation and want to be connected; when we experience others as relational beings; when we're aware of others' true hearts; when we feel compassionate concern regarding what others are thinking and feeling; when we experience others as a source of joy (as opposed to problems to be solved or resources to be used); when we are glad to be with them; when we both want to offer attunement and are able to offer attunement; when we are patient and tolerant (as opposed to impatient, intolerant, and irritable); when we are flexible and creative even when unexpected circumstances require that we change our plans at the last minute; when we perceive the relationships involved to be more important than any problems we might be trying to solve, and when we perceive others as allies, and want to join with them to explore, understand, and collaborate (as opposed to perceiving others as adversaries, and tending toward judging, interrogating, and trying to "fix" the situation); *I guarantee that the damaging effects of our triggering will be greatly reduced, and that we will especially be more able to deal with any relational conflict contributing to the problem.*

Yet another strategic reason to focus on our relational connection circuits is that it's often possible to reestablish access to our relational circuits even in situations in which we do not have the time, emotional space, or other resources necessary for fully resolving any underlying trauma contributing to the problem. For example, when Charlotte and I get in a conflict that triggers me and causes me to lose access to my relational circuits, I try to flex my schedule so that I can take a break for my regular exercise walk. However, with the resources available in this context I am usually not able to expose and fully resolve the underlying traumatic memories. Many of the issues that get stirred up by conflict with Charlotte are not simple issues anchored in a single, moderate-sized traumatic memory, but rather deep issues, such as lingering pockets of attachment trauma associated with the two-year-old separation from my parents, or thematic issues, such as the chronic feeling of anxiety anchored in thousands of memories throughout my childhood. Sometimes I am able to complete small pieces of the healing journey in the course of my walk, but these kinds of problems do not get fully, permanently resolved in the course of an exercise walk when I am having to facilitate ministry for myself while simultaneously crossing streets and navigating urban traffic.

In contrast, I usually *am* able to successfully use the tools for reestablishing access to my relational circuits, even with the same limitations of ministering to myself, crossing streets, and navigating urban traffic. As I combine calming, receiving attunement from the Lord, and deliberate appreciation *I am almost always able to regain access to my relational connection circuits.* And with my relational circuits back on line, even though the underlying memories have not yet been fully resolved, it is much less difficult to recognize and acknowledge my triggering, and I can be much more constructive as Charlotte and I work to resolve our conflict.

A Side Note—Taking the Lord's Light into Places of Darkness

Before moving on, I'd like to make a really important side note point regarding our relational circuits. One of the most important missions to which the Lord calls us is working with him to take his light into places of darkness. There's nothing wrong with gathering together with our church family to celebrate in sharing the Lord's light with each other, but he also wants us to take his light into the dark places where it's needed the most, like Betsy and Corrie ten Boom taking his light into the horrors of the Ravensbrück Nazi concentration camp during World War II. Thankfully, the Lord has provided a way for us to do this. To the extent we're able to walk through each day connected to the living presence of Jesus, the power and light of his living presence goes with us and shines through us *no matter how dark or difficult the situations we encounter*; and to the extent we're able to maintain access to our positive relational memories, we carry our memory-anchored security and joy with us as well, again, no matter how dark or difficult the situations we encounter.

This is where our relational circuits come in: carrying light with us in these ways works well when we're in relational mode, but losing access to our relational circuits will greatly hinder our connection to the Lord and completely cut us off from our memory-anchored security and joy. Therefore, *staying in relational mode* is one of the most important things we can do toward the end of being able to carry the Lord's light *with us* into difficult church meetings, economic turmoil, urban ghettos, religious persecution, oppressive social systems, or any other dark places we might go.

24

Additional Resources and Insights (Advanced Topics)

Let's take a moment for another satellite overview. In part 1, I presented basic information about psychological trauma, and then also discussed implicit memory, the Verbal Logical Explainer, and central nervous system extrapolation. In part 2, I presented an initial discussion of how to recognize and neutralize psychological trauma and VLE confabulated explanations. In part 3, I talked about exacerbating factors that can make it much more difficult to recognize and neutralize traumatic implicit memory and VLE confabulations. And here, in part 4, I have been describing additional resources and insights that are helpful for working with both straightforward and more difficult situations. I have already discussed additional insights regarding the importance of taking responsibility for *our own* stuff, additional resources for recognizing when our traumatic memories are getting stirred up (focusing especially on learning to recognize when we fall into non-relational mode), and tools for regaining access to our relational circuits for situations in which triggering has caused us to fall into non-relational mode. Now I would like to present several advanced interventions that can be especially helpful in the messy, difficult situations caused by the exacerbating factors described in part 3.

Advanced topics warning: I encourage you to skip the rest of this chapter (for now) if many of the concepts presented in *Outsmarting Yourself* are new to you and you are reading through the book for the first time, trying to get the big picture. At this point in your learning journey, slowing down to study these advanced concepts and tools will hinder you from getting the more important overview understanding of how all the pieces fit together. Come back to this material after you have been through the whole book at least once, you feel that you have a good understanding of the basic principles and tools, and you are ready to learn more about principles and tools for working with the messy, difficult situations caused by the exacerbating factors described in part 3.

Apply "Recognize and Acknowledge Our Implicit Memory and VLE Confabulations, and Then Make Behavioral Choice Based on Truth" to Second-Level Triggering[1]

Another piece of good news with respect to complex, difficult situations is that we can apply "recognize and acknowledge our implicit memory and VLE confabulations, and then make behavioral choices based on truth" to second-level triggering. Even when those around us do *not* start with helping us get our relational circuits back on by first attuning to our triggered pain, we can take even more responsibility for our traumatic implicit memory by recognizing second-level exacerbating reactions and then again making behavioral choices based on truth. For example, I usually feel blamed, accused, and invalidated when Charlotte forgets to attune first and jumps straight to suggesting that I might be triggered; but I have been increasingly able to recognize this second layer of triggering as it wells up inside of me, and I can feel that recognizing and understanding these exacerbating phenomena help me choose to respond constructively *even though my subjective experience is still an intense implicit memory perception of being blamed, accused, and invalidated, and even though I still feel intense impulses toward angry, defensive retaliation.*

Furthermore, just knowing about implicit memory, triggering, the Verbal Logical Explainer, and second-level negative reactions is tremendously helpful. For example, it has been my experience that just knowing about the way in which external-locus-of-control dynamics can get triggered forward has been tremendously helpful in recognizing and neutralizing this problem. When traumatic memories carrying this component get activated, I can *feel* that having a clear understanding of this implicit memory external-locus-of-control phenomena helps me to recognize it for what it is, and then at least partially neutralize it by making behavioral choices based on truth. For example, in the middle of being intensely triggered by the flooded car disaster, recognizing that my triggering included young child external-locus-of-control dynamics helped me get over the hump with respect to acknowledging that the problem was on my side, and then asking the Lord for help (as opposed to remaining stuck in the place of believing that the problem was on his side, and then passively waiting for him to fix it).

---

1. As you probably remember from the discussion of exacerbating factors, second-level triggering is the activation of a variety of specific, memory-anchored negative reactions in response to the suggestion that we might be triggered (chapter 11).

Receive Attunement Regarding
Second-Level Triggering

In the same way that receiving attunement reestablishes access to our relational connection circuits while we're thinking about and feeling the pain from the initial trigger, receiving attunement reestablishes access to our relational connection circuits while we're thinking about and feeling the pain from second-level triggering. For example, just as we can talk to the Lord, receive his attunement, and reestablish access to our relational connection circuits while feeling the pain stirred up by the initial trigger, we can talk to the Lord, receive his attunement, and regain access to our relational connection circuits while feeling the pain stirred up when it feels like the person suggesting we're triggered is blaming us, or the pain stirred up when it feels like this person will use our acknowledgment of being triggered to dismiss our valid concerns. If we recognize what's happening, and then deliberately talk to the Lord and receive his attunement regarding each of the second-level negative reactions, we will be able to regain access to our relational connection circuits *even while still dealing with the painful second-level reactions.* And when we get our relational circuits back on line, even though we are still feeling pain from the second-level triggering, we will feel much stronger and the triggered content will feel much less powerful.

The key is that we need to recognize that second-level issues are getting stirred up, and then deliberately focus on the painful thoughts and emotions associated with our second-level negative reactions (as opposed to focusing on and fighting with the triggers). We need to get words for our pain (for example, "It feels like I'm being blamed and invalidated, and I feel powerless and unable to defend myself."), we need to share this with the Lord (or some other friend who can offer attunement), and we need to receive the attunement they offer. Just as with the primary trigger, trying to fix the problem by focusing on the second-level triggers will actually get in the way of regaining access to our relational circuits.

Furthermore, just as with the traumatic content associated with the initial trigger, receiving attunement and regaining access to our relational circuits *while still connected to the traumatic content underlying the second-level issues* will contribute to the process of permanently resolving them.

Once we have received attunement regarding each of the second-level negative reactions (in the context of some other friendship and/or our relationship with the Lord), it should be much easier to go back into the original situation even though nothing has changed with respect to how the other person is relating to us (even though the other person is still relating to us in ways that trigger second-level reactions).

Self-Validation and Agreement, in the Context of Acknowledging the True Source of the Implicit Memory Content

As mentioned earlier, in the original painful experience we want others to validate the difficulty of the situation. When this comes forward as part of the triggered memory content we will want others to validate our perception that the implicit memory pain is real and valid *in the present*, and that the size and intensity of our reactions are therefore reasonable *in the present*. In the original experience we will also want others to agree with our assessment of the situation, and when this comes forward as part of the triggered memory content we will want others to agree with our VLE confabulated explanations about how triggers in the present are the true source of the implicit memory pain. Unfortunately, the people around us cannot do this with integrity, and when they refuse we will usually feel frustrated, disappointed, invalidated, disbelieved, and misunderstood.

When I am triggered, others do not satisfy this desire-for-validation-and-agreement part of the traumatic implicit memory, and I am consequently feeling frustrated, disappointed, invalidated, disbelieved, and misunderstood, I have learned to remind myself that the full extent of my pain, the intensity of my reactions, and my assessment of the situation will probably all make sense *in the context of the original trauma*. I think of this as my adult self in the present offering validation and agreement to my child self from inside the traumatic memories. When I can remember to do this it helps me avoid getting tripped up by the absence of validation and agreement, and thereby makes it easier to recognize and acknowledge my triggering.

I commented earlier that I sometimes respond with angry resistance when I suggest to myself that I might be triggered, and that this happens when my thought (that I might be triggered) comes with a non-relational attitude of judgment, blame, and invalidation. However (as just described), this negative reaction can be avoided if, *instead of judging, blaming and invalidating,* my adult self in the present is able to *attune* to my child self from inside the traumatic memories by acknowledging unresolved trauma as the true source of the implicit memory content, and then offering validation and agreement in this context.

Part Five

Helping *Others* Who Are Triggered

Parts 2, 3, and 4 have all focused on addressing *our own* triggering and VLE confabulations: a brief summary regarding tools for permanently resolving the underlying trauma, an initial discussion of recognizing and acknowledging our own triggering and confabulations, discussion of exacerbating factors that can make things much more difficult, and, most recently, discussion of insights and tools that can help us in the situations where exacerbating factors make things especially difficult. Now we are going to shift our focus, and talk about insights and tools that will assist us in helping *others* who are triggered.

25

Make Sure to Start with Offering Attunement

The insights discussed earlier regarding relational connection circuits and attunement also have tremendous implications for situations in which we're trying to help others who are triggered, and in our assessment the most important, most strategic application is: *when trying to help a person who is triggered, make sure to attune to him and help him get back into relational mode **before** suggesting that triggering could be contributing to his distress.* As Charlotte and I have examined this point in our relationship, we have noticed that things go MUCH better if we truly attune to the other *before* addressing the question of triggering; and we have also noticed that things consistently go badly when we do not start with attunement.

For example, on some occasions when I get triggered and drop into non-relational mode, Charlotte feels spontaneous compassionate concern for what I am thinking and feeling, and she is glad to be with me even though I am upset and non-relational. In these situations she listens to me, understands my internal experience, empathizes with me, acknowledges my pain, and cares for me. As I *feel* that she is with me, that she is glad to be with me, and that she hears me, understands me, empathizes with me, and cares for me, my relational circuits come back on line; and then *after* I have gotten back into relational mode, she gently suggests that I might be triggered and offers to pray with me to address this possibility. In these situations, even though I can also feel the desire for her to validate my perception that the situation in the present is the true source of all my pain, to validate the intensity of my reactions, and to agree with my VLE confabulated interpretations, and even though I feel a wave of disappointment and frustration when she does not, her attunement usually means a lot more than her lack of agreement *and since I'm receiving attunement I do not also feel invalidated, disbelieved, and misunderstood on top of the disappointment and frustration.* Furthermore, as described above, getting back into relational mode gives me much stronger emotional resources with which to deal with my disappointment and frustration. When Charlotte points out my triggering *after* first attuning to me and helping me get back into relational mode, I am almost always able to receive her suggestion, surrender my VLE confabulations, and acknowledge my traumatic implicit memory.

In contrast, sometimes when I get triggered and lose access to my relational circuits, Charlotte feels like I am blaming her, or at least that there is a mess to be cleaned up, and she tries to get me to recognize and acknowledge my triggering as part of defending herself and/or as part of cleaning up the mess. In these situations she is trying to manage me as opposed to truly attuning to me. Furthermore, when we look at these situations carefully we discover that she is also triggered and that she has also lost access to her relational circuits. When she's triggered and non-relational, and she's trying to get me to recognize and acknowledge my triggering as part of managing me, any not-heard-not-understood-not-cared-for aspect of the original trauma gets intensely triggered, any aspect of the original trauma in which I felt blamed and invalidated gets activated, any aspect of the original trauma in which my admissions were used to dismiss valid concerns gets activated, and things quickly go from bad to worse.

And when we think about it, these observations regarding the importance of starting with attunement make complete sense. Except for implicit memory pain around not receiving validation and agreement, *all of the second-level negative components are inherently incompatible with attunement.* For example, if a child's parents are truly attuned to her they will not blame her for causing abuse; if a child's parents are truly attuned to her they will not use admission of responsibility to dismiss valid concerns; and if a child's parents are truly attuned to her it will be safe for her to admit anything she has done wrong.

Our perception is that when we are *not* triggered, we are operating in *relational mode,* and we are *truly attuned,* our suggestion regarding the possibility of triggering will be totally clean of even the subtlest hints of these negative dynamics. Conversely, our observations are that when we suggest triggering *without* first offering attunement, we are usually also triggered and non-relational; and when we suggest the possibility of triggering while even subtly triggered and non-relational, our suggestion will always be contaminated with varying amounts of second-level negative dynamics. Furthermore, our observations are that only the slightest traces of these second-level negative dynamics are needed to activate any pieces of these dynamics from the original trauma. Therefore, it makes sense that starting with truly offering attunement, and then gently suggesting the possibility of triggering only after attunement has been received, usually avoids the second-level negative reactions; and it makes sense that pointing out clues indicating triggering, without first offering attunement, consistently takes the problem to a whole new level.

More good news is that we have found these insights to be very valuable even in the situations where one of us being triggered and non-relational triggers the other to the point of becoming non-relational, so that we both end up triggered and without access to our relational connection circuits. For example, let's say (just for the sake of this example) that Charlotte is triggered and non-relational, I feel she is blaming me for her traumatic implicit-memory pain, this triggers me to the point that I also drop into non-relational mode, and my immediate impulse is to defend myself by making sure she recognizes and acknowledges how most of her distress is really coming from underlying traumatic memories. If I go ahead with this initial impulse, and focus on her triggering with an attitude contaminated by my triggering and without the benefit of my relational connection circuits, we quickly discover a whole new realm of difficulty.

However, I can pull this whole situation out of the fire if, at this point, I remember these insights regarding relational connection circuits, attunement, and how to avoid the second-level negative reactions. First, I remember that I should start with helping her get back into relational mode by offering attunement, and I therefore stop myself before jumping into my original plan of beginning with pointing out all the evidence indicating that she's triggered. Then, when I try to offer attunement and realize that the ingredients for attunement are not present in my heart (for example, I am *not* glad to be with her), and when I notice that my immediate impulse is to become defensive, I realize that *I* am also triggered and operating in non-relational mode. (If I have any doubts, I can take a moment to confirm this by going over the checklist.) At this point I go through the exercises to get my relational circuits back on line, and then after getting *myself* back into relational mode I acknowledge my own triggering and offer attunement in order to help Charlotte regain access to her relational circuits. Finally, with these pieces all in place, I can address her triggering with a much greater chance of success—I gently suggest that she might be triggered, point out the clues that support this, and offer to pray with her.

So let's apply some Scripture at this point. We all know the verse: "Husbands, love your wives, just as Christ loved the Church."[1] Let's apply this to a totally hypothetical situation: Charlotte starts the fight by getting triggered by some totally innocuous, innocent behavior on my part. In her triggered state she gets angry, unreasonable, and non-relational, and then

---

1. *The Holy Bible: New International Version.* (Grand Rapids: Zondervan, 1984), Ephesians 5:25.

focuses on my behavior, blaming me for her traumatic implicit memory. This triggers me, and then I get angry, defensive, and non-relational. At this point, one option for me is to punish her with sullen, silent emotional withdrawal until she admits that *she* started it, does the work to get *her* relational circuits back on line, acknowledges *her* unreasonable triggered thoughts and emotions, and then offers attunement so that I can more easily acknowledge and deal with my stuff. Another option is for *me* to get *my* relational circuits back on first, *even though she started it*, and then make things easier for her by acknowledging my triggering and offering attunement. Hmmm. "Husbands, love your wives, just as Christ loved the Church." What do you think Jesus would do?

And just in case someone thinks husbands are getting special treatment, we can look at Ephesians 5:1–2 (NRSV), "Therefore be imitators of God . . . and live in love, as Christ loved us and gave Himself up for us," or 1 John 3:16 (Living Bible), "We know what real love is from Christ's example in dying for us. And so we also ought to lay down our lives for our Christian brothers." These verses obviously make space for everybody to get in on the action when it comes to loving others in this humble, vulnerable, sacrificial way.

Along these lines, Charlotte and I have actually come up with an odd kind of competition that creates a win/win situation with respect to conflicts in our relationship. The first person to get back into relational mode, acknowledge triggering, and offer attunement "wins" and gets to wear the "maturity hero" medal. On one hand, it's much more difficult, sacrificial, humbling, and vulnerable to wrestle myself back into relational mode, acknowledge my triggered stuff, and offer attunement *even while she's still non-relational and operating out of traumatic implicit memory*; but I get the satisfaction of winning and being recognized as the maturity hero. On the other hand, it's humbling in another kind of way for Charlotte to win and prove herself to be the maturity hero; but I get the benefit of her regaining access to her relational circuits, acknowledging her triggered stuff, and coming to me with attunement.[2]

---

2. Just in case you're wondering: "Do they really walk around the house wearing a maturity hero medal?" No, we don't—we don't have an actual, physical maturity hero medal. But we do pause for a moment to explicitly recognize the "winner," and then acknowledge him/her as the maturity hero with respect to the particular conflict that has just been resolved.

26

Advanced Attunement Interventions (Advanced Topics)

Advanced topics warning: If many of the concepts presented in *Outsmarting Yourself* are new to you and you are reading through the book for the first time, trying to get the big picture, I encourage you to skip this chapter for now. At this point in your learning journey, slowing down to study these advanced techniques will hinder you from getting the more important overview understanding of how all the pieces fit together. Come back to this material after you have been through the whole book at least once, you feel that you have a good understanding of the basic principles and tools, you have developed some skill with respect to offering attunement, and you want to add some advanced attunement interventions to your toolbox for helping in situations where the person is trying to get you to validate his triggered reactions and pressuring you to agree with his VLE's confabulated explanations regarding the problems that are triggering him.

As we become more skilled with respect to staying in relational mode and offering attunement, we can learn to offer attunement in specific, strategic ways that will be especially helpful in situations that are more difficult.

Attunement without Validation or Agreement

When someone is triggered and the desire for validation of the difficulty of his situation is coming forward as part of the triggered memory content, he will want us to validate his perception that the implicit memory pain is real and valid *in the present,* and that the size and intensity of his reactions are therefore reasonable *in the present.* And if the desire for agreement with his assessment of the situation is coming forward as part of the triggered memory content, he will want us to agree with his VLE confabulated explanations about how triggers in the present are the true source of the implicit memory pain. Unfortunately we cannot do this with integrity, and he will usually feel disappointed and frustrated when he does not receive the desired response. He will also often feel misunderstood, experience the *absence* of validation as *active invalidation,* and experience the *absence* of agreement as *active disagreement/disbelief.*

The most helpful intervention in this situation is to make sure to start with offering attunement. If we look carefully at the ingredients that go into attunement—hearing him, correctly understanding his internal experience, connecting emotionally and empathizing, so that we are with him in his pain, caring about him, and being genuinely glad to be with him—we will notice that none of these require the kind of validation or agreement that I am talking about here. Therefore, even though we are *not* able to validate his pain or reactions as reasonable in the present, and even though we are *not* able to agree with his VLE confabulated explanations, *we can still offer attunement.* When someone is triggered and we offer attunement without validation or agreement, our attunement will usually mean a lot more than our lack of validation or agreement, he will usually feel disappointment and frustration *but without also feeling misunderstood, invalidated, and disbelieved,* and regaining access to his relational circuits will give him much stronger emotional resources with which to deal with his disappointment and frustration.

We have found this intervention of deliberately offering attunement, *even when we cannot offer validation or agreement,* to be tremendously helpful in many difficult situations. To be able to do this we cannot be triggered, we must be operating in relational mode, we need an especially clear grasp of attunement, and there is a skill component that takes some practice to learn, but it's all worth it. Furthermore, attempting this intervention provides valuable information regarding *our* triggering and relational circuits. When I am *not* triggered, I am in relational mode, I truly care for the person, and I am genuinely glad to be with him, offering attunement feels like the most natural and obvious response, even in situations where I cannot honestly validate or agree. However, there are times when I feel immediate internal resistance to the idea of offering attunement, and I feel like I need to make sure he knows I am *not* validating his perceptions or agreeing with his assessments *before* I can offer attunement. Whenever I have had these reactions it has always turned out that I was triggered and had lost access to my relational connection circuits. Sometimes this was subtle and hard to spot, but I have always found it to be true if I looked closely enough.

As you are learning the skill of offering attunement without agreement, it is helpful to be aware of the reality that some situations will be much more challenging than others. In some cases the triggered need for validation and agreement will be less intense, the person will be less blended with the trauma memory package, and her maturity skills will be much stronger. In these situations the person will be able to get over the small bump of frustration and disappointment with relative ease as she receives your attunement and regains access to her relational circuits. However, there are other situations in which the person will be intensely triggered to traumatic memories that include major components of invalidation, she will have minimal insight due to being profoundly blended with the content from the underlying memories, and she will be operating out of child maturity skills corresponding to the age of the original trauma. In these situations the person will have an intense and persistent perceived need for you to validate and agree, and she will not be satisfied with your initial attempts at offering attunement without agreement. I have had Immanuel sessions in which the client repeatedly asked for explicit validation and agreement, and persisted in pushing for this even after I had gone through several rounds of offering attunement. When you encounter more intense and difficult situations, you will need to have more capacity and skill in order to navigate them successfully.

One specific intervention I have found helpful in especially difficult situations is to give special attention to helping the person clarify and get words for what he is thinking and feeling. I have found that I can often redirect the person's demands for validation and agreement with additional questions to help him accurately focus and then articulate the full measure of his thoughts and emotions. Helping him to accurately focus what he is thinking and feeling, and then to articulate this, will dramatically increase the chance that he will be able to recognize what's *really* bothering him,[1] that you will be able to attune to what's really bothering him, that he will be able to receive your attunement, and that he will then regain access to his relational connection circuits.

In especially difficult situations I also deliberately attune to the person's intense desire for validation and agreement, and to his frustration, disappointment, and perception of being misunderstood regarding *not* receiving this validation and agreement.[2] With those who have embraced our understanding of psychological trauma, implicit memory, VLE confabulation, etc., explicitly naming and discussing this aspect of the whole scenario can be part of helping him feel heard and understood (and is therefore part of offering attunement).

---

1. The story I shared in part 1, about my sister, Emily, helping her daughter to recognize that she was missing Charlotte and me provides an excellent example.

2. Again, we are talking about not receiving validation of his perception that the implicit memory pain is real and valid *in the present*, and that the size and intensity of his reactions are therefore reasonable *in the present*. And we are talking about not receiving agreement with his VLE confabulated explanations regarding how *triggers in the present* are the true source of the implicit memory pain.

When you encounter situations that are beyond your current skill level, *focus your attention on keeping yourself in relational mode* even though the other person persists in being upset with you for not providing the desired validation and agreement.

Provisional Validation and Agreement

With those who have embraced our understanding of psychological trauma, implicit memory, etc., there is yet another intervention that can be helpful. You can offer *provisional* validation and agreement—you can anticipate the validation and agreement you will probably be able to offer once the memory pieces have been found and put into place. For example, when trying to help someone recognize that his present experience is being affected by trauma that has come forward as implicit memory, (after starting with attunement) I will make comments along the lines of:

> I think the intensity of your fear and shame, the intensity of your angry reactions, your sense that your wife's behavior has been irreparably hurtful and inappropriate, and your perception that there's nothing you can do that will make any difference—I think it's all gonna make sense as soon as we get all the pieces in place. My intuition tells me that some of this stuff may be coming from memory, and if I'm right about this then everything's gonna make sense and fit together when we find those pieces and put them where they belong—I think when we find the memories where some of this stuff is coming from, and put that together with what happened this afternoon, I'll stand there with you and say: "Wow. Your reactions are completely understandable!"[3]

Anticipating the validation and agreement you will probably be able to offer, once the memory pieces are in place, is an honest, accurately nuanced way of saying, "Your thoughts, emotions, intensity, reactions, and interpretations *are not crazy*," (*misplaced* from old memories into the present, but *not invalid or crazy*).

---

3. This intervention is usually quite helpful when working with someone who has been triggered by something or someone *other than you*, but it does not go over as well if you *are* in the middle of whatever is triggering the person.

27

Simplify the System by Dealing with Stuff on *Our* Side of the Equation

The reader will probably remember that I commented earlier, regarding our teaching examples, that real-life situations are messier and more difficult to sort out because there's almost always triggering and imperfection on both sides. That is, there is almost always something that *we* are contributing to the overall package of messiness and difficulty. Furthermore, we have the most legitimate authority and power to implement changes regarding any aspect of the problem being affected by *our* memories, reactions, thoughts, emotions, and behaviors. Therefore, there is almost always something to be gained by focusing on *our* side of the equation.

Eliminate Any Triggering, Immaturity, or Other Dysfunction That We Are Contributing

One way to simplify the system, making things less messy and less complicated, is to eliminate any ways in which *our* triggering, immaturity, or other dysfunction are contributing. No matter what kind of interpersonal difficulty we are dealing with, simplifying the system by resolving any part of the problem that we are contributing will always help.

For example, during the first ten years of our marriage Charlotte and I noticed that there were certain issues we were unable to resolve—issues that we would discuss (argue about) over and over again, without ever coming to satisfying resolution. In fact, after repeating each of these arguments three to four times per year for ten years, we were so familiar with them that either of us could have described the points that the other would bring forward, and we could have described the seemingly unresolvable endpoints at which each of these "discussions" would terminate before they had even begun. With each of these familiar unresolvable arguments, I would come to a familiar conviction that *I* was right about certain key points, and that we were unable to resolve the conflict because *Charlotte's* thoughts and emotions were unreasonable regarding these points; whereas Charlotte would come to an opposite familiar conviction that *her* formulation was correct, and that *my* unreasonable thoughts and emotions were preventing a reasonable, satisfying solution.

As we came to understand psychological trauma, and how unresolved content comes forward as "invisible" implicit memory that feels true in the present, we were able to recognize that the stuck points in our familiar unresolvable conflicts were being caused by distorted, unreasonable thoughts and emotions coming from traumatic implicit memory content. Exposing and resolving the underlying trauma proved to be fairly straightforward with several of our familiar arguments, and, to our happy amazement, these long-standing "unresolvable" conflicts quickly collapsed as we dealt with the traumatic memories. However, we were not able to resolve all of our long-standing, recurrent arguments so easily, and the points of unresolvable conflict in these remaining arguments then became the differences between our formulations regarding triggering. That is, each of these remaining arguments had specific points where we each thought the *other* person's traumatic implicit memory was the key problem, and that the key to resolution was for the *other* person to acknowledge and resolve his/her triggered, distorted, traumatic implicit memory content.[1]

I especially remember one of these remaining arguments because Charlotte always seemed to win. I was convinced that her triggered stuff was contributing just as much "unresolvable conflict" to the situation as my triggered stuff; but somehow my stuff always seemed bigger, messier, and much easier to spot, whereas her stuff always seemed to be subtle and hard to put your finger on. Working with raw material that was so much more robust, her VLE always came up with much stronger explanations for why my traumatic implicit memory was the key problem, and for why any triggering on her part was relatively unimportant. *With this real-life complexity and messiness of* ***my*** *dramatic triggering obscuring the view, she was never able to perceive the size or importance of* ***her*** *traumatic implicit content.* For several years this same scenario played out each time this particular issue came up. It frustrated me to feel like she never fully owned *her* contribution to the problem, but as much as I hated to admit it, I could also see the dramatic, messy evidence pointing to the presence and importance of my triggering, and we would always eventually end up working on another piece of toxic memory content contributing to my part of the problem.

And then, one day, this issue came up and I was completely calm. I was thinking clearly, my relational circuits were on, and there was no evidence of triggering on my side. In fact, I remember being a bit disoriented by the

---

1. Or, at least it felt like the other person's traumatic implicit memory was *more* of the problem, and that he/she should take responsibility for being more of the problem by working on his/her triggered, distorted toxic implicit memory content first.

strangeness of experiencing this familiar argument from such a different perspective. As I quietly and gently pointed out clues indicating that she was triggered, and that her triggering seemed to be the key to the remaining difficulties, Charlotte actually became more upset than usual as she tried to get things to go back into their old, familiar patterns. Even so, I remained calm, I felt concern for her, and I continued with genuine efforts to find good resolution. At this point another change occurred on Charlotte's side of the experience. With the messiness and complexity of my dramatic triggering out of the way, Charlotte had a new thought that came to her with striking clarity: "There's only one crazy person in the room, and it's not Karl." With the messiness and complexity of my triggering out of the way, Charlotte was able to perceive the unresolved issues on her side more clearly, we were able to work on her stuff, and we finally resolved the last pieces of this particular "irreconcilable" difference.

Own Any Parts of the Other Person's Concerns That *Are* Valid

Another way to help simplify real-life complicated, messy situations is to own any parts of the other person's concerns that *are* valid. I know that when Charlotte and I have been in conflict, we have been surprised by how much it has helped when even one of us has been able to humbly and honestly acknowledge even part of the problem perceived by the other.

For example, several years ago, as part of our ongoing healing journey as a couple, Charlotte challenged me with the concern that I would sometimes bully her. At first I was quite offended by this: "How can you make such an ugly accusation when I never get violent? When I never even make the slightest *hint* of threatening violence? When I never even raise my voice?!" She clarified that I would bully her with my anger, in that I would get angry when I didn't get what I wanted in certain situations, it was very unpleasant to be with me when I was angry, and I would therefore bully her by threatening to punish her with my unpleasant anger if we didn't do things my way. I could not honestly own this either. First of all, I knew that my triggered reactions weren't voluntary—I knew that I didn't *choose* to feel the disappointment and anger that welled up when I would get triggered by things not going my way in certain situations. And I was very consciously aware of being *tempted* to deliberately punish her when I would feel this triggered anger and disappointment, but then battling inside to choose to *not* indulge in this. For example: being tempted to indulge in extended emotional withdrawal, but then choosing to reengage even when I didn't feel like it; or being tempted to drop little comments that would be subtle but still mean, but then choosing to refrain from this even though I really wanted to; or even being tempted to punish her by withholding small attentions and considerations, but then choosing to continue to offer these even though I didn't feel like it. Furthermore, I correctly perceived that Charlotte was triggered when she brought this concern—that some of her energy, thoughts, and emotions were coming from traumatic implicit memory.

However, as I challenged myself with painful honesty and humility I realized that her intuition was correctly perceiving a much more subtle form of bullying. I wouldn't withdraw and refuse to talk to her, I wouldn't drop little mean comments, I wouldn't even stop emptying the trash or refuse to wash the dishes; but I *would* be grumpy and unhappy, I knew this was unpleasant for her, *and I would indulge in remaining grumpy and unhappy even when I knew I could climb out if I wanted to.* Instead of embracing the adult maturity behavior of engaging in clean negotiations, owning my disappointment and talking about it openly when I did not get what I wanted, and then choosing to have a good attitude in relating to Charlotte even though I was disappointed; I would indulge in the infant/child maturity[2] behavior of broadcasting grumpy unhappiness, both as my primary way of communicating disappointment and as a way of motivating Charlotte to give me what I wanted. Furthermore, I could clearly perceive a decision point, where I knew I *could* choose to climb out of my grumpy disappointment and embrace a more pleasant attitude in being with Charlotte, but instead I would choose to linger in my grumpy unhappiness as a very subtle way of punishing her.

When I was finally able to acknowledge this subtle form of bullying, and agree that her concern was certainly valid with respect to this immature and hurtful behavior, reconciliation regarding this particular conflict took a huge step forward.

This proposed intervention also provides additional diagnostic information because owning the parts that are valid will be relatively easy if you are *not* triggered and you are operating in *relational mode*; however, if you *are* triggered and you have dropped into *non-relational mode* it will seem incredibly difficult even to own the parts of the other person's concern that you know are true. If we think for a minute, we can see how this points to a practical application: when someone is bringing concerns to you, and some of what they present is distorted but other parts of their concerns are valid, if you have difficulty acknowledging the valid parts of what they are

---

2. When we are infants or very young (preverbal) children, the only way we have to communicate that we want/need something to be different, and the only way we have to motivate others to care for us, is to engage in some form of messy behavior (such as crying, clinging, screaming, hitting, etc.).

saying, *then you are probably triggered and you have probably lost access to your relational connection circuits.* And this is very valuable information because there is something you can do about it—you can get back into relational mode, and then come back and simplify the situation by owning every concern that you know is true.

Note that "simplifying the system by eliminating any triggering, immaturity, or other dysfunction on your side" and "simplifying the system by owning any concerns that are valid" are very similar but not identical. Simplifying the equation by eliminating your own stuff requires actually finding the underlying roots and *resolving* them, whereas simplifying the equation by owning any concerns that are valid just requires that you *acknowledge* your stuff. It is obviously ideal to permanently resolve the underlying roots, but our experience is that it can be very helpful to just acknowledge that some part of the other person's concern is valid, even before the roots of your problematic contribution have been identified and resolved.

28

Final Thoughts Regarding Others Who Are Triggered

Before concluding this discussion of how to help others who are triggered, I would like to offer several final thoughts.

Whenever Possible, Refer Questions Regarding Possible Triggering to God

If a person has a good relationship with the Lord, it is usually best to refer questions regarding the possibility of triggering to him. Instead of trying to point out evidence that the person is triggered, simply ask: "Would you be willing to ask, 'Lord, *if* there is any component of this pain/upset that is coming from unresolved trauma, would you please bring forward the memories that are contributing?'" A recent experience of my own provides a good example of the way in which this simple question can be tremendously helpful. I was working with a woman who had been terribly wronged by a friend, but she was also intensely triggered, and the triggered implicit memory content was greatly hindering her ability to deal with the situation in a good way. I had foolishly suggested the possibility that she might be triggered *before* first attuning to her and helping her get back into relational mode, and, not surprisingly, she felt painfully invalidated and responded with angry defensiveness. Thankfully, she was also a person of tremendous integrity who had a very close relationship with the Lord, and when I asked if she would be willing to ask the Lord to show her if memories were contributing to any part of her pain, she realized that there could be no valid reason for refusing this proposal. In fact, my question helped her to realize that the Lord was the one person she *could* trust to address this tremendously vulnerable question. She asked the Lord for guidance, he helped her identify and resolve the underlying memories, and she was then much more able to deal with the difficult situation in a life-giving way.

In other situations, I have used the following variation on the same theme: "I realize that some part of your distress is a reasonable response to the situation in the present; but since we know that it always helps to identify and resolve any triggered component, why don't we start with asking the Lord to help us recognize and resolve any part of your distress that comes from old stuff? Even if only 10 percent is from implicit memory, it will be easier to deal with the remainder of the problem once this piece has been removed."[1]

Especially *Unhelpful*

Sometimes it can be valuable to think backwards. That is, it can be valuable to identify things that would be especially problematic, so that we can be sure to avoid them. When trying to help someone who is triggered, the following approaches are especially *un*helpful:

- Repeatedly insist that we know more about what the person is thinking and feeling than she does.

- Don't acknowledge that there are two people in the conversation.

- Keep insisting that we are right and she is wrong with respect to her thoughts and emotions.

Once again, this brings us back to relational circuits. If our relational circuits are on line and functioning properly, we will feel compassionate concern regarding the other person's thoughts and emotions, and our true hearts will provide good guidance with respect to the gentlest, most helpful ways to talk about the possibility that the other person is triggered. In contrast, if we are operating in non-relational mode we will be much more likely to fall into one or more of the unhelpful behaviors just described.

PLEASE Don't Let Your VLE Misuse This Information

My verbal-logical-explainer has been thrilled to get all this new, fascinating, research-based information about implicit memory, confabulation, and central nervous system extrapolation. Just the other day Charlotte got triggered, and understanding these phenomena made it so much easier to see how the distorted thoughts and emotions from *her* traumatic implicit memory were contributing to the disagreement we were having. Once upon a time all I could offer were vague, general comments about why I thought her unresolved issues were the real problem, but working with this new information is *so* much more satisfying. Not only was I able to see and point out a variety of specific clues indicating that she was triggered,

---

1. Note that it is still best to start by offering attunement until the person has gotten back into relational mode. These specific interventions have been helpful in messy situations where I failed to do this, but addressing the difficult issue of possible triggering will go even more smoothly if you use these gentle interventions after first offering attunement and helping the person regain access to his relational circuits.

I was also able to explain why she was having so much difficulty recognizing and acknowledging her triggering. I was even able to point out the holes in her VLE confabulated attempts to blame her triggered thoughts and emotions on me. Unfortunately, instead of submitting to my brilliant formulation and agreeing that the whole problem would be resolved if she would just deal with her stuff, Charlotte perceived that *I* was triggered, that distorted content from *my* traumatic implicit memory was contributing to our disagreement, and that I was using all this new information about implicit memory, the VLE, and CNS extrapolation as part of my attempt to defend myself and blame her. Eventually, we were both able to acknowledge that we were both triggered, but my "new and improved" VLE confabulations actually made the process more difficult.

The moral of this story is: "PLEASE don't let your VLE misuse this information." Your VLE will want to use the information from this book as a new,

---

SURGEON GENERAL'S WARNING:
Letting Your VLE Misuse This Information
Is Hazardous to Your Relationships.

---

powerful resource in the never-ending effort to explain why the problems in front of you are always somebody else's fault. In most difficult situations, *all* the people involved, *including you*, will be at least subtly triggered, and your VLE will want to use the information from this book to help explain why the *whole* problem is being caused by the other people's triggering, VLE confabulated explanations, immaturity, etc. PLEASE don't let your VLE use this information to justify your triggered reactions, defend your confabulated explanations, and blame and/or invalidate others. If you do indulge in this subtle but deadly trap, you would be better off if you had never learned about implicit memory, the VLE, and central nervous system extrapolation.

Just so you won't beat yourself up when you fail, I will confess that I have already caught myself doing this on a number of occasions. The earlier example was somewhat exaggerated to make the point, but slightly less dramatic scenarios have certainly occurred in real life. And I'm pretty sure you will also occasionally fall into this trap, no matter how hard you try to avoid it. As described earlier, *the key is to be on the lookout for any place where you are focusing on someone else's triggering without first attuning; and when you recognize this pattern, check for clues that **you** are triggered,* *especially checking the status of your relational connection circuits, and then take care of **your** stuff before turning your attention back to the other person.*

The ideal is for all of the people involved in a given situation to understand this material, and for each person to be voluntarily, proactively embracing the humbling challenge of exposing and neutralizing his own traumatic implicit memory and VLE confabulations. It has been an incredible gift to Charlotte and me to be able to do this in our marriage (at least most of the time). However, there will be many situations in which one or more players have not yet encountered this information regarding implicit memory, etc. In these difficult scenarios it can sometimes be very helpful (ask the Lord for wisdom) to share this information about traumatic implicit memory, VLE confabulation, etc. If you decide to do this, *make sure that you lead by example* after sharing the information. If you want to be especially humble, heroic, and helpful, spend the first several months after introducing this material repeatedly owning your own stuff, without even hinting that the other person has at least as much triggering and VLE confabulation as you do. This humble, heroic approach will be extremely difficult for most of us, but if you can do it, it will also be extremely helpful.

We Cannot Override Another's Choice to Turn Away from Relational Connection

Sadly, a person can choose to indulge in bitterness and/or self-pity and/or rebellion in ways that turn away from relational connection. If a person persists in these choices he will not be able to receive attunement and he will remain in non-relational mode regardless of how well we apply the principles and tools just described. In these situations there is nothing we can do to override his free-will choices—we cannot force him to receive our attunement, regain access to his relational circuits, and return to constructive, life-giving interactions. However, even in these especially unhappy situations, we *can* focus on keeping ourselves in relational mode even though we feel helpless and powerless,[2] we can ask the Lord for grace to persist in loving those who are hurting us, and we can ask the Holy Spirit to work in the person's heart in the mysterious ways that only the Lord understands.

Emphatic caveat: When I am subtly triggered and non-relational people respond poorly to my attempts at pseudo-attunement, and it is soberingly easy for me to then conclude that they are making a deliberate choice to turn away from relationship. Therefore, if we think someone is persisting in a deliberate choice to refuse attunement and turn away from relational

---

2. Working on any helpless/powerless traumatic memories that are getting stirred up is often part of keeping myself in relational mode in these difficult situations.

connection, we need to take a time-out to check our relational connection circuits, impliment any interventions necesssary to make sure that we are *strongly* in relational mode, and then carefully reevaluate the situation. At the very least, we need to make sure that the person has a chance to experience genuine attunement in a context where we are truly in relational mode. And remember, **if you feel judgmental toward the other person, then you have lost access to your relational circuits and you are** *not* **in relational mode.**

Part Six

Summary, Synthesis, and Answers to Frequently Asked Questions

29

Summary Points and Synthesis Conclusions

In closing, I would like to offer a combination of summary points and synthesis conclusions:

- Trauma occurs when we fail to successfully process painful experiences, and this failure to successfully process results in active toxic content that is carried in the memories for these traumatic experiences.

- Under certain circumstances, and especially during childhood, we can fail to process painful events that may seem minor; and this means that psychological trauma can sometimes be caused by relatively small painful events. Traumatic memories are therefore much more common than most people realize, and the manifestations of unresolved trauma can therefore be much more subtle than most people realize.

- When traumatic memories are activated, the toxic content they carry comes forward and powerfully affects our perceptions, thoughts, beliefs, emotions, abilities, and choices.

- This traumatic, toxic content comes forward as "invisible" implicit memory, *so that it feels true in the present, and is not recognized as coming from underlying unresolved trauma.* Our VLEs come up with explanations that focus on the triggering stimuli in the present. Our central nervous system extrapolators fill in most of the holes in the VLE confabulated explanations, and good old denial and self-deception take care of anything that is left over. The end result is that we usually believe the explanations that the VLE makes up, accept the implicit memory content as true in the present, and blame the triggers as if they are the original source of the implicit memory content that is actually coming from the underlying traumatic memories—we blame the triggers as if they are the true and complete reason we're feeling bad.

- If we perceive that a specific person is responsible for the triggering situation, we will only feel heard, validated, safe, and ready for reconciliation if she takes full responsibility for the implicit memory traumatic content. This creates an irreconcilable difference because she cannot honestly do so.

- If we are triggered by some aspect of our interactions with the Lord, then all of the above dynamics will result in traumatic implicit memory content and VLE confabulations undermining our relationship with him. Our perception is that *traumatic implicit memories and VLE confabulations combine to create some of the most important blockages hindering people from perceiving the Lord's presence and from connecting with him more intimately.*

- Recognizing, acknowledging, and taking responsibility for our traumatic implicit memories and VLE confabulations helps us choose righteous behavior, even before anything *feels* different.

- Recognizing and acknowledging our traumatic implicit memories and surrendering our VLE confabulations opens the door to the possibility of finding and resolving the underlying traumatic memories. Until we recognize and acknowledge our traumatic implicit memories and surrender our VLE confabulations, we are not even asking the question: "Should I deal with underlying memories?"

- When we are able to identify the underlying traumatic memories, the moment the pieces all come together so that it *feels* true that our pain is really coming from the memories, *all the negative thoughts and emotions we had transferred onto others drop off of them.* For example, it no longer feels true that bad Charlotte is causing my pain by beating me at Scrabble and making insensitive comments, and I once again perceive her as my ally instead of the source of my pain. I may still feel the negative thoughts and emotions from the trauma, but it no longer feels true that Charlotte is causing them.

- When we successfully work through a traumatic memory, this particular package of toxic content is *permanently* resolved so that it will never again cause trouble.

- An especially powerful point of good news is that Jesus understands the healing process, he wants to help us heal, and for those who are able to establish a strong, interactive connection with him, *healing for traumatic memories becomes surprisingly simple as the Lord leads the person through each step of the process.*

- There are exacerbating factors (such as maturity from the age of memory and second-level triggering) that can make it much more difficult to recognize, acknowledge, and take responsibility for our traumatic implicit memory and VLE confabulations. Fortunately, being aware of these exacerbating factors enables us to at least partially neutralize them.

- Learning to recognize when we lose access to our relational circuits is both the easiest-to-use and the most effective tool for helping us recognize the times when we are triggered.

- Recognizing that we have lost access to our relational connection circuits, and then choosing to take deliberate steps to get them back on line, will dramatically reduce the negative effects of our traumatic implicit memory and VLE confabulations. Furthermore, understanding with respect to relational circuits and attunement, and specific tools that apply this understanding (for example, attunement without agreement), can further neutralize the exacerbating factors discussed in part 3.

Finally, I would like to make several comments specifically regarding traumatic implicit memory, VLE confabulations, and relationships.

- When we are trying to help another person who is triggered, it is extremely important to help him get his relational circuits back online by offering attunement *before* suggesting the possibility of triggering. Having the resources associated with relational mode back on line will make it much easier for him to surrender VLE confabulations and acknowledge traumatic implicit memory.

- No matter what kind of interpersonal difficulty we are dealing with, simplifying the system by eliminating any triggering, immaturity, or other dysfunction on *our* side will always help.

- As Charlotte and I have applied the principles and tools presented in this book, we have experienced steadily increasing joy in our marriage. And this makes sense: *relational connection is the source of joy, and relational conflict breaks relational connection. Applying these principles and tools to resolve and prevent relational conflict will therefore result in much more joy.*

- As mentioned earlier, God has created us to be relational beings, and this seems to be one of the most important aspects of his plan for us. The enemy, not surprisingly, therefore makes a special effort to attack relationships. *Understanding and applying the principles and tools presented in this book can help us to outwit the devil's schemes to disrupt the body of Christ through relational conflict.*

- Our most important relationship is our relationship with the Lord—the relational connection that God designs and desires to be the foundation and center of our lives. The most costly effects of traumatic implicit memory content and VLE confabulations are injuries to our relationship with the Lord, and the most important purpose for understanding and applying the principles and tools presented in this book is therefore to prevent and/or repair these injuries. *Understanding and applying these principles and tools will help us to outwit the devil's schemes to disrupt the relational connection that God designs and desires to be the foundation and center of our lives.*

How many of you have watched *Star Wars,* and thought, "I wish I could be a Jedi knight, defending the innocent and battling evil in heroic confrontations"? How many of you have watched the *Lord of the Rings,* and thought, "I wish I could stand beside Aragorn, fighting the forces of darkness in an heroic and righteous quest"? Well, I haven't seen any death stars, orcs, or trolls lately, but our true enemy makes the *Star Wars* emperor and Middle Earth's Sauron look like my grandmother, and Jesus—our commander, who is always standing beside us—makes Aragorn look like a Cub Scout (a good and heroic Cub Scout, but a Cub Scout nonetheless). We have our opportunities if we choose to accept them. For example, every single one of us will face the challenge of being triggered and non-relational while in conflict with others who are also triggered and non-relational, *and often in situations where they started it!* In these situations, you can be courageous and heroic in choosing to get *your* relational circuits back on first, acknowledging *your* triggering, and then offering attunement.

Men, if you want to be courageous and heroic in serving your wives, your children, your friends, and your communities, then be courageous and heroic in the battle to expose and neutralize your triggered traumatic content and VLE confabulations. Women, if you want to be courageous and heroic in serving your husbands, your children, your friends, and your communities, then be courageous and heroic in the battle to expose and neutralize your triggered traumatic content and VLE confabulations. Believers, if you want to be courageous and heroic in serving the Lord, then be courageous and heroic in the battle to expose and neutralize your triggered traumatic content and VLE confabulations. *Let us be courageous and heroic in exposing and neutralizing our triggered traumatic content and VLE confabulations, so that we can foil the enemy's schemes for division and fulfill the Lord's plan for thriving relationships, healthy community, and a unified, relational church that will take his love to the world.*[1]

---

1. You may think I'm being melodramatic in my use of "courageous" and "heroic," but if you take me up on this challenge you'll discover that I'm not overstating my case. In fact, once you have gotten some practice with recognizing and acknowledging your stuff, and have

We invite you to join us in the following prayer:

Lord, we thank you for the Immanuel truth that you are always with us, and we ask that you would help us to perceive your presence.

Lord, we want to be courageous and heroic in the battle to expose and neutralize our triggered traumatic content and VLE confabulations—give us the grace to do so.

Lord, we want to foil the enemy's schemes for division—give us the grace to do so.

Lord, we want to cooperate with your plan for thriving relationships, healthy community, and a unified, relational church that will take your love to the world—please give us the courage, the grace, and the love that we will need to fulfill this vision.

Amen.

---

strengthened your capacity for vulnerability, if you are feeling especially courageous and heroic you can take the step of *inviting* others to help you in the narcissistically mortifying process of exposing your triggered traumatic content and confabulated explanations.

30

Frequently Asked Questions

Are You Saying That All Painful Thoughts and Emotions Come from Underlying Traumatic Memories?

After our many, many, many comments about the pervasiveness and importance of triggering and traumatic implicit memory content, some ask if we believe that *all* painful thoughts and emotions come from underlying traumatic memories. The simple answer is no. Sometimes real problems in the present cause painful thoughts and emotions that are valid and appropriate in the present. As already discussed at great length, we are convinced that triggered traumatic implicit memory content contributes to our painful thoughts and emotions much more than most of us realize, but we are also convinced that sometimes real problems in the present cause painful thoughts and emotions that are fully valid and appropriate in the present.

A very important point to remember when trying to figure out whether your pain is truly caused by problems in the present or whether it is triggered is that most painful situations include a mixture of both. One especially common scenario is for real problems in the present to cause painful thoughts and emotions that are valid and appropriate in the present, but then these thoughts and emotions resonate with unresolved trauma, so that traumatic memory content gets activated and comes forward as well. The end result is a situation in which "invisible" traumatic implicit memory is contributing to the person's painful thoughts and emotions, and at the same time some of the pain is fully legitimate and appropriate in the present.

Charlotte's and my experience with a miscarriage provides a good example. We had gone in for the three-month visit that is a routine part of prenatal care in our ob/gyn's practice, and at the end of our appointment Dr. Phillips[1] said, "The ultrasound room is open—if you want, we can just take a quick peek." As soon as Dr. Phillips began rubbing the ultrasound probe on Charlotte's abdomen, we could see our child on the screen. Even as early as twelve weeks, we could easily make out the head, rib cage, arms, and legs of a small body. We could count the ribs, and could even see fingers and toes on our child's hands and feet. Charlotte and I were excitedly pointing and exclaiming about the many details so clearly visible on the screen, but I

---

1. Not her real name.

noticed that Dr. Phillips was very quiet. Then she said, "What's concerning me is that I can't find a heartbeat." Even as she was finishing her sentence, I realized that she had been going back and forth through the rib cage for the last several minutes, and a beating heart would have been easy and obvious to see. Advanced ultrasound confirmed that our child had died.

This was obviously very painful, and we experienced intense grief and disappointment that was fully valid and appropriate in the present. However, this pain corresponding to our real loss in the present also resonated with grief and disappointment carried in unresolved trauma, and caused the old pain to come forward as well. For the first couple weeks after the miscarriage, we were intensely triggered every day and spent a lot of time working through traumatic implicit memory content that was being brought to the surface. And then, as we worked through more and more of the old pain, our grief in the present felt increasingly free from triggered contributions. Eventually we got to a place where we were still grieving, but we were *not* triggered, and we felt quiet joy in being together. It was actually quite strange. We were sad and crying, but it felt very clean. Even as we were crying, we felt peaceful. And even as we were feeling grief, we were also glad to be together. Some may find this hard to believe, but we felt grief at losing our child, a peaceful calm, and joy from being glad to be with each other all at the same time.

"Brain Science, Psychological Trauma, and the God Who Is with Us ~ Part II" provides additional thoughts regarding painful thoughts and emotions that are fully valid and appropriate in the present (as opposed to coming from traumatic implicit memory). See especially the section in the pre-introduction titled, "Right-hemisphere emotions, left-hemisphere emotions, and other emotional experiences," and the section toward the end titled, "Painful experiences, with optimal scenario of moving through the pathway smoothly and successfully."

Can the Immanuel Approach Be Used with Children?

The really, really short answer is yes.

Now for a somewhat longer answer. As described in chapter 7, we are getting a steady stream of very encouraging stories from people who are using the Immanuel approach for emotional healing with children. Furthermore, we are now also getting stories from parents who are incorporating the Immanuel approach into day-to-day family life. For example, Dr. Ian M., a friend of ours and psychologist in Winnipeg, Canada, has been teaching his children about the Immanuel approach for life. He has talked to them about the truth that Jesus (Immanuel) is always with us, he has taught them how to perceive the Lord's presence and establish an interactive connection, he has taught them that they can turn to Jesus and engage with him as a living person when they encounter difficulties in life, and they have discovered that the Lord can and does respond to them—in their hearts/to their spirits. With this foundation in place, Ian can easily use the Immanuel approach as part of day-to-day parenting interactions.

For example, he was at the stove one evening, frying hamburger for dinner, when his four-year-old daughter, Selah, came into the kitchen and informed him that she needed a drink of juice. When he told her that he would be glad to get her a drink, but that she would have to wait a few minutes until he was done with the hamburger, she responded with, "No, I need a drink of juice right now!" And when he repeated that she would have to wait a few minutes, she began to escalate into tantrum mode, with crying, tears, and increasingly intense demands of "I need a drink now! I need juice right now! I need juice *now, **now, Now, NOW!***"

At this point Ian knelt down in front of his daughter, face to face, eyes to eyes, and said, in a gentle, soft voice, "Honey, would you be willing to ask Jesus what he wants to say to you?" Immediately her crying stopped, and Selah held up her hand towards Ian and said, "Okay Dad, be quiet." Not in a harsh way, but more with an intended meaning along the lines of, "It's Jesus' turn to talk now. Please be quiet so I can hear him." She paused, completely still and quiet for maybe ten seconds, and then said, "Jesus said that I need to be patient and I need to wait." When Ian asked, "Okay, so what are you going to do?" She respond promptly with, "I'm gonna do what Jesus asked me to do, Dad—I'm gonna be patient and wait."

Selah then just stood beside Ian, smiling, watching, and waiting quietly and patiently for him to finish frying the hamburger. It seemed to Ian that Selah continued to perceive Jesus' lingering presence and feel connected to him as she was waiting, and she seemed quite pleased that she now had what she needed to be able to wait. Quite impressive, really, when you consider that she had to wait five to ten minutes before he was able to get her the juice, and this is a very long time for a four-year-old who was escalating to a tantrum with demands for immediate action only moments earlier.

As of November 2011, the summary from all the information we have gathered is that even very young children can embrace the Immanuel approach to life,[2] and when they do this it provides an ideal foundation

---

2. The Immanuel approach to life is based on the same principles as the Immanuel approach to emotional healing, and uses the same tools, but it is much more comprehensive. The wider Immanuel approach to life *includes* healing for psychological trauma, but clearly recognizes that this is only *one part* of God's agenda for working in our lives. For example, the Lord also wants to build our capacity, grow our maturity, and spend time "just" being with us as a

for routine parent-child interactions (and any other aspects of day-to-day life). Our cumulative information to date also indicates that the Immanuel approach for emotional healing is particularly safe and effective when working with children to resolve psychological trauma. Special safety and effectiveness for emotional healing work makes sense, since helping the child establish an interactive connection with the Lord at the beginning of the session, coaching her to focus on Jesus and keep going back to Jesus throughout the session, and having the initial positive connection as a safe place she can go back to if she gets stuck, would all be expected to contribute to making the Immanuel approach especially gentle and safe. For these reasons, we strongly encourage using the Immanuel approach when working with children. We especially encourage using the Immanuel approach, with generous initial time "just" being with Jesus, if the child has had negative experiences with any other emotional healing tools.

We are hoping to eventually present a much more thorough discussion of using the Immanuel approach with children. In the meantime, see the essay, "The Immanuel Approach/Theophostic-Based Emotional Healing with Children," for what we currently have available.

Can the Immanuel Approach Be Used with Non-Christians?

This may surprise some readers, but we have seen consistently positive results when using the Immanuel approach with any non-Christians who are willing to try it. In fact, willingness to try it seems to be the only prerequisite.[3] When discussing the option of using the Immanuel approach with someone who is not yet a Christian, I explain what would be involved and then offer an invitation along the lines of, "You don't have to agree with me, and you don't have to believe this stuff, but would you be willing to try it? Would you be willing to let me pray in this way, let Jesus be with you (if he actually exists), and then simply describe whatever happens?" Initially I didn't know what to expect, but I decided to go ahead and try it and I've been thrilled with the results. Almost every non-Christian who has been willing to "just

---

friend. Furthermore, the Immanuel approach to life takes the tools for helping us connect with the Lord outside of special "sessions," with the ultimate goal of helping us get to the place where we perceive the Lord's presence, and *abide* in an interactive connection with Jesus, as our usual, normal, baseline condition as we walk through life each day. For a much more detailed discussion of these points, see "Brain Science, Psychological Trauma, and the God Who Is with Us ~ Part I: A Psychiatrist's Journey–A Brief Introduction to the Immanuel Approach."

3.   Note that "willingness to try it" does not mean going through the motions externally, but with no agreement or cooperation internally.

go ahead and try it" has eventually[4] been able to perceive the Lord's presence and then experience some kind of positive interaction with him. We now have a number of stories in which people were willing to try the Immanuel approach, even though they were not yet Christians, and then decided to give their lives to the Lord after having powerful, beautiful encounters with Jesus in the context of the emotional healing session.

Dr. Wilder's recent Immanuel approach training seminar in Asia, described earlier,[5] provides a good example. As you may remember, two of the people attending the seminar started the week as non-Christians. However, even though they were not Christians they were still willing to try the exercises; and by the end of the week both of them had experienced the Lord's living, personal, Immanuel presence, received healing from him, and decided to follow him. Our May 2009 seminar in Panama provides another example. As you may remember, a non-Christian mental health professional found one of the flyers for the seminar and decided to attend. However, even though he was not a Christian he was still willing to participate in the Immanuel approach group exercise that we included at the end of the seminar; and he was astonished by the results—he experienced God as a loving father for the first time in his life, he went to several traumatic memories and received profound healing in each of them, and then he ended the exercise by deciding to follow the Lord. Rhonda and Danny Calhoun's experience with Sarah and Claire provides a third example. As you may remember, when her non-Christian friend asked her for help, Sarah suggested they try Immanuel prayer. However, even though she was not a Christian she was still willing to try it; and after "close encounters of the Jesus kind," she said yes in response to a direct invitation from the Lord to be part of his family.

Another phenomenon that we have observed with respect to non-Christians is that many of them have chosen to turn away from Jesus in response to traumatic experiences with Christians/Christianity. The good news is that when we identify this history and help them resolve it, they often embrace Jesus gladly. As I write this, I'm working with two people who are having exactly this experience. In a recent session with one of these people, he commented spontaneously, "Everything that has felt true about God, for my whole life, . . . [describes many details, all negative]—it's totally different than what I'm experiencing with the Jesus I'm encountering in these prayer

---

4. An initial block of troubleshooting has been necessary in many of these sessions, before the person was able to perceive Jesus' presence, and then more troubleshooting is sometimes necessary before the person is able to have positive interactions with him.

5. See chapter 7, pages 78 and 79.

sessions, . . . [describes many details, all positive]." At the end of another recent session he popped out with, "Wow! This is actually *good* news!"

Is the Immanuel Approach Consistent with/Supported by Scripture?

As the Immanuel approach has become more widely known, people have appropriately raised the question, "Is it Biblical?" Our perception is that the Immanuel approach, for emotional healing and for life,[6] is clearly consistent with and strongly supported by the Christian Scriptures.

A FEW BASICS

To begin with, well known verses unambiguously teach that the Lord is always with us, that we should expect to be able to perceive his presence, and that he wants us to have a living, interactive relationship with him. For example:

- In Matthew 28:19–20, Jesus says, "Therefore go and make disciples of all nations, baptizing them in the name of the Father and of the Son and of the Holy Spirit, and teaching them to obey everything I have commanded you. And surely I am with you always, to the very end of the age."

- In John 14:21, Jesus says, "Whoever has my commands and obeys them, he is the one who loves me. He who loves me will be loved by my Father, and I too will love him and show myself to him."

- In John 15:4-5, Jesus says, "Abide in me as I abide in you. Just as the branch cannot bear fruit . . . unless it abides in the vine, neither can you unless you abide in me. I am the vine, you are the branches. Those who abide in me and I in them bear much fruit, because apart from me you can do nothing." NRSV

- In Revelation 3:20, Jesus says, "Listen! I am standing at the door, knocking; if you hear my voice and open the door, I will come in to you and eat with you and, you with me." NRSV

SCRIPTURAL SUPPORT FOR DELIBERATE APPRECIATION

Deliberate appreciation is included in the Immanuel approach process at several points;[7] and, as described in chapter 19 (pages 203–206), this

---

6. For comments regarding the wider Immanuel approach to life, see footnote 2, above.

7. For a detailed discussion of the points at which deliberate appreciation is included in the Immanuel approach process, see "Brain Science, Psychological Trauma, and the God Who Is with Us ~ Part I: A Psychiatrist's Journey – A Brief Introduction to the Immanuel Approach,"

component of the Immanuel approach is strongly supported by many scriptural references.

SCRIPTURAL SUPPORT FOR PRIORITIZING A LIVING,
INTERACTIVE CONNECTION WITH GOD
An interactive connection with Jesus is foundational for the Immanuel approach process. Furthermore, our ultimate goal with the Immanuel approach is getting to the place where we perceive the Lord's presence, and *abide* in an interactive connection with Jesus, as our usual, normal, baseline condition as we walk through life each day. To put this another way, in both the Immanuel approach to emotional healing and the wider Immanuel approach to life,[8] the number-one, highest priority is to be *with* God. According to the team of more than fifty people who have spent five years preparing *The Renovare Spiritual Formation Bible*,[9] being "with God" is the central, organizing theme of the whole Bible. Quoting directly from the general introduction:

> . . . the unity of the Bible is discovered in the development of life "with God" as a reality on earth, centered in the person of Jesus. We might call this the Immanuel Principle of life.

So, according to these scholars and authors, the entire Bible happens to support this particular point.

ADDITIONAL DISCUSSION REGARDING SCRIPTURAL SUPPORT
For extensive additional discussion, see the "Biblical Basis" page of www .immanuelapproach.com, and also Appendices 3 through 10 in Patricia A. Velotta, *Immanuel: A Practicum* (Libertyville, IL: This Joy! Books, 2011).

How Do You Include the Immanuel Approach in the Care of People with Clinical Mental Illnesses? In the Care of People Taking Psychiatric Medications?

These important questions are addressed extensively in the essays below (all available as free downloads from www.kclehman.com).

- "ADD/ADHD and Emotional Healing"

---

and "Brain Science, Psychological Trauma, and the God Who Is with Us ~ Part V: The Immanuel Approach, Revisited" (available as free downloads from www.immanuelapproach.com).

8. For comments regarding the wider Immanuel approach to life, see footnote 2, above.

9. *The Renovare Spiritual Formation Bible: New Revised Standard Version with Deuterocanonical Books*, Editor: Richard J. Foster; General Editors: Gayle Beebe, Lynda L. Graybeal, Thomas C. Oden, Dallas Willard; Consulting Editors: Walter Brueggemann, Eugene H. Peterson. (New York, NY: HarperCollins Publishers), 2005.

- "Bipolar Disorder and the Immanuel Approach/Theophostic®-based Emotional Healing: General Comments and Frequently Asked Questions"

- "Depression & the Immanuel Approach/Theophostic®-based Emotional Healing: General Comments and Frequently Asked Questions"

- "The Immanuel Approach, Theophostic®, Mental Illness, and Medication"

- "Mind and Brain: Separate but Integrated"

- "Mood, Monthly Cycle, and the Immanuel Approach/Theophostic®"

- "Obsessive-Compulsive Disorder (OCD) and the Immanuel Approach: General Comments and Frequently Asked Questions"

- "The Place of the Immanuel Approach/Theophostic®-based Emotional Healing in the Treatment of Clinical Disorders"

- "Psychosis and Psychotic Symptoms: Definitions and Diagnostic Considerations"

- "Schizophrenia and the Immanuel Approach/Theophostic®-based Emotional Healing: General Comments and Frequently Asked Questions"

How/Where Can I Get Training Regarding the Immanuel Approach?

It probably won't surprise anybody to hear that an increasing number of people have been contacting us with questions along the lines of: "I would like to use the Immanuel approach in my _____(psychotherapy practice, ministry, church, small group, family, marriage, etc.). How/where do I get training that will enable me to do this?" As mentioned earlier, at this time we do not have any kind of training institute, we do not offer internships/apprenticeships, and we are not providing any regular schedule of seminars designed to train people to use the Immanuel approach. In the absence of these kinds of Immanuel approach training packages, appendix C offers a summary of the resources that *are* currently available, and then describes how to use these resources in putting together a do-it-yourself Immanuel approach training program.

We do, occasionally, provide training events related to the Immanuel approach, and all relevant information regarding these seminars will be posted on the "Events" page of the Immanuel approach website (www.immanuelapproach.com). As we become aware of others providing training related to the Immanuel approach, we will post brief descriptions of the individuals/ministries providing training, along with contact information, in the "Trainers" section on the "Training" page of this same website. Information regarding trainers will also be increasing-ly available through the Immanuel network directory (accessed from the "Referrals" page of www.immanualapproach.com), as self-identified trainers post profiles.

How/Where Can I Find Someone to Facilitate Immanuel Approach Emotional Healing for Me?

It probably won't surprise anyone to hear that we also receive many, many requests for assistance in finding a therapist/emotional healing minister who can facilitate Immanuel approach emotional healing. We are working hard to train Immanuel approach facilitators, and to post information regarding these people on the "Referrals" page of our Immanuel approach website (www.immanuelapproach.com), but the small number of facilitators we are currently aware of are profoundly unable to provide sessions for the large number of people who want them. At least for now, many people will have to find or recruit their own facilitators. See appendix C, part III ("Finding/ Recruiting Your Own Immanuel Approach Facilitator") for our thoughts regarding how one might pursue doing so.

What about Plain Old Sin?

At one of our seminars, after we finished presenting this material a gentleman in the audience asked, "So what about plain old sin? Does all this stuff about trauma, triggering, implicit memory, the VLE, central nervous system extrapolation, immaturity, and non-relational mode explain away sin as a cause for hurtful behavior?" I'm not a theologian, and so can't provide a systematic theological discussion, but I would like to offer a couple of thoughts. First, I perceive that we can sin by choosing to persist in non-relational mode. That is, when the Lord or others in our community are offering attunement, we can make a sinful choice to refuse their attunement by turning away in bitterness and/or self-pity and/or rebellion. And in my experience, this sinful choice to persist in non-relational mode seems to be closely associated with choices to engage in various combinations of immature, inconsiderate, selfish, self-centered, judgmental, mean, and negligent behavior.

My second thought is just an observation. When I'm free of triggering and in relational mode, I rarely engage in sinful behavior. That is, when I correctly perceive reality; when my spontaneous, normal experience is to feel relationally connected and to feel the desire for connection; when I experience others as relational beings, I am aware of others' true hearts, I feel compassionate concern regarding what others are thinking and feeling, I perceive the presence of others as a source of joy, and I'm glad to be with them; when I both want to offer attunement and am able to offer attunement; when I'm flexible and creative even when unexpected circumstances require that I change my plans at the last minute, and little things don't "get under my skin;" when my spontaneous, normal experience is to perceive others as allies, even in difficult interpersonal situations; when I want to join with them in the collaborative process of exploring the situation together; when I want to understand their perspectives; and when I want to join with them in the collaborative process of working together to find a mutually satisfying solution, *I rarely engage in immature, inconsiderate, selfish, self-centered, judgmental, mean, or negligent behavior.*

In contrast, when I'm triggered into non-relational mode, I find myself constantly slipping into sinful behavior. That is, when "invisible" traumatic implicit memory feels true in the present and gets directed at and/or blamed on those around me; when my spontaneous experience includes the absence of feeling relationally connected and I don't even want to be connected; when I don't perceive others as relational beings, I'm not aware of other's true hearts, I don't feel compassionate concern regarding what others are thinking and feeling, I'm not glad to be with them, and I don't experience their presence as a source of joy; when I don't want to offer attunement and I'm not able to offer attunement; when I'm rigid and unable to think outside the box; when even small problems irritate me; when I perceive others as adversaries in difficult interpersonal situations; when I tend towards judging, interrogating, and focusing on trying to "fix" the situation, and when I perceive others as resources to be used or problems to be solved, *I constantly find myself falling into various combinations of immature, inconsiderate, selfish, self-centered, judgmental, mean, and negligent behavior.*

From a very concrete, practical perspective with respect to sin: engaging in regular, ongoing work to resolve traumatic memories, so that I am less often triggered, and taking deliberate steps to spend as much time as possible in relational mode, have been two of the most effective interventions I have ever found for actually reducing my sinful thoughts and behaviors.

What Is the Relationship between the Immanuel Approach and Theophostic® Prayer Ministry?

My perception is that the Immanuel approach and Theophostic® Prayer Ministry (TPM) share many of the same foundational principles. Many aspects of the process are also similar. I started with Theophostic® Prayer Ministry, and progressively developed the Immanuel approach as I modified my understanding and techniques so that they would address the priority of intimacy with God over relief of symptoms, so that they would establish perception of Jesus' tangible presence and an interactive connection with him as the foundation for the process, so that they would address issues related to capacity, so that people (especially lay ministers) could learn them more easily and safely, and so that they would also incorporate new understanding regarding the pain-processing pathway. For a much more detailed description of my journey from Theophostic® to the Immanuel approach, and for additional discussion of how they are related, see "Brain Science, Psychological Trauma, and the God Who Is with Us ~ Part I: A Psychiatrist's Journey—A Brief Introduction to the Immanuel Approach."

I. **"Brain Science, Psychological Trauma, and the God Who Is with Us"**
Essay Series: As has been mentioned earlier, the series of essays titled "Brain Science, Psychological Trauma, and the God Who Is with Us," parts 1 through 6, provide a much more detailed discussion of many of the points presented in *Outsmarting Yourself.*[1] For those of you who do not want to go through the whole three hundred-plus pages, here is a quick guide to help you find subjects that may be of special interest.

A. **The Pain-Processing Pathway:** For a thorough, detailed discussion of the pain-processing pathway, see part 2.

B. **Relational Connection Circuits and Attunement:** For discussion of relational connection circuits, and how you can help a person bring them back on by being with him in his pain, hearing him, understanding him, and attuning to him, see especially part 2, the discussions of synchronization, interpersonal attunement, and mutual mind (pages 23–26); the discussions of relational connection joy and returning to joy (pages 31–38); and the discussions of staying with negative emotions and maintaining/reestablishing relational connection joy (pages 46–52).

C. **Deliberate Recall of Previous Positive Connections:** For discussion of the value of deliberately recalling past positive experiences with the Lord, see especially part 5.

D. **Deliberate Appreciation:** For discussion of the value of deliberately appreciating the Lord's goodness and how he has cared for you, see especially part 5.

E. **Explicit Invitation and Request:** For discussion of explicitly inviting the Lord to be with you in your pain, and asking the Lord to help you perceive his presence, see especially the "Immanuel Interventions" section in part 5.

F. **Immanuel Connection Troubleshooting:** For discussion of how to identify and resolve the psychological and spiritual issues that hinder you from establishing an interactive connection with the Lord, see especially the sections on Immanuel intervention troubleshooting in part 5.

G. **Sharing Your Heart with Jesus:** For discussion of recognizing what's in your heart, and then expressing it directly to Jesus, see especially part 5.

H. **Traumatic Memories and How to Access Them:** For discussion of traumatic memories, and how to identify the specific memories underlying a given triggered reaction, see especially the discussion of traumatic memories

---

1. All of this material is available for free download from www.kclehman.com.

being qualitatively different and the discussion of traumatic memories being difficult to access in part 3, the discussion of how to access traumatic memories in part 4, and the discussion of "describe everything that comes into your awareness (your brain works better in community)" in part 5.

I. The Immanuel Approach to Emotional Healing: For discussion of the Immanuel approach to permanently resolving traumatic memories, see especially parts 1 and 5.

II. **Other Essays from www.kclehman.com:** There are several additional essays from our kclehman website that will also be especially helpful in providing expanded discussion of the material presented in this book.

A. **Self-Pity and Bitterness:** For discussion of self-pity and bitterness, and especially discussion of how to surrender them, see "Judgments and Bitterness as Clutter That Hinders Prayer for Emotional Healing," and "Deadly Perils of the Victim Swamp: Bitterness, Self-Pity, Entitlement, and Embellishment."

B. **More Immanuel Connection Troubleshooting:** For additional discussion of how to identify and resolve the psychological and spiritual issues that hinder you from perceiving the Lord's attuning presence, see "Immanuel, an Especially Pernicious Blockage, and the Normal Belief Memory System."

III. *Outsmarting Yourself* **Website (www.outsmartingyourself.com):** The *Outsmarting Yourself* website has been created primarily to provide information about the book, to assist those who are wanting to tell others about this resource, and to assit those who are trying to decide whether to purchase a copy. However, it also presents supplementary material that complements the information in the book. For example, the "Key Concepts" page provides very nice, concise summaries of each of the key concepts presented in the book, and the "FAQ" page provides answers to a number of additional questions that we have received and answered since the book was published.

IV. **Immanuel Approach Website (www.immanuelapproach.com):** We are continually working on the Immanuel approach website in an effort to provide the best possible resources for helping people to learn about the Immanuel approach, receive their own healing through the Immanuel approach, use the Immanuel approach to facilitate healing for others, train others with respect to the Immanuel approach, and embrace the wider Immanuel approach to life.[2] Some of the resources already available include:

---

2.   The Immanuel approach to life is based on the same principles as the Immanuel approach to emotional healing, and uses the same tools, but it is much more comprehensive. The wider Immanuel approach to life includes healing for psychological trauma, but clearly recognizes that this is only one part of God's agenda for working in our lives. For example, the Lord also wants to build our capacity, grow our maturity, and spend time "just" being with us as a friend. Furthermore, the Immanuel approach to life takes the tools for helping us connect with the Lord outside of special "sessions," with the ultimate goal of helping us get to the place where

- a "Getting Started" page, presenting a *small* handful of essays that have been specifically chosen to provide a manageable, easy-to-understand introduction for those who are just getting started with respect to learning about the Immanuel approach;

- a "Biblical Basis" page, providing extensive discussion of the biblical support for the Immanuel approach;

- a "Referrals" page, providing information regarding others who are providing Immanuel approach sessions;

- a "Trainers" section (on the "Training" page), presenting information regarding others who are providing Immanuel approach training;

- a "Testimonies" page, where we share encouraging stories from people who are using the Immanuel approach for working with psychological trauma, and who are often also embracing the wider Immanuel approach to life;

- and an "FAQs" page, with answers to frequently asked questions such as Can the Immanuel approach be used with children?, Does the Immanuel approach work with non-Christians?, and How do you include the Immanuel approach in the care of people with clinical mental illnesses?

V. *Share Immanuel* Booklet:[3] As mentioned earlier, this 2010 booklet by Jim Wilder and Chris Coursey provides a very brief discussion of the theory behind the Immanuel approach, and then also presents a brief description of the Immanuel approach exercises that are the safest and easiest to learn, the safest and easiest to use, and the safest and easiest to teach.

VI. Supplementary Essays for *Share Immanuel* Booklet: Dr. Wilder is planning to write several essays specifically designed to provide supplementary material for the *Share Immanuel* booklet. These are not yet available, but watch the www.lifemodel.org website for these to be released (we hope sometime in 2012).

VII. *Healing* module of *Thriving: Recover Your Life*: As I write this (August 2012), Ed Khouri and team are working diligently on the development of the *Healing* module of the *Thriving: Recover Your Life* program.[4] When this is finally released (we hope sometime in 2013), it will provide an excellent resource

---

we perceive the Lord's presence, and abide in an interactive connection with Jesus, as our usual, normal, baseline condition as we walk through life each day. For a much more detailed discussion of these points, see "Brain Science, Psychological Trauma, and the God Who Is with Us ~ Part I: A Psychiatrist's Journey–A Brief Introduction to the Immanuel Approach."

3.   E. James Wilder and Chris M. Coursey, *Share Immanuel* (Pasadena: Shepherd's House Inc., 2010). Available through www.lifemodel.org.

4.   We work closely with those developing the *Thriving* material (Pastor Ed Khouri, Dr. E. James Wilder, Pastor David Takle, and Pastors Chris and Jen Coursey), **but we do not produce or distribute the material and we are not involved with coordinating and/or keeping track of *Thriving* groups**. For more information regarding *Thriving* groups, the *Restarting, Forming, Belonging,* and *Healing* modules, and other *Thriving* materials, see www.thrivingrecovery.org.

for learning the Immanuel approach. The current plans are for the lecture content to include systematic teaching about each of the building blocks[5] of the Immanuel approach, and the exercises at the end of each session will include practice with these building blocks. The later session exercises will then lead the participants in progressively putting the pieces together to end up with the complete Immanuel approach package, including the resolution of traumatic memories.

VI. *Immanuel: A Practicum:*[6] This 2011 book by Pastor Patti Velotta focuses on very practical teaching regarding how to facilitate Immanuel approach sessions. (It does not try to duplicate the discussions regarding theory and supporting evidence provided in our essays.) The extensive appendices presenting strong biblical support for the Immanuel approach supplement the comments we make in our website essays and in chapter 19 of this volume regarding the ways in which the Immanuel approach is consistent with Scripture. See appendix C for additional description of *Immanuel: A Practicum.*

---

5.   As described in parts 1 and 5 of the "Brain Science, Psychological Trauma, and the God Who Is with Us" essay series, some of the building blocks of the Immanuel approach include the initial steps of 1) calming and deliberate appreciation to prepare the brain for relational connection, 2) recalling previous experiences of positive connection with the Lord, and 3) taking time to reenter these memories, and then reestablishing a present, living, interactive connection with the Lord in this context.

6.   Patti Velotta, *Immanuel: A Practicum*, (Libertyville, IL: This Joy! Books, 2011).

Detailed Outline

In the first edition of *Outsmarting Yourself,* appendix B provided an outline of the logical flow of the book that was much more detailed than the basic outline provided by the table of contents. The initial intention was to provide the more detailed outline as an additional resource for those who would be wanting to study and/or teach the material in much greater depth (such as graduate students and/or professors). However, our perception is that this resource has been used by only a very small percentage of readers, and now that the *Outsmarting Yourself* website is also available, we have decided to move the detailed outline to the "Look Inside" page of the website (www.outsmartingyourself.org). Please let us know if you would prefer the detailed outline to be included as appendix B in the book. We will consider bringing the detailed outline back into the book if we get a lot of readers requesting this (and if we ever publish a third edition).

Where/How Do I Get Training
Regarding the Immanuel Approach?

An increasing number of people have been contacting us with questions along the lines of: "I would like to use the Immanuel approach to emotional healing in my _____ (psychotherapy practice, ministry, church, small group, family, marriage, etc.). How/where do I get training that will enable me to do this?" Unfortunately, at this time we do not have any kind of training institute, we do not offer internships/apprenticeships,[1] and we are not providing regularly scheduled seminars designed to train people to use the Immanuel approach.[2] In the absence of this kind of Immanuel approach training package, we offer the following thoughts regarding do-it-yourself Immanuel approach training programs.

I. **Resources Available and Thoughts Regarding How to Use Them:** I would like to start with briefly describing the resources that *are* currently available, and then offering a few thoughts regarding how to use each of these resources in your do-it-yourself program.

   A. **Other Trainers:** Even though this section is about do-it-yourself Immanuel approach training, the ideal is certainly to learn directly from someone who is already knowledgeable and experienced regarding the Immanuel approach. There's nothing like going to a training event where you can watch a live demonstration, get practical tips for the specific circumstances in which you will be practicing, and then have a calm, confident, experienced trainer checking in with each small group as you are actually taking the step of facilitating your first session. Fortunately, even though we are not offering regularly scheduled training events ourselves, there is a small but steadily growing handful of others who are providing Immanuel approach training, such as pastor Patti Velotta and our friend Mark. As we become aware of trainers that we know personally, we will post brief descriptions of the individuals/ministries providing training, along with contact information, in the "Trainers" section on the "Training" page of our Immanuel approach website, www.immanuelapproach.com. Information regarding trainers will also be increasingly available through the Immanuel approach

---

1. Our essays occasionally refer to mentoring groups. These groups must be kept small for a variety of reasons, and due to our limited availability we are only able to provide two of them. Therefore, unfortunately, we are not able to offer this kind of mentoring to the general public.

2. We do, occasionally, provide training events related to the Immanuel approach, and all relevant information regarding these seminars will be posted in the "Events" section of the "Training" page of the Immanuel approach website (www.immanuelapproach.com).

network directory (accessed from the "Referrals" page of this same website) as self-identified trainers post profiles.

B. *The Immanuel Approach (to Emotional Healing and to Life)*: Our new book, *The Immanuel Approach (to Emotional Healing and to Life)*, now provides one of the best resources for do-it-yoursef Immanuel approach training.[3]

As discussed earlier, each time a traumatic memory gets activated we get another chance to complete previously unfinished processing tasks, and if we are able to successfully complete these tasks the traumatic memory will be permanently resolved. Furthermore, if we have sufficient understanding with respect to how traumatic memories work, we can deliberately activate them, deliberately set up the conditions so that they can be modified, and then deliberately finish the processing tasks. As also discussed earlier, the Lord knows all this stuff and he wants to help us get healed. For people who are able to perceive the Lord's presence clearly, establish an adequate interactive connection with him, stay synchronized with him, and receive help from him, the potentially complicated process of emotional healing can become very simple. *The Lord* can help the person access the memories, he can set up the conditions so that the memories can be modified, and he can help the person successfully complete the remedial processing tasks; and the Lord can do all of this without *us* needing to explicitly manage any of the details. With people who are able to perceive the Lord's presence clearly, establish an adequate interactive connection with him, and receive guidance from him, all we do is help them perceive the Lord's presence, help them connect with him and synchronize with him, help them *stay* synchronized with him, coach them to keep asking him for guidance regarding the next step they need to take, and coach them to engage with the Lord directly whenever they encounter problems in the process.

When working with these people who are able to perceive the Lord's presence, establish an adequate interactive connection with Jesus, and let him lead the process, this book provides most of what you need to know for facilitating the Immanuel approach. If you already have good right-brain interpersonal skills, maturity,[4] high capacity for being with people displaying negative emotions, and good spiritual discernment, then studying *The Immanuel Approach (to Emotional Healing and to Life)* and watching one or more of the Immanuel approach live-session DVDs may be enough to get you started. (Some people also like to include some of the practical tips and encouragement from Patti Velotta's, *The Immanuel Approach: A Practicum*, described below.)

---

3. At the time of this writing (winter 2014), *The Immanuel Approach (to Emotional Healing and to Life)* is still in process. However, as each chapter is completed the draft version is being posted on the "Getting Started" and "Resources" pages of www.immanuelapproach.com.

4. I use the combination of "right-brain interpersonal skills" and "maturity" to be more accessible to the average reader. For those who want to be more precise and who are familiar with "Brain Science, Psychological Trauma, and the God Who Is with Us ~ Part II," you can substitute the more accurate "right hemisphere pain-processing pathway maturity skills."

We have also found that our clients are able to cooperate with the process more easily when they have a basic understanding of what we are trying to do. We therefore ask them to read the first three chapters, as an introduction to the Immanuel approach, before we start working with them. It is a significant chunk of reading, but we also encourage our clients to read through to at least chapter eighteen. Reading chapters seventeen and eighteen especially help people embrace the "describe everything that comes into your awareness" part of the Immanuel approach process.

C. **Immanuel Approach Website (www.immanuelapproach.com):** We are continually working on the Immanuel approach website, www .immanuel approach.com, in an effort to provide the best possible resources for helping people to learn about the Immanuel approach, receive their own healing through the Immanuel approach, use the Immanuel approach to facilitate healing for others, train others with respect to the Immanuel approach, and embrace the wider Immanuel approach to life.[5] Some of the resources already available include:

- a "Getting Started" page, presenting the video clips, essays, and chapters from *The Immanuel Approach (for Emotional Healing and for Life)* that we suggest for those who are just getting started with respect to learning about the Immanuel approach;

- a "Biblical Basis" section on the "Resources" page, providing extensive discussion of the biblical support for the Immanuel approach;

- a "Referrals" page (including the network directory), presenting information regarding trainers, facilitators, and people who are interested in Immanuel approach study/practice groups;

- a "Testimonies" page, which shares encouraging stories from people who are using the Immanuel approach for working with psychological trauma, and who are often also embracing the wider Immanuel approach to life;

- a "Special Subjects/Advanced Topics" section of the "Resources" page, providing more in-depth and specialized resources for mental health professionals, people in full time ministry, and others who are working with more advanced, complicated situations.

---

5. The Immanuel approach to life is based on the same principles as the Immanuel approach to emotional healing, and uses the same tools, but it is much more comprehensive. The wider Immanuel approach to life includes healing for psychological trauma, but clearly recognizes that this is only one part of God's agenda for working in our lives. For example, the Lord also wants to build our capacity, grow our maturity, and spend time "just" being with us as a friend. Furthermore, the Immanuel approach to life takes the tools for helping us connect with the Lord outside of special "sessions," with the ultimate goal of helping us get to the place where we perceive the Lord's presence, and abide in an interactive connection with Jesus, as our usual, normal, baseline condition as we walk through life each day. For a much more detailed discussion of these points, see chapter three, "More Introduction (A Psychiatrist's Journey)" in *The Immanuel Approach (to Emotional Healing and to Life)*.

- and an "FAQs" page, with answers to frequently asked questions such as "Can the Immanuel approach be used with children?," "Does the Immanuel approach work with non-Christians?," and "How do you include the Immanuel approach in the care of people with clinical mental illnesses?"

B. **Advanced Material, Including the "Brain Science, Psychological Trauma, and the God Who Is with Us" Essays:** Unfortunately, some people are not yet able to establish an adeqaute interactive connection with the Lord, stay synchronized with him, and receive guidance from him; and when working with these people it is very helpful for us to understand many details regarding traumatic memory and the processing pathway, and to deliberately apply this information as we lead the session. Note that many recipients are *initially, briefly* unable to establish the interactive Immanuel (God-with-us) connection that makes it possible for the Lord to lead, but then are able to identify and resolve the blockages that hinder Immanuel connection with a reasonable amount of the basic troubleshooting described in chapters twelve and thirteen of the new book. And, again, the good news is that the average lay person can facilitate for these recipients. However, some people have complex blockages that are anchored to specific traumatic memories, and in these situations the recipient often needs to do substantial healing work as part of removing the blockages. When facilitating for these people, who have to work on traumatic memories without the benefit of the interactive Immanuel connection that makes it possible for the Lord to lead the sessions, *you* will need to lead the process.

Parts 2, 3, and 4 of the "Brain Science, Psychological Trauma, and the God Who Is with Us" essay series discuss the specific processing tasks in the pain-processing pathway, describe how to deliberately activate traumatic memories, and describe how to set up the conditions so that they can be modified. To the extent the people you work with are *not* able to perceive the Lord's presence clearly, establish an adequate interactive connection with him, stay synchronized with him, and receive guidance from him, you will need to apply this information about the pain-processing pathway, trauma, and emotional healing as you lead the session.

Mastering this material is a LARGE task, but it is an appropriate investment for anyone who is routinely working with people who have severe, complicated trauma, who have complex blockages, and who are not able to maintain an adequate interactive connection with Jesus through the emotional healing process. A strategic approach that I especially encourage is for mental health professionals and others engaged in full-time emotional healing work to master this material, along with other emotional healing principes and tools such as EMDR, Theophostic, and the material in the "Advanced Topics/Special Subjects" section of the "Resources" page of www. immanuelapproach.com. My first goal with this strategic approach is to have an adequate number of advanced facilitators who can work with recipients who have particulary complex blockages. Another goal with this approach is for the people with more advanced training and experience to provide consultation and backup for lay people, who want to use the Immanuel approach but don't have space in their lives to master the more advanced principles and tools. In our experience, there are many lay ministers who are willing to facilitate emotional healing in part-time volunteer settings, *if there is someone available to provide consultation and backup when they encounter more difficult cases.* Therefore, a small number of people able to provide this consultation and backup can be part of empowering a much larger force of part-time volunteer lay ministers.

C. **The Book You Are Holding in Your Hands (*Outsmarting Yourself: Catching Your Past Invading the Present and What to Do about It*), and/or the DVD Set, *Psychological Trauma, Implicit Memory, and the Verbal Logical Explainer (VLE):*[6]** As discussed in the essay "Unresolved Issues in the Therapist/Facilitator: One of the Most Important Hindrances to Emotional Healing,"[7] the *facilitator's* unresolved issues getting stirred up is one of the most important hindrances to effective emotional healing work. This book and DVD set presents a combination of fascinating brain science insights and examples from my own life that will hopefully increase your awareness of the ways in which your own stuff gets stirred up as you facilitate emotional healing sessions. This book and DVD set especially describe the ways in which we are traumatized by painful events that seem small, the ways in which these "small" traumas subtly affect us, and the ways in which our Verbal Logical Explainers keep this humbling reality out of our conscious awareness. Furthermore, this book and DVD set provide an easy-to-use tool that will help you recognize when you are triggered and when your relational circuits are off-line. The material presented in this book and DVD set will be especially valuable if you are having "unexplained" difficulty with facilitating the Immanuel approach, if you do a lot of emotional healing work, and if you are working with difficult situations.

D. ***Share Immanuel* Booklet:**[8] This 2010 booklet by Jim Wilder and Chris Coursey provides a very brief discussion of the theory behind the Immanuel approach, and then also presents a brief description of the Immanuel approach exercises that are the safest and easiest to learn, the safest and easiest to use, and the safest and easiest to teach.[9] It is important to note that the *Share Immanuel* booklet is designed to be part of a larger training

---

6. For information regarding availability, cost, ordering, shipping, etc for the *Psychological Trauma, Implicit Memory, and the Verbal Logical Explainer (VLE)* four-DVD set, see the store page at www.kclehman.com.

7. Available as a free download from www.kclehman.com.

8. E. James Wilder and Chris M. Coursey, *Share Immanuel*, (Pasadena, CA: Shepherd's House Publishing, 2010). Available through www.lifemodel.org.

9. These "safest and easiest" Immanuel exercises may take more time than some of the tools described in our longer essays, but they are designed so that they can be used safely by people with no mental health training, and designed so that they can be used safely in group settings.

program. For example, during his recent training in Asia (described earlier), Dr. Wilder used these booklets as *one part* of the teaching to describe and explain the Immanuel exercises. And one of the most important purposes for these booklets was to help participants share with others about the Immanuel approach *after having experienced several Immanuel encounters themselves.* A few people may be able to understand and successfully go through the Immanuel process with only the content from *Share Immanuel;* however, if people use this booklet as their primary/only resource, many will probably have the frustrating (triggering?) experience of feeling as if their understanding is inadequate (especially if they are actually trying to do the Immanuel process). Most people will have a better experience if they use this booklet in combination with supplementary material that can provide additional discussion, explanations, and examples.

E. **Supplementary Essays for the *Share Immanuel* Booklet:** Dr. Wilder is planning to write several essays specifically designed to provide supplementary material for the *Share Immanuel* booklet. These are not yet available, but watch the Life Model (www.lifemodel.org) and Immanuel approach (www.immanuelapproach.com) websites for these to be released (we hope sometime in 2014).

F. ***Immanuel: A Practicum:***[10] This 2011 book by Pastor Patti Velotta focuses on very practical teaching regarding how to facilitate Immanuel approach sessions. (It does not try to duplicate the discussions regarding theory and supporting evidence provided in our Immanuel approach book and essays.) Some have found Wilder and Coursey's *Share Immanuel* to be particularly understandable and usable, others have found the way I present material regarding the Immanuel approach to be especially easy to understand and apply, and there are still others who have found *Immanuel: A Practicum* to be the best fit for the way they think and work. The extensive appendices presenting strong biblical support for the Immanuel approach are also excellent—a valuable supplementary resource, going far beyond the comments we make in our website essays and in chapter 19 of this volume regarding the ways in which the Immanuel approach is consistent with Scripture.

G. **Live-Session DVDs:** As we learn to facilitate Immanuel approach emotional healing sessions, it is important to understand and apply certain concepts and principles. The left sides of our brains have been designed to learn and carry this kind of information, and we can learn this cognitive, conceptual information through language-based teaching, such as listening to a lecture or reading a book. As we learn to facilitate Immanuel approach emotional healing sessions there is also an interpersonal, behavioral *skill* component that we must master. For example, interpersonal, behavioral skill is required to be able to simultaneously communicate compassion, offer attunement, and supply firm redirection as I coach a client to keep engaging with Jesus

---

10. Patti Velotta, *Immanuel: A Practicum*, (Libertyville, IL: This Joy! Books, 2011).

as she works through a traumatic memory. The right sides of our brains have been designed to learn and carry this kind of information, and the best way to learn this interpersonal, behavioral skill information is to observe someone else successfully executing the task we are trying to learn—to have somebody else model "this is what it looks like." Putting all of this together: the best way to learn the right-brain interpersonal behavioral skill component of facilitating the Immanuel approach is to directly observe someone else actually doing it. The ideal is to have experienced mentors that you can observe; but, unfortunately, opportunities to observe experienced mentors facilitating live sessions can be hard to find. The good news is that our live-session DVDs are an excellent alternative source for this "this is what it looks like" modeling.

Furthermore, in addition to "this is what it looks like" modeling for how to facilitate, our live-session DVDs also provide "this is what it looks like and feels like" information regarding various other aspects of the Immanuel approach.[11] For example, "this is what it looks like and feels like when a person perceives God's presence," "this is what it looks like and feels like when the recipient is experiencing an interactive connection with Jesus," "this is what it looks like and feels like when the Lord comes with correction/guidance/ healing," and "this is the kind of fruit you see when a person has been able to work with the Lord to accomplish healing." See the "Live Session DVDs" section on the "Training" page at www.immanuelapproach.com for a brief session summary and a written commentary providing extensive explanatory comments for each of our live-session DVDs, and see the "Getting Started" page for free download previews of each of these DVDs. (The relevant section of the www.immanuelapproach.com Store page provides information regarding availability, prices, ordering, shipping, etc.)

1. **Immanuel approach sessions:** We now have nine live-session DVDs that provide examples of the Immanuel approach to emotional healing, including the initial steps of positive memory recall, deliberate appreciation, and refreshing connection with Jesus. Furthermore, most live-session DVDs beyond #29 in the Live Ministry Series will try to demonstrate the most

---

11.   Our earlier live-session DVDs portray Theophostic®-based emotional healing sessions, as opposed to emotional healing sessions using the Immanuel approach. However, since Theophostic®-based emotional healing and the Immanuel approach share many important principles and techniques, even the earlier Theophostic®-based sessions provide "this is what it looks like and feels like" for many aspects of the Immanuel approach. Regarding "Theophostic®-based": We use the term "Theophostic®-based" to refer to therapies/ministries that are built around a core of Theophostic® principles and techniques, but that are not exactly identical to Theophostic® Prayer Ministry as taught by Dr. Ed Smith. Our own therapy/ministry prior to 2007 would be a good example—it was built around a core of Theophostic® principles and techniques, but it sometimes also included material that is not a part of what we understand Dr. Smith to define as Theophostic® Prayer Ministry (such as "Immanuel Interventions," our material on dealing with curses, spiritual strongholds, generational problems, and suicide-related phenomena, and our material on journaling, spiritual disciplines, capacity, community, and medical psychiatry).

current iterations of the Immanuel approach.[12] If you have read parts 1 and 5 in the "Brain Science, Psychological Trauma, and the God Who Is with Us" essay series, but are having trouble getting started, I would strongly encourage you to look at the following sessions:

- *Maggie #2: "If I Leave, She Could Die"* (Live Ministry Series #12)

- *Renae: Healing Helps Parenting* (Live Ministry Series #17)

- *Rita #3: Jesus Is Better Than Candy* (Live Ministry Series #18)

- *Maggie #3: Labor and Delivery Trauma* (Live Ministry Series #19)

- *Steve: "Just" Be with Jesus* (Live Ministry Series #21)

- *Bruce: Loss of Parents, Sibling Conflict, Daughter's Illness* (Live Ministry Series #22)

- *Ian: "I'm not enough"* (Live Ministry Series #24)

- *Charlie: "See, this works!"* (Live Ministry Series #27)

- *Bob: Safety Net Demonstration* (Live Ministry Series #29)

- Most live session DVDs beyond #21 in the Live Ministry Series.

These full-length sessions can also be helpful in giving your clients a very realistic picture of what to expect. The condensed-version sessions are very faith building, inspirational, and helpful for introducing people to the Immanuel approach; but when a person is wanting to actually receive Immanuel emotional healing, it is helpful for them to have realistic expectations regarding the flow of an hour and a half session (as opposed to expecting to go through the process in fifteen minutes, as portrayed in the condensed versions).

2. **Immanuel intervention troubleshooting sessions:** We have three live-session DVDs that provide examples of extended troubleshooting with people who are initially unable to perceive the Lord's presence. These three sessions show you what it looks like to keep turning to Jesus for guidance and help when the person is repeatedly unable to perceive his presence, and they are especially valuable in combination with chapters twelve, thirteen, and twenty-six in *The Immanuel Approach (to Emotional Healing and to Life)*. If you have studied these chapters on troubleshooting but are still having difficulty in helping people identify and resolve the blockages hindering them from perceiving the Lord's presence and/or connecting with him, I would strongly encourage you to look at *Doug: "Immanuel Intervention," Intermediate* (Live Ministry Series #9), *Eileen: "Immanuel Intervention," Intermediate* (Live Ministry Series #7), and *Rita #1: Advanced Immanuel Intervention* (Live Ministry Series #26).

---

12.   I am currently working on several older sessions that provide especially good examples of specific issues and/or troubleshooting techniques. Therefore, an occasional live-session DVD beyond #29 will present an older session that does not demonstrate the newest Immanuel approach principles and process.

3. **Other live-session DVDs:** The many other live-session DVDs include smaller blocks of troubleshooting regarding various aspects of the Immanuel connection not working. For example, *Dawn: Disarming the Lure of Affirmation* (Live Ministry Series #16), *Rocky: Father-Son Wounds* (Live Ministry Series #6), and *Patricia: First Session with Internal Parts* (Live Ministry Series #3) all include places where we identify and then resolve guardian lies that initially hinder the person from perceiving the Lord's presence and/or fully being able to receive from him, and *Rita #2: Resolution of Bitterness toward Mother* (Live Ministry Series #14) includes troubleshooting where we identify and resolve blockages caused by bitterness and demonic interference.

4. **Condensed versions of live sessions:** The condensed versions of the live sessions are not so good for actually learning to facilitate the Immanuel approach process, but many have found them to be valuable for inspiration, encouragement, and building faith. The condensed sessions are also one of the best ways to introduce people to the Immanuel approach. At fifteen to twenty minutes each, they require a very modest time investment that most are willing to make, and the powerful healings during the sessions and striking fruit apparent at the follow-up interviews tend to be very effective in convincing people that this is an approach to emotional healing that merits further investigation.

H. *Forming,*[13] *Restarting,* and *Belonging* **Groups:** I have never actually participated in one of these groups, but from what I understand the exercises at the end of each group session provide opportunities to practice many of the building blocks of the Immanuel approach. For example, the exercises in *Restarting* [14] and *Belonging* [15] include practice with the initial steps of the Immanuel process: 1) recalling previous experiences of positive connection with the Lord, 2) deliberate appreciation to prepare the brain for relational connection, and 3) taking time to reenter these memories in order to re-establish an interactive connection with the Lord in the present.

I. *Healing* **module of** *Thriving: Recover Your Life*: As I write this (June 2014), Pastor Ed Khouri and team are working diligently on the development of the *Healing* module of the *Thriving: Recover Your Life* program. When this is released (we hope sometime in 2015), it will provide an excellent resource for learning the Immanuel approach. The current plans are for the lecture content to include systematic teaching about each of the building blocks of the Immanuel approach, and the exercises at the end of each session will

---

13. David Tackle, Edward M. Khouri, and E. James Wilder, *Forming* (Pasadena, CA: Shepherd's House Publishing, 2012).

14. Edward M. Khouri and E. James Wilder, *Restarting* (Pasadena, CA: Shepherd's House Publishing, 2007).

15. Edward M. Khouri and E. James Wilder, *Belonging* (Pasadena, CA: Shepherd's House Publishing, 2011).

include practice with these building blocks.[16] The later session exercises will then lead the participants in progressively putting the pieces together to end up with the complete Immanuel approach package, including the resolution of traumatic memories.

Note: We work closely with those developing the *Thriving* material (Pastor Ed Khouri, Dr. E. James Wilder, Pastor David Takle, and Pastors Chris and Jen Coursey), **but we do not produce or distribute the material, and we are not involved with coordinating and/or keeping track of *Thriving* groups.** For more information regarding *Thriving* groups, the *Restarting, Forming, Belonging,* and *Healing* modules of *Thriving, Recover Your Life,* and other *Thriving* materials, see www.thrivingrecovery.org.

J. **"This Is What It Looks Like" Models:** As mentioned above in the discussion of our live-session DVDs, the best way to learn the right-hemisphere skill component of facilitating the Immanuel approach is to watch someone else do it. In the ideal do-it-yourself Immanuel approach training package, you will find someone who is already getting good results with the Immanuel approach and who can provide a live "this is what it looks like" model. It may not always be possible to find this, but it is ideal and I encourage you to ask the Lord for guidance and then actively watch for opportunities in which you can observe effective facilitators.[17] As mentioned above, our live-session DVDs can provide "this is what it looks like" modeling to some extent.

Unfortunately (or fortunately, depending on your perspective), at this early point in the journey regarding the Immanuel approach, the Lord may be calling *you* to be one of the pioneers—one of the people who embraces the special challenge of helping to lead the way in learning and practicing something new. If this is the case, then may the Lord bless you to go forth with both boldness and humility, and then to provide modeling for others.

K. **Consultation and Backup:** In the ideal do-it-yourself Immanuel approach training package, you will also find someone who can provide consultation and backup as you learn. You can experiment and practice much more comfortably if you have someone you can go to when you encounter things you don't understand and/or don't know how to handle. Ideally, you want to find someone who has high capacity, who has good right-brain maturity skills, who does their own healing work, who has a lot of experience with

---

16.   As described in chapters two through eleven in *The Immanuel Approach (to Emotional Healing and to Life)*, some of the building blocks of the Immanuel approach include the initial steps of 1) recalling previous experiences of positive connection with the Lord, 2) deliberate appreciation to prepare the brain for relational connection, 3) taking time to reenter/reconnect with these memories, and 4) in the context of being inside a memory for a previous positive experience, reestablish an interactive connection with the Lord in the present. And then, throughout the rest of the session, 5) focus on Jesus and engage with him directly regarding every question, issue, and problems that comes up.

17.   For example, some of the training events provided by the people/ministries in the "Trainers" section of the "Training" page of www.immanuelapproach.com include live demonstrations.

facilitating emotional healing, and who understands the pain-processing pathway, psychological trauma, defenses, troubleshooting, etc. This is the ideal, but anyone with more capacity, maturity, experience, and understanding than yourself will be helpful. One very specific possibility is to find someone you trust and respect from the "Referrals" or "Training" pages of the Immanuel approach website (www.immanuelapproach.com), and then pay her for consultation time as you need it.

Again, at this early point in the journey regarding the Immanuel approach, the Lord may be calling you to be one of the pioneers—one of the people who embraces the special challenge of helping to lead the way in learning and practicing something new. If this is the case, then may the Lord bless you to go forth with both boldness and humility, and then to provide consultation and backup for others.

L. **Observation and Coaching:** Yet another piece of the ideal do-it-yourself Immanuel approach training package is a coach who can observe you work and then offer feedback/constructive criticism. It is especially valuable to have someone else help us with identifying our blind spots. This is another ideal resource that may be difficult to find, but I encourage you to ask the Lord for guidance and then actively watch for opportunities. One possibility available to anyone with a video camera is to record sessions and then provide observation for yourself by watching your own sessions. You will be amazed by how many things you will notice, when watching the film, that you were unaware of during the actual session. (You would also be amazed by the clumsy, suboptimal facilitating displayed in the tapes of some of my sessions. Watching these tapes has been both painfully humbling and tremendously educational. The good news is that the people in these sessions still received healing from the Lord, in spite of my many imperfections. And in case you're wondering, I have not yet had the courage to include one of these sessions in our collection of training DVDs.)[18]

Once again, the Lord may be calling you to be one of the pioneers. If this is the case, then I gladly pray even more blessings for you as you go forth with both boldness and humility, and then provide observation and coaching for others.

M. **Discussion/Practice Groups:** Discussion/practice groups are a very good idea. Pursue this option wherever possible. *The Immanuel Approach (to Emotional Healing and to Life)*, the live-session DVDs, and the "Psychological Trauma, Implicit Memory, and the Verbal Logical Explainer" DVDs should be especially good resources for discussion/practice groups. Note: it should be safe to practice the Immanuel approach in the context of discussion/practice groups if you use the safety nets and exercise instructions described

---

18. Another possibility is to find someone you trust and respect from the "Referrals" or "Training" pages of the Immanuel approach website, and then pay her for consultation time to provide observation and coaching for you.

in chapters fourteen and twenty-four of the new book.[19] Without skilled one-on-one Immanuel intervention troubleshooting, some people may not be able to perceive the Lord's presence, and will therefore be disappointed when they are not able to fully participate in the later steps of the process. Never the less, it is very important to abide by these group exercise safety nets unless your group is full of experienced facilitators.[20]

II. Go Back to the Basics If You Feel Overwhelmed: If you encounter complex situations that feel overwhelming, go back to three of the most trustworthy, basic principles:

A. Care for Your Own Connection with the Lord: When you encounter complicated situations, *there is no substitute for sensing the Lord's presence and receiving his guidance.* Do whatever you need to do to optimize the quality of your own, personal relationship and interactive connection with the Lord.

B. Build an Increasingly Strong and Accurate "Knowing" with Respect to Who the Lord Is and How He Works: One of the most important (and sometimes one of the most challenging) tasks of the facilitator is to help the person discern whether the content coming into her awareness is from the Lord or from some other source. As discussed at length in chapter twenty-nine of the new book, one of the best ways to recognize counterfeits is to start with a strong and accurate "knowing" with respect to the Lord's true character and heart. That is, if you have a deep, clear, accurate sense of who God is and how he works, you can quickly, intuitivey recognize counterfeits because they just don't feel right.

C. Get Your Own Healing: One of the most important things you can do to prepare for dealing with complex healing situations is to keep getting your own healing. As discussed at length in "Unresolved Issues in the Therapist/ Facilitator: One of the Most Important Hindrances to Emotional Healing,"[21] getting your own healing, and thereby removing blockages that hinder your connection with the Lord, is one of the most important things you can do to optimize your ability to perceive the Lord's presence and receive his guidance. Getting your own healing is therefore one of the most important things you can do to address principle number one—caring for your own, personal connection with the Lord. As also discussed at length in the same essay, getting your own healing, and thereby resolving toxic content that otherwise gets transferred onto the Lord, is one of the most important things you

---

19. This same material is also presented in the essay, "Immanuel Approach Exercises for Groups and Beginners, available as a free download from either the "Resources" or "Getting Started" pages of www.immanualapproach.com.

20. Groups with severe trauma and poor discernment can still get into trouble, but most discussion/practice groups should be able to practice safely if they carefully apply the safety nets recommended for group exercises.

21. Available as a free download from www.kclehman.com.

can do to address principle number two—growing in your ability to recognize counterfeits by knowing the genuine. Yet another point discussed at length in the essay just referenced is that getting your own healing will neutralize issues that impair your discernment in a variety of other ways.[22] Furthermore, being triggered and losing access to your relational circuits greatly impairs your interpersonal skills as well as greatly reducing your capacity for being with others in emotional distress, and getting your own healing will increasingly protect you from both of these liabilities.

III. Finding/Recruiting Your Own Immanuel Approach Facilitator: As mentioned earlier, we also receive many, many requests along the lines of "Can you help me find a therapist/emotional healing minister who can facilitate Immanuel approach emotional healing for me?" We are working hard to train Immanuel approach facilitators, and to post information regarding these people on the "Referrals" page of the immanuel approach website, but this relatively small group of facilitators is profoundly unable to provide sessions for the large number of people who want them.[23] Therefore, an important part of the answer to these requests is for people to find or recruit their own Immanuel approach facilitators.

With respect to *finding* your own facilitator, contact the Christian therapists in your area and ask them if they are familiar with our Immanuel approach to emotional healing, whether they have experience in using it, and whether they have seen good results. Ideally, you will find someone who is already experienced and getting good results. Another way to find your own facilitator is to look for a group running the *Healing* module of the *Thriving: Recover Your Life* program described above. Just as the group exercises in the *Healing* module are a good place to learn to facilitate for others, they are also a good place to receive Immanuel healing for yourself.

With respect to *recruiting* your own Immanuel approach facilitator, find someone with good right-brain interpersonal skills, maturity,[24] high capacity for being with people displaying negative emotions, and good spiritual

---

22. See also "'Triggered' Positive Thoughts and Emotions" (available as a free download from www.kclehman.com) for additional discussion of how unresolved issues can impair your discernment, and, correspondingly, how healing can improve your discernment by resolving these issues.

23. For example, when we put up the new Immanuel network directory (see the "Referrals" page of www.immanuelapproach.com), I had hoped that large numbers of facilitators would quickly post profiles, and that this would make it much easier for folks to find a facilitator. However, it turns out that many well trained, experienced facilitators have chosen to not post profiles because they are already swamped with more requests than they can care for. Consequently, many who would like to receive Immanuel approach sessions are still having difficulty in finding facilitators, and this problem will probably continue for some time.

24. Again, I use the combination of "right-brain interpersonal skills" and "maturity" to be more accessible to the average reader. For those who want to be more precise and who are familiar with "Brain Science, Psychological Trauma, and the God Who Is with Us ~ Part II," you can substitute the more accurate "right hemisphere pain-processing pathway maturity skills."

discernment. Ideally, this person will also already have training and experience with other techniques that are effective in working through the unresolved content carried inside traumatic memories (such as EMDR or Theophostic®-based emotional healing). Then use any legal, ethical method you can find (prayer, requests, argument, begging, payment, barter, calling in old debts, leveraging relationship connections, etc.) to get them to learn the Immanuel approach. Along these lines, the condensed versions of the live sessions are one of the best ways to introduce people to the Immanuel approach. At fifteen to twenty minutes each they require a very modest time investment that most are willing to make, and the powerful healings during the sessions and striking fruit apparent at the follow-up interviews tend to be very effective in convincing people that this is an approach to emotional healing that merits further investigation.[25] Even shorter preview clips from the live-session DVDs (five to seven minutes each) are also now available as free downloads from the Immanuel approach website; and although they are very brief, they still give the viewer a feel for the healing and fruit that we see with Immanuel approach sessions.

Note that it is okay to be very direct in asking a therapist whether she is already familiar with the Immanuel approach, whether she has experience with it, whether she has seen good results, or even whether she would be willing to learn it and give it a try. If a therapist is threatened and/or offended by these direct questions it is because she is triggered, *and this is not your fault.* Some really good therapists might be initially triggered and then get over it; but if the person you talk to is not able to handle this direct initial discussion, then you don't want to work with him. It is also okay to move to somebody new if the person you are working with does not seem able to facilitate the Immanuel approach as described in these essays and as portrayed in the live-session DVDs.

The bulimia case study posted on our kclehman website[26] provides an important example. Mary would not have received life-changing healing if she had not been willing to move on to someone else when the first two therapists were not able to provide what she was looking for.

Also, while recruiting someone who is already trained and experienced as a therapist may be necessary for more severe and/or complicated trauma, many less severe, less complicated traumatic memories can be resolved in the context of lay people facilitating for each other. That is, the "someone" with good

---

25. There are currently seven sets of condensed sessions available: *Live Emotional Healing Ministry ~ Four Condensed Sessions* (Live Ministry Series #8), *Live Emotional Healing Ministry ~ Four MORE Condensed Sessions* (Live Ministry Series #10), *Live Emotional Healing Ministry ~ Condensed Sessions, 3rd Set,* (Live Ministry Series #15), and *Live Emotional Healing Ministry ~ Condensed Sessions, 4th Set* (Live Ministry Series #20), *Live Emotional Healing Ministry ~ Condensed, with Subtitles,* (Live Ministry Series #23), *Live Emotional Healing Ministry ~ Condensed Sessions, 5th Set* (Live Ministry Series #25), and *Live Emotional Healing Ministry ~ Condensed Sessions, 6th Set* (Live Ministry Series #28). We recommend starting with the first, fourth, and fifth sets if you will be sharing them with others as a first introduction to the Immanuel approach. These DVDs can be obtained through the store page of www.kclehman.com.

26. See "Freedom from Bulimia: Case Study/Testimony," available as a free download from www.kclehman.com.

right-brain interpersonal skills, maturity, high capacity for being with people displaying negative emotions, and good spiritual discernment might be a lay person, such as a close friend, a member of your prayer group, or your spouse. For example, in our church there are several groups of lay people that have gotten together to facilitate Immanuel approach emotional healing for each other, and this has gone fairly well. We also know of several different couples who have learned to facilitate Immanuel healing for each other. In fact, my current perception is that lay people practicing with each other in the context of do-it-yourself Immanuel approach study/practice groups will be one of the primary ways in which the general public will be able to receive Immanuel approach emotional healing.

Safety note: If you and your prayer partner/the others in your group are all beginners, we recommend that you use the "safety nets" and exercise instructions described in chapters fourteen and twenty-four of *The Immanuel Approach (to Emotional Healing and to Life)*.[27] Even if you are facilitating one-on-one sessions for each other, as opposed to trying group exercises, we still strongly encourage you to use the group exercise "safety nets" when you are just getting started.[28]

IV. Additional Thoughts Regarding Do-It-Yourself Immanuel Approach Training Programs:

A. **Beginners Can Use Group Exercise "Safety Nets" as They Practice:** As just mentioned, if you are a beginner, and you want to start practicing but you do not have an experienced facilitator to provide backup, you can use the "safety nets" described in chapters fourteen and twenty-four of the new book. For example, lay people who want to learn to use the Immanuel approach with their friends and family should be able to practice safely with these "safety nets" in place.[29]

B. **Wide Range with Respect to Difficulty, It's Okay to Say, "This one is too much for me.":** It's helpful to recognize that there is a wide range with respect to complexity and difficulty. Working with people who have minor trauma is easier than working with people who have severe trauma. Working with people who have trauma from adulthood or later childhood is easier than working with people who have early childhood trauma. Working with people who have simple and/or failing defenses is easier than working with

---

27.   This same material is also presented in the essay, "Immanuel Approach Exercises for Groups and Beginners," available as a free download from either the "Resources" or "Getting Started" pages of www.immanualapproach.com.

28.   People with severe trauma and poor discernment can still get into trouble, but most healing partners/learning groups should be able to practice safely if they carefully apply the safety nets recommended for group exercises.

29.   Once again, if the people involved have severe trauma and poor discernment they can still get into trouble, but most beginners should be able to practice safely if they carefully apply the safety nets recommended for group exercises.

people who have complex, strong, and well-maintained defenses. Working with people who have high capacity and well-developed maturity skills is easier than working with people who have low capacity and poor maturity skills. And most importantly, working with people who have memories for past positive experiences with Jesus, who can establish a strong interactive connection with him in the present, and who can obtain guidance and help from Jesus through the process are much easier to work with than people who have difficulty with one or more of these pieces.

Remember that some emotional healing sessions are very simple and straightforward, and that it is okay to stay with emotional healing work appropriate to your level of experience, training, maturity, capacity, and discernment. If you are working with someone and you realize you don't know how to handle the problems you are encountering, it's okay to say, "This one is too much for me," and then either refer the person to a more skilled facilitator or agree to postpone work with that particular person until you feel adequately prepared. Again, it is perfectly okay to say, "I'm just a beginner, so I need to stay with emotional healing work that is more straightforward." You can even do this with respect to different issues in the same person. For example, if you and a friend/colleague are learning by practicing on each other and you encounter a particular issue that is beyond your current level of skill, you can simply acknowledge this and then find a more manageable target, either referring her to a more skilled facilitator to address the complex issue or agreeing to postpone work on that particular target until you feel adequately prepared. I would greatly prefer that you start learning to facilitate, even though you only feel comfortable working with easy problems, than that you indefinitely postpone practicing with the Immanuel approach because you are too intimidated by the possibility of encountering problems that are too difficult.

C. **Interpersonal Skills, Capacity, Maturity, and Discernment:** You will probably have noticed that I repeatedly mention right-brain interpersonal skills, capacity for being with people who are in emotional distress, maturity, and spiritual discernment as things that are important for being able to successfully facilitate Immanuel approach emotional healing. You will probably also have noticed that I mention getting your own healing as being important in order to prevent impairment. I am hoping to eventually write more about how to actively cultivate these assets specifically as part of focused preparation for facilitating emotional healing. As I am able to do this, the new material will be posted on the Immanuel approach website (included in the "Where/How Do I Get Training Regarding the Immanuel Approach?" essay, and also posted in other appropriate places on the website). In the meantime, THRIVE provides a lot of good general material regarding how to deliberately cultivate right-brain skills, capacity, and maturity.[30] The essay, "Brain

---

30. See www.thrivetoday.org for information regarding seminars and other training material provided by THRIVE.

Science, Psychological Trauma, and the God Who Is with Us ~ Part II," also includes good material regarding right-brain skills, capacity, and maturity.

D. **"Homework" for Those Intending to Receive Emotional Healing:** I am also hoping to eventually write more about "homework" that can help a person prepare for engaging in Immanuel approach emotional healing work, and this material will also be posted on the Immanuel approach website (again, included in the "Where/How Do I Get Training Regarding the Immanuel Approach?" essay, and also posted in other appropriate places on the website).

Additional Clues That Indicate Triggering

As discussed in the main body of the text, it is *really* important to recognize and take responsibility for our triggering. When we embrace the challenge of recognizing and taking responsibility for our triggering we provide tremendous benefits—to ourselves, to our friends, to our spouses, to our families, to our colleagues, and to our communities. And when we fail to recognize or take responsibility for our triggers, there are incredibly expensive consequences that affect every sphere of our lives.

I. Watch for Specific Indicators of Being Triggered: Physicians learn to watch for specific signs and symptoms as the diagnostic indicators for particular diseases. In the same way, you can learn to watch for the specific "signs and symptoms" that indicate being triggered.

    A. Loss of Access to Relational Connection Circuits: As described in the main body of the text, learning to recognize loss of access to our relational circuits is the most valuable and easiest-to-learn tool for recognizing when we are triggered, and this tool will enable us to recognize our triggering in most situations. However, as also described earlier, there are some situations where it is helpful to have additional tools for identifying that traumatic implicit memory has been triggered forward. The additional indicators, discussed below, can be helpful in these situations.

    B. Exaggerated Reaction to the Specific Situation: One of the most consistent indicators that I am triggered is that I will have an exaggerated reaction to the specific situation that triggers me. *When I am triggered, the intensity of my reaction will fit the original situation from the unresolved traumatic memory, as opposed to the situation in the present.* The more dramatic this is, the easier it is to spot. An easy-to-remember way to express this is, "Small infraction, big reaction."[1]

    C. Maturity Level Reduced from Baseline: To the extent that I am blended with the memory for an unresolved traumatic event, I will display the maturity level from the age of the triggered memory. For example, when I am blended with a memory carrying infant or child maturity, my perspective will be very entitled and self-centered. Another clue signaling that I am blended with unresolved childhood trauma derives from the observation that we experience tasks at the appropriate maturity level to be challenging but

---

1. Note that attachment pain can also cause you to experience exaggerated responses to difficult situations in the present. Attachment pain playing in the background will "turn up the volume" with respect to your reactions to any other problems you encounter.

satisfying, whereas tasks from a maturity level beyond the one we are actually at feel burdensome. Therefore, if we feel burdened and/or overwhelmed by tasks that are usually satisfying, this is a clue that we are triggered. For example, the parent/elder maturity task of caring for my God sons when they are being difficult feels satisfying when I am at my optimum non-triggered maturity baseline, but feels burdensome if I am triggered to a lower level of maturity.

Both Charlotte and I have observed this to be so reliable that it is now often the first clue we recognize to indicate that one or the other of us is subtly triggered. If we notice infant or child thoughts, attitudes, and reactions, we stop and ask, "Am I triggered?" And in almost all of these situations, we are eventually able to identify implicit memory content from experiences that match the age of the maturity clues we had observed.

D. **Capacity and Other Resources Reduced from Baseline:** If I am triggered, to the extent that I am blended with the triggered memory I will respond to problems in the present from the ego state contained in the memory. Therefore, *to the extent that I am blended with memory from unresolved trauma, I will be working with the impaired capacity, impaired faith, impaired creativity, impaired flexibility, etc., corresponding to the ego state contained in the memory.* For example, if I am deeply blended with a triggered five-year-old playground memory of being frightened and overwhelmed, I will respond to problems in the present with the resources of a frightened and overwhelmed five-year-old.[2]

E. **General Irritability:** When I am not triggered, I have a large capacity for irritating situations—I can take a lot of frustration, inconvenience, disappointment, and unpleasant behavior on the part of others without getting upset. When I am not triggered, I have a surprising amount of patience even when I'm exhausted and physically uncomfortable. However, this all changes dramatically when I am triggered. When I'm triggered, I respond to the smallest inconvenience, disappointment, or unpleasantness with anger and judgment. Even if I'm exhausted and/or in pain, I'm only irritable if I'm *also* triggered.[3]

When I am not triggered, I would describe myself as being tolerant; but when I am triggered, I would have to describe myself as irritable. In fact, irritability has been such a reliable indicator that I have learned to take a "trigger-check time-out" whenever I notice that I'm reacting to small things that don't usually bother me. Whenever I notice that I'm irritable, I pause and deliberately check for other indicators of triggering, and I almost always (always?) discover that I am indeed triggered.

---

2. Note that this impairment can be subtle if I am only slightly blended and/or if the underlying traumatic memory is minor.

3. I have been amazed to realize that I can be exhausted and physically ill, but still be fully synchronized, untriggered, and living out of my true heart. My perception is that fatigue, physical illness, and physical pain often result in irritability because they make us much more vulnerable to triggers and/or directly activate unresolved trauma.

As discussed earlier, traumatic memories usually include loss of access to our relational circuits; and when traumatic memories coming forward cause us to lose access to our relational circuits, we go from being patient and tolerant to being impatient, intolerant, and irritable. In addition to losing access to our relational circuits, I think there are also several other factors that contribute to the way in which triggering causes irritability. By definition, a traumatic event will always involve a situation we were not able to handle in a good way. Therefore, when we are triggered we are blended with the memory of a situation that we could not handle. And when we are blended with the thoughts and emotions from a painful situation that was too much for us, then even the smallest additional hassle feels like a big deal. Furthermore, traumatic memories are often childhood memories and, as described above, to the extent that I am blended with traumatic memories I will respond to problems in the present from the ego state contained in the memories. It should not surprise me that I respond to minor annoyances with irritability instead of grace when I realize that I am trying to handle these "minor" annoyances with the dramatically impaired resources of a traumatized child.[4]

Our increased emotional reactivity when triggered is similar to our increased physical reactivity when physically injured. When our physical bodies are completely healthy, someone can bump into us and we hardly even notice it. However, if we have a bruise or skin abrasion, even the slightest contact, on the spot where we are already injured, will produce a surprising amount of pain and a surprisingly intense reaction. Similarly, if we are triggered, so that an emotional wound is active, even the slightest emotional "bump" will produce a surprising amount of pain and a surprisingly intense reaction.

F. **Vocabulary:** With memories for experiences that included thoughts formulated as words, the vocabulary of the words coming forward with the memory will match the age of the original trauma. Childish words from early experiences usually get edited into adult vocabulary before we actually speak them out loud, but with a little practice we can learn to spot the internal thoughts that first come forward in the vocabulary of our childhoods, and the specific vocabulary will tell us about the underlying memories. For example, when I have thoughts that include, "You're just a poo-poo head!" I can be pretty sure I'm dealing with implicit memory from kindergarten or first grade.

G. **Thoughts and Emotions Inconsistent with Reference Points:** As previously discussed, when thoughts and emotions from unresolved trauma are triggered forward, *the thoughts and emotions from the memories will feel true and reasonable in the present*. However, if you look at the present situation carefully and honestly, you will realize that the triggered thoughts and emotions are actually not consistent with well-established reference points. For example, twenty years of marriage have provided me with thousands of

---

4. Again, attachment pain can also increase your overall reactivity and irritability.

data points that all agree in establishing the compelling reference point that Charlotte is trustworthy. So if I am in the middle of a conflict with Charlotte and I notice that it feels true that she is engaging in some kind of sneaky, deliberate deception, the incompatibility between this new suspicion and her well-established trustworthiness strongly indicates that my thoughts and emotions are being contaminated by traumatic implicit memory content.

Scriptural truths are one of the best sources of reference points that can help us in exposing triggered thoughts and emotions. For example, many biblical passages clearly agree in establishing that the Lord is always with us and that he watches over us with careful love. He may still allow pain into our lives, for reasons that we do not yet understand, but he is always with us and he cares for us with amazing tenderness and love. However, when I was sitting in the middle of the huge car repair problem, it felt true that the Lord was either absent through negligence or that he was deliberately withholding assistance through some kind of perverse spitefulness. In this situation, the striking incompatibility between my negative perceptions and the Scriptural reference points clearly indicated that my thoughts and emotions were being distorted by triggered content from underlying traumatic memories.

H. **Focusing on the Trigger Does Not Resolve the Problem:** If the painful thoughts and emotions you experience are actually implicit memory content from underlying trauma, then focusing on the trigger in the present, as if it is the true problem, will never result in a good *long-term* solution. For example, if you have wounds about being unappreciated that are consistently triggered in the average job setting, triggered thoughts and feelings related to these wounds will eventually come forward regardless of where you are working. Your VLE will always come up with an explanation for why some aspect of your job is the problem: "This job isn't a good fit for my gifts and interests," "My supervisor is _____ (fill in the blank)," "My co-workers are _____ (fill in the blank)," "The support staff are _____ (fill in the blank)," "The employer doesn't provide adequate training," etc. But no matter where you work—job after job after job—the same triggered thoughts and feelings will eventually come forward. In contrast, if the true problem really is in the present, then moving to a new job might provide a lasting solution. For example, if you experience persistent frustration and lack of satisfaction because your gifts and interests are not well suited for your current employment, you can move to a job with a better fit and the problem will go away. You will experience lasting satisfaction at the new job, as opposed to the same old problem returning as you begin to bump into triggers in the new job setting.

This diagnostic criteria can be misleading in short-term situations because sometimes it is possible to come up with a trigger-focused plan that simply tries to avoid the trigger. This will provide temporary relief, and you might even tell yourself, "See! It wasn't my stuff—I just needed to find new friends and get away from that terrible Jim Wilder. As long as I don't have to deal with his irritating _____ (fill in the blank), I'm fine." But it will only be a matter of time before you will start bumping into new triggers, and the old, familiar triggered thoughts and emotions will return.

I. **Negative Reaction to the Suggestion That You Might Be Triggered:** As described in the discussion of "second-level triggering" in Part III, an inherent part of trauma is not having the necessary resources. If the person who is going through a painful experience has an adult who is with her, attuned to her, hearing her, validating her, connected to her, etc., she will almost never be traumatized. Therefore, most traumatic memories will include the absence of being heard, validated, understood, and attuned to. If the possibility of triggering is suggested with the least bit of challenge, blame, judgment, or even just lack of attunement, it can specifically activate this part of the original pain. As also described in the earlier discussion of second-level triggering, many traumatic experiences include being actively blamed, invalidated, ignored, not heard, and not understood. When active blame, invalidation, or some other form of misattunement was part of the original experience, then suggesting the possibility of triggering will often provide additional activation for this particular piece of the original traumatic experience.

The point relevant to our current discussion is that if we are triggered, so that implicit memory content from unresolved trauma is already active in the present, then second-level triggering will usually cause us to have a negative reaction to the suggestion that we might be triggered. In my own experience, there have been some situations in which this phenomena has been painfully obvious, but also other situations in which it has been difficult to spot. In the sitautions where it has been difficult to spot, I started out with subtle triggering smouldering quietly in the background, so that I was not even consciously aware of it, and I responded to the suggestion that old trauma might be affecting me with only a mild flash of irritation and defensiveness—both the triggering and the negative reaction were subtle. But even in these situations where I responded to the suggestion of possible triggering with only mild irritation and defensiveness, when I have examined things carefully I have almost always been able to find evidence indicating that I had indeed been triggered to start with.

Conversely, in situations where I am truly free of triggered traumatic memory content, the suggestion that I might be triggered almost never bothers me. Instead of feeling irritation, defensiveness, or outrage, I usually feel calm, nondefensive openness to exploring the question, and respond with something along the lines of, "I'm wondering what makes you think I'm triggered?"

J. **Recognize a Familiar Package:** Over time, one can increasingly learn to recognize packages that have been encountered repeatedly in the past. For example, there is a whole package of thoughts, emotions, and even physical sensations that come forward with any unresolved trauma splinters from the extended separation from my parents at two years old. Thoughts, such as "He/they won't come," "There's no excuse for their refusal to help me," and

"There's nothing I can do about it"; emotions, such as loneliness, hopeless-ness, powerlessness, and anger; and physical sensations, such as the heavi-ness and fatigue that go along with feeling hopeless and powerless. This par-ticular collection of thoughts, emotions, and physical sensations has come forward on the many occasions that my two-year-old separation trauma has gotten triggered, and eventually I came to recognize the whole, overall pack-age as a specific, familiar subjective experience. Now, whenever I feel this particular subjective experience package, I know that I am triggered (and that I am triggered to these specific memories).

Splinters of unresolved trauma from my many grade-school memories of being frightened by bullies provide another example. When these memo-ries get activated, I have an overall sense of being physically unsafe, I have a subtle perception of being small (as if I were seven or eight years old), I feel the physical tension and alertness associated with the fight-or-flight response, I have thoughts such as, "They won't be reasonable—they'll be upset with me no matter what I do," and I can usually also notice specific fears that some-one is going to yell at me and/or physically strike me. This particular collec-tion of thoughts, emotions, and physical sensations has come forward on the many occasions that my memories of being bullied have gotten triggered, and eventually I came to recognize the whole, overall package as a specific, familiar subjective experience. Now, whenever I feel this particular subjec-tive experience package, I know that I am triggered (and that I am triggered to these specific memories).

K. **Negative Emotions, Animosity toward People We Are Usually Glad to Be With:** As described earlier in part 4, when we lose access to our relational circuits we no longer experience the presence of others as a source of joy, and we no longer feel the spontaneous gladness to be with others. However, this change can sometimes be subtle, and it is especially difficult to notice when we are still glad for the practical benefits others are providing. In contrast, *when traumatic implicit memory is activated and pointed at specific people, we can feel negative emotions and animosity toward people we are usually glad to be with*, and this provides a clue that is much easier to spot.

For example, Charlotte is the person I am most consistently glad to be with. If I lose access to my relational circuits, I no longer perceive her as a source of relational joy, but this can be subtle if she is not the source of any of the triggers that are stirring me up, and it can be especially difficult to notice if she's providing practical help in dealing with the painful situa-tion. However, if I'm triggered and some of the traumatic implicit content is pointed toward Charlotte, then I experience negative thoughts and emotions focused on her. Whenever I have negative thoughts and emotions pointed toward Charlotte, this is usually easier to notice than simply the lack of rela-tional joy, and I am almost always triggered. And whenever I experience intense negative thoughts, intense negative emotions, and actual animosity toward Charlotte, this is much easier to notice, I am always triggered, and I am always transferring traumatic content onto her.

L. **Unable to Perceive the Lord's Presence, Establish an Interactive Connection, or Feel Emotionally Connected to Him:** Being triggered can hinder our ability to perceive the Lord's presence, get in the way of establishing an interactive connection, and prevent us from feeling emotionally connected to him. Note that traumatic memories getting stirred up will not always hinder our interactions with the Lord in these ways. That is, in some situations we will still be able to perceive the Lord's presence and/or establish an interactive connection and/or feel emotionally connected even though we are triggered. However, *once we have gotten to the place where perceiving the Lord's presence and feeling connected to him has become our baseline, then when we are not able to perceive the Lord's presence and/or establish an interactive connection and/or feel emotionally connected to him, triggered traumatic content is almost always contributing to the problem.*

As we become more and more able to perceive the Lord's presence, establish an interactive connection, and feel emotionally connected to him, then noticing the lack of these things can become an increasingly valuable clue for recognizing when we are triggered. This can become an especially valuable clue if we deliberately practice recognizing what it feels like when we *do* perceive the Lord's presence, have an interactive connection, and feel emotionally connected; if we deliberately practice recognizing what it feels like when we do *not* perceive the Lord's presence, have an interactive connection, or feel emotionally connected; and if we then also deliberately practice being aware of whether we are (or are not) perceiving the Lord's presence, abiding in an interactive connection, and feeling emotionally connected to him as we go through each day.

M. **Consequences of Failed Processing Tasks:**[5] Many of the indicators of triggering discussed above could fit into the larger concept of "consequences of failed processing tasks." By our definition, trauma comes from painful experiences that have not successfully completed their journey through the processing pathway, and the toxic content carried in traumatic memories is directly related to the processing tasks that have not yet been completed. For example, if a person is not able to successfully complete the level 3 processing task of maintaining access to her relational circuits through a given painful experience, then the traumatic content carried in the memory for this experience will include lack of access to her relational circuits—the direct and inherent result of failure with respect to this level 3 task. If a person is not able to successfully complete the level 4 processing task of finding a satisfying way to navigate the situation, then the traumatic content carried in the memory for this experience will include feeling inadequate—the direct and inherent result of failure with respect to this level 4 task. If a person is not able to successfully complete the level 5 processing task of making sense out

---

5. The comments in this section will make much more sense for those who are already familiar with our teaching regarding the processing tasks at each of the five levels of the pain-processing pathway. For additional information regarding these processing tasks, see "Brain Science, Psychological Trauma, and the God Who Is with Us ~ Part II."

of the painful experience, then the traumatic content carried in the memory for this experience will include confusion—the direct and inherent result of failure with respect to this level 5 task. And if a person is not able to successfully complete the level 5 processing task of correctly interpreting the meaning of the experience, then the traumatic content carried in the memory for this experience will include distorted interpretations and the associated distorted emotions—the direct and inherent results of failure with respect to this level 5 task.

As described in chapter 2, when a traumatic memory is activated by some stimuli in the present (triggered), the unresolved toxic content comes forward as implicit memory that feels true in the present. *And this toxic traumatic content will include the direct and inherent consequences of any failed processing tasks from the original experience.*

Note that it is also possible that the person is in a painful situation that she is unable to process *in the present*, and that the consequences of failed processing are being generated by failed processing *in the present*, but my experience is that disruptive phenomena associated with failed processing are usually implicit memory content from unresolved trauma. Therefore, consequences of failed processing tasks, such as lack of access to relational connection circuits, feeling inadequate, confusion, distorted interpretations, and inappropriate emotions driven by distorted interpretations, are all clues that indicate probable triggering.

II. Learn to Recognize the Overall Subjective Experience of Being Triggered:

An approach to learning to recognize your own triggering that many find helpful is learning to recognize the overall subjective experience of being triggered—learning to recognize "this is what I *feel like* when I'm triggered" at a very subjective, intuitive, gestalt level. Learning to recognize a person provides a good analogy. When we first meet a new acquaintance, especially in contexts where we are meeting many new people at the same time, we might try to remember the person by focusing on a handful of specific details. For example, "She was tall, she had red hair, she wore thick black glasses, she had three earrings in her right ear, and she had a tattoo on her left forearm." But as we become more familiar with a person, we very quickly learn to recognize her face, as a whole: "That's just Stephanie—I remember her face." And most[6] of us experience that, in the long run, learning to recognize the person's face, as a whole, is much more effective than trying to remember a bunch of identifying features.

---

6. People with certain neurological disorders are unable to recognize a person's face as a unified, recognizable whole, and therefore use collections of identifying features as the only way of recognizing others. Not surprisingly, these people have much more trouble with mis-identifying their acquaintances. For an excellent discussion of this interesting phenomenon, written for the lay public, see Oliver Sacks, "Chapter Four: Face Blind," in *The Mind's Eye*, large print edition (New York: Random House, 2010), pages 107-144.

A. **Spontaneous Association through Many Repetitions:** In my personal experience this has happened mostly by accident. I started out with a very deliberate, explicit, left-brain process: I would notice that I felt bad, ask the question, "What's wrong? Could traumatic implicit memory be causing this bad feeling?" and then systematically check for clues that would indicate whether or not I was triggered. As I went through this process many hundreds of times over several years, a much more right-brain, intuitive component developed through the normal neurological learning process of repeated association. That is, through many, many repetitions, I increasingly associated the overall subjective experience of being triggered with the logical conclusion, "I'm triggered." Now, my first conscious awareness regarding the possibility of being triggered will often be the thought, "I *feel* triggered," and then I will confirm this thought by checking for specific indicators. My hope is that the rest of you will be able to learn this intuitive, right-hemisphere component much more quickly by being much more deliberate. My suggestion is to learn to recognize when you are triggered by watching for the specific clues, and then, on occasions when you recognize that you're triggered, take time to deliberately notice the overall subjective experience. Take time to ask yourself the question, "What does it *feel like* when my thoughts and emotions are being affected by traumatic implicit memory?"

B. **Deliberate "What Does This Feel Like?" as You Learn Indicators of Triggering:** One might also learn the left-hemisphere systematic approach and the right-hemisphere intuitive approach simultaneously—as you are learning to recognize and watch for each of the specific clues that indicate triggering, deliberately include a component of "what does this *feel* like?" This will not be applicable with a few of the indicators, but this component can easily be included for most. Although I didn't do it this way myself (as I stumbled through the bushes in the process of pioneering these tools), some may find this approach to be more efficient for learning the intuitive, right-hemisphere component of being able to recognize the overall subjective experience of being triggered.

1. **Loss of access to relational circuits:** The many aspects of losing access to your relational circuits contribute strongly to the overall subjective experience of being triggered. Learn to recognize what it feels like to fall into non-relational mode.

2. **Exaggerated reaction to the specific situation:** Learn to recognize what it feels like when you are overreacting.

3. **Maturity level reduced from baseline:** Reduced maturity level contributes to the overall subjective experience of being triggered. Learn to recognize what it feels like to be operating out of entitled, self-centered infant and child maturity. Learn to recognize what it feels like to be burdened and/or overwhelmed by maturity tasks that are usually satisfying.

4. **Capacity and other resources reduced from baseline:** Learn to recognize the overall subjective experience of having your capacity and other re-

sources reduced from baseline. What does it feel like to work with the impaired capacity, impaired faith, impaired creativity, impaired flexibility, etc., corresponding to the ego states contained in childhood memories?

5. **General irritability:** How does it feel when you are experiencing the generalized irritability of being triggered? Learn to recognize this subjective experience.

6. **Vocabulary:** Learn to recognize what it feels like when your thoughts come forward in the vocabulary of your childhood? In my experience, a common subjective feeling aspect of this phenomena is the sense that I can't find words to adequately express my thoughts and emotions, and then frustration with this inability.

7. **Thoughts and emotions inconsistent with reference points:** Sometimes, while I am still in the middle of being triggered, I am able to recognize that my triggered thoughts and emotions are inconsistent with well-established reference points, and the process of recognizing this truth is an interesting experience.[7] Most of my conscious awareness is filled with the triggered thoughts and emotions, and the intense subjective perception that they are true and valid in the present. At the same time, I am also aware of well-established reference points that are totally incompatible with the thoughts and emotions coming from traumatic implicit memory.[8] And even as the triggered thoughts and emotions *feel* intensely true and valid in the present, at some deeper level I know they are distorted. Simultaneously, even as the reference points feel distant and weak, at some deeper level I know they are true. At this point I usually have a thought along the lines of, "This all shows that I'm just triggered," at some deep level I know this thought is true, and it infuriates me because it feels so invalidating and misattuning.[9]

The overall subjective experience you have, as you see incompatibilities between reference points and your triggered thoughts and emotions, may not be exactly the same as mine; but the key is for you to learn to recognize your personal version of this package as a possible component of your overall subjective experience of being triggered.

---

7. Note that sometimes the insight/self-awareness (that triggered thoughts and emotions are inconsistent with reference points) will come later, when you are no longer triggered. In these situations, the insight/self-awareness experience will feel very different, and is *not* a part of the overall subjective experience of actually being triggered.

8. For example, in the middle of the car repair mess it felt *intensely* true that God was failing to help me due to some combination of negligence and/or incompetence and/or perverse spitefulness; and at the same time I knew that many data points, including many of my own experiences and a host of Bible verses, all agreed on the established truth that the Lord is perfectly loving, competent, and always with me.

9. Sometimes this insight comes with more internal attunement—more along the lines of "These thoughts and emotions are all valid, but just not in the present," and then I feel much less resistance. Hopefully, as I continue to grow and heal, I will become increasingly able to offer this insight to myself in this more gentle way.

8. **Focusing on the trigger does not resolve the problem:** The moment of realizing, "Hey, this all looks familiar! This is exactly the picture that developed at the last seven places I worked—this is the problem I thought I solved each time I moved," is definitely an overall subjective experience that you can learn to recognize. Becoming aware of the truth that the painful thoughts and emotions you have been trying to eliminate are coming from somewhere inside of you is also an overall subjective experience you can learn to recognize. However, neither of these insight/self-awareness experiences tend to happen when you are actually triggered. Therefore, learning to recognize the overall feeling of these experiences will contribute to your growing self-awareness, but it will *not* contribute to learning to recognize the overall subjective experience of actually being triggered.[10]

9. **Negative reaction to the suggestion that you might be triggered:** Learn to recognize what it feels like when you respond to the suggestion of possible triggering with defensiveness and/or indignation and/or offense and/or outrage.

10. **Recognize a familiar package:** Learn to recognize the overall subjective experience of your specific memory packages—what does it feel like to be blended with specific packages of unresolved trauma, such as two-year-old memories of being separated from your parents, or eight-year-old memories of being bullied on the playground?

11. **Recognize body sensations associated with being triggered:** An important part of learning to recognize the overall subjective experience of being triggered is learning to recognize the body sensations associated with specific memory packages. For example, when my playground memories of being bullied are triggered forward, I feel muscle tension throughout my body, I feel an anxious hyperalterness, I feel a knot in my stomach, and I have an odd, hard-to-describe physical sensation of being small and vulnerable.

12. **Negative emotions, animosity toward people we are usually glad to be with:** How does it feel when you have negative thoughts and emotions, and even animosity, toward people you are usually glad to be with? Learn to recognize this subjective experience.

13. **Unable to perceive the Lord's presence, establish an interactive connection, or emotionally connect with him:** Being unable to perceive the Lord's presence and/or unable to establish a relational connection and/or unable to emotionally connect with him can definitely be part of the overall subjective experience of being triggered. As described in more detail below, you can deliberately practice recognizing what it feels like when you *are* able to per-

---

10. Learning to recognize the "What does it feel like?" component of these two insight/self-awareness experiences *will* increase your ability to spot the "Focusing on the trigger will never solve the problem" clue, but since these experiences are not part of actually being triggered, learning to recognize them will *not* help you recognize the overall subjective experience of being triggered.

ceive the Lord's presence, establish an interactive connection, and emotionally connect, and you can also deliberately practice recognizing what it feels like when you are *not* able to perceive the Lord's presence and/or establish an interactive connection and/or emotionally connect to him.

14. **Consequences of failed processing tasks:** Learn to recognize what it feels like to lose access to your relational circuits, learn to recognize what it feels like to be unable to handle a situation in a way that is satisfying, learn to recognize what it feels like to be confused, and learn to recognize what it feels like to believe the different distorted interpretations associated with your various unresolved traumatic memories.

C. **Shalom and Joy vs *Not* Shalom and Joy:** There is yet another way to develop the right-hemisphere, intuitive ability to recognize the overall subjective experience of being triggered. We can learn to be more and more consciously aware of what it feels like when we are completely free of triggering, emotionally present, operating in relational mode, and living from the heart Jesus gave us. I would summarize this overall subjective experience as a combination of *joy* and the rich biblical concept of *shalom*. One way to do this is to identify a number of specifics regarding the overall subjective experience of being in this non-triggered, relational mode place of shalom and joy. For example:

> We are aware of ourselves and others;
> We are glad to be with others, and their presence gives us joy;
> We are patient, with high frustration tolerance;
> We have good mind-sight (we are able to accurately perceive and understand what others are thinking and feeling);
> We are playful;
> We are creative and flexible;
> We are life giving, and being life giving is satisfying;
> We can easily perceive the Lord's presence and establish an interactive connection with him;
> We feel emotionally connected to the Lord.

We can then watch deliberately for when these pieces are in place, and learn to recognize what our overall subjective experience feels like when these things are true about ourselves. After learning to recognize what it feels like to be in this place of shalom and joy, we can deliberately watch for it, and thereby train ourselves to become more and more consciously aware of when we are living in shalom and joy. Finally, after becoming more consciously aware of when we *are* living in shalom and joy, we can deliberately watch for times when this is *not* the case, and thereby train ourselves to become more and more consciously aware of when we are not living in shalom and joy. Whenever we realize that we are not experiencing this optimal baseline of shalom and joy, we should assume that we are triggered until proven otherwise.

Some people find this approach to be very helpful, but my personal experience has been mixed. On the plus side, there have been times when this "notice when I'm *not* feeling shalom and joy" approach exposed subtle triggering. On these occasions, I had been consciously aware of enjoying a sustained time of shalom and joy, and noticing the loss of this shalom and joy was the clue that helped me realize that traumatic implicit memory had been triggered forward in a very subtle way.

On the negative side, I find that I'm still subtly triggered much of the time, and that this undermines the value of noticing that I'm not living in shalom and joy. When subtle triggering is smouldering in the background for hours (or days) at a time, so that I spend large blocks of time at a *baseline* that is not shalom and joy, noticing that I'm not living in shalom and joy only tells me that triggered traumatic memory is smouldering subtly in the background. This is valuable information, and has helped me realize the extent to which subtle triggering still smoulders in the background of my day-to-day life, but since I am already at a baseline of not shalom and joy, noticing that I am not living in shalom and joy won't help me to recognize when new triggers stir up additional traumatic memory. In contrast, the indicators of triggering discussed earlier *will* tell me when new triggers stir up additional trauma.

Another point on the negative side (in my experience) is that the "notice when I'm *not* living in shalom and joy" approach lacks power to convince against resistance. When I am really triggered, and angrily resisting the thought that I might be triggered, just noticing that I'm not experiencing shalom and joy has only been marginally effective in convincing me that I am being affected by traumatic implicit memory. In contrast, I have been much more able to accept the humbling truth in these difficult situations, even in spite of intense resistance, when I have been able to line up six or eight specific indicators, all in agreement regarding the presence of traumatic implicit memory.

III. Recognition of Specific Clues *and* Awareness of Overall Subjective Experience: Having made all these comments regarding the value of learning to recognize the overall subjective experience of being triggered—what it *feels* like to be triggered—I still find that it is helpful to be able to recognize the specific indicators of triggering discussed earlier.

When I notice that I'm feeling bad (*not* shalom and joy), and then notice that I *feel* triggered, it is still usually valuable to be able to reinforce/confirm this thought by checking with respect to specific clues. Occasionally the situation will be so clear that I don't feel the need for any additional confirmation or reinforcement—as soon as I have the thought that I might be triggered, I clearly recognize the overall subjective experience of being triggered, and there is no doubt in my mind. But in most situations I still find it helpful to be able to check a few specific indicators to confirm the initial suspicion that my thoughts and emotions are being affected by triggered implicit memory. Unless the triggering is *really* dramatic, I still find problems in the present that are easy to focus on as possible causes for my negative thoughts and emotions, my VLE still comes up with explanations that seem convincing, and my central nervous system extrapolator still does a good job of filling in the holes. Furthermore, implicit memory content still *feels* true and valid in the present, in spite of my thorough cognitive understanding of the phenomenon. When I'm triggered, I still experience an intense subjective pressure toward "these thoughts and feelings are true and valid in the present—I'm upset because _____ (fill in the blank, describing why the trigger is the real problem)." In these situations, I usually have the initial thoughts "I feel bad, I wonder if I'm triggered?" and then, "My overall subjective experience right now does feel like triggering," but when all of these other factors push toward focusing on the triggers as the real problem, it is very helpful to be able to reinforce my initial thoughts by checking for specific indicators of triggering.

Another way to say this is that the strongest approach is to use *both* recognition of specific clues *and* awareness of the overall subjective experience of being triggered. And you will be surprised by how often you need the full power of this "industrial strength" approach.

IV. Attachment Pain, Differential Diagnosis between Attachment Pain and Triggering: Attachment pain is the unique pain we feel when separated, either temporarily or permanently, from key attachment figures, such as family members and close friends. The unresolved content in traumatic memories can include attachment pain, so that the experience of attachment pain in the present can be caused by triggering; but attachment pain can also be caused by truth-based separation or loss in the present, such as when a spouse dies (or is just out of town for a couple weeks).

For this discussion, the main point with respect to attachment pain is that it can cause some of the same observable effects as triggering, such as generalized irritability and exaggerated negative reactions in response to relatively minor provocation. This is practically relevant because the most important care for a person with truth-based attachment pain in the present is to help them build stable, healthy, emotionally connected relationships, and this is not the case for situations where the distress is primarily coming from triggered traumatic memories. Therefore, when asking "am I triggered?" one should also ask "could this be attachment pain as opposed to triggering?"

Pending a much more detailed discussion, I will offer several quick thoughts:

A. Most Attachment Pain Includes at Least a Component of Memory-Based Pain: My observation is that most (all?) of us still have some traumatic memories that include attachment pain. Due to the phenomenon of resonance activation in our memory association networks, any significant attachment pain in the present will also trigger these attachment pain memories. Therefore, any time we are experiencing marked attachment pain, even when initiated by truth-based losses in the present, it will include at least a component of pain from underlying traumatic memories. Practically, this means that even when a person is experiencing attachment pain from separation and/or loss in the present, some of their distress can usually be relieved by helping them identify and resolve any memory-based pain.

B. **Watch for Attachment Pain with Separation and/or Loss:** We should spend a lot more time thinking about where attachment pain might fit in when there has been separation and/or loss that would be expected to cause attachment pain.

C. **Look for Clues That Would Be Present for One, but Not the Other:** The real short summary regarding differential diagnosis between implicit memory content coming forward from traumatic memories and present-based attachment pain is: "look for clues that would be present for triggering but not for present-based attachment pain." For example, grade-school vocabulary is often noticed when childhood memories are activated, but this is not something you would expect to see with present-based attachment pain.

D. **Connecting with the Lord and Receiving His Attunement Are Always a Good Idea:** Establishing an interactive connection with the Lord, and receiving attunement from him, are two of the most helpful interventions for both unresolved traumatic memories and present-based attachment pain, so it is always a good idea to deliberately include these in the treatment plan (for those who are able to perceive the Lord's presence).

V: Miscellaneous Comments, Related Issues:

A. **The Overall Subjective Experience Can Be Very Different from One Triggered Implicit Memory Package to the Next:** It is important to remember that we can experience a variety of different triggered implicit memory packages, and that each of these packages can feel very different from the next. For example, much triggering involves loss of access to our relational circuits, and any time this is the case all of the clues corresponding to non-relational mode will be present. But this is not always the case—sometimes you will still be in relational mode, even though you're triggered. As another example, consider the memory packages for my two-year-old separation trauma and for my eight-year-old experiences of being bullied. While many of the same indicators of being triggered will be present when either of these memory packages are activated, the overall subjective experience of being blended with the two-year-old memories will feel very different from the overall subjective experience of being blended with the eight-year-old memories.

The point here is to realize that there can be many different pictures for what it looks like and feels like to be triggered. If you become very familiar with the packages of traumatic implicit memory that you encounter most frequently, and are immediately able to recognize your overall subjective experience when these familiar packages get triggered forward, remember that there are probably still other memory packages—packages that you will *not* recognize so quickly, and that will not feel so familiar. Another way to put this: don't slip into the trap of thinking, "If I don't recognize one of my familiar implicit memory packages, then I'm not triggered."

B. **Triggering Can Be the Beginning of Healing:** The good news is that many of us have grown since the original traumatic events. Our adult selves in the present often *do* have adequate capacity and maturity skills to successfully process the traumatic memories, especially if we are with others who can help us. When triggering opens a memory of an unresolved traumatic experience, the person who now has adequate resources can embrace this as an opportunity for growth and healing. Triggering can be the beginning of appropriate processing and healing. Instead of letting the triggered content disrupt our lives and destroy our relationships, we can get healing.

C. **Two Significant Patterns Regarding Triggered Traumatic Implicit Memory Content and VLE Confabulations:** As mentioned in chapter 16, I have observed two significant patterns in the course of carefully studying triggered traumtic implicit memory content and the VLE confabulations we come up with to explain it.

   1. **It's easy to spot the big ones, but most of us miss the little ones:** It's easy to spot the most glaring examples, but most of us don't even stop to ask the question with respect to the many, many less dramatic cases of triggered traumatic implicit memory and VLE confabulations.

   2. **It's easy to spot if you know about it and look for it:** As described in more detail in chapter 16, it's easy to spot these phenomena if you look for them, know how to recognize them when you see them, and think systematically and logically about your VLE explanations. However, most of us don't even know these phenomena exist. And we don't see what we don't know exists, don't look for, and don't know how to recognize. A common experience among medical personnel provides a good analogy. When medical professionals learn about a new illness they suddenly see it everywhere. Sometimes this is just the product of overactive imaginations, but often the truth is that people with the illness in question had been walking around in front of them for years, but they missed these cases because they hadn't known the illness was there, hadn't known how to recognize it, and hadn't been looking for it.

D. **Not All Pain Is from Triggered Traumatic Memories:** It is important to remember that painful thoughts and emotions sometimes actually *are* caused by problems in the present. As discussed in much more detail in chapter 29, a common scenario is for real problems in the present to cause painful thoughts and emotions that are valid and appropriate in the present; but then these thoughts and emotions resonate with unresolved trauma, so that traumatic memory content gets activated and comes forward as well. The end result is a situation in which "invisible" traumatic implicit memory is *contributing* to the person's painful thoughts and emotions, and the person is *also* experiencing some pain that is fully legitimate and appropriate in the present.

E. **The Reality Regarding Triggering Can Be Overwhelming and Hard to Accept:** As mentioned in chapter 16, one common stumbling block that can hinder people from accepting and using these principles and tools is that the reality revealed with respect to triggering can be so overwhelming that it is hard to accept. As Charlotte and I have carefully observed ourselves and those around us, our observation is that subtle, low-grade triggering is especially pervasive and chronic. Our perception is that most people are triggered a lot of the time, and that a soberingly high percentage of people are triggered most of the time. This may be hard for many to accept. We encourage you to make your own observations, and to ask God for help in perceiving (and accepting) whatever truth the evidence reveals.

As Charlotte and I have pressed into this with respect to ourselves, we have found the reality regarding how often we are impaired by triggering to be painfully humbling. However, once we got over the initial bump of severe narcissistic mortification, we have found these insights and tools to be TREMENDOUSLY valuable. We have also discovered the truths revealed to be ultimately hopeful, in that every place where we are impaired by triggering is a place where we will experience dramatic improvement as we expose and neutralize our triggered implicit memory and VLE confabulations.

Additional Explanation Regarding
Disorganized Attachment and the
Shalom-for-My-Body Calming Techniques

We develop disorganized attachment patterns when we are repeatedly put in traumatic situations where one of our primary caregivers does things that are overwhelming, frightening, and chaotic—situations where the person that we want
to go to for comfort and safety is actually the source of our distress. When this
happens, we simultaneously experience *both* an intense attachment drive to be with
the person who is our primary caregiver *and* an intense self-protection drive to get
away from this same person as the source of our distress. In a relationship with
disorganized attachment, we feel that we need to be with the person, *and* that we
need to get away from the person. We feel that something terrible will happen if
we leave the person, *and* that something terrible will happen if we stay with them.
In a relationship with disorganized attachment, we feel that we must stay with the
person to be okay, *and* we know the person is unsafe and will hurt us. In any experience or memory that includes the disorganized attachment dilemma (the person we
need to comfort and protect us is the source of our distress), in addition to feeling
fearful we will also feel profoundly confused and disorganized.[1]

There are many toxic aspects to disorganized attachment, and one of these is
that it disrupts the usual synchronized, reciprocal connection between the sympathetic and parasympathetic nervous systems. To better understand this aspect of
disorganized attachment, let's refresh our memories regarding the sympathetic
and parasympathetic nervous systems. The *sympathetic* nervous system is responsible for *activating* the many aspects of physical arousal associated with intense
emotions. For example, when we encounter danger the sympathetic nervous system
activates the physiological changes associated with the fear and anger of the fight-
or-flight response—the increased alertness, the increased muscle tension, the
increased blood flow, and a variety of other physical reactions that prepare our
bodies to either fight or flee. The sympathetic nervous system is like the gas pedal.
As the direct counterpart of the sympathetic nervous system, the *parasympathetic*
nervous system is responsible for *calming* the many aspects of physical arousal
associated with intense emotions. The parasympathetic nervous system is like the
brake pedal.

The sympathetic and parasympathetic nervous systems are designed to be
complementary—we step on the gas pedal when we want to stir things up in preparation for intense activity, and we step on the brake pedal when we want to calm
things down. In fact, there is usually a synchronized, reciprocal connection between

---

1. For additional explanation and discussion regarding disorganized attachment, see
"Brain Science, Emotional Trauma, and the God Who Is with Us ~ Part II."

the sympathetic and parasympathetic nervous systems, so that stimulation of the sympathetic system causes a decrease in the activity of the parasympathetic system, and stimulation of the parasympathetic system causes a decrease in the activity of the sympathetic system. However, severe and complicated trauma (especially including disorganized attachment) can disrupt this synchronized connection, so that the interactions between the two systems are chaotic and unpredictable. In fact, in disorganized attachment we can get stuck in a place where the sympathetic and parasympathetic systems are being stimulated simultaneously. That is, we have one foot stuck on the gas pedal and the other foot stuck on the brakes.

Fortunately, the shalom-for-my-body calming techniques seem to be uniquely helpful for calming a person when his non-relational upset includes disorganized attachment.[2] Our current understanding regarding this benefit is that the physical components of Shalom-for-My-Body systematically alternate between stimulating the sympathetic nervous system and stimulating the parasympathetic nervous system,[3] and this rapid alternation between stimulating the sympathetic and parasympathetic systems somehow reestablishes connection and reciprocal synchronization. Then, after synchronized connection has been reestablished, ending with parasympathetic stimulation will activate the relaxation response and calm the system.[4]

Several additional theoretical considerations also contributed to development of the shalom-for-my-body techniques:

- **EMDR and alternating left/right stimulation:** Eye movement desensitization and reprocessing (EMDR) is one of the most research-supported treatments for psychological trauma, and it is believed that alternating between right-hemisphere and left-hemisphere stimulation is an important neurological component contributing to the technique's effectiveness. With respect to Shalom-for-My-Body, yawning to the left and then yawning to the right, and also the alternating left/right chest taps, are intended to contribute this alternating left-hemisphere/right-hemisphere stimulation component from EMDR.

- **Vagus stimulation and chest tap/rub:** According to Dr. Van der Kolk, stimulation of the vagus nerve activates the thalamus in a way that helps "unstick" neurological systems that have gotten tangled in unsuccessful attempts at processing painful experiences, and thereby contributes to helping successful processing move forward.[5] With respect to Shalom-for-My-Body, tapping

---

2. For example, a person will experience disorganized attachment if he has memories for traumatic experiences that included disorganized attachment, and then one of these memories gets triggered, bringing disorganized attachment forward into the present as part of the memory package.

3. For example, rapidly breathing in stimulates the sympathetic system, and then slowly breathing out stimulates the parasympathetic system.

4. This theory is consistent with initial clinical observations, and Dr. Bessel van der Kolk is currently developing experiments that will provide careful empirical testing.

5. Summary of information from recent presentations by Dr. Bessel van der Kolk, per private communications with Dr. E. James Wilder (phone conversation 9/24/2010, e-mail 12/2/2010).

and rubbing the upper chest—one of the few places on the body where skin sensory receptors map to the vagus nerve—accomplishes this vagus-thalamus stimulation.

- **Yawning:** According to a number of neuroscientists, yawning produces a variety of beneficial neurological effects, including activation of ". . . areas of the brain that are directly involved in generating social awareness and creating feelings of empathy."[6]

---

6.   For a brief discussion of the neurologically beneficial effects of yawning, written for the lay person and summarizing thirty-four yawn-related research studies, see Andrew Newberg and Mark Robert Waldman, *How God Changes Your Brain* (New York: Ballantine Books, 2009), pages 155–159.

Additional Interventions for Calming

As with the shalom-for-my-body techniques, components focusing on the physical body are also prominent in these additional interventions for calming. I have chosen these interventions for the same reason Wilder and Khouri designed the shalom-for-my-body techniques around prominent physical components—the physical components are simple, concrete interventions that we can choose to apply even when we are intensely upset and our brains are significantly impaired by being in non-relational mode. Furthermore, physical body interventions can produce surprisingly dramatic benefits for the whole body-mind-spirit system. Our bodies, minds, and spirits are so intimately connected that calming one will usually also produce powerful calming effects for the others. In fact, Dr. Edmund Jacobson's fascinating research (described in more detail below) shows that it is almost impossible to have an anxious mind if your body is fully and deeply relaxed.

Just as with the shalom-for-my-body calming exercises, the meditative prayer, deep breathing,[1] and progressive muscle relaxation[2] exercises presented here all produce the physiological "relaxation response" that helps calm intense emotions

---

1. For a very understandable discussion of Dr. Benson and colleagues' extensive work with respect to breathing exercises, meditative prayer, and the relaxation response, see Herbert Benson and Miriam Z. Klipper, *The Relaxation Response,* updated and expanded edition (New York: HarperCollins, 2000) and Herbert Benson, *Beyond the Relaxation Response* (New York: Berkley Books, 1984).

2. The reader will remember that the relaxation response is essentially the opposite of the sympathetic nervous system stimulation associated with the fight-or-flight response. Carefully documented case studies show that prolonged use of daily progressive muscle relaxation produces lasting benefits for many illnesses that are caused and/or exacerbated by excessive sympathetic activity. See, for example, the many case studies described in Edmund Jacobson, *You Must Relax: Practical Methods for Reducing the Tensions of Modern Living,* fifth edition (New York: McGraw-Hill, 1976), and Edmund Jacobson, *Progressive Relaxation: A Physiological and Clinical Investigation of Muscular States and Their Significance in Psychology and Medical Practice,* second edition, Midway Reprint (Chicago: University of Chicago Press, 1974), pages 357–411, 422–423. Furthermore, laboratory research demonstrates that progressive muscle relaxation consistently produces decreased norepinephrine levels in the blood, decreased skin conductance, decreased heart contractility, decreased blood pressure, and decreased heart rate. (See, for example, Dennis M. Davidson et al., "Effects of Relaxation Therapy on Cardiac Performance and Sympathetic Activity in Patients with Organic Heart Disease," *Psychosomatic Medicine* vol. 41, no. 4 (June 1979): pages 303–309; F. D. McGlynn et al., "Relaxation Training Inhibits Fear and Arousal During In Vivo Exposure to Phobia-cue Stimuli," *Journal of Behavior Therapy and Experimental Psychiatry* vol. 30, no. 3 (September 1999): pages 155–168; E. Jacobson, "Variation of Blood Pressure with Skeletal Muscle Tension and Relaxation," *Annals of Internal Medicine* vol. 12, no. 8 (February 1939): pages 1194–1212; and E. Jacobson, "Variation of Blood Pressure with Skeletal Muscle Tension and Relaxation. II. The Heart Beat," *Annals of Internal Medicine* vol. 13, no. 9 (March 1940): pages 1619–1625.) Both of these sets of data indicate that progressive muscle relaxation also produces the physiological relaxation response studied by Dr. Benson.

by calming the physical reactions associated with intense emotions. As noted in the comments regarding Shalom My Body, this relaxation response is especially relevant to our discussion, since it is especially effective in calming the fear and anger at the center of the fight-or-flight reaction, and these are the negative emotions that most powerfully push us into non-relational mode.

In addition to the prominent physical components that focus most directly on calming the body/brain, these calming techniques also include components that directly calm the mind and spirit. With respect to the mind, simply directing our attention *to* the practical details of the calming interventions provides a mental focus that takes our attention *away* from the upsetting situations that cause us to fall into non-relational mode in the first place. For example, with the breathing exercises, focusing *on* our breathing directs and holds our attention *away* from the issues, problems, and triggers that are upsetting us. With meditative prayer, focusing *on* a combination of our breathing and a simple prayer directs and holds our attention *away* from the issues, problems, and triggers that are causing our negative emotions. And with the muscle relaxation exercises, focusing *on* our muscles directs and holds our attention *away* from the issues, problems, and triggers that are producing the fear, anger, shame, etc. that are pushing us into non-relational mode. As I have been experimenting with each of these calming tools, I have been pleasantly surprised by the effectiveness of this simple component of each of these techniques. In fact, my assessment is that the mental focus component (directing and holding my attention *away* from the issues, problems, and triggers that were causing me to be upset) has usually been the most tangibly effective part of the intervention.

With respect to the spirit, even though secular practitioners use deep breathing and progressive muscle relaxation without any spiritual component, these exercises can easily be modified to incorporate simple prayer. The physical components of each of these calming techniques become more and more routine with ongoing practice, and as these components become increasingly routine (thereby requiring less and less attention), we can add a component of simple prayer.

As mentioned in the main text, another important point regarding these additional interventions for calming is that most people need to practice them for a while under ideal conditions before being able to use them in difficult situations. However, if you invest the initial time and effort required to become skillful with these techniques, they can be powerful resources for calming even in messy, difficult situations where you are upset, triggered, and non-relational, where you have less time, and where the environment is distracting and uncomfortable.[3]

I. Meditative Prayer: One fairly simple and consistently effective calming resource is a simple form of meditative prayer much like the basic contemplative prayer

---

3. See, for example, Herbert Benson, *The Relaxation Response*, updated and expanded (New York: HarperCollins, 2000), especially pages xix, xxii, 132, 133; Herbert Benson and William Proctor, *Beyond the Relaxation Response* (New York: Berkley Books, 1984), especially pages 127, 129, 131, and 136–140; and Edmund Jacobson, *You Must Relax: Practical Methods for Reducing the Tensions of Modern Living*, fifth edition (New York: McGraw-Hill, 1976), especially pages 59, 60, 147, 164, and 197–216.

taught by church leaders and by Christian mystics throughout the ages.[4] There are also a variety of other ways to engage in meditative prayer, but the following guidelines should enable you to experiment with this very simple form that many have found to be a powerful calming resource.

With respect to decreasing your baseline sympathetic arousal so that you are more resistant to getting triggered into non-relational mode, and with respect to building skill with calming techniques so that you can use them effectively in increasingly difficult situations, the time required to experience benefits from regular practice sessions is quite variable. Dr. Benson reports that some experience full benefits in as little as two weeks, but that for others benefits can increase slowly for as long as a year. He also observes that most people will experience significant physiological benefits corresponding to decreased baseline sympathetic stimulation (such as decreased blood pressure) within four to six weeks.[5]

A. **Choose a Prayer to Use as Your Focus:** Choose a simple prayer that is easy to remember, easy to pronounce, and that you can say quietly to yourself during one breath. Within these limitations, use any phrase or Scripture which is particularly meaningful to you. It is okay to experiment some initially in order to find a prayer that is comfortable for you. However, you will eventually want to decide on a prayer that you can use each time, so that as you practice you can relax more and more into the Lord's care without having to think so much about the words you are saying. Furthermore, if you use the same prayer each time, your mind and body will learn to associate this prayer with relaxation. This conditioned response will increase the beneficial power of the prayer.[6] Examples: "Lord Jesus Christ, have mercy on me," "Come, Holy Spirit," "Lord Jesus, please help me," "The Lord is my shepherd," (Ps. 23) "Jesus saves," or just "Jesus."

You can also use a pair of phrases, one for the breath in and the second for the breath out. For example, "I thank you that you are here with me Lord," and "Help me to perceive your presence more clearly." Or even a two-phrase couplet distributed over two breaths, such as (first breath, inhale) "You are good, Lord," (first breath, exhale) "all the time"; (second breath, inhale) "and all the time, Lord," (second breath, exhale) "you are good."

B. **Make Yourself as Comfortable as Possible:** Ideally, your entire body, including your head, should be supported. Lying down on a sofa or bed, or sitting in a reclining chair, are good ways to obtain complete support. Also, placing

---

4. For a brief summary of the similarities between traditional Christian contemplative prayer and this meditative prayer calming technique, see Herbert Benson, *The Relaxation Response,* updated and expanded (New York: HarperCollins, 2000), pages 80–96.

5. Herbert Benson, *Beyond the Relaxation Response* (New York: Berkley Books, 1984), page 121.

6. Actually, these benefits can still apply if you alternate between two or three prayers that you use repeatedly. The key is to avoid constant change, in that this will require more effort with respect to remembering the content and also prevent the beneficial conditioned response connection between the specific prayer(s) and physical relaxation.

a pillow (or two) under your knees can be helpful if you have trouble with lower back strain.

Obviously, if you are upset and in non-relational mode, and you are using meditative prayer as part of regaining access to your relational circuits, you may be riding on the bus supervising three children on the way home from a long visit to the Museum of Science and Industry. When you are in messy, difficult situations where the ideal is not possible, then just do the best you can to be as comfortable as possible. Fortunately (as noted above), with practice you can effectively use this calming technique in increasingly uncomfortable situations. However, when you are engaging in regular, ongoing practice sessions, as part of building skill with calming techniques and decreasing your baseline sympathetic arousal, then you should take the time to find an ideal setting where you can be as comfortable as possible, in a fully supported, reclining position.[7]

C. **Minimize Distractions and Interruptions:** A setting free from distractions and interruptions is ideal. Sudden loud noises and human voices (including the TV) are especially distracting, so pay special attention to minimizing these. A pair of good earplugs can be very helpful.[8] Interruptions, such as the telephone ringing or someone walking into the room unexpectedly, are also very disruptive, so take deliberate steps to minimize these as well.

As already mentioned, if you are upset and in non-relational mode, and you are using meditative prayer as part of regaining access to your relational circuits, you may be on the bus with your children on the way home from the museum. Again, when you are in messy, difficult situations then just do the best you can with respect to distractions. Fortunately (as mentioned above), with practice you can effectively use this calming technique in increasingly distracting situations as well as in increasingly uncomfortable situations. For example, people have been able to use this kind of meditative prayer while exercising, while sitting at their desk at the office, while in classrooms during examinations, while receiving chemotherapy, and while riding on jostling, noisy public transportation. Furthermore, in many difficult situations it is possible to excuse yourself, and then find a place more conducive to this meditative prayer calming exercise.

As with physical comfort, when you are engaging in regular, ongoing practice sessions, as part of building skill with calming techniques and decreasing your baseline sympathetic arousal, you should take the time

---

7. If you have a tendency to fall asleep during your meditative prayer practice sessions, then experiment with kneeling, sitting, or other positions that are as comfortable as possible while still helping to avoid sleep.

8. This may seem like such a small thing as to be almost silly, but the right pair of ear plugs can make a big difference. I have tried many different brands, and they vary widely with respect to both comfort and effectiveness. If I had tried the worst brand first, and not known that others were so much better, I would have quickly discarded the inexpensive but extremely valuable ear plug resource. Also, a little Vaseline rubbed onto the surface of the ear plugs can help if you have trouble with ear plugs causing soreness in your ear canals.

to find an ideal setting where distractions and interruptions can be minimized as much as possible.

D. **Make Ten- to Twenty-Minute Sessions a Part of Your Daily Routine:** When you are engaging in regular, ongoing practice sessions, as part of building skill with calming techniques and decreasing your baseline sympathetic arousal, Dr. Benson recommends continuing the meditative prayer for a set period of time (ten to twenty minutes) once or twice each day. The ideal scenario is to incorporate these regular practice sessions into your daily routine (like brushing your teeth or taking a shower).

With respect to the messy, difficult situations where you are using meditative prayer as part of regaining access to your relational circuits, you obviously don't plan these times of crisis and can't schedule the ideal twenty minutes of uninterrupted quiet for meditative prayer calming interventions. Once again, do the best you can. Fortunately (as mentioned above), many find that they can learn to use this type of meditative prayer whenever the need arises and for as much time as they have available. For those who have engaged in regular practice, so that they have increased skill and also the benefit of a positive conditioned response, five minutes (or even less) can produce significant calming.

E. **Practice on an Empty Stomach:** It seems that food digestion after meals tends to disrupt deep relaxation, so avoid scheduling your regular practice sessions after meals. If it's possible, the best plan is to schedule your practice sessions for times when your stomach is empty, such as immediately before meals.

F. **Close Your Eyes:** This one is pretty self-explanatory.

G. **Relax Your Muscles:** Relax the different muscle groups in your body, starting with your feet and moving upward to your calves, thighs, abdomen, chest, arms, shoulders, neck, and head. Tension in the muscles of the face and scalp are especially common with intense negative emotions, so take special care to relax these muscle groups. If you have difficulty with muscle tension interfering with your prayer time, use the progressive relaxation exercises described below to gain skill with respect to muscle relaxation.

H. **Coordinate Your Breathing with Your Simple Prayer:** Become aware of your breathing. Breathe slowly and deeply. When you are breathing slowly and deeply, begin to coordinate your breathing with your simple prayer. Some prefer to say part of their prayer as they breathe in and then the remainder as they breathe out. Others prefer to breathe in quietly and then say their prayer as they exhale. As mentioned in point A, it is important to choose a simple prayer that can be said quietly and easily in one of these two ways. Also, you can either speak your prayer audibly or just say the prayer silently in your thoughts. I find it difficult to speak audibly as I am breathing in, so I use the silent-thought method for the part of the prayer associated with breathing in, and then speak quietly the part of the prayer associated with breathing out.

I. **Maintain the Focus of Your Attention on Your Breathing and Prayer:** As described above, directing and holding the focus of your attention *on* your breathing and prayer, and thereby *away* from the issues, problems, and triggers that are upsetting you can be a very important part of the intervention. Also, it would actually be more accurate to say, "keep bringing the focus of your attention back to your breathing and prayer," since everybody has the experience of frequently, spontaneously, involuntarily drifting back to whatever it was that was upsetting them in the first place. In my experience, noticing that my attention has drifted back to the initial issues, problems, and triggers (*again*), and then gently redirecting my focus to my breathing and prayer, has been the most challenging part of the exercise. Fortunately, this is a skill that we can learn, so this challenge gets progressively easier with practice.

Regarding the exact focus for your attention, experiment to find what works best for you. You might find that it works best to use your breathing as your primary focus, with a very, very simple prayer (such as just the one word, "Jesus") subtly in the background. You might find that it works best to use your prayer as you primary focus, with a vague awareness of your breathing in the background. Or you might find that it works best for your breathing and your prayer to share the focus of your attention more evenly (this has been my experience).

J. **Maintain a Nonjudgmental Attitude Toward Yourself, Especially with Respect to Distracting Thoughts:** As just mentioned, everybody has trouble with repeatedly drifting back to the issues, problems, and triggers that caused their upsetting negative emotions in the first place. In fact, even when you are just practicing the exercises in a calm, quiet environment, distracting thoughts and/or worries are a very common problem. Don't be surprised if initially it is difficult to maintain meditative prayer for more than a few moments. Your ability to maintain the focus of your attention on your breathing and prayer will improve with time and practice.

One of the keys for preventing upsetting or distracting thoughts from becoming a much bigger disruption is to take a nonjudgmental attitude toward yourself with respect to distractions. Whenever you notice you have begun thinking about something else, don't punish yourself with thoughts of being a failure; rather, just gently bring your attention back to your breathing and your simple prayer. If worries come to mind, remind yourself, "I can think about that when I'm finished with my prayer time. Now the priority is to calm down and get back into relational mode." It is important to gently put worrisome or distracting thoughts aside, or to simply let them pass on by, and then gently bring the focus of your attention back to your breathing and prayer *without judging yourself or fighting the distractions.* When you judge yourself and/or try to fight the upsetting or distracting thoughts, they become much more disruptive.

A little trick that has helped me is to *explicitly embrace* the process of dealing with distractions as part of the exercise—as part of the new skill that you are trying to learn. Whenever I notice that I have become distracted (again), I say to myself, "Ah, I have just practiced the skill of becoming more mindful of when my attention wanders, and now I get to practice the skill of gently bringing my attention back to the target that I have actually chosen to focus on."

K. **End Your Prayer Time Smoothly:** When you are engaging in regular, on-going practice sessions, as part of building skill with calming techniques and decreasing your baseline sympathetic arousal, it is ideal to end your prayer time smoothly. If you use a timer or alarm clock to signal the end of your time, make sure to find an alarm that is not jarring or startling. Anticipation of the jolt from the alarm will interfere with the relaxation. A gentle timer or alarm clock, with a quiet chime or soft music as the "time's up" signal, will allow you to be free from worrying about the time but without jolting you out of your prayer. An alternative technique is to keep a clock or watch easily visible and to peek occasionally as you think about the time. When you are finished with your prayer time, continue to sit quietly with your eyes closed for one or two minutes before moving into the rest of your day.

It will obviously be more difficult to end the prayer time smoothly in the messy, difficult situations where you are using meditative prayer as part of getting back into relational mode. Once again, do the best you can.

II. Deep Breathing: Another simple and effective calming resource is the following basic deep breathing exercise.

A. **Make Yourself as Comfortable as Possible:** As described in the section regarding meditative prayer, above.

B. **Minimize Distractions and Interruptions:** As described in the section regarding meditative prayer, above.

C. **Make Regular Five-Minute Sessions a Part of Your Daily Routine:** When you are engaging in regular, ongoing practice sessions, as part of building skill with calming techniques and decreasing your baseline sympathetic arousal, Dr. Edmund Bourne recommends a practice session of at least five minutes each day. If possible, find a regular time for your practice sessions so that your breathing exercises become a habit.[9]

With respect to the messy, difficult situations where you are using deep breathing as part of regaining access to your relational circuits, you obviously don't plan these times of crisis and can't schedule the ideal five minutes of uninterrupted quiet for deep breathing exercises. Once again, do the best you can. Fortunately, many find that they can learn to use deep breathing whenever the need arises and for as much time as they have available. For those who have engaged in regular practice, so that they have increased skill

---

9. Edmund J. Bourne, *The Anxiety and Phobia Workbook*, second edition (Oakland, CA: New Harbinger Publications, 1995), page 72.

and also the benefit of a positive conditioned response, even two to three minutes can produce significant calming.

D. **Practice on an Empty Stomach:** As described in the section on meditative prayer above.

E. **Close Your Eyes:** Again, this one is pretty self-explanatory.

F. **Relax Your Muscles:** As described in the section on meditative prayer above.

G. **Inhale:** Inhale slowly, through your nose, and count slowly to five as you inhale.

H. **Pause:** Pause and hold your breath, again to a slow count of five.

I. **Exhale:** Exhale slowly, through your nose or mouth, to a slow count of five (or more if it takes you longer). Make sure to exhale fully.

J. **Two Normal Breaths, and Then Repeat:** After exhaling completely, take two breaths in your normal rhythm, and then repeat the breathing cycle just described in steps G through I.

K. **Continue the Exercise for at Least Five Minutes:** This should involve going through at least ten cycles of inhale-five, hold-five, exhale-five. As you continue the exercise, you may notice that you sometimes breathe more deeply and can count higher, or that you sometimes count higher when you exhale than when you inhale. Don't worry about these variations, and just allow them to occur if/as they happen spontaneously. Remember to take two normal breaths between each cycle. If you start to feel light-headed, take a thirty-second break and then resume the exercise.

L. **Keep Your Breathing Smooth and Regular:** Throughout the exercise, keep your breathing smooth and regular. (Avoid gulping in breaths or breathing out suddenly.)

M. **Maintain the Focus of Your Attention on Your Breathing and Prayer:** As described in the section regarding meditative prayer above.

N. **Maintain a Nonjudgmental Attitude toward Yourself, Especially with Respect to Distracting Thoughts:** As described in the section regarding meditative prayer above.

O. **End Your Deep Breathing Time Smoothly:** As described in the section regarding meditative prayer above.

P. **Incorporate Simple Prayer (optional):** As you practice regularly, the practical, physical aspects of the deep breathing component will become increasingly routine. When you get to the point that your breathing rhythm is smooth, you are not having trouble with either hyperventilating or feeling like you aren't getting enough air, and you feel like you could maintain slow, smooth breathing, including the pauses, without needing to count, you have the option of weaving a simple prayer into the exercise. If you do decide to incorporate prayer into this deep breathing exercise, then choose a simple prayer as described in the section on meditative prayer above.

For sessions including the prayer component, begin the breathing exercise as already described. Once you are comfortably established in your familiar deep breathing rhythm, begin to coordinate your breathing with your simple prayer. Some prefer to say part of their prayer as they breathe in and then the remainder as they breathe out. Others prefer to breathe in quietly and then say their prayer as they exhale. Also, you can either speak your prayer audibly or just say the prayer silently in your thoughts. I find it difficult to speak audibly as I am breathing in, so I use the silent-thought method for the part of the prayer associated with breathing in, and then speak quietly the part of the prayer associated with breathing out.

As you probably already realize, if you decide to include the prayer component, then this breathing exercise becomes a variation of the meditative prayer described earlier, with the primary difference being an increased focus on the breathing component.

For any readers who want to pursue deep breathing calming techniques more vigorously, a huge collection of research and other resources is easily available. (The Google search I just did for "deep breathing exercises" yielded 2,940,000 links.)

III. Progressive Muscle Relaxation: In an ingenious series of experiments, Dr. Jacobson meticulously recorded the electrical activity in specific muscles as study subjects engaged in a wide variety of mental activities, such as generating predetermined mental images, engaging in carefully defined imaginary physical activities, imagining spoken interactions, and even thinking about abstract concepts. He then analyzed the patterns of muscle tension and was able to demonstrate that *every mental activity studied, including deliberately generated negative thoughts and emotions, consistently produced measurable tension in the muscles that would logically correspond to the mental activity in question.* For example, if he instructed you to imagine being in a restaurant and asking the waiter to bring the bill, the recording of tensions in the muscles associated with speech would exactly match the imagined interaction. That is, as you were imagining the interaction, measurable tension in your speech muscles would reveal that you were "talking" internally. An observation of particular interest was that *almost all activity of the mind included mental images and/or mental speech, and that these internal, mental activities always corresponded to measurable tension in the muscles that move the eyes and/or the muscles responsible for speech.*

Furthermore, Dr. Jacobson demonstrated that a person could consistently "relax" the thoughts and emotions in her mind by using progressive relaxation techniques to systematically decrease tension in the muscles that would otherwise be activated by the thoughts and emotions. In fact, he observed that completely blocking activity in a given group of muscles would often completely block any thoughts or emotions that would be associated with tension in those muscles (for as long as the muscles remained relaxed). And he observed that this phenomena was also especially pronounced when the systematic relaxation carefully included the muscles associated with eye movement and speech.[10] Putting this all together, Dr. Jacobson's research shows that *systematic, deep relaxation of our voluntary muscles will consistently produce powerful calming effects on our minds.*[11]

With respect to decreasing your baseline sympathetic arousal so that you are more resistant to getting triggered into non-relational mode, and with respect to building skill with calming techniques so that you can use them effectively in increasingly difficult situations, the time required to experience benefits from regular practice sessions is quite variable. Dr. Jacobson reports that most will notice increased skill and significant decrease in baseline tension with several months of regular practice. He also notes that in some situations, such as with chronic high blood pressure, benefits can increase slowly but steadily over the course of years.[12]

---

10.   From my own observations, I would add that activity in your muscles of facial expression is especially closely linked to the emotions you are feeling at any given moment, and that relaxing these muscles is therefore especially important in "relaxing" intense negative emotions.

11.   E. Jacobson, "Electrical Measurements of Neuromuscular States During Mental Activities: I. Imagination of Movement Involving Skeletal Muscle," *American Journal of Physiology,* vol. 91, no. 2 (1930): pages 567–608; E. Jacobson, "Electrical Measurements of Neuromuscular States during Mental Activities: II. Imagination and Recollection of Various Muscular Acts," *American Journal of Physiology* vol. 94, no. 1 (1930): pages 22–34; E. Jacobson, "Electrical Measurements of Neuromuscular States During Mental Activities: III. Visual Imagination and Recollection," *American Journal of Physiology,* vol. 95, no. 3 (1930): pages 694–702; E. Jacobson "Electrical Measurements of Neuromuscular States during Mental Activities: IV. Evidence of Contraction of Specific Muscles During Imagination," *American Journal of Physiology,* vol. 95, no. 3 (1930): pages 703–712; E. Jacobson "Electrical Measurements of Neuromuscular States During Mental Activities: V. Variation of Specific Muscles Contracting during Imagination," *American Journal of Physiology,* vol. 96, no. 1 (1931): pages 122–125; E. Jacobson, "Electrical Measurements of Neuromuscular States during Mental Activities: VII. Imagination, Recollection and Abstract Thinking Involving the Speech Musculature," *American Journal of Physiology,* vol. 97, no. 1 (1931): pages 200–209; and E. Jacobson, "Electrophysiology of Mental Activities," *American Journal of Psychology,* vol. 44, no 2 (October 1932): pages 677–694. **For a brief summary of this extensive research, written for the layperson,** see Edmund Jacobson, *You Must Relax: Practical Methods for Reducing the Tensions of Modern Living,* fifth edition (New York: McGraw-Hill, 1976), pages 189–196 and 239–253.

12.   See, for example, the case study described on pages 145–146 of Edmund Jacobson, *You Must Relax: Practical Methods for Reducing the Tensions of Modern Living,* fifth edition (New York: McGraw-Hill, 1976), and the case studies described on pages 357–394 of Edmund Jacobson, *Progressive Relaxation: A Physiological and Clinical Investigation of Muscular States and Their Significance in Psychology and Medical Practice,* second edition, Midway Reprint (Chicago: University of Chicago Press, 1974) .

A. **General Conditions/Parameters:** With respect to general conditions and parameters, most of the guidelines described above for meditative prayer and deep breathing also apply to progressive muscle relaxation.

1. **Make yourself as comfortable as possible:** As described above in the section on meditative prayer.

2. **Minimize distractions and interruptions:** As described above in the section on meditative prayer. Again, when you are in messy, difficult situations then just do the best you can with respect to distractions. Fortunately (as mentioned above), with practice you can effectively use progressive muscle relaxation in increasingly distracting situations as well as in increasingly uncomfortable situations.

3. **Make thirty-minute practice sessions a part of your daily routine:** When you are engaging in regular, ongoing practice sessions, as part of building skill with calming techniques and decreasing your baseline sympathetic arousal, all current protocols I reviewed recommend daily practice sessions that usually require thirty minutes for beginners. Again, the ideal scenario is to incorporate these regular practice sessions into your daily routine (like brushing your teeth or taking a shower).

With respect to the messy, difficult situations where you are using progressive muscle relaxation as part of regaining access to your relational circuits, you obviously don't plan these times of crisis and can't schedule the ideal thirty minutes of uninterrupted quiet for muscle relaxation calming sessions. Once again, do the best you can. Fortunately, the exercises will flow more smoothly and quickly with practice. (Most people report that the time required to go through the exercises can eventually be reduced to fifteen minutes.) Furthermore, Dr. Jacobson reports that after sufficient practice with isolating and relaxing individual muscle groups, one can skip the component exercises and simply relax all of the muscle groups simultaneously. This can be accomplished in as little as one to two minutes. Dr. Jacobson also reports that you can learn to accomplish deep muscle relaxation without the contraction part of the exercise,[13] which is nice if you are in public. (If you spend ten seconds in intense contraction of all your muscle groups simultaneously, bystanders might think you are having a seizure.)

4. **Practice on an empty stomach:** As described above in the section on meditative prayer.

5. **Close your eyes:** Again, this one is pretty self-explanatory.

---

13. Edmund Jacobson, *Progressive Relaxation: A Physiological and Clinical Investigation of Muscular States and Their Significance in Psychology and Medical Practice*, second edition, Midway Reprint (Chicago: University of Chicago Press, 1974), pages 43, 63, and 80; Edmund Jacobson, *You Must Relax: Practical Methods for Reducing the Tensions of Modern Living*, fifth edition (New York: McGraw-Hill, 1976), pages 164 and 179.

6. **Maintain the focus of your attention on your breathing and prayer:** As described in the section regarding meditative prayer, above.

7. **Maintain a nonjudgmental attitude toward yourself, especially with respect to distracting thoughts:** Distracting thoughts and/or worries are a very common problem, especially when you are upset and using progressive muscle relaxation to help yourself get back into relational mode. Don't be surprised if initially it is difficult to maintain focus on the sensations of muscle tension and relaxation (or on the optional simple prayer) for more than a few moments. Concentration will improve with time and practice. As much as possible, take a nonjudgmental attitude toward these distracting thoughts. Whenever you notice you have begun thinking about something else, don't punish yourself with thoughts of being a failure. Rather, gently come back to focusing on the sensations of muscle tension and relaxation (or on the optional simple prayer). If worries come to mind, remind yourself, "I can think about that when I'm finished with my muscle relaxation. Right now the priority is to calm down and get back into relational mode." It is important to gently put worrisome and distracting thoughts aside, or to simply let them pass on by, as opposed to fighting them.

8. **End your time of muscle relaxation smoothly:** As described above in the section on meditative prayer.

9. **Incorporate simple prayer (optional):** As you practice regularly, the practical, physical aspects of the progressive muscle relaxation exercises will become increasingly routine. When you get to the point that you can remember the sequence of muscle groups with minimal mental effort, you can carry out the various instructions with minimal mental effort, and you are familiar with the sensations of tension and relaxation (and especially aware of the difference between them), you have the option of weaving a simple prayer into the exercise. If you do decide to incorporate prayer, then choose a simple prayer as described in the section on meditative prayer above.

None of the authors I read regarding progressive muscle relaxation have mentioned breathing, but I recommend maintaining slow, steady breathing throughout the exercises, and then you can coordinate the simple prayer with your breathing. Some prefer to say part of their prayer as they breathe in and then the remainder as they breathe out. Others prefer to breathe in quietly and then say their prayer as they exhale. Also, you can either speak your prayer audibly or just say the prayer silently in your thoughts. I find it difficult to speak audibly as I am breathing in, so I use the silent-thought method for the part of the prayer associated with breathing in, and then quietly speak the part of the prayer associated with breathing out.

My understanding of progressive muscle relaxation is that it is important to be aware of the tension, and especially the relaxation, in each muscle group. Therefore, I recommend that you continue to focus a small part of your awareness on your muscles, even after you have practiced to the point that you can go through the exercises with very little conscious attention to the specific instructions. I try to focus most of my attention on the prayer, while also maintaining a subtle awareness of my muscles in the background.

Finally, I found that I can use my simple prayer to help with keeping time. I practiced with my prayer until I developed a steady, consistent rhythm, and then noted that one cycle of (inhale) "You are good, Lord," (exhale) "all the time," (inhale) "and all the time, Lord," (exhale) "you are good," required ten to twelve seconds. So as a way of keeping time, I tense each muscle group for one cycle through my prayer, and then relax each muscle group for the time it takes to go through two cycles.

B. **Additional Guidelines for Progressive Muscle Relaxation:** The core of progressive muscle relaxation is to first tense and then relax, in succession, a series of muscle groups, with the goal being to produce deep muscle relaxation throughout the entire body. Apply the following additional guidelines as you tense and relax each of the specific muscle groups in the sequence below.

1. **Tense vigorously for about ten seconds:** When you tense each muscle group, do so vigorously (but without straining) for about ten seconds.

2. **Focus on sensations associated with tension:** As you tense each muscle group, focus on the muscles, paying special attention to the physical sensations associated with the building tension.

3. **Release and relax:** After the ten seconds of tension, release each muscle group suddenly, and then allow the muscles to relax as fully as possible for the next twenty seconds.

4. **Focus on sensations associated with relaxation:** As you relax each muscle group, focus on the muscles, paying attention to the physical sensations associated with the deepening relaxation. Especially notice the difference between how the muscles feel as they are relaxing and how they felt when they were tensed.

5. **Redirect your attention gently:** If your attention wanders from focusing on your muscles, gently bring it back to the muscle group you're working with.

6. **Keep other muscle groups relaxed:** While working with a particular muscle group, try to keep all of the other muscle groups relaxed as much as possible. Most people initially have difficulty with isolating the different muscle groups in this way, but this skill steadily grows with practice.

7. **Repeat the tension cycle if necessary:** You will tense and relax most muscle groups once, but if you can still feel lingering tension in a particular set of muscles after the first cycle, you can repeat the tension and relaxation two

or three times. Allow an additional twenty seconds of deliberate relaxation between each cycle.

8. Use an audio recording of the directions (optional): Some people find it helpful to make an audio recording of the directions for specific muscle groups, incorporating the time intervals for both contraction and relaxation, so that they don't have to read the instructions or keep track of time as they are going through the exercises. This is especially helpful for early practice sessions.

C. Directions for Specific Muscle Groups: When Dr. Jacobson first developed progressive muscle relaxation more than seventy-five years ago, he recommended a series of more than two hundred exercises that required months of daily hour-long sessions to complete. Thankfully, since Dr. Jacobson's pioneering work in the 1920s, we have found that much simpler protocols can produce many of the same benefits.[14] The tension component is included to help the person focus on a particular muscle group, and to help the person learn to recognize the sensations associated with both muscle tension and muscle relaxation. It has also been discovered that relaxation following intense contraction is usually more complete than when the person tries to relax her muscles from a resting baseline;[15] however, the initial tension phase becomes less and less necessary as the person gains skill with respect to the relaxation response, and can eventually be eliminated completely. The sequence below has been adapted from several of the most popular protocols currently in use,[16] with several of my own contributions

---

14.   Many authors writing about abbreviated protocols for PMR claim that they provide *all* of the same benefits. I have found many research studies verifying that abbreviated protocols provide *many* of the same benefits but no research actually verifying *all* of the same benefits. Also, McGuigan and Lehrer, two doctors who have worked extensively with Jacobson's longer protocols, argue (somewhat convincingly) that they still produce superior results. See Douglas A. Bernstein, Charles R. Carlson, and John E. Schmidt, "Progressive Relaxation: Abbreviated Methods," in *Principles and Practice of Stress Management,* third edition, eds., Paul M. Lehrer, Robert L. Woolfolk, and Wesley E. Sime (New York: Guilford Press, 2007), pages 88–122 for a summary of the steps by which various clinicians have condensed Jacobson's original protocols to the current much briefer exercises, and also for discussion of the theory and research supporting the effectiveness of the current, condensed protocols. See F. J. McGuigan and Paul M. Lehrer, "Progressive Relaxation: Origins, Principles, and Clinical Applications," in *Principles and Practice of Stress Management,* third edition, eds., Paul M. Lehrer, Robert L. Woolfolk, and Wesley E. Sime (New York: Guilford Press, 2007), pages 57–87 for arguments that Jacobson's more extensive protocols still produce superior results.

15.   D. A. Bernstein and T. D. Borkovec, *Progressive Relaxation Training: A Manual for the Helping Professions* (Champaign, IL: Research Press, 1973), page 20; and Gordon L. Paul, *Insight Versus Desensitization in Psychotherapy* (Stanford, CA: Stanford University Press, 1966), page 118.

16.   See, for example; Edmund J. Bourne, *The Anxiety and Phobia Workbook,* second edition (Oakland, CA: New Harbinger Publications, 1995), pages 73–76; Rolf G. Jacob and William E. Pelham, "Behavior Therapy," in *Kaplan and Sadock's Comprehensive Textbook of Psychiatry,* eighth edition, eds., Benjamin J. Sadock and Virginia A. Sadock (Baltimore, MD: Lipincott Williams & Wilkins, 2004), page 2531; and Douglas A. Bernstein, Charles R. Carlson, and John

specifically designed to increase efficacy with respect to calming negative thoughts and emotions.[17]

1. **Three long, deep breaths:** Focus on your breathing as you take three long, deep breaths, inhaling smoothly and slowly and then exhaling smoothly and slowly with each breath.

2. **Feet:** Tense the muscles in your feet by curling your toes downward while keeping your feet flat (*not* pointing your whole foot downward).[18] Maintain tension for about ten seconds, release suddenly, and then relax for about twenty seconds.

3. **Lower legs:** Tense the muscles in your lower legs by simultaneously pulling your toes upward, toward your head, and clenching your calf muscles. Maintain tension for about ten seconds, release suddenly, and then relax for about twenty seconds.

4. **Thighs:** Tense your thighs by straightening your legs out stiffly, and simultaneously clenching the muscles on both the fronts and backs of your thighs. Maintain tension for about ten seconds, release suddenly, and then relax for about twenty seconds.

5. **Buttocks:** Tighten your buttocks so that they are firm and push against the surface upon which you are resting. Maintain tension, release suddenly, and then relax.

6. **Lower back:** Tense your lower back by arching it forward. Maintain tension, release suddenly, and then relax. (You may omit this muscle group if you have trouble with lower back pain.)

7. **Stomach:** Tighten your stomach muscles by contracting them as if you are starting to do a sit-up, or by "making them hard," as if you are preparing for someone to hit you in the stomach. Maintain tension, release suddenly, and then relax.

8. **Chest:** Tighten your chest muscles by simultaneously clenching your pectoral muscles, your lats (the large muscles on your sides, immediately beneath your arms), and the muscles of your chest wall. Maintain tension, release suddenly, and then relax.

9. **Upper back:** Tighten the muscles of your upper back by pulling your shoulders back as far as possible (as if you are trying to make your shoulder blades touch each other). Maintain tension, release suddenly, and then relax.

E. Schmidt, "Progressive Relaxation: Abbreviated Methods," in *Principles and Practice of Stress Management,* third edition, eds., Paul M. Lehrer, Robert L. Woolfolk, and Wesley E. Sime (New York: Guilford Press, 2007), pages 88–122.

17.   The order has also been rearranged to enhance the logical flow, hopefully making the sequence easier to remember.

18.   If you have trouble with cramps, curl your toes upward instead of downward.

10. **Hands and forearms:** Clench your fists and focus on tensing all of the muscles in your forearms. Maintain tension, release suddenly, and then relax.

11. **Upper arms, front:** Bring your forearms up toward your shoulders, and tense your biceps by "making a muscle" with both arms. Maintain tension, release suddenly, and then relax.

12. **Upper arms, back:** Straighten your arms, lock your elbows, and tense your triceps (the muscles on the backsides of your upper arms) by clenching them. Maintain tension, release suddenly, and then relax.

13. **Sides of neck:** Tighten the muscles on the sides of your neck by pulling your shoulders up, as if you are trying to make them touch your ears. Maintain tension, release suddenly, and then relax.

14. **Back of neck:** Tense the muscles in the back of your neck by pulling your head way back, as if you are trying to bring the back of your head between your shoulder blades. Maintain tension, release suddenly, and then relax. (Be gentle with this muscle group if you have neck pain and/or have had neck injuries.)

15. **Front of neck:** Tense the muscles in the front of your neck by pushing your chin down against your chest. Maintain tension, release suddenly, and then relax.

16. **Jaw:** Tighten your jaw muscles by opening your mouth as wide as possible (so that you stretch the muscles around the hinges of your jaw). Maintain tension, release suddenly, and then relax. When you relax, let your jaw hang loose so that your mouth hangs open.

17. **Forehead and scalp:** Tighten the muscles of your forehead and scalp by raising your eyebrows as far as possible. Maintain tension, release suddenly, and then relax.

18. **Muscles around eyes and nose:** Tense the muscles around your eyes and nose by closing your eyes tightly and wrinkling your nose. Maintain tension, release suddenly, and then relax.

19. **Muscles associated with eye movement:** With your eyes still closed, move your eyes as far as they will go to the right, and hold this for five seconds. Move them as far as they will go to the left, and hold this for five seconds. Move them up as far as they will go, and hold this for five seconds. Move them down as far as they will go, and hold this for five seconds. Then relax the muscles that move your eyes, as fully as possible, for twenty seconds.

Many find it difficult to maintain relaxation in the muscles associated with eye movement. (Dr. Jacobson notes that success with this particular relaxation target usually requires considerable practice with his techniques.) In experimenting with this, I discovered that when I first relax the muscles of eye movement, my eyes settle so that I am "looking" forward and slightly down. And I discovered that calmly maintaining my focus on the patterns of light and color on the insides of my eyelids, at this place where my attention first settles, is a simple but effective way to shut down the activity of my eye movement muscles.

20. **Muscles associated with speech:** First imagine saying something, and notice the small tensions and movements in the muscles associated with speech (tongue, lips, jaw, throat, neck, chest, diaphragm) that correspond to the imagined speech. Then try to relax these muscles as fully as possible for twenty seconds.

21. **Muscles of facial expression:** First notice the movements and tensions in your facial muscles as you smile, frown, and generate expressions of sadness, disgust, anger, and fear. Then try to relax all muscles of facial expression as fully as possible for twenty seconds.

22. **Muscle groups with lingering tension:** Mentally scan through your body for any feelings of lingering tension, and then go through an additional one or two tension-relaxation cycles for any muscle groups that are not yet fully relaxed.

23. **Relaxation imagery:** Finish the exercise by imagining a wave of relaxation starting at the top of your head, and then spreading slowly, down through your body, to the tips of your toes.

For any readers who want to pursue the progressive muscle relaxation technique more vigorously, an extensive array of research and other resources is easily available. (The Google search I just did for "progressive muscle relaxation" yielded 222,000 links.)

Glossary

attachment.

Emotional **attachment**/bonding is the deep, enduring emotional connection between us and specific people that we know and that are important to us. This emotional attachment, or bonding, is one of the most important phenomena in our emotional and social experience. Children internalize their attachment experiences with their parents (primary caregivers), and these internalized parental attachments then serve as the foundation for all future relationships. When our attachments/emotional bonds are joy based, we want to be near the people we are attached to, and we go to them for comfort and protection in times of distress.

attachment, dismissive.

Dismissive attachment is established by repeated experiences of having your parents ignore you, reject you, dismiss the importance of emotional connection, or disparage the importance of emotional connection. For example, if you are growing up in an emotional desert of being persistently ignored and/or rejected, you can come to the self-protective conclusion: "If I can't get it, it won't hurt so bad if I don't need it or want it." You then try to teach yourself, both consciously and unconsciously, to not need or want emotional connection. In most cases, you develop dismissive attachment because your parents have predominantly dismissive attachment. If this is the case, they will make it much easier for you to adopt this same form of attachment. In addition to ignoring and/or rejecting your attempts to connect with them, they will model dismissive attachment by appearing not to need or want emotional connection—they won't initiate emotional intimacy, they won't ask for it, and they won't express distress at not having it. Sometimes they will make it even easier for you to adopt the dismissive style of attachment by explicitly dismissing and/or disparaging the importance of emotional connection with comments such as, "Don't come cryin' to me. If I came home crying, my father would whip me till I stopped. If you're gonna cry, go to your room till you're done," or "What do you want a hug for? Only sissies and faggots need hugs." Or they might pick up a book such as *Raising an Emotionally Intelligent Child*,[1] and comment, "All that touchy-feely therapy crap is just a waste of time and money."

In a **relationship with dismissive attachment,** you do *not* feel felt, seen, understood, or connected. You have the sense that if you share your heart with vulnerability and transparency, the other person will ignore or disparage your

---

1. John Gottman with Joan DeClaire, *Raising an Emotionally Intelligent Child* (New York: Simon & Schuster, 1997). This is actually an excellent book, despite what might be said about it by people with dismissive attachment.

attempt to initiate emotional intimacy (as opposed to see you, understand you, attune to you, and respond appropriately to what you share). In a relationship with dismissive attachment, you have a deep, subjective, intuitive *feeling* that emotional intimacy is not seen as important and that your needs for relational connection will be ignored or disparaged.

attachment, disorganized.

Disorganized attachment is established by repeated experiences of a primary caregiver doing things that are overwhelming, frightening, and chaotic—experiences where the primary caregiver that you want to go to for comfort and safety is actually the source of your distress. When this happens, you *simultaneously* experience *both* an intense attachment drive to be with the person who is your primary caregiver *and* an intense self-protection drive to get away from this same person as the source of your distress. In a **relationship with disorganized attachment**, you feel that you need to be with the person, *and* that you need to get away from the person. You feel that something terrible will happen if you leave the person, *and* that something terrible will happen if you stay with him. In a relationship with disorganized attachment, you feel that you must stay with the person to be okay, *and* you know the person is unsafe and will hurt you. In any experience or memory that includes the disorganized attachment dilemma (the person you need to comfort and protect you is the source of your distress), in addition to feeling fearful you will also feel profoundly confused and disorganized.

attachment, distracted.

Distracted attachment is established by repeated experiences of having your parents be unpredictable with respect to relational, emotional connection. On some occasions when you come to them with the need and desire for emotional connection, they see you, understand you, share your emotions, join you in your experience, want to be with you, and respond appropriately to the situation you are bringing to them. However, on other occasions when you come to them with the need and desire for emotional connection, they are distracted and emotionally unavailable. In these situations, they might pretend to be with you and attune to you, but you can tell that they are not fully present—you can tell that they are not really attuning to you, and they do not respond with what you need for the unique situation you are bringing to them.

In a **relationship with distracted attachment**, you know what you are looking for and you know that it's possible, but on any given occasion you don't know whether or not you will get the attuned emotional connection that you need. In a relationship with distracted attachment, you never know what you are going to get—you cannot *depend* on the person for attuned connection. In a relationship with distracted attachment, you have a deep, subjective sense of insecurity regarding whether attuned emotional connection will be available when you need it.

attachment pain.

Attachment pain is the unique pain we feel when separated (either temporarily or permanently) from key attachment figures, such as family members and close friends. The unresolved content in traumatic memories can include attachment pain, so that attachment pain in the present can be caused by triggering; but attachment pain can also be caused by truth-based separation or loss in the present, such as when a spouse dies.

attachment, secure.

Secure attachment is established by repeated experiences of having your parents be available when you need them, repeated experiences of having your parents attune to you (see you, understand you, share your emotions, join you in your experience, and be glad to be with you), repeated experiences of having your parents respond appropriately to the unique situations you bring to them, and repeated experiences of successful repair after some kind of conflict has caused a rupture in the relationship. In a relationship with secure attachment you *feel* seen, understood, felt, loved, connected, and relationally safe. You feel safe to share your heart with vulnerability and transparency, and expect that the other person will see you, understand you, attune to you, and respond appropriately to what you share. In a **relationship with secure attachment**, you are aware that conflict can arise, but you are confident that problems can be resolved. You have a deep, subjective, intuitive *feeling* that the relationship is safe and stable. In a relationship with secure attachment, you have a deep, subjective sense of security that emotional connection and attunement will be available when you need them.

If your parents do *not* consistently attune to you and respond appropriately to you, and if you do not consistently experience successful repair after some kind of conflict has caused a rupture in the relationship, then instead of developing secure attachment you will develop one or more of the forms of insecure attachment.

attunement.

Attunement is an especially important form of interpersonal emotional connection, currently at the center of a lot of research and writing. For the purposes of *Outsmarting Yourself*, we can use the following simple, functional definition: I am successfully *offering* **attunement** if I see you, hear you, correctly understand your internal experience, *join* you in the emotions you're experiencing, genuinely care about you, and am glad to be with you; and you are successfully *receiving* my **attunement** if you *feel* seen, heard, and understood, if you *feel* that I am *with* you in your experience, and if you *feel* that I care about you and that I am glad to be with you. As discussed in chapter 18, the Lord has designed our brains so that if something causes us to fall into non-relational mode, receiving attunement will quickly, smoothly, and consistently bring us back into relational mode.

autobiographical memory. *See* memory, autobiographical.

blending, psychological blending, psychologically blended.

Psychological blending is when implicit memory content *blends together* with the mental content corresponding to our experiences in the present, so that we *do not perceive any subjective difference* between the implicit memory content and content corresponding to the present. For example, when I am **psychologically blended** with childhood memories, instead of standing in my untriggered, adult ego state and thinking about autobiographical memories from the childhood experiences as if they were part of my past history, I will experience the childhood implicit memory thoughts and emotions as *blended together* with the thoughts and emotions from my adult ego state. I will *not perceive any subjective difference* between the implicit memory content and the content corresponding to my current adult experience, and the implicit memory thoughts and emotions will *feel true in the present.*

capacity.

When we refer to the **capacity** of a physical system, we're referring to how much it can hold or how much it can carry. For example, the capacity of a bucket refers to how much liquid it can hold before overflowing, the capacity of a bridge refers to how much weight it can carry before it collapses, and the capacity of an electrical circuit refers to how much current it can handle before blowing a fuse or burning out components. When we refer to **capacity in the context of emotional healing,** we're referring to the capacity of the person's biological brain, nonbiological mind, and spirit—we're referring to how much biological, psychological, and spiritual intensity a person can handle before some part of his combined brain-mind-spirit system "blows a fuse," and causes the person to malfunction and/or disconnect in some way.

confabulation. *See* Verbal Logical Explainer (VLE) and confabulation.

contingent interaction/communication.

Contingent interaction/communication means that our responses are directly related to (*contingent upon*) what the other is experiencing and communicating. For example, if I meet my godson in the park and he comes running to me with a big smile, a *contingent* interaction would be to greet him with, "Hey! It's good to see you! It looks like you're having a good day." And if I'm walking through the park and I see him standing by himself and crying, a contingent interaction would be to kneel down beside him and quietly ask, "What's the matter? Tell me what happened." In contrast, if I see him alone and crying, a *non*contingent interaction would be to ignore his distress and greet him with, "Hey! It's good to see you! Isn't this a beautiful day?" For excellent additional discussion of contingent interactions, see Daniel J. Siegel and Mary Hartzell, *Parenting from the Inside Out* (New York: Jeremy P. Tarcher/ Putnam, 2003), especially pages 80–85.

dismissive attachment. *See* attachment, dismissive.

disorganized attachment. *See* attachment, disorganized.

distorted interpretations (lies).

Unsuccessful processing of a painful experience often results in **distorted interpretations** regarding the meaning of the experience. These distorted interpretations (lies) are then stored as part of the memories for the inadequately processed painful experiences. The memories that carry the unprocessed content from the trauma also carry the distorted interpretations (lies) that are associated with the traumatic events. The trauma-associated lies contribute to the toxic power that unprocessed trauma exerts on the person's life, and trauma-associated lies can also hinder the process of trying to resolve the traumatic memories.

distracted attachment. *See* attachment, distracted.

emotional healing. *See* Immanueal approach.

explicit memory. *See* memory, explicit.

extrapolate.

"**Extrapolate**" is the scientific, technical term for making educated guesses—for studying information we *do* have, and then using this information to make educated guesses about the answers to related questions regarding which we *do not* yet have direct, confirmed information. For example, if we are observing a woman driving her car, and we verify that she has traveled one mile at two minutes, three miles at six minutes, and five miles at ten minutes, then based on this known data (represented by the bolded line in figure G.1), we can *extrapolate*

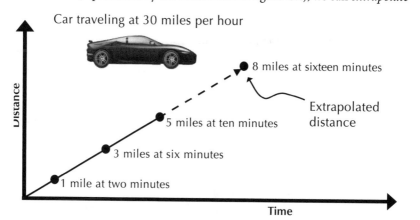

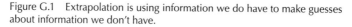

Figure G.1   Extrapolation is using information we do have to make guesses about information we don't have.

(represented by the grey, dashed line) that she will probably have traveled eight miles by the time she has been on the road for sixteen minutes. Similarly, if a person hates broccoli but loves apples, dislikes carrots but enjoys oranges, avoids peas but likes strawberries, detests cauliflower but loves pears, and has an aversion to beans but delights in raspberries; we can *extrapolate* to make the educated guess that she will dislike other vegetables, such as brussels sprouts and radishes, and that she will like other fruits, such as pineapples and peaches.

As described in chapter 4, Charlotte using her graphics software to repair a damaged photograph provides another good example. She makes an *educated guess* that missing material from the damaged spot probably looked a lot like parts of the picture immediately adjacent to the flaw, and therefore repairs the scene by filling in the hole with a sample from this nearby material.

Immanuel approach to emotional healing.

When we encounter pain, our brain-mind-spirit system always tries to process the painful experience. There is a specific pathway that this processing attempt will follow, and there are specific processing tasks that we must complete as we travel along this pathway. When we are able to successfully complete this processing journey, we get through the painful experience without being traumatized—we emotionally and cognitively "metabolize" the experience in a healthy way, and instead of having any toxic power in our lives, the adequately processed painful experience contributes to our knowledge, skills, empathy, wisdom, and maturity. Unfortunately, various problems and/or limitations can block successful processing; and when we are not able to complete the processing journey, then the painful experience becomes a traumatic experience, and the memory for this traumatic experience will then carry unresolved toxic content.

The good news about the pain-processing pathway and traumatic memories is that each time a traumatic memory gets activated, we get another chance to finish the processing. With the right resources and tools, a person can work through a traumatic memory, successfully completing the processing tasks she was not able to accomplish at the time of the original experience. When this has been done, the package of toxic content associated with this particular traumatic memory is permanently resolved so that it will never again cause trouble. More good news is that traumatic memories are consistently accessible to deliberate activation, under the right conditions. This means that we can proactively find them and open them up, so that we can work on traumatic memories strategically in the context of emotional healing sessions.

Even more good news is that God knows all this stuff, and he wants to help us get healed. For people who are able to perceive the Lord's presence, connect with him, and receive help from him, this potentially complicated process can become very simple. The Lord can lead the process, help the person access the memories, and help the person successfully complete the remedial processing tasks, without us needing to explicitly manage any of these details. With the basic version of the **Immanuel approach to emotional healing**, all the facilitator needs to do is:

• establish the foundation for the session by helping the recipient to perceive the Lord's presence and establish an interactive connection with him;

• coach the recipient to turn to Jesus, focus on Jesus, and engage with Him directly at every point in the session, regarding every issue that comes up, and regarding every difficulty that arises;

• if the agenda is to work with trauma, help the recipient to connect with Jesus inside any traumatic memory that comes forward, and then continue to coach her to turn to Jesus, focus on Jesus, and engage with him directly at every point, regarding every issue, and regarding every difficulty;

• if the person is not able to connect with Jesus when she first goes inside the traumatic memory, if she loses her connection with Jesus at any point later in the session, if the process becomes stuck for any other reason later in the session, or if you feel like you are getting in over your head, use the "safety net" troubleshooting tool (help the recipient return to the initial positive connection with Jesus, and then, in the context of this safe and comfortable place, coach the person to engage directly with Jesus regarding the point of difficulty). [2]

• if you are running out of time and the traumatic memory is still not fully resolved, use the end of session "safety net" (help the recipient return to the initial positive connection with Jesus). Even though she was not able to fully resolve the trauma, she will be fine if she ends the session in the initial positive connected with Jesus.[3]

implicit memory. *See* memory, implicit.

interactive connection with the Lord.

I am experiencing an ***interactive* connection with the Lord** when I perceive his presence in some way, and it feels true that we are having a living, real-time, mutual, contingent *interaction*. When I am experiencing an interactive connection, it feels true that the Lord sees, hears, and understands the emotions and thoughts I am experiencing and communicating, and it also feels true that he is offering contingent responses to my emotions and thoughts.

---

2. For additional discussion of the "safety net" troubleshooting tool, see "Immanuel Approach Exercises for Groups and Beginners," available as a free download from the "Getting Started" page of www.immanuelapproach.com.

3. For additional discussion of the end of session "safety net," see "Immanuel Approach Exercises for Groups and Beginners," available as a free download from the "Getting Started" page of www.immanuelapproach.com.

maturity skills, psychological/spiritual maturity skills.

As a person develops physically, she encounters many physical skills that she must master in order to thrive physically. For example, she must learn to co-ordinate her feet and legs and trunk in the complex skills of walking and running; she must learn to coordinate the movements of her fingers and thumbs in the many complex skills of manipulating objects with her hands; she must learn to coordinate the movements of her teeth, tongue, lips, and vocal cords in the complex skill of talking; etc. These are physical skills that you learn during the process of physical development—skills that you learn as you grow in physical maturity. Mastering these physical skills is an important part of maturing physically. Similarly, as a person develops psychologically/spiritually, she encounters many psychological/spiritual skills that she must master in order to thrive psychologically/spiritually. For example, she must learn to handle painful emotions—to stay emotionally connected, to maintain (or regain) access to her relational circuits, and to think and behave appropriately while feeling painful emotions; she must learn to be aware of and care for her own needs; she must learn to be aware of and care for the needs of others; etc. These are **psychological/spiritual skills** that you learn during the process of psychological/spiritual development—skills **that you learn as you grow in psychological/spiritual maturity**. Mastering these psychological/spiritual skills is an important part of maturing psychologically/spiritually.

When checking to see whether this theory fits your experience, it is important to remember that the subjective experience of using most of these skills is more like the subjective experience of walking than the subjective experience of doing long division. You can be aware of and understand these skills with your logical, analytical, linguistic left-hemisphere neurological circuits; but the actual skill is not learned by or carried in your left prefrontal cortex, and therefore does not *feel, subjectively,* like a logical, analytical, language-based skill.[4] You can have a logical, analytical, language-based understanding of walking, but this left-hemisphere understanding is not what actually enables you to walk. The subjective experience of most of these psychological/spiritual maturity skills is very similar. You can be aware of them and understand them with your logical, analytical, linguistic left-hemisphere circuits, but the actual skills are not learned by, or carried in, your left prefrontal cortex. In fact, most of the time we use these skills so smoothly and intuitively that our logical, analytical, linguistic left hemisphere is hardly even aware of them.

When checking to see whether this theory fits your experience, it is also important to remember that we learn some of the most important psychological/spiritual maturity skills very early in childhood, so that we do not have any conscious autobiographical memory of the actual learning process. This is another way in which these maturity skills are more like walking than long division—you have conscious autobiographical memory for learning

---

4.   For those of you who are already familiar with the five levels of brain function, yes, these are left prefrontal cortex level 5 circuits and left prefrontal cortex level 5 skills.

how to do long division, but not for learning how to walk. See "Brain Science, Psychological Trauma, and the God Who Is with Us ~ Part II" essay series for additional discussion regarding maturity skills (available as a free download from www.kclehman.com).

memory, autobiographical.

Autobiographical memory is memory for the *story* of your life. For example, let's say that you were woken up this morning by the paper boy throwing the newspaper through your living room window at 5:30 a.m., and that you spent the next hour picking up broken glass. Your memory for this *story* about what happened to you this morning would be *autobiographical* memory. Remembering the meaning of the word "autobiography" helps me to remember the definition of autobiographical memory. If I wrote a book about the story of my life, it would be called an *autobiography*; similarly, memory for the story of my life is *autobiographical* memory.

memory, explicit.

Explicit memory recall is what we all think of as "remembering." Explicit memory *feels* like "normal" memory. When I recall events through the explicit memory system, I can *feel, subjectively,* that I'm remembering something from my personal past experience. For example, if I ask you, "What did you do this morning?" you will tell me about being awakened by the paper boy throwing the newspaper through your living room window at 5:30 this morning, and how you spent the next hour picking up broken glass, and you will *feel, subjectively,* that you are remembering something from your personal past. This *conscious, autobiographical* memory about your personal experiences is explicit memory.

memory, implicit.

Implicit memory is all memory phenomena that *does not* include the subjective experience of "I'm remembering something from my personal past experience." Implicit memory content *does not* feel like "normal" memory. When the implicit memory systems are activated, our minds and brains recall memory material, but it does not *feel, subjectively,* like explicit autobiographical memory. Since implicit memory does not *feel* like what we think of as memory, we usually *do not* have any awareness that we are remembering or being affected by past experience when we recall and/or use learned information through one of the implicit memory systems.[5] When this happens, the person perceives that the implicit memory material, such as the beliefs and emotions associated with a childhood traumatic event, *are true in the present.* We sometimes refer to implicit memory as "invisible" memory, since it usually affects us *without being "seen" by our conscious minds.*

---

5. You can learn to recognize the subjective experience of implicit memory being activated with a lot of deliberate practice, but most people have very little awareness or insight regarding implicit memory phenomena.

Note: Even if we are *cognitively* aware that we are being affected by some kind of memory phenomena (for example, we learn to recognize emotional triggering as an implicit memory phenomena), we still don't have the *subjective* experience of "I'm remembering something from my personal past experience."

mis-attuning, mis-attunement, mis-attunement pain:

Mis-attunement can be thought of as the opposite of attunement. For example, let's say you are in distress, but unfortunately you are with a friend who does not have the capacity or maturity skills to offer attunement, and he is becoming increasingly uncomfortable with your distress. Eventually, in order to make his own discomfort stop, he gives you a big smile and states, "Don't feel bad—just think happy thoughts!" That is, instead of understanding your situation, being empathetically *with* you in your pain, and being *glad* to be with you (even when you are in pain), he tries to make his own discomfort go away by just telling you to be different. This would be *mis*-attunement. When we are in distress, and a friend misses attunement in this way, the resulting unpleasant subjective experience is what I call **mis-attunement pain**. Similarly, this unpleasant experience could be described as *painfully **mis-attuning***.

nervous system, "the big picture."

The nervous system can be divided into the **central nervous system** (the brain and the spinal cord) and the **peripheral nervous system**, which includes everything outside of the brain and the spinal cord. The peripheral nervous system can then be divided into the **pyramidal (voluntary) nervous system**, which is responsible for all voluntary muscle movements, and the **autonomic (involuntary) nervous system**. If you want to lift your foot, your pyramidal (voluntary) nervous system will carry the conscious command from your brain to the muscles in your leg. In contrast, your autonomic (involuntary) nervous system cares for the many bodily functions that do not normally come into conscious awareness, such as maintaining an appropriate heart rate, regulating your blood pressure, and producing saliva in preparation for a meal. The autonomic nervous system is then divided into the **sympathetic branch**, the **parasympathetic branch**, and the **enteric (or gastrointestinal) branch**.

nervous system, parasympathetic.

As the direct counterpart of the sympathetic nervous system, the **parasympathetic nervous system** is responsible for calming the many aspects of physical arousal associated with intense emotions.

nervous system, sympathetic.

The **sympathetic nervous system** is responsible for activating the many aspects of physical arousal associated with intense emotions. For example, when we encounter danger, the sympathetic nervous system activates the physiological changes associated with the fear and anger of the fight-or-flight response—the increased alertness, the increased muscle tension, the increased blood flow, and a variety of other physical reactions that prepare our bodies to either fight or flee.

non-relational mode. *See* relational connection circuits.

pain-processing pathway.

When we encounter pain, our brain-mind-spirit system always tries to process the painful experience. There is **a very deliberate pathway that this pain processing attempt will follow,** and there are specific processing tasks that we must complete as we travel along this pathway, such as maintaining organized attachment, staying connected, staying relational, navigating the situation in a satisfying way, and correctly interpreting the meaning of the experience. When we are able to successfully complete this processing journey, we get through the painful experience without being traumatized—we emotionally and cognitively "metabolize" the experience in a healthy way, and instead of having any toxic power in our lives, the adequately processed painful experience contributes to our knowledge, skills, empathy, wisdom, and maturity. Unfortunately, various problems and/or limitations can block successful processing; and when we are *not* able to complete the processing journey, then the painful experience becomes a traumatic experience, and the memories for these traumatic experiences carry unresolved toxic content.

parasympathetic nervous system. *See* nervous system, parasympathetic.

psychological/spiritual maturity skills. *See* maturity skills.

relational connection circuits, relational mode, non-relational mode.

We have been created to be relational beings—we have been created to be in relationship with God and with each other. Our minds and spirits have been created to desire relationship and to function best in relationship, and the Lord has actually designed specific circuits in our biological brains to serve this longing and need for connection—our **relational connection circuits.** When these brain circuits are functioning as designed, our spontaneous, normal experience will be to feel relationally connected and to feel the desire for connection. We will experience others as relational beings, we will be aware of others' true hearts, we will feel compassionate concern regarding what others are thinking and feeling, we will perceive the presence of others as a source of joy, and we will be glad to be with them. We will both want to offer attunement and be able to offer attunement, we will be flexible and creative even when unexpected circumstances require that we change our plans at the last minute, and little things won't "get under our skins." When these brain circuits are functioning as designed, our spontaneous, normal experience will be to perceive others as allies, even in difficult interpersonal situations; and as part of this allied attitude we will want to join with them in the collaborative process of exploring the situation together, we will want to understand their perspectives, and we will want to join with them in the collaborative process of working together to find a mutually satisfying solution. Charlotte refers to this way of living as "operating in **relational mode**."

Unfortunately, there are certain problems and conditions that can cause us to temporarily lose access to these brain circuits. When this happens we operate in **non-relational mode**. Our spontaneous experience in non-relational mode will include the *absence* of feeling relationally connected, and we won't even want to be connected. We will *not* perceive others as relational beings, we will *not* be aware of others' true hearts, we will *not* feel compassionate concern regarding what others are thinking and feeling, and we will *not* be glad to be with them or experience their presence as a source of joy. We will *not* want to offer attunement or be able to offer attunement, we will be rigid and unable to think outside the box, and we will find little problems to be much more irritating. When we are operating in non-relational mode and we encounter difficult interpersonal situations, instead of perceiving others as allies we perceive them as adversaries, and instead of wanting to join, explore, understand, and collaborate, we will tend toward judging, interrogating, and focusing on trying to "fix" the situation. Furthermore, when we lose access to our relational connection circuits in the context of being upset with a specific friend or family member, instead of perceiving that person's presence as an emotional resource we will perceive him as the problem.

When we lose access to the parts of our brains responsible for processing relational connection (that is, when we fall into non-relational mode), we temporarily lose the relational aspect of every area of our lives. We not only lose the ability to be relationally connected to those around us in the present, we also lose the ability to think relationally, and we even lose the relational connection components of our memories.

relational mode. *See* **relational connection circuits.**

relational connection joy.

When you look at someone's face, and you can see from her expression and from the sparkle in her eyes that she likes you and that she is glad to be with you, the attachment circuits in your right-hemisphere emotional/social processing system will respond with joy. A warm, wonderful feeling bubbles up in your heart, you are glad to be alive, and you are especially glad to be with the person who is glad to be with you. This joy response wells up inside you very quickly, it is not voluntarily, and it is not caused by cognitive beliefs. It is important to understand that this joy response is also a psychological and spiritual phenomena, in addition to the biological phenomena produced by your neurological attachment circuits. For the purposes of all the material we are developing and any discussions we are a part of, Dr. Wilder and I define joy as the biological, psychological, and spiritual experience produced when you are in attuned relational connection with another person, and you can perceive from the expression on the person's face that she is glad to be with you.

Note that this relational, right-hemisphere joy is not the same thing as pleasure, fun, or happiness. Joy can be associated with pleasure, fun, and happiness—people who are joyful are often also happy, having fun, and experiencing pleasure, and people who are happy, having fun, and experiencing pleasure are often also joyful—but joy is not the same thing as happiness, fun, or pleasure. I deliberately refer to this relational, right-hemisphere joy as relational connection joy in order to remind the reader that joy is inherently connected to relationship, and that we are not using joy simply as a synonym for pleasure, fun, or happiness.

Ideally, a person will build a growing memory bank of "I'm glad to be with you" experiences during her early childhood, and thereby internalize the important "I'm glad to be with you" relationships in her life. This allows her to carry these relational connections with her, so that she can stand on a memory-based foundation of "I'm glad to be with you" relational connection, and the consequent relational connection joy, even when she is alone. When a child receives optimal care, and her brain/mind/spirit system therefore develops as the Lord intended, she will carry with her a deep, stable, memory-anchored awareness that there are others who know her, love her, and are glad to be with her; and the corresponding deep, stable, memory-anchored relational connection joy will be the background, baseline, and foundation for every other aspect of her life.

People who have spent many years trying to compensate for lack of true relational joy by pursuing pleasure may even have a hard time telling the difference between the two. One way to learn to recognize relational connection joy is to watch for times when all of the checklist questions from chapters 15 and 16 indicate that you are in relational mode, and then carefully observe and ponder the subjective quality of the good feelings you get when you notice that others are glad to be with you.

For additional discussion of relational connection joy, see "Brain Science, Psychological Trauma, and the God Who Is With Us ~ Part II: The Processing Pathway for Painful Experiences and the Definition of Psychological Trauma."

secure attachment. *See* attachment, secure.

sympathetic nervous system. *See* nervous system, sympathetic.

trauma (psychological trauma), traumatic memory.
A painful experience becomes a traumatic experience (a **psychological trauma**) when we are *not* able to successfully complete one or more of the tasks in the pain-processing pathway. Therefore, *our definition of trauma is a painful experience that has not been fully processed.* If we do not get help processing

a traumatic event at the time it occurs, the experience will be stored in this unprocessed state and becomes a **traumatic memory**. Traumatic memories are qualitatively different than non-traumatic memories—traumatic memories carry toxic content from unresolved painful experiences, and they are processed, stored, and retrieved differently than memories for experiences that have been fully resolved. When these memories are activated at any point in the future, implicit memory content from the unresolved trauma comes forward and *feels true in the present*. For example, implicit memory content from unresolved traumatic events might include unprocessed physical sensations, unresolved negative emotions, feelings of inadequacy, confusion, and distorted interpretations (lies); and this implicit memory content will disrupt our ability to function as it comes forward and invisibly blends with our experience in the present.

In contrast, when we *are* able to successfully complete all of the tasks in the pain-processing pathway, *we can go through a painful experience without being traumatized*. We emotionally and cognitively "metabolize" the experience in a healthy way, and memory for the experience is stored as **non-traumatic memory**, where it contributes to knowledge, skills, wisdom, maturity, and conscious autobiographical memory for our personal history. Non-traumatic memories do *not* carry any toxic content. When these memories are activated at any point in the future, they contribute valuable resources as opposed to interfering with our ability to function.

trigger, triggered, triggering.

A **"trigger"** is any stimulus in the present that activates memory content. Technically, a trigger can activate both traumatic and non-traumatic memories. For example, an angry comment from your spouse may activate traumatic memories of being frightened by bullies on the playground, whereas a favorite song might activate positive memories from the special evening you spent with your spouse on your last anniversary. However, most people use "trigger," "triggered," and "triggering" in relation to traumatic memories.

With respect to psychological trauma, we are **"triggered"** when something in the present causes our brains/minds to open traumatic memories, so that unresolved content from these memories is activated. When unresolved traumatic experiences are activated, various aspects of the experiences, such as unprocessed physical sensations, unresolved negative emotions, feelings of inadequacy, confusion, and distorted interpretations come forward and *feel true in the present*. Whenever implicit memory content from unresolved trauma is active in the present, we are triggered; and whenever we are triggered, implicit memory content from unresolved trauma is active in the present.

We use **"triggering"** to refer to the overall phenomena of people being triggered. For example, "Triggering is one of the biggest causes of conflict at family reunions," or "There sure is a lot of triggering going on in our difficult council meetings about the new pastor."

"Trigger," "triggering," and **"triggered"** can also be used as verbs. For example, "If I watch a documentary about kids with dyslexia, it will probably *trigger* my memories of having difficulty with learning to read," "Watching this documentary about kids with dyslexia is really *triggering* my memories of having difficulty learning to read," and "When I watched the documentary about kids with dyslexia, it really *triggered* my memories of having difficulty learning to read."

Verbal Logical Explainer (VLE) and confabulation.

When dealing with unresolved traumatic content coming forward as invisible implicit memory, there are two intriguing, subtle, and ubiquitous phenomena that make the situation even more difficult. The first of these "particular phenomena" is the part of our brain/mind/spirit that I call our **Verbal Logical Explainer**, or VLE. The VLE's job is to come up with explanations that help us organize and make sense out of our experiences and the world around us. Most of the time this is a good thing. Our VLEs are constantly coming up with explanations that help us make sense out of our lives, and they usually work so quickly and smoothly that we don't even notice them. In fact, your VLE is busily working at this very moment, making sense out of your experience as you read this paragraph. For example, your VLE is explaining to you that you are looking in the glossary of a book titled *Outsmarting Yourself*, reading about the Verbal Logical Explainer and confabulation (as opposed to other things you might be doing, such as watching a soap opera, hang gliding in Hawaii, or driving to work in rush hour traffic).

Our VLEs also usually start with basically adequate, accurate data and come up with basically valid explanations. However, if our VLEs start with distorted and/or inadequate data, they can come up with profoundly flawed explanations. For example, if my VLE starts with thoughts and emotions that are actually from childhood memories of bullies cutting in front of me during playground activities, but these thoughts and emotions are coming forward as "invisible" implicit memory *so that they feel true in the present and I have no awareness of their real origin*, my VLE will make up explanations for how these thoughts and emotions are being caused by *circumstances in the present*, such as people using the merge lane to go to the front of the line in a construction zone.

The second of these "particular phenomena" is **confabulation**. Confabulation is a special kind of fabrication in which the person makes something up based on her best guess regarding what might be the answer, but with *no conscious awareness that she is just guessing* and with *no deliberate intent to deceive*. Confabulation is most dramatically seen in people who have severely damaged explicit memory combined with minimal conscious awareness of their explicit memory deficit, such as people with Korsakov's syndrome. However, we all engage in much more subtle forms of confabulation when our VLEs are unknowingly working with raw material that includes "invisible" implicit memory content.

With respect to unresolved trauma and implicit memory, the relevant point is that our VLEs will quickly and smoothly come up with confabulated explanations for why and how our *current circumstances* are causing us to experience any triggered thoughts and emotions (thoughts and emotions that are actually content from unresolved trauma coming forward as implicit memory). And, unfortunately, the confabulated, flawed VLE explanations feel very much like valid VLE explanations. Without a lot of deliberate practice, most of us don't seem to perceive any difference between valid explanations and flawed, confabulated explanations.

Bibliography

Anand, Bal K., and John R. Brobeck. "Localization of a 'Feeding Center' in the Hypothalamus of the Rat." *Proceedings of the Society for Experimental Biology and Medicine* vol. 77 (1951): pages 323–4.

Beck, Aaron T., and Brad A. Alford. *Depression: Causes and Treatment,* second edition. Philadelphia, PA: University of Pennsylvania Press, 2009.

Benson, Herbert, and Miriam Z. Klipper. *The Relaxation Response,* updated and expanded. New York: HarperCollins, 2000.

Benson, Herbert, and William Proctor. *Beyond the Relaxation Response.* New York: Berkley Books, 1984.

Bernstein, Douglas A., and T. D. Borkovec. *Progressive Relaxation Training: A Manual for the Helping Professions.* Champaign, IL: Research Press, 1973.

Bernstein, Douglas A., Charles R. Carlson, and John E. Schmidt. "Progressive Relaxation: Abbreviated Methods." Chapter 5 in *Principles and Practice of Stress Management,* third edition, edited by Paul M. Lehrer, Robert L. Woolfolk and Wesley E. Sime. New York: Guilford Press, 2007.

Bourne, Edmund J. *The Anxiety and Phobia Workbook,* second edition. Oakland, CA: New Harbinger Publications, 1995.

Carter, C. Sue. "Biological Perspectives on Social Attachment and Bonding." Chapter 5 in *Attachment and Bonding,* edited by C. S. Carter, L. Ahnert, K. E. Grossmann, S. B. Hardy, M. E. Lamb, S. W. Porges, and N. Sachsher. Cambridge, MA: MIT Press, 2005.

Chapman, Loren J. "Illusory Correlation in Observational Report." *Journal of Verbal Learning and Verbal Behavior* vol. 6 (1967): pages 151–55.

Claparede, Edouard. "Recognition and 'Me-ness.'" in *Organization and Pathology of Thought* edited by D. Rapaport. New York: Columbia University Press, 1951. Translated from E. Claparede. "Recognition et Moiete." *Archives de Psychologie* vol. 11 (1911): pages 79–90.

Clark, David A., and Aaron T. Beck. *Cognitive Therapy of Anxiety Disorders: Science and Practice.* New York: The Guilford Press, 2010.

Coren, Stanley, Lawrence M. Ward, and James T. Enns. *Sensation and Perception,* sixth edition. Hoboken, NJ: Wiley & Sons, 2004.

Dattilio, Frank M. *Cognitive-Behavioral Therapy with Couples and Families: A Comprehensive Guide for Clinicians*. New York: The Guilford Press, 2010.

Davidson, Dennis M., Mark A. Winchester, C. B. Taylor, Edwin A. Alderman, and Neil B.Ingels, Jr. "Effects of Relaxation Therapy on Cardiac Performance and Sympathetic Activity in Patients with Organic Heart Disease." *Psychosomatic Medicine* vol. 41, no. 4 (June 1979): pages 303–9.

Dickens, Charles. *A Christmas Carol*. New York: New American Library, 1984.

Friesen, James G., E. James Wilder, Anne M. Bierling, Rick Koepcke, and Maribeth Poole. *The Life Model: Living from the Heart Jesus Gave You—The Essentials of Christian Living* revised 2000-R. Van Nuys, CA: Shepherd's House Publishing, 2004.

Gazzaniga, Michael S., and Joseph E. LeDoux. *The Integrated Mind*. New York: Plenum Press, 1978.

Gottman, John M., and Joan DeClaire. *Raising an Emotionally Intelligent Child*. New York: Simon & Schuster, 1997.

Gottman, John M., and Clifford I. Notarius. "Decade Review: Observing Marital Interaction." *Journal of Marriage & the Family* vol. 62, no. 3 (November 2000): pages 927–47.

Gottman, John M., and Nan Silver. *The Seven Principles for Making Marriage Work*. New York: Three Rivers Press, 1999.

Hamilton, David L., and Terrance L. Rose. "Illusory Correlation and the Maintenance of Stereotypic Beliefs." *Journal of Personality and Social Psychology* vol. 39, no. 5 (1980): pages 832–45.

Hunt, James Henry Leigh. "Song of Fairies Robbing an Orchard." Public domain, author life dates: (1784–1859).

The Holy Bible: New International Version. Grand Rapids, MI: Zondervan, 1984.

The Holy Bible: New Revised Standard Version. Nashville, TN: Thomas Nelson Publishers, 1989.

Insel, Thomas R., James T. Winslow, Zouxin Wang, and Larry J. Young. "Oxytocin, Vasopressin, and the Neuroendocrine Basis of Pair Bond Formation." *Advances in Experimental Medicine and Biology* vol. 449 (1998): pages 215–24.

Jacob, Rolf G., and William E. Pelham. "Behavior Therapy." *Kaplan and Sadock's Comprehensive Textbook of Psychiatry*, eighth edition, edited by Benjamin J. Sadock and Virginia A. Sadock. Baltimore, MD: Lippincott, Williams & Wilkins, 2004.

Jacobson, E. "Electrical Measurements of Neuromuscular States during Mental Activities: I. Imagination of Movement Involving Skeletal Muscle." *American Journal of Physiology* vol. 91, no. 2: pages 567–608.

Jacobson, E. "Electrical Measurements of Neuromuscular States during Mental Activities: II. Imagination and Recollection of Various Muscular Acts." *American Journal of Physiology* vol. 94, no. 1: pages 22–34.

Jacobson, E. "Electrical Measurements of Neuromuscular States during Mental Activities: III. Visual Imagination and Recollection." *American Journal of Physiology* vol. 95, no. 3: pages 694–702.

Jacobson, E. "Electrical Measurements of Neuromuscular States during Mental Activities: IV. Evidence of Contraction of Specific Muscles during Imagination." *American Journal of Physiology* vol. 95, no. 3: pages 703–12.

Jacobson, E. "Electrical Measurements of Neuromuscular States during Mental Activities: V. Variation of Specific Muscles Contracting during Imagination." *American Journal of Physiology* vol. 96, no. 1: pages 122–25.

Jacobson, E. "Electrical Measurements of Neuromuscular States during Mental Activities: VII. Imagination, Recollection and Abstract Thinking Involving the Speech Musculature." *American Journal of Physiology* vol. 97, no. 1: pages 200–9.

Jacobson, E. "Electrophysiology of Mental Activities." *American Journal of Psychology* vol. 44 (October 1932): pages 677–94.

Jacobson, Edmund. *Progressive Relaxation: A Physiological and Clinical Investigation of Muscular States and Their Significance in Psychology and Medical Practice*, second edition, Midway Reprint. Chicago: University of Chicago Press, 1974.

Jacobson, Edmund. *You Must Relax: Practical Methods for Reducing the Tensions of Modern Living*, fifth edition. New York: McGraw-Hill, 1976.

Jacobson, E. "Variation of Blood Pressure with Skeletal Muscle Tension and Relaxation." *Annals of Internal Medicine* vol. 12, no. 8 (February 1939): pages 1194–1212.

Jacobson, E. "Variation of Blood Pressure with Skeletal Muscle Tension and Relaxation. II. The Heart Beat." *Annals of Internal Medicine* vol. 13, no. 9 (March 1940): pages 1619–25.

Jensen, Bernard. *Iridology: Science and Practice in the Healing Arts* vol. 2. Winona Lake: Whitman Publications, 1982.

Johnston, Dierdre. "A Series of Cases of Dementia Presenting with PTSD Symptoms in World War II Combat Veterans." *Journal of the American Geriatric Society* vol. 48 (2000): pages 70–72.

Keverne, E. B., and K. M. Kendrick. "Oxytocin Facilitation of Maternal Behavior in Sheep." *Annals of the New York Academy of Science* vol. 652 (1997): pages 83–101.

Khouri, Edward M., and E. James Wilder. *Belonging*. Pasadena, CA: Shepherd's House, forthcoming.

Khouri, Edward M., and E. James Wilder. *Restarting*. Pasadena, CA: Shepherd's House, 2007.

Kraemer, David J. M., C. Neil Macrae, Adam E. Green, and William M. Kelley. "Sound of Silence Activates Auditory Cortex." *Nature* vol. 434 (March 10, 2005): page 158.

Lehman, Karl D. *Bob: Safety Net Demonstration*. Live Ministry Series #29. Evanston, IL: Karl and Charlotte Lehman, 2013. DVD.

Lehman, Karl D. "Brain Science, Psychological Trauma, and the God Who Is with Us ~ Part I: A Psychiatrist's Journey—A Brief Introduction to the Immanuel Approach," last modified February 6, 2013, http://www.kclehman.com.

Lehman, Karl D. "Brain Science, Psychological Trauma, and the God Who Is with Us ~ Part II: The Processing Pathway for Painful Experiences and the Definition of Psychological Trauma," last modified February 4, 2011, http://www.kclehman.com.

Lehman, Karl D. "Brain Science, Psychological Trauma, and the God Who Is with Us ~ Part III: Traumatic Memories vs Nontraumatic Memories," last modified February 4, 2011, http://www.kclehman.com.

Lehman, Karl D. "Brain Science, Psychological Trauma, and the God Who Is with Us ~ Part IV: Conditions and Resources Necessary for Resolving Traumatic Memories," last modified February 4, 2011, http://www.kclehman.com.

Lehman, Karl D. "Brain Science, Psychological Trauma, and the God Who Is with Us ~ Part V: The Immanuel Approach, Revisited," last modified July 7, 2013, http://www.immanuelapproach.com.

Lehman, Karl D. "Brain Science, Psychological Trauma, and the God Who Is with Us ~ Part VI: Special Subjects and Frequently Asked Questions," last modified February 4, 2011, http://www.kclehman.com.

Lehman, Karl D. *Bruce: Loss of Parents, Sibling Conflict, Daughter's Illness*. Live Ministry Series #22. Evanston, IL: Karl and Charlotte Lehman, 2012. DVD.

Lehman, Karl D. *Charlie: "See, this works!"* Live Ministry Series #27. Evanston, IL: Karl and Charlotte Lehman, 2012. DVD.

Lehman, Karl D. "Dad/God Isn't All-Knowing or All-Powerful: A Case Study and Discussion," last modified October 5, 2011, http://www.kclehman.com.

Lehman, Karl D. *Dawn: Disarming the Lure of Affirmation.* Live Ministry Series #16. Evanston, IL: Karl and Charlotte Lehman, 2008. DVD.

Lehman, Karl D. "Deadly Perils of the Victim Swamp: Bitterness, Self-Pity, Entitlement, and Embellishment," last modified May 5, 2006, http://www .kclehman.com.

Lehman, Karl D. *Doug: "Immanuel Intervention" (intermediate).* Live Ministry Series #9. Evanston, IL: Karl and Charlotte Lehman, 2006. DVD.

Lehman, Karl D. *Eileen: "Immanuel Intervention" (intermediate).* Live Ministry Series #7. Evanston, IL: Karl and Charlotte Lehman, 2006. DVD.

Lehman, Karl D. "Emotional Healing and Personal Spiritual Growth: A Case Study and Discussion," last modified February 4, 2011, http://www.kclehman .com.

Lehman, Karl D. "Freedom from Bulimia: Case Study/Testimony," last modified November 5, 2009, http://www.kclehman.com.

Lehman, Karl D. *Ian: "I'm not enough."* Live Ministry Series #24. Evanston, IL: Karl and Charlotte Lehman, 2012. DVD.

Lehman, Karl D. "Immanuel, an Especially Pernicious Blockage, and the Normal Belief Memory System," last modified June 8, 2012, http://www.kclehman .com.

Lehman, Karl D. *Immanuel, an Especially Pernicious Blockage, and the Normal Belief Memory System.* Evanston, IL: Karl and Charlotte Lehman, 2006. two-DVD set.

Lehman, Karl D. *The Immanuel Approach (to Emotional Healing and to Life).* Libertyville, IL: This Joy! Books, in print. Note that as each chapter is completed the draft version will be posted on the "Getting Started" page of www. immanuelapproach.com.

Lehman, Karl D. "Internal Dissociated Parts Presenting as Jesus," last modified December 11, 2009, http://www.kclehman.com.

Lehman, Karl D. "Judgments and Bitterness as Clutter That Hinders Prayer for Emotional Healing," last modified November 21, 2009, http://www.kclehman .com.

Lehman, Karl D. *Live Emotional Healing Ministry ~ Four Condensed Sessions.* Live Ministry Series #8. Evanston, IL: Karl and Charlotte Lehman, 2006. DVD.

Lehman, Karl D. *Live Emotional Healing Ministry ~ Four MORE Condensed Sessions.* Live Ministry Series #10. Evanston, IL: Karl and Charlotte Lehman, 2007. DVD.

Lehman, Karl D. *Live Emotional Healing Ministry ~ Condensed Sessions, 3rd Set,* Live Ministry Series #15. Evanston, IL: Karl and Charlotte Lehman, 2008. DVD.

Lehman, Karl D. *Live Emotional Healing Ministry ~ Condensed Sessions, 4th Set.* Live Ministry Series#20. Evanston, IL: Karl and Charlotte Lehman, 2009. DVD.

Lehman, Karl D. *Live Emotional Healing Ministry ~ Condensed Sessions, 5th Set.* Live Ministry Series#25. Evanston, IL: Karl and Charlotte Lehman, 2012. DVD.

Lehman, Karl D. *Live Emotional Healing Ministry ~ Condensed Sessions, 6th Set.* Live Ministry Series#28. Evanston, IL: Karl and Charlotte Lehman, 2012. DVD.

Lehman, Karl D. *Live Emotional Healing Ministry ~ Condensed with Subtitles.* Live Ministry Series#23. Evanston, IL: Karl and Charlotte Lehman, 2009. DVD.

Lehman, Karl D. *Maggie #2: "If I leave, she could die."* Live Ministry Series #12. Evanston, IL: Karl and Charlotte Lehman, 2008. DVD.

Lehman, Karl D. *Maggie #3: Labor and Delivery Trauma.* Live Ministry Series #19. Evanston, IL: Karl and Charlotte Lehman, 2009. DVD.

Lehman, Karl D. "Non-Christian/Occult Spiritual Activities," last modified October 18, 2006, http://www.kclehman.com.

Lehman, Karl D. *Patricia: First Session with Internal Parts.* Live Ministry Series #3. Evanston, IL: Karl and Charlotte Lehman, 2004. DVD.

Lehman, Karl D. *Psychological Trauma, Implicit Memory, and the Verbal Logical Explainer.* Evanston, IL: Karl and Charlotte Lehman, 2009. Four-DVD set.

Lehman, Karl D. *Renae: Healing Helps Parenting.* Live Ministry Series #17. Evanston, IL: Karl and Charlotte Lehman, 2009. DVD.

Lehman, Karl D. *Rita #2: Resolution of Bitterness toward Mother.* Live Ministry Series #14. Evanston, IL: Karl and Charlotte Lehman, 2008. DVD.

Lehman, Karl D. *Rita #3: Jesus Is Better than Candy.* Live Ministry Series #18. Evanston, IL: Karl and Charlotte Lehman, 2009. DVD.

Lehman, Karl D. *Rocky: Father-Son Wounds.* Live Ministry Series #6. Evanston, IL: Karl and Charlotte Lehman, 2006. DVD.

Lehman, Karl D. *Steve: "Just" Be with Jesus.* Live Ministry Series #21. Evanston, IL: Karl and Charlotte Lehman, 2011. DVD.

Lehman, Karl D. "'Triggered' Positive Thoughts and Emotions," last modified December 15, 2009, http://www.kclehman.com.

Lehman, Karl D. "Unresolved Issues in the Therapist/Facilitator: One of the Most Important Hindrances to Emotional Healing," last modified September 26, 2009, http://www.kclehman.com.

McGlynn, F. D., Peter M. Moore, Steven Lawyer, and Rhonda Karg. "Relaxation Training Inhibits Fear and Arousal During In Vivo Exposure to Phobia-Cue Stimuli," *Journal of Behavior Therapy and Experimental Psychiatry* vol. 30, no. 3 (September 1999): pages 155–68.

McGuigan, F. J., and Paul M. Lehrer. "Progressive Relaxation: Origins, Principles, and Clinical Applications." *Principles and Practice of Stress Management,* third edition, edited by Paul M. Lehrer, Robert L.Woolfolk, and Wesley E. Sime. New York: Guilford Press, 2007.

Newberg, Andrew, and Mark Robert Waldman. *How God Changes Your Brain.* New York: Ballantine Books, 2009.

Paul, Gordon L. *Insight Versus Desensitization in Psychotherapy.* Stanford, CA: Stanford University Press, 1966.

Rubin, Zick. "Measurement of Romantic Love." *Journal of Personality and Social Psychology,* vol. 16, no. 2 (1970): pages 265–73.

Sacks, Oliver. *An Anthropologist on Mars.* New York: Vintage Books, 1995.

Sacks, Oliver. *The Man Who Mistook His Wife for a Hat.* New York: HarperCollins, 1970.

Sacks, Oliver. *The Mind's Eye,* large print edition. New York: Random House, 2010.

Sadock, Virginia A., and Benjamin J. Kaplan, eds. *Kaplan and Sadock's Comprehensive Textbook of Psychiatry,* eighth edition. Baltimore, MD: Lippincott Williams & Wilkins, 2004.

Sanbonmatsu, David M., Frank R. Kardes, and Paul M. Herr. "The Role of Prior Knowledge and Missing Information in Multiattribute Evaluation." *Organizational Behavior and Human Decision Processes* vol. 51 (1992): pages 76–91.

Siegel, Daniel J., and Mary Hartzell. *Parenting From the Inside Out.* New York: Jeremy P. Tarcher/Putnam, 2003.

Tackle, David, Edward M. Khouri, and E. James Wilder. *Forming.* Pasadena, CA: Shepherd's House Publishing, 2011.

Taylor, Kenneth Nathaniel, *The Living Bible: Paraphrased.* Wheaton, IL: Tyndale House, 1973.

Turner, Rebecca A., Margaret Altemus, Teresa Enos, Bruce Cooper, and Teresa McGuinness. "Preliminary Research on Plasma Oxytocin Levels in Healthy, Normal Cycling Women: Investigating Emotional States and Interpersonal Distress." *Psychiatry* vol. 62, no. 2 (summer 1999): pages 97–113.

Uvnas-Moberg, Kerstin. "Oxytocin May Mediate the Benefits of Positive Social Interaction and Emotions." *Psychoneuroendocrinology* vol. 23, no. 8 (1998): pages 819–35.

Van Achterberg, Margriet E., Robert M. Rohrbaugh, and Steven M. Southwick. "Emergence of PTSD in Trauma Survivors with Dementia." *The Journal of Clinical Psychiatry* vol. 62, no. 3 (2001): pages 206–7.

Velotta, Patti. *Immanuel: A Practicum.* Libertyville, IL: This Joy! Books, 2011.

Viorst, Judith. *Alexander and the Terrible, Horrible, No Good, Very Bad Day.* New York: Aladdin Paperbacks, 1972.

Wilder, E. James. *The Complete Guide to Living with Men.* Pasadena, CA: Shepherd's House Publishing, 2004.

Wilder, E. James and Chris M. Coursey. *Share Immanuel.* Pasadena, CA: Shepherd's House Publishing, 2010.

Willard, Dallas. *The Divine Conspiracy: Rediscovering Our Hidden Life in God.* New York: HarperCollins, 1998.

Zimmer, Carl. "A Career Spent Learning How the Mind Emerges From the Brain." *The New York Times* (Tuesday, May 10, 2005): page F3. http://www.nytimes.com/2005/05/10/science/10prof.html

Index

A

Abraham (biblical patriarch), 7

aging, declining coping mechanisms and, 68

agreement. *See* validation

Andre the Giant, 195–197

anger
    attunement and, 229
    bullying and, 253
    calming and, 220
    cheaters and, 11
    glaring and, 142
    with God, 61, 225
    relaxation response and, 326
    shalom-for-my-body exercises and, 210
    telling the Lord about, 180

anxiety
    calming and, 220
    implicit memory and, 21, 32
    relational connection circuits and, 131
    relaxation and, 325
    triggering and, 94, 131

appreciation
    versus attunement, 222
    as biblical, 205–208
    cognitive therapy and, 189–191
    decision to use, 232
    difficulty with, 225, 227
    greater ease of over time, 205
    Immanuel approach and, 190, 294, 297
    live appreciation exercise and, 197–199
    of the Lord, 197–199
    neurobiology and, 188–189
    non-relational mode and, 187–191, 227, 228

appreciation *continued*
    with other interventions, 223, 227, 228–232
    positive memories and, 149–151, 163
    recommended resources and, 283
    as relational circuit intervention, 187–191
    sequence of, 231
    specific memories and, 191–200
    as stand-alone intervention, 223
    time and space required for, 230–231
    triggering and, 204

asking for help, 100–101

attachment
    attachment pain and, 305, 307, 318–319, 345
    attunement and, 344
    childhood origins of, 343–345
    definition of, 343
    dismissive, 126, 130, 151, 209, 343–344
    disorganized, 211, 323, 344
    distracted, 344
    flexibility and creativity and, 143
    joy-based, 343
    relational connection circuits and, 111, 161
    relationship with God and, 112
    secure, 345
    types of, 343–345

attunement
    in absence of validation, 248–250
    advanced interventions for, 247–250
    versus appreciation, 222
    attachment and, 344–345
    availability of, 223
    versus calming, 222

blockages *continued*
    child development and, 101
    emotional healing and, 57
    exposing and resolving, 183–186, 291, 295, 299
    inability to perceive the Lord's presence and, 68, 266
    separation trauma and, 55
Bourne, Edmund, 331
brain science
    attunement and, 165
    hunger and, 130
    left versus right sides of brain and, 113, 289, 313, 323
    levels of brain function and, 350
    maintaining relational mode while feeling negative emotions and, 159
    maturity and, 350–351
    oxytocin and, 188–189
    recommended resources and, 283, 291
    yawning and, 324
"Brain Science, Psychological Trauma, and the God Who Is with Us" (Lehman), 6
bulimia, 301
bullying, 34, 41, 253, 310
butterfly exercise, 48–49

C

Calhoun, Rhonda and Danny, 82, 275
calming
    amid grieving, 272
    attunement and, 180, 222
    building skill with, 325–326
    decision to use, 232
    deep breathing and, 331–333
    Immanuel approach and, 286
    maturity and, 222
    meditative prayer and, 327–331
    non-relational mode and, 225, 227
    ongoing practices for, 225

calming *continued*
    with other interventions, 224–226, 228, 229–232
    practice and, 214
    progressive muscle relaxation and, 333–341
    relational connection circuits and, 163, 209–214
    relaxation response and, 210, 325–326
    shalom-for-my-body exercises and, 210–213, 322–323
    simple interventions for, 209
    as stand-alone intervention, 224–226
    time and space required for, 230–231
    types of negative emotions and, 220
Campbell, Kim, 77, 78
capacity. *See also* maturity
    attunement and, 111
    definition of, 346
central nervous system extrapolation
    definition of extrapolation and, 347
    perceptual interpretation and, 43–47
    Verbal Logical Explainer (VLE) and, 67, 95, 259, 265, 318
cheating, 11, 12
children, Immanuel approach with, 81, 82–84, 272–274
Christmas Carol, A (Dickens), 153
church, psychological trauama in, 6–9
Claire and Sarah's story
    Immanuel approach with children and, 82–83
    Immanuel approach with non-Christians and, 82–83, 275
Claparede, Edouard, 19–20
cognition, central nervous system extrapolation and, 44
cognitive therapy, 189

"I really appreciate Dr Lehman's new book. He writes so clearly, leaving no details hanging where you wonder, "Now is this what he means?" Instead, he explains exactly what he means. Sometimes the sentences get r-e-a-l-l-y long, but I have been able to understand and stay connected because the explanations make sense. The content of the book flows very smoothly without jumping from one topic to another. Everything flows in a logical, clearly understood pattern. And to top it all off, Dr Lehman stops occasionally and says, "Here is what you've just read/learned and here is what you will read/learn next." I appreciate that! I think anyone reading Dr Lehman's book will find him a safe, highly competent leader, not only because of his intense understanding of the subject matter, but because he shares the messy details of his own life and marriage with us. I feel Dr Lehman is a guide who can be trusted. I know he understands what I am experiencing. Thus he becomes a shepherd guide worth following as I explore my own issues so I can experience joy, healing, and growth."

Edith Buller-Breer
Lay person pursuing her own healing journey and helping others with theirs
"Full time mom"

"I am an avid student with a great desire to understand how our brains function in the complex dynamics present in human relationships. Having read numerous books on the subject, I can honestly say that *Outsmarting Yourself* by Dr. Karl Lehman is by far the best! This book goes far beyond the step by step process of inner healing and takes you to the why and how of those processes. Dr. Lehman shares his wealth of knowledge and experience in inner healing in such a way that even novices can understand and apply it to their lives and the lives of others. I highly recommend this book to everyone I know—it's that good! "

Rhonda Calhoun
Co-founder and co-director, Harvest Home and Our Father's Farm ministries
Author of many books, including *The Bride, Blessed are the Poor, Simon Peter and the Master, Simon Peter and the Savior,* and *Simon Peter and the King*

"*Outsmarting Yourself* is a relational life-preserver! This book is a must-read for every person who has a relationship with another human being. Karl and Charlotte candidly share from their personal experience, present fascinating corroborating information from mainstream scientific research, and provide useful solutions to keep our relational windshields free from dirt and grime! I want everyone I know to read this book! "

Rev. Chris M. Coursey
THRIVE Training Director

"Since I did not have any background or training in counseling, I was delighted to find that Dr. Lehman clearly defined each of his terms before using them in context. In this way, he built an easily climbable ladder by which I was equipped to descend into a foundational understanding of Immanuel healing prayer which went far beneath the surface I hoped to scratch as a non-professional. I have received this well-written book as a gift —a strong base on which to build my practice of Immanuel healing prayer as both a participant and minister of hope and healing in the presence of Christ. THANK YOU!"

Cyd Holsclaw

Director of Discipleship at Life on the Vine Community Church, Long Grove, IL

"We got a copy of *Outsmarting Yourself* at the THRIVE conference a few months ago, and it has been a HUGE blessing. We have read through once and are going back over it. It has already been instrumental in bringing change and healing, and many of Dr Lehman's ideas have become part of our everyday lingo."

Sally Schuman
Director, Time of Life Ministries
Time of Life group member

"What Dr. Lehman has done is nothing short of spectacular. By integrating the most recent findings on brain science with the most spiritually dynamic teachings on faith, he has produced a book that is uncompromising to both academically rigorous traditional mental health care practitioners and theologically sound biblically based counselors. By doing the work to carefully integrate these two pieces, the author has broken down the false separation that has dichotomized many Christians for generations.

Over decades of professional work combining faith-based interventions and state of the art mental health care, Dr. Karl and Pastor Charlotte have developed an approach to emotional healing that consistently resolves traumatic memories, and their resultant irrational beliefs and maladaptive behaviors. Since learning the Immanuel approach while in Dr. Lehman's mentoring group for the past six years, I have employed this approach in my practice as a pastoral counselor and as a wilderness adventure counselor. The transformation that occurs when people are able to process and resolve their painful experiences is life-changing....And even though this has not been a primary focus of the Lehman's work, when those involved in sports begin to remove reactive triggering, their ability to perform increases in direct proportion to the resolution of irrational beliefs and unhelpful behaviors that had previously been caused by unresolved pain. I have used the Immanuel approach in my work as a life coach with athletes and coaches, and have seen dramatic, measurable positive results. Both athletes and coaches consistently discover increased capacity to perform as they eliminate self sabotaging thoughts and behaviors.

In this landmark book, Dr. Lehman presents insights and tools gleaned from over 25 years of combining rigorous medical psychiatry with biblically based spiritual truths. As you read Outsmarting Yourself, you will discover that Karl discounts neither his scientific medica background, nor his deep faith in the God of the Bible. In fact, you will find that both your understanding and faith will grow as a result of learning and applying the principles and tools in Outsmarting Yourself."

Mark Hattendorf, Ph.D.
NCAA 2x Division I All-American, psychologist
Pastoral counselor, wilderness adventure counselor, life coach

"I have been using the concepts and tools in Outsmarting Yourself for several years in my own life, in my counseling, and in our recovery ministry. Understanding the Verbal Logical Explainer (VLE), being "triggered," and the Immanuel approach to emotional healing has been invaluable in helping individuals and couples work through painful issues, resolve conflict, and experience deep healing. This book is a must read for anyone who wants to really understand why they respond the way they do and how to escape their destructive patterns. Dr. Lehman's material strikes a unique balance as it contains both cutting edge brain science as well as personal examples that illustrate the points so well even my thirteen-year-old daughter thoroughly enjoyed and even grasped most of the content. You will find this book a blessing both for yourself and for those with whom you minister, counsel, or simply share life."

Darrell Brazell

Pastor and Director of New Hope Fellowship & Recovery Ministries

"Dr Lehman's work is original and fascinating, humbly written in plain English, which makes him rare in the field of psychiatry. Hats off!"

Karen Struble, Ph.D.

Adjunct Professor of Psychology, Montreat College

"New! Profound and urgently needed! For only the second time in thirty years I have read something that is fundamentally original, very practical, and solves critical problems (Dr. Allan Schore's books were the first such experience). Throughout my career as a counselor, whenever I worked with conflicts in which the people involved did not share the same sense of reality about the problem, nothing helped for long regardless of what I did. The "hurt" parties were almost always offended by my attempts to help, and eventually walked out of the talks with the relationships being lost. In *Outsmarting Yourself* Dr. Karl Lehman provides a brilliant integration of brain science and God's healing that guides beginners and experts alike through simple interventions for correcting the ways our brains create distortions in our perceptions of reality; and when we then share the same sense of reality we can finally sort out conflicts that had previously been irreconcilable. Here is the road map for helping yourself and others out of the messiest relational tangles in life. This is a book for everyone you know who has a broken relationship in their life or in their church. We are about to see some people reunited!"

Jim Wilder, Ph.D.
Psychologist with thirty years of clinical experience
Director, Shepherd's House,
Developer of *Thriving: Recover Your Life*
Author of several books, including *The Complete Guide to Living with Men*

About the Author
Karl Lehman, M.D.

Dr. Lehman is a board-certified psychiatrist with twenty-five years and more than forty thousand hours of clinical experience. He has worked tenaciously throughout his career to integrate his personal Christian faith with medical science, modern mental health care, and his rigorous scientific training; and he has especially worked to integrate faith-based emotional healing with insights provided by psychological and neurological research. Working closely with Dr. E. James Wilder, Dr. Lehman developed the Immanuel approach (to emotional healing and to life). In addition to observations from his clinical work, regular consultation with colleagues, and extensive ongoing study of a wide range of research literature,

Dr. Lehman is also deeply committed to his own growth and healing. He is constantly learning through the application of emotional healing principles and tools in his personal journey. Furthermore, Dr. Lehman has been married for more than twenty years, and he and Charlotte work as a team to apply everything they learn about growth and healing in the context of their marriage. This combination of decades of clinical experience, extensive ongoing study, regular collaboration with colleagues, and regular emotional healing work in his own life has provided an especially strong foundation from which to discover important new insights.

Karl and Charlotte live in Evanston, Illinois. They have enjoyed many books together as Charlotte reads out loud while Karl washes the dishes, and they have a larger collection of nature documentaries than the local library. Charlotte is a runner and completed the Chicago Marathon in 2008. Karl especially enjoys the beauty of creation as manifested in his salt water aquarium.